C0-DUR-112

SUCCESSFUL RESIDENTIAL MANAGEMENT

Editorial Consultants
Julia A. Banks, CPM®
Enis L. Hartz, CPM®
Connie J. Patterson, CPM®
Michael B. Simmons, CPM®

Joseph T. Lannon
Publishing and Curriculum Development Manager

Caroline Scoulas
Senior Editor

Joseph P. Parsons
Project Editor

Barbara Kamanitz Holland, CPM®

Successful Residential Management

The Professional's Guide

Institute of Real Estate Management
of the NATIONAL ASSOCIATION OF REALTORS®
430 NORTH MICHIGAN AVENUE • CHICAGO, ILLINOIS 60611

Library of Congress Cataloging-in-Publication Data

Holland, Barbara Kamanitz.
Successful residential management : The professional's guide / Barbara Kamanitz Holland.
p. cm.
Includes index.
ISBN 1-57203-005-4
1. Real estate management--United States. 2. Rental housing--United States--Management. I. Title.
HD1394.5.U6H65 1995
333.5'068--dc20 94-28556
CIP

Printed in the United States of America

2 3 4 5 6 7 8 9 10 Printing/Year 03 02 01 00 99 98 97 96

To my loving husband, Andy Holland,
the wind beneath my wings.

Contents

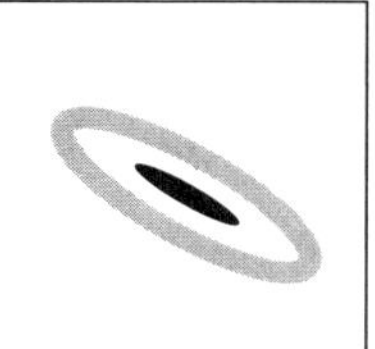

Preface

In writing any textbook, certain important objectives must be achieved:

- The information provided has to be at the "cutting edge"—communicating philosophies, policies, and procedures and providing guidelines and forms that are not only valuable today, but will remain so for years to come.
- It must meet the needs of its target audience—in this case, site practitioners—helping them to become more effective professionally. The information provided should add to their professional growth and development.
- It has to be realistic in response to the questions, "Do real people implement these policies, procedures, guidelines, and strategies?" and "Do successful, effective site managers not only share these same beliefs and goals, but implement them in their daily practice?"
- The complement to the issue of realism is one of control. The diversity of management styles and approaches must be acknowledged. Therefore, in this book I have striven to present information that is not only part of the site managers' functions and responsibilities, but something they can share with the property manager and the owner.

There are also a number of themes that I have tried to articulate throughout this book. They pertain to management theory, organizational behavior, and styles of management.

Effective site management depends on an understanding of the "big picture." With the exception of the first, second, and last chapters, each chapter of this book is devoted to a specific aspect of residential management; however, it would be misleading to represent each of these chapters as free-standing or independent of the others. At the conceptual level, each chapter represents a function of management that is related to the rest—simultaneously supplementing *and* complementing the other areas of site management. For example, procedural changes in marketing strategies will ultimately affect the other areas of the property, from leasing to finances to maintenance and repairs. Understanding this *interdependent* relationship and communicating it to the staff is one of the site manager's most important roles.

Interpersonal skills are equally important. The ability to communicate effectively and motivate people is a basic concern of property owners. Resident relations and resident retention must be of primary importance to the on-site team. The costs and benefits of good versus bad resident relations can profoundly affect a property's financial condition, which, in turn, affects its physical condition and ability to retain residents.

Bringing technical and interpersonal skills together is one of the central tasks of site management. To be an effective site manager, you must not only understand the conceptual level of management, but you need to balance technical and interpersonal or "people" skills. The technical skills are the "how to's." The people skills are the basis for personal interactions between the site manager and the staff, the residents, the owners, and the management company. These two levels come together when site managers understand the difference between delegating tasks and doing them themselves and recognize that they cannot do everything alone. Doing the job right means not only communicating and delegating, but motivating on-site staff to have positive attitudes about their work so they will act, not react.

In order to build an effective team, employees must be motivated and retained because employee turnover imposes high costs throughout site management. Employee retention is partially based on people skills. Studies have shown that most people are not dismissed from their jobs because of technical deficiencies, but because they could not work well with their co-workers or supervisors. Therefore, motivating staff is an especially important part of building a viable team—

one that plans and shares goals based on mutual respect. The result will be a working environment that promotes energy, enthusiasm, and suggestions.

Employees will remain with the company if they have opportunities to grow professionally. Continual improvement requires the ability to accept positive criticism. This requires a certain type of person who views constructive criticism or a suggestion for improvement not as a rebuke, but as an opportunity to learn and grow. People who are able to phrase constructive criticisms positively usually also possess strong leadership skills, and site managers must be such people.

Finally, all of these pieces are brought together in a management style that is based on an understanding of why you are in the business, what your mission is, who your customers are, and how to satisfy their sometimes divergent needs and requirements. The management theory that explicitly addresses all of these questions is known as Total Quality Management, or TQM. Throughout this book, I have tried to bring its lessons to real estate management.

In real estate management, the primary customer is the property owner, and the secondary customer is the resident. Ultimately, the owner's investment goals will not be met without the financial support provided by the residents. Therefore, meeting residents' needs—and retaining residents—becomes a fundamental objective. In many ways, resident retention is, in fact, more important than leasing apartments. By fostering good resident relations from the start, resident retention moves to the front of real estate management concerns. The result is a property that produces more income and increases in value. The success of a residential property depends on continuous improvement and doing things well the first time. Technology now profoundly affects the real estate management industry, and it will continue to do so in the future. Automation of record keeping, routine use of office computers, and quantitative marketing studies have all changed real estate management. Nevertheless, some fundamental aspects of this industry remain unchanged. Continual improvement and conscientious efforts to retain residents will benefit the property in many ways. Learning how to motivate, persuade, and communicate are skills that take time, effort, and personal commitment to develop. In doing so, attitude and aptitude go hand in hand.

Finally, there is the fiduciary relationship with the client, which is dictated by ethical and legal requirements. The requirements of this relationship include loyalty, disclosure, confidentiality, reasonable care, diligence, and accounting. To meet the increasingly stringent standards of the agency relationship, all those involved in real estate management must commit themselves to continued education and professionalism. I hope that this book will help serve that purpose.

ACKNOWLEDGEMENTS

I wish to express my appreciation to many close associates for their invaluable assistance. I would like to thank my partners, Merle Thompson, GRI, and Marilyn Burke, ARM®, for their support and encouragement; Tom Comstock, Director of Facilities Engineering, H & L Realty and Management Company, for assisting me with the maintenance chapter; Greg Billigan, Maintenance Supervisor, H & L Realty and Management Company, for his comments on the maintenance chapter; the H & L Realty and Management Company office staff for their support of my "extracurricular activities"; Steve Kawa, Risk Management Consultant, Inc., for reviewing the risk management chapter; Roger Foster, CRB, president of the Foster Day Corporation, and Gary Allhiser, Great Visions Consulting, for introducing me to Total Quality Management; Dr. Elaine Weiman, for reviewing the entire manuscript; and my family—my daughters Michelle and Danielle and my husband Andy—for their patience and understanding and for tolerating the many hours spent working on the book and not with them. All three were a source of constant encouragement and support.

The editorial consultants for this project provided insightful comments that make this a better book. A special thank you to Julia A. Banks, CPM®, of Banks and Company in Denver, Colorado; Enis L. Hartz, CPM®, of Hartz and Associates in Mount Holly, New Jersey; Connie J. Patterson, CPM®, of Polinger Shannon & Luchs Company in Bethesda, Maryland; and Michael B. Simmons, CPM®, of Community Realty Management in Pleasantville, New Jersey.

I wish to thank the staff members at IREM who gave their unflagging attention to this project. Especially, I would like to thank Joyce Travis Copess, Staff Vice President, Education and Communications, for her support and for her belief, confidence, and faith in me. I also wish to express my deep appreciation to Joseph T. Lannon, Publishing and Curriculum Development Manager, and Caroline Scoulas, Senior Editor, who coordinated the project and successfully guided the book into print. Finally, I would like to thank Joseph P. Parsons, Project Editor, for revising and editing the entire manuscript and shaping the text into a comprehensive guide for contemporary residential managers.

Barbara Kamanitz Holland, CPM®

About the Author

Barbara Kamanitz Holland, CPM®, is president and co-owner of H&L Realty and Management Company of Las Vegas, Nevada. She is the executive officer responsible for the development and growth of the property management, commercial brokerage, and leasing divisions. The company's portfolio comprises more than 3,000 residential units and 350,000 square feet of commercial and office space. Ms. Holland has been involved in real estate management since 1971, when she was director of property management for Revest Company in Hartford, Connecticut.

Ms. Holland was awarded the CPM designation in 1978, and she has been an active member of the Institute of Real Estate Management at both the national and local levels since then. She was the first Las Vegas ARM® Chairman in 1981, and the first Las Vegas IREM president in 1984. Nationally, she has served as Vice Division Director, chairman and member of the Publishing Committee, member of the editorial board of the *Journal of Property Management,* and course board director. Ms. Holland has been twice elected to IREM Governing Council and served as a Regional Vice President during 1993–1994. She is a recipient of the Institute's Professional Achievement Award and a member of its Academy of Authors.

In addition to her activities for IREM, Ms. Holland maintains professional affiliations with the NATIONAL ASSOCIATION OF REALTORS, the Women's Council of REALTORS, the National Association of Home Builders (NAHB), the National Apartment Association (NAA), and the Nevada Apartment Association. She is currently President-Elect of the

Greater Las Vegas Association of REALTORS and a member of its Board of Directors. She has also served on the Board of Directors of the Nevada Association of REALTORS for ten years.

Ms. Holland's teaching experience with IREM includes Course 101, Successful Site Management; Course 301, Marketing and Management of Residential Property; and Managing Single-Family Homes and Small Residential Properties, a seminar based on her book, *Managing Single-Family Homes.* She has also taught numerous courses and seminars for the Nevada Real Estate Commission and the Nevada Association of REALTORS.

In addition to *Managing Single-Family Homes,* Ms. Holland is co-author of *Landlord-Tenant Law in Nevada* and a frequent contributor to the *Journal of Property Management (JPM).* In 1991, she was recipient of the JPM Article of the Year Award for "Agency and Legal Liability." Ms. Holland holds a B.A. degree from the University of Massachusetts—Amherst and an M.A. degree from the University of Connecticut.

About the Institute of Real Estate Management

The Institute of Real Estate Management (IREM) was founded in 1933 with the goals of establishing a Code of Ethics and standards of practice in real estate management as well as fostering knowledge, integrity, and efficiency among its practitioners. The Institute confers the CERTIFIED PROPERTY MANAGER® (CPM®) designation on individuals who meet specified criteria of education and experience in real estate management and subscribe to an established Code of Ethics. Similar criteria have been established for real estate management firms that are awarded the ACCREDITED MANAGEMENT ORGANIZATION® (AMO®) designation. The ACCREDITED RESIDENTIAL MANAGER® (ARM®) service award is presented to individuals who meet specified educational and professional requirements in residential site management and subscribe to a Code of Ethics.

The Institute's membership includes more than 9,400 CPM members, nearly 3,500 ARM participants, and almost 665 AMO firms. In the United States, CPM members manage 6.2 million multifamily rental housing units plus 1.5 million condominiums and 103,700 units in cooperative ownership properties; CPM members also manage 1.2 million subsidized housing units. In addition, they manage 4.8 billion square feet of office space and 1.0 billion square feet of retail space in shopping centers.

For more than sixty years, IREM has been enhancing the prestige of property management through its activities and publications. The Institute offers a wide selection of courses, seminars, periodicals, books, and other materials about real estate management and related topics.

To obtain a current catalog, write to:

Institute of Real Estate Management
430 North Michigan Avenue
P.O. Box 109025
Chicago, IL 60610-9025

or telephone (312) 661-1953

About This Book

As the publisher of *Successful Residential Management: The Professional's Guide,* the Institute of Real Estate Management had two goals: (1) to develop a comprehensive textbook for the newly revised course, "Successful Site Management," and (2) to provide a general text-reference for professional site managers. These goals established a thematic concept that has become an integral part of the book.

The cover design incorporates images of two major construction materials—a brickwork pattern representing a masonry building exterior and a woodgrain pattern representing finished flooring. The equal representation of these materials suggests the site manager's role as a "balancer." The bullseye in the title represents the achievement of success through utilization and application of the skills and knowledge acquired from reading this book. The bullseye image is repeated as a chapter opening icon to remind the reader that residential site managers are, above all, goal oriented, and that the goal is to be successful—"on target."

While this book is intended as a general survey text, it reaches out specifically to two distinct groups of readers—those seeking to become residential site managers or to enhance their knowledge of site management and those who will use this text to teach others about site management. While it is necessary to distinguish the various responsibilities of the site manager, it is also important to understand that the overlap and interdependence of the different responsibilities make the whole greater than the mere sum of its parts. The chapters of this book reflect this bigger picture.

Specific Contents

The first two chapters are intended to establish a context. Chapter 1 describes the different ways real estate—including and especially rental apartment properties—can be owned. It distinguishes the different kinds of goals owners have for their real estate investments and demonstrates how ownership and owners' goals define how a property will be managed. Chapter 2 presents an overview of the site management function and defines the characteristics of successful residential site managers. It also outlines the specific responsibilities of the position they assume.

The next two chapters characterize fundamental aspects of real estate management in general—people and finances. Chapter 3 describes the procedures for recruiting, hiring, training, and evaluating the performance of employees who work at the site, as well as related administrative issues (e.g., payroll). Termination of employment and the various laws that impact employers are also addressed. Because real estate management is a people-intensive activity, communication is emphasized and methods for handling employee problems are discussed. Chapter 4 elaborates the financial issues faced by site managers, emphasizing the need to maximize the bottom line and providing tips for minimizing income losses and controlling operating expenses. Budgets, accounting and record-keeping procedures, and reports to the owner are also addressed.

Three chapters focus on residents, and all are directed to the twin goals of lease renewal and resident retention. Chapter 5 discusses marketing strategies and includes analysis of the marketplace, planning and budgeting, and positioning the property. Chapter 6 presents a full picture of the leasing process, with its requirements for selling skills and closing strategies, and discusses related administrative activities (qualification of applicants, move-in procedures, etc.). Once residents are in place, there will be countless interactions with members of the management team—chapter 7 addresses resident relations with an emphasis on communication.

Chapter 8 explores the maintenance function: Periodic inspections are the basis for specific maintenance work on the building as a whole, but residents' service requests often define the work done inside occupied apartments. Planning, scheduling, and preventive maintenance are emphasized.

Chapter 9 summarizes the various approaches to risk management, including the role and importance of insurance. Chapter 10 outlines the various laws that affect real estate management in general and residential site management in particular, including lease clauses, eviction proceedings, and civil rights issues. In chapter 11, the many specific responsibilities discussed in the preceding chapters are brought together again as parts of the larger process of site management.

Throughout the text, the interrelationship of the various site management functions is highlighted. Communication is critical to both employee relations and resident relations. Cost savings and inventory controls are introduced as financial issues, but they are applied in the context of maintenance. Decisions related to marketing, leasing, rents, and insurance coverages have an economic impact as well. Discriminatory practices are prohibited in the employment of personnel, the marketing and leasing of apartments, and personal interactions with residents. In order to fulfill these responsibilities successfully, residential site managers must have excellent planning, technical, and communication skills, and they must demonstrate professionalism.

For Students and Teachers

Successful Residential Management is designed to be reader-friendly. Although it is a textbook, the reader is often addressed as "you" to personalize the educational experience. The text is enriched with more than 80 illustrations. Various types of forms used in site management are presented as numbered exhibits, and unnumbered boxed elements summarize and highlight relationships as well as provide supplementary background information.

To help readers review what they have learned, each chapter concludes with a summary followed by lists of "key terms" and "key concepts"—items that have been highlighted in the text (with italic type)—and a series of "key points" (questions) that focus on the main ideas developed in the chapter. Chapters 3 through 10 include a special boxed list that itemizes the site manager's practical responsibilities within the particular function being discussed. The array of specific responsibilities is summarized in a boxed list in chapter 2, where they are introduced. The Glossary defines specific terms used in the text, often providing additional details, and the Index guides readers to individual topics.

The ARM® Program

The Institute of Real Estate Management (IREM) has been educating professional site managers for more than twenty years. The ACCREDITED RESIDENT MANAGER (ARM) program, launched in 1975, includes three critical components—experience, education, and accreditation. While it evolved out of earlier educational efforts, the ARM program was the Institute's response to a 1971 Cornell University study that demonstrated a specific need for resident manager training as well as a charge to IREM from the U.S. Department of Housing and Urban Development (HUD) to develop a defined program.

The ARM program defined the specific skills or "competencies" required of site managers, provided a mechanism to train people and measure the success of that training, and established a specific award—the ACCREDITED RESIDENT MANAGER (ARM) service award. Specially trained CPM® members of IREM serve as the faculty, and courses are sponsored by local IREM chapters and offered nationwide. Because the word "resident" in the program name implied that individuals who received the award always lived on site (a situation less common today than when the program began), the name of the program was changed to ACCREDITED RESIDENTIAL MANAGER® in 1990 to better characterize the recipient's role as a multifamily housing manager. The ARM service award is conferred on individuals who meet specific educational requirements (including completion of course 101, Successful Site Management, or an equivalent), have accumulated a certain level of experience (including performance of specific residential management functions and responsibility for a defined number of housing units), and agree to abide by the ARM Code of Ethics (established standards of practice that govern residential managers' relations with the property owner-clients and management firms that employ them and guide the management of operations at their assigned properties). ARM participants maintain their status by paying annual dues and being reaccredited every two years (continuing education is required).

The benefits of participating in the ARM program include acknowledgment of the individual's professional expertise, increased opportunities for higher compensation and career advancement, and opportunities to exchange information with others who specialize in residential management. Numerous educational opportunities, books, periodicals, and pamphlets are available to program participants through IREM, many at a discount.

Achievement of the ARM service award is a milestone in the residential manager's career and a stepping stone toward professional advancement. (Many ARM participants have gone on to achieve the CERTIFIED PROPERTY MANAGER® designation from IREM.) At present, there are nearly 3,500 active participants in the program, and about 250 applicants are preparing for the award at any one time.

The Role of the Site Manager

Each chapter of *Successful Residential Management: The Professional's Guide* provides information about the site manager's role and responsibilities. These characterizations are not intended to be absolutes; some of them anticipate the site manager's role in the future. Some site managers may contract directly with an owner to manage an apartment property, in which case they may have a greater level of responsibility for site personnel, financial administration, and leasing decisions than described here. Site managers employed by a management company may report to a supervisor at a central office—usually a property manager who has overall responsibility for a portfolio of similar properties—and they may have more or less direct responsibility for some of the activities outlined in this book.

The need for professional management of real estate is growing, and the responsibilities of site managers are growing as well. In the future, it is expected that their financial responsibilities will be expanded and that they will have increasing latitude in making budgeting, marketing, and leasing decisions. The Institute of Real Estate Management is striving to prepare individuals to accept these challenges by providing educational vehicles, such as this book, to help them acquire the skills needed to be successful residential site managers.

The Publisher

RESIDENTIAL

MANAGEMENT

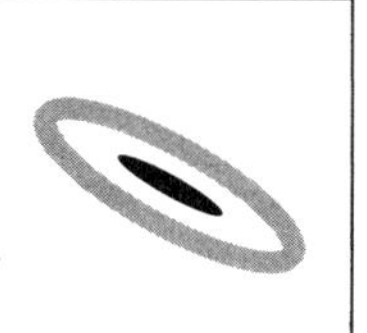

1

Ownership and Management of Real Estate

About a third of U.S. households are renters. In fact, most Americans spend a good part of their lives in rented apartments until they are able to buy houses of their own. Renters not only spend a considerable portion of their income on apartments, they consider them home. They expect their homes to be pleasant and relaxing, and when there is a problem within the apartment, they expect to be able to call the landlord and receive a prompt response to their request. For the most part, apartment residents take service and a pleasant atmosphere for granted. When their expectations are not met, however, they may or may not complain to the management, but they will probably be reluctant to renew their leases. Keeping residents satisfied is a full-time job that is also a challenging and exciting professional career. This is one of the aspects of residential site management.

Today's site managers are concerned with much more than leasing apartments and collecting rents. While these are both important tasks, the site manager also plays a critical role in maximizing the return on the owner's investment through successful management of the day-to-day operations of the property. Site managers are responsible for implementing policies and procedures that the owner and the property manager develop. They also train and supervise the on-site staff, coordinate and schedule the work of on-site personnel and independent contractors, and inspect all work done by independent contractors and vendors prior to payment. Site managers also work on the front line of resident relations, dealing directly with residents' questions and complaints.

The site manager is responsible for keeping the financial and administrative records of a property. This becomes especially important during marketing efforts, for example, when the site manager is able to identify the most effective advertising campaigns—information used by the property manager and owner to determine where advertising dollars are best spent. By keeping track of what initially brought prospective residents to the property—curb appeal, newspaper advertising, or signage—the site manager monitors the strengths of the property and various marketing approaches. These are then used to the property owner's best advantage.

One of the site manager's most important responsibilities is motivating the staff to be as efficient and productive as possible and creating a pleasant atmosphere for the residents, both of which contribute directly to the profitability of the property. To be truly effective, a site manager will do more than create a pleasant atmosphere; he or she will strive to develop a genuine sense of community among the residents and the on-site staff. This can be very demanding because site managers are responsible to many different people. They have a *fiduciary responsibility* to the owner (i.e., they are responsible for managing the residential property wisely and attempting to meet the owner's investment goals), and they have legal and ethical responsibilities to both the owner and the residents. This means that site managers have to balance the investment goals of the owner, the physical needs of the property, and the residents' desires and expectations with the reality of the property's financial condition.

As the critical link in the property management chain, a site manager's decisions have a direct impact on the profitability and value of the property. Decisions about leasing, maintenance, or resident relations have a long-term impact on the property itself and the solvency of the property management firm. The site manager is responsible for maintaining desired occupancy levels, but his or her approach to doing this will determine the success of the property. For example, filling the apartment with residents who are not carefully screened will reduce vacancy, but it might also increase delinquencies. Thus, the site manager must consider all of the owner's goals and how best to meet them.

TYPES OF OWNERSHIP AND THEIR GOALS

Like most endeavors, effective real estate management depends on planning. Management planning takes into account income and expense projections, staffing, marketing, leasing, maintenance, security, and risk management. The contemporary site manager must be knowledgeable about rent collection, budgeting, hiring and dismissing personnel, employee training, resident relations, housing laws, landlord-tenant law, security, insurance, and communication, all the while keeping in mind both the objectives of the owner and the expectations of the residents. Thus, the site manager's goals are to maintain and increase property value and foster a home-like residential atmosphere.

To meet these many challenges, the site manager must possess conceptual, technical, and interpersonal skills. Conceptual skills enable one to visualize the "big picture" and see how myriad factors affect the owner's goals for the residential property. Technical skills are the means by which the goals will be achieved; however, "technical" solutions to management challenges are often shaped by the availability of funds, and the site manager must understand how to achieve goals within the limits of a budget. Interpersonal skills are also critical: The site manager must be able to motivate site employees to achieve specific goals and communicate effectively with residents.

Forms of Ownership

Ownership of income-producing real estate is first and foremost a business venture. It is a very attractive form of investment that accounts for literally trillions of dollars in the U.S. economy. There are several forms of ownership, and each one has unique characteristics and income tax implications. While sole proprietors and corporations are among the more "traditional" types of real estate owners, the

U.S. Real Estate by Asset Class

	Dollar value (billions)	Percent
Residential	*6,122*	*69.8*
Retail	1,115	12.7
Office	1,009	11.5
Manufacturing	308	3.5
Warehouse	223	2.5
Total	**8,777**	**100.0**

Reproduced with permission from *Managing the Future: Real Estate in the 1990s* (Chicago: Institute of Real Estate Management Foundation, 1991), p. 28.

growth of ownership by institutions (banks, insurance companies, pension funds), real estate investment trusts (REITs), and governmental agencies has changed the face of property management and created a growing need for real estate management professionals. Because real estate competes with other types of investments, real estate professionals are especially important. Changing tax laws and competition for investment dollars underscore the importance of property management and the site manager's role in *value enhancement* in all aspects of site management.

Sole Proprietorship. This is a common form of real estate ownership. In a sole proprietorship, an individual investor may own a single apartment building or several smaller ones (two or three units per building). As a sole proprietor, the owner is fully responsible for the property's operation including liability for income shortfalls or operational problems. Profits from the investment are taxable income for the individual. In this ownership form, a single apartment building usually represents a sizable investment or perhaps the investor's entire portfolio. Often the owner is responsible for maintenance and leasing of the apartments as well as all other aspects of management. On the other hand, sole proprietorships represent unique opportunities because a site manager employed by an individual owner may

Residential Real Estate Investment Ownership

	Dollar value (billions)	Percent
Partnerships	673	60.0
Government	173	15.4
Not-for-profit	104	9.3
Individual	71	6.3
Other*	101	9.0
Total	**1,122**	**100.0**

*Includes foreign owners, REITs, institutional investors, and other miscellaneous owners.

Reproduced with permission from *Managing the Future: Real Estate in the 1990s* (Chicago: Institute of Real Estate Management Foundation, 1991), p. 32.

report directly to the owner as opposed to a property management firm. These site managers may make the majority of decisions about the property, in concert with the owner's objectives.

The advantage of sole proprietorship is its simplicity: Profits, losses, and tax benefits pass directly to the owner. There are also disadvantages of sole proprietorship to the owner, including limited availability of capital or credit lines, a lack of (or limited) technical knowledge, and inflexibility regarding different management styles and management operations. Decision making may be subjective and without a clear organizational structure or consistent theme, which can make the site manager's job more challenging.

Partnership. Acquisition of larger-scale income properties requires larger amounts of investment capital. Because such amounts are often beyond the financial reach of many individuals, two or more investors may pool their funds to form a partnership. In a *general partnership*, each partner contributes a certain amount of capital and receives a proportionate share of any profits. General partners are also responsible for the investment's losses. Their liability is said to be unlimited—they are personally responsible for the debts created by

Forms of Real Estate Ownership

Ownership Form	Taxation Status	Investor Liability
Sole Proprietorship	Single	Unlimited
General Partnership	Single	Unlimited
Limited Partnership	Single	Limited
Corporation	Double	Limited
REIT	Modified single	Limited

the partnership, and each general partner is liable for the actions of the others.

In cases where it is impossible for each partner to contribute a sufficient share of funds to capitalize a partnership, a *limited partnership* may be formed. In a limited partnership, one or more general (managing) partners are joined by several limited partners who contribute capital but have no say in the management and no liability beyond their capital investment.

Like a sole proprietorship, profits (and losses) are passed directly to the partners based on their proportionate investment and are taxable to the individuals as ordinary income. One potential disadvantage of a partnership is the possibility that a single partner may make a decision about the property without first consulting or receiving the consent of the other partners. Site managers who work for partnerships must balance the needs and desires of all the partners when (or if) there are differences among them. These situations are commonly addressed by real estate managers. An additional administrative responsibility for the site manager may be the need to prepare multiple copies of reports when there are several partners. In limited partnerships, the general partners receive detailed reports on the property while limited partners receive only summaries.

Syndication. A real estate *syndicate* is a specialized form of limited partnership. The participants in a syndicate may be individuals, general or limited partnerships, joint ventures, unincorporated associations, or corporations. In its simplest form, syndication pools both capital and experience for a property's success. The advantage of syndication is that a formal agreement can be made between people or business entities of different backgrounds to accomplish a specific goal. Syndication is also flexible: A syndicate can be formed to purchase a particular property, or it can rely on the experience of a syndicator to acquire a promising property; if more funds are needed, additional partnerships can be sold. Prior to enactment of the Tax Reform Act of 1986, syndicates were popular as tax shelters. Typically, one or more general partners "managed" the investment property or a portfolio of properties for perhaps hundreds or even thousands of individual investors. The Tax Reform Act of 1986 reduced or eliminated the deductions that made syndicates so appealing to investors, and the level of investment in them has diminished greatly since then. The appeal of syndications now lies in their potential for cash flow and liquidity.

Corporation. Another approach to raising investment capital is to form a corporation and sell shares. A corporation is recognized by federal and state governments as an independent legal entity that can be a party to lawsuits or file for bankruptcy protection in the same way as an individual. A corporation differs from a sole proprietorship in that a corporation has continuity of life; the legal entity survives the comings and goings—and deaths—of its officers. Unlike the sole proprietor, however, the liability of the corporate stockholders—the owners of the corporation—is limited to the amount of capital they invested. The officers of the corporation (including its board of directors) are responsible for the management of any real estate acquired by the corporation, and investment proceeds (profits) may be distributed to the stockholders as dividends. Corporations are unique in that they pay income taxes on their profits, and their stockholders pay income taxes on the dividends; this amounts to double taxation.

Residential properties may be held by corporations for investment purposes or acquired in the course of their business activities. A corporation may also hold a real estate portfolio to house employees who are transferred from place to place. A site manager working for a corporation may have more administrative duties than he or she would under some other forms of ownership. For example, preparation of records for the government, the board of directors, and the corporation's shareholders may be required. The board of directors may have to approve specific projects, and accounting practices for the property may have to conform to those used by the corporation, even though they may not be well-suited to real estate management. The corporation may also require information for inclusion in a corporate annual report, adding to the administrative responsibilities of the site manager. In general, these responsibilities fall to a property manager who may rely on a site manager for assistance.

Real Estate Investment Trusts (REITs). REITs pool the capital of many individual investors and invest the funds in real estate (equity trusts), lend it by way of real estate mortgage loans (mortgage trusts), or combine the two forms (hybrid trusts). By pooling the resources of many investors and investing in several properties, REITs spread the risk across a larger number of investors, reducing the respective risk to individuals. REITs are popular because if they comply with certain requirements of the U.S. Internal Revenue Code, they can distribute profits to shareholders (investors) without paying federal income tax. This eliminates the double taxation associated with corporate ownership. In addition to this tax benefit, REITs can use depreciation deductions to shelter income that would otherwise be taxable to shareholders.

Management Impact of Different Types of Owners

Although tax laws and other statutes define the forms of ownership as businesses, ownership by institutions (insurance companies, banks, etc.), common-interest realty associations (condominiums, cooperatives, and planned unit developments or PUDs), and governmental agencies will create different expectations and demands of the site manager and the on-site staff. While site management responsibilities may remain fundamentally the same, the conceptual aspects of multiple owners for single properties are different and so are the technical approaches to meeting the owners' goals.

Institutional Ownership. Many large pension funds and insurance companies have in-house real estate portfolio management operations, an indication of the attractiveness of real estate as an investment. Pension funds usually invest in real estate because of expectations of solid performance (and the poorer performance of other investment alternatives). Alternatively, they may loan money to investors who purchase real estate. If the borrowers default, the pension fund becomes the reluctant owner of the property. Like pension funds, banks and other lending institutions often acquire real estate portfolios through borrowers' default or foreclosure. Real estate portfolios are held in the real estate owned (REO) departments of lending institutions.

The real estate manager's responsibilities will vary according to the type of institutional owner and its goals. For example, a pension fund may invest in real estate with the expectation of a healthy return on its investment, the goal being to maximize cash flow and increase the value of the property. By contrast, a lending institution that acquired a property through default may only want to maintain the status quo and avert further losses in anticipation of a quick sale of the property. However, if the goal is to make a distressed property profitable again, the lender may require eviction of nonpaying residents and rehabilitation of the property to reestablish it in the marketplace.

Site managers must be flexible and adaptable because different owners may have very different goals and expectations. For example, institutional owners may insist that the site manager use the institution's policies, procedures, and forms. If the site office is automated (computerized), this may also mean converting to the owner's computer software and formats.

Condominium and Cooperative Ownership. In a *condominium,* the residents' units are individually owned, while the common areas of the building—the lobby, exterior walls, and hallways—are jointly owned. Condominium residents own the space within their units extending up to the walls, ceilings, and floors between the respective condominiums. The "common" walls, ceilings, and floors are jointly owned, but each owner/resident is responsible for maintaining the portions of these shared elements that are within or part of their respective units.

A condominium is formed when a group of property owners files a declaration of condominium with the local land-records office. The owners are required to form a condominium owners' association and elect a board of directors, which is responsible for the management of the condominium. The declaration of condominium states the percentage of ownership represented by each individual unit. These percentages also determine each owner's respective assessment to cover the operating expenses of the property. Individual owners may sell or mortgage their units as they see fit or rent them to someone else (if association bylaws permit). Real estate taxes are assessed on each unit rather than on the property as a whole, leaving each owner responsible for property taxes. Unit owners are often required by association covenants, conditions, and restrictions (CC&R) to carry homeowner's insurance unless there is a master policy for the association (in which case, individual residents can obtain additional coverage for personal contents of their units). Management decisions about the property, including major financial outlays, are made by the condominium association or its board, but a real estate manager may be required to attend board meetings and provide management services to the board.

The site manager of a condominium may be an employee of a property management company or hired directly by the board of directors. He or she may be responsible for collecting assessments, paying operating expenses, and maintaining the common areas of the condominium, including grounds, lobbies and hallways, parking areas, and recreational facilities. Individual owners are responsible for maintenance and repair of their units.

Although the organizational structure of the condominium association may provide clear lines of communication and authority, problems can develop that defy this structure. There may be times when members of the board and other individual owners are in conflict, and different instructions may be given to the site manager. In addition, some members of the condominium association may attempt to sidestep board requirements and expect the site manager and the on-site staff to do special favors or respond to maintenance requests without following the usual protocol. Situations such as these place the site manager in the difficult position of either defying policies and procedures or not responding to an owner's or board member's request. To avoid conflicts of interest, the site manager should receive approval from the board to have separate management agreements with owners who rent their units. Because of the potential for problems, the site manager of a condominium must be both assertive and tactful and be aware of the "politics" within the association.

By contrast, in a *cooperative,* individual residents buy shares of the corporation, which entitle them to occupy a residential unit. The corporation holds the mortgage and title to the property. Real estate taxes are assessed on the property as a whole. The cooperative itself is run by a board of directors, and each shareholder pays a monthly assessment to cover building expenses such as the mortgage, real estate taxes, insurance, and maintenance and repairs. As in a condominium, the site manager is responsible for common area maintenance and repairs, inspection of the property, and implementing the policies of the cooperative corporation. The same drawbacks that exist working for a condominium are inherent in this form of ownership.

Planned Unit Developments (PUDs). Planned unit developments combine aspects of a conventional neighborhood subdivision with some of the characteristics of condominium ownership. PUDs are usually governed by homeowners' associations, which are comparable to condominium associations. Although some residents may be renters, most purchase their homes and the land on which they sit as well as an interest in the common area within the PUD (roads, parks, recreational facilities). Homeowners pay monthly assessments to maintain the common areas only. They are responsible for all interior and exterior maintenance of their own property, including, for example, painting, roof replacement, landscaping, and snow removal.

The site manager may be responsible for collection of assessments and supervision of maintenance and repair of rental units (if owned by the association), building exteriors, roads, and amenities. Zoning of PUDs often sets an overall density limit that allows clustering of units to provide for common open space and establishes standards for the exterior of residential units. The site manager may be responsible for inspection of work done to make certain it conforms to PUD zoning requirements.

Government Ownership. Government entities involved in real estate include the Resolution Trust Corporation (RTC) and the U.S. Department of Housing and Urban Development (HUD), as well as the Federal Housing Administration (FHA), a division of HUD. The RTC was established by Congress to dispose of financially distressed properties in the real estate portfolios of bankrupt savings and loan associations (S&Ls). In the case of the S&L bailout during the late 1980s and early 1990s, the RTC took back or foreclosed properties and arranged for interim management while real estate brokers attempted to sell them. Because the disposal of properties can take a long time,

Objectives of Ownership

- Periodic return
- Capital appreciation (value enhancement)
- Income tax advantage
- Pride of ownership

the RTC places them in the hands of asset managers who establish management policies and procedures until investors buy them.

Similar to the REO properties owned by institutions, the site manager's responsibilities can range from maintaining the status quo to value enhancement. Often the decision-making process is slower and more complicated than private ownership. Finally, the site manager must become familiar with the government's extensive operating manuals and paperwork requirements.

Objectives of Ownership

The objectives of real estate ownership vary. *Owners by choice* purchase residential real estate based on its potential to generate income. However, not all ownership is motivated by profits. An individual may inherit a relative's real estate holdings; a corporation may acquire another company's property as part of a merger or buy-out, or a lending institution may gain possession of an apartment building following default of the borrower. Such *owners by circumstance* may choose to manage the real estate or dispose of it. However, banks have been known to collapse financially, leaving the government to take over their real estate portfolios. Government involvement in real estate ownership and management, in general, is not motivated by profits.

Real estate holds many attractions for investors. Although it is said to be an "illiquid" investment because it cannot be readily converted to cash, real estate provides both tangible (financial) and intangible benefits for the investor. The financial benefits include periodic return, capital appreciation, and income tax advantages, while the intangible benefits derive from pride of ownership.

Periodic Return. The income produced by a property in a given period of time is its periodic return. (This is also known as cash flow, a concept that will be discussed in detail in chapter 4.) The real estate manager has a direct influence on this through preservation, maintenance, and improvement of the physical asset; by increasing income through higher rents, lower turnover and delinquency rates, and fewer or smaller concessions; and by controlling or reducing operating costs. Periodic return is also influenced by prevailing market conditions that are outside the manager's control (e.g., interest rates, lack of refinancing alternatives, improvement or deterioration of a neighborhood).

Capital Appreciation and Value Enhancement. Owners also evaluate a property's capacity for capital appreciation—its ability to increase in value over time. An investor wants to be able to sell the property for more than its original purchase price. Capital appreciation is generally a long-term goal; it is achieved by producing as much income as possible, controlling costs, and maintaining, preserving, or improving the physical property. The greater the positive difference between income and expenses, the greater the potential for capital appreciation. The market value of the property can also increase if the economy of the neighborhood or region improves, if property in the area becomes more desirable, or if the property itself is rehabilitated.

In evaluating real estate, investors look for good location, quality construction, architectural appeal, potential to increase in value over time, favorable lease terms with established tenants, sufficient income to pay expenses and service debt, an acceptable purchase price, an absence of encumbrances (e.g., liens against the property), and good management.

Income Tax Advantage. A primary advantage for real estate owners is income tax deductions for mortgage interest, *depreciation,* and operating expenses. Depreciation is a property's gradual loss of value due to its physical deterioration and obsolescence. Under the *Economic Recovery Tax Act of 1981 (ERTA),* property owners are allowed to deduct a certain percentage of the value of the property from their income each year as depreciation. This is known as a capital cost recovery deduction. ERTA enables property owners to deduct a larger amount in the early part of the investment period than the actual depreciation each year, creating a tax shelter. This acts as an incentive for owners to hold property for longer periods and reclaim the costs of capital improvements via depreciation deductions. Deductible operating expenses include real estate taxes; property insurance; utilities (gas, electricity, water, and telephone); maintenance and repairs; painting and refurbishing of the building and grounds; advertising and promotional costs; wages, salaries, and related personnel costs; and legal, management, and accounting fees.

Pride of Ownership. Property ownership represents financial success, and its appeal is enhanced by the fact that real estate is more tangible than stock certificates or other forms of investment. When the owner enhances the property's appearance through reinvestment of income into maintenance and repairs and capital improvements—rather than taking the highest immediate financial return possible—he or she demonstrates pride of ownership. Improvements will attract new residents who may pay higher rents. In turn, higher rents increase the net operating income of the property, contributing to capital appreciation. Because the costs of repairs and maintenance can be deducted from taxable income for the year in which they were made, and depreciation of capital improvements is deductible over several years, pride of ownership is also linked to the tangible financial benefits of ownership.

Additional Reasons for Ownership. Many investors acquire residential real estate for speculative purposes. These *turnaround investments* occur when an investor sees the possibility of quick profit in a property that has the potential for rehabilitation. The investor will improve management and maintenance, renovate the property, and maximize rental income with the objective of reselling it at a profit. However, not all investors seek substandard properties; some purchase apartment buildings on the assumption that trends in the local market or favorable changes in a neighborhood will cause a property's value to increase with only minimal changes to its management and minor cosmetic improvements being needed.

MANAGEMENT CONSIDERATIONS BY PROPERTY TYPE

Just as the responsibilities of the site manager vary according to the form of ownership and the owner's goals, they also depend on the

Professionally Managed Residential Property

- Apartment buildings
  —low-rise
  —garden style
  —mid-rise
  —high-rise
- Government-assisted housing
- Single-family homes
- Manufactured housing communities
- Housing for the elderly
- Retirement communities

NOTE: *Townhouses* are like single-family homes in that they have two or more levels of living space and separate entrances; but, depending on ownership and other factors, they may be rented and managed as apartments or as single-family homes.

type of property as well as its size, location, and condition. A large apartment building and a portfolio of single-family homes will have different effects on the scope of the site manager's duties, the number of on-site personnel, and the way the site manager interacts with residents. Also to be considered are the owner's goals and the management duties spelled out in the management agreement.

Conventional Apartments

In urban and suburban settings, many different types of rental apartment properties are found. *Low-rise apartment buildings* are generally not more than five stories tall, and some are only two or three stories tall with first-floor apartments one-half flight below ground level.

Garden or *terrace* apartments are often located in suburban areas where land is comparatively less expensive. Garden apartment complexes may cover several acres and consist of numerous low-rise buildings having as few as four apartments each. A separate building may house a management office, laundry facilities, and recreational facilities. Garden apartment complexes often have numerous amenities and appeal to residents who favor their landscaped grounds.

In urban areas, *mid-rise apartment buildings* are very common. They are generally six to nine stories tall, with elevators and many standard amenities such as trash chutes, laundry rooms, and storage rooms. Parking may be provided as open lots or on the ground floor of the building itself. The layout of each floor of a mid-rise building is virtually identical, with kitchens, bedrooms, and bathrooms stacked one above the other, and all units on each floor opening onto a common hallway.

High-rise apartment buildings are designed to maximize the use of available space. They are typically ten or more stories tall and may be as tall as office buildings. High-rise apartment buildings are similar in configuration to mid-rise buildings and often provide additional amenities such as enclosed parking on lower levels, health clubs, and even restaurants and grocery stores.

Government-Assisted Housing

The most visible form of government involvement in real estate is *government-assisted housing.* Broadly defined, this is any residential rental property in which the lessor receives part of the rent payment from a governmental agency. Such housing subsidies may be either resident based or property based. In the first case, the government pays a portion of the resident's rent to the owner or management company. In the second case, the government buys down a portion of the owner's mortgage—thus reducing the interest rate on the loan—and in return, the owner reduces the rent charged to residents.

One specific form of government-assisted housing, *Section 8 housing,* is privately owned residential rental units participating in the low-income rental assistance program that was created by the 1974 amendments to Section 8 of the 1937 Housing Authority Act. Under this program, HUD pays a rent subsidy to the owner or manager on behalf of qualified low-income residents so they may limit the portion of their income paid out as rent.

Under another type of program, the local housing authority leases a portion of a rental complex from the owner or uses a voucher system to pay a percentage of the residents' rent. The result is *mixed-income housing* that provides more choices for low- and moderate-income residents. This differs from *public housing,* which is generally owned and managed through local or state agencies.

Real estate managers face special demands in government-assisted housing. They must carefully balance the interests of private owners, governmental agencies, residents who receive subsidies, and those who do not, and they may have to deal with tenant associations. In addition to the ordinary management responsibilities, real estate managers must also be aware of applicable regulations and the required submission of forms and reports to federal, state, and local housing authorities. Government-assisted housing is generally limited in its expenditures for operations by the lower rental income collected, which affects both the budget and what can be accomplished at the property.

Government-assisted housing requires site managers who are sensitive to economic, social, ethnic, and linguistic differences that may exist within the community. Interactions with residents have added social, fiscal, and political dimensions that make site management of government-assisted properties more demanding: While these site managers must be especially open-minded, optimistic, and enthusiastic, the same qualities are necessary to site management in any sort of housing.

Other Residential Properties

The site manager responsible for a portfolio of *single-family homes* faces a particularly challenging task because the portfolio may consist of numerous houses at scattered sites. Having to travel between units means the site manager has less time to devote to each individual property, although this can be minimized by managing a number of units within a prescribed zone. Marketing and leasing also can be demanding for this reason.

If the units in a property management portfolio are owned by different investors, the site manager faces additional administrative duties. Tracking expenses can be complicated, and setting up a separate bank account for each individual unit may not be feasible. (In such situations, trust accounts would be established, each consisting of a set number of owner accounts.) Financial reports must be prepared for different owners according to their needs. Maintenance tasks are often complicated because the materials used differ from one house to another according to what was installed by the contractors who built them (e.g., appliances and locks). All told, the range and implementation of operating duties for a single-family home portfolio may be greater (and different) than that for a typical apartment community. Despite these seeming disadvantages, single-family home portfolios can be very rewarding for real estate management companies, which often realize higher management fees and leasing fees, in addition to the relatively high rents residents will pay for privacy and comfort.

Townhouses have their own entrances but share a common wall with an adjacent unit. They offer the convenience of rental housing along with the privacy of single-family homes. Managing townhouses combines many aspects of single-family home management with that of apartments.

Residents of *manufactured housing communities* either rent the land on which their own mobile homes are installed, or they rent both the land and the home. (The term "mobile home park" is no longer in vogue.) Depending on its type, a manufactured housing community may be managed along the lines of a condominium, a PUD, or an apartment community. Residents are usually assessed fees for utilities and sewerage usage, either directly or as part of the rent. The site manager must monitor both utility and sewerage usage by residents and enforce limits on the duration of guests' stays to avoid overtaxing the community's facilities.

The site manager of a manufactured housing community may be an employee of either the owner or a management company. In addition to the ordinary site management responsibilities, the manager supervises installation of mobile homes, awnings, skirting, and landscaping and may be required to develop social programs for community residents. He or she also routinely deals with mobile home dealers or manufactured housing vendors, set-up crews, and accessory vendors and must therefore develop and maintain good relations with them. The site manager must have a broad working knowledge of landlord-tenant law and local laws governing the physical condition of manufactured housing and related facilities.

Property management at an *elderly housing* facility often includes arrangements for independent or assisted living and provision of food service, maid and laundry services, transportation options, and recreational amenities, as well as medical, psychological, and social services for residents in addition to overall management and maintenance of the building. Management of elderly housing is characterized by more diverse services and greater interaction with residents and their families than occurs in other types of housing and requires more specialization of the site manager and the management company.

As long as they are able to function independently, many retirement-age people prefer to remain in their own homes rather than move to a retirement community or housing specially designed for the elderly. However, rising costs and the demands of housekeeping, as well as family pressures and health and safety considerations, may prompt senior citizens to relocate to housing that better serves their needs even though the costs of living in elderly housing facilities can be quite high. Numerous housing alternatives for the elderly exist:

- Retirement communities—self-contained entities with medical, financial, recreational, and shopping facilities close to residential areas.
- Congregate living—private living quarters with access to services needed by people who are not completely independent.
- Lifecare facilities—residents receive housing and necessary health care for the remainder of their lives in return for a fee.
- Nursing homes—facilities that provide continuous, but not acute, medical care for residents.

In order to be classified as housing for the elderly under the Fair Housing Amendments Act of 1988, a residence must be intended for and solely occupied by persons age 62 or older, or 80 percent of all units in a facility must be occupied by at least one person who is age 55 or older. The community must have significant facilities and services specifically designed to meet the physical and social needs of older persons, and there must be written policies and procedures that demonstrate an intent to provide housing for the elderly. Unless these guidelines are met, others (nonseniors) cannot be excluded from living there.

PRINCIPLES OF REAL ESTATE MANAGEMENT

Real estate management is a profession in which someone other than the owner supervises the operation of a property according to the owner's objectives. The purpose of property management is to maximize the return on the investment over the owner's intended holding period. This is accomplished by defining the investor's objectives in the course of drafting the management plan and the operating budget; how long the investor plans to hold the property will determine many of the management strategies, policies, and procedures employed by the real estate manager or management company.

The property management profession is characterized by several fundamental responsibilities that are common to residential and commercial properties. They are to implement budgets, collect rents, pay operating expenses, implement marketing plans, negotiate leases, maintain and inspect the property, respond to tenants' needs, hire and supervise personnel, and report to owners.

Real estate management is a growing field. This growth has been fueled by three distinct trends:

1. The expanding U.S. population and its requirements for space have increased the total number of buildings.
2. Real estate is considered an attractive investment that provides equal or better returns than many other types of assets, and its strength has widened the range of buildings considered for investment purposes.
3. Property owners have recognized that professional management enhances their investment.

A site manager may be hired by an owner to manage a single property, but more often the individual is an employee of a property management company with which the owner has a contract. A *management agreement* is a legal contract between the owner and the property management firm that authorizes the management company to act on behalf of the owner—i.e., as the owner's *agent.*

A management agreement will identify the parties involved—the property owner (principal) and the real estate manager or management company (agent)—as well as the property to be managed. It will also state the duration of the agreement (commencement and expirations dates). It may or may not provide for automatic renewal of the agreement, but it should state conditions for cancellation or renewal.

Under the management agreement, the owner is obligated to insure the building and is responsible for compliance of the property with governmental regulations such as environmental laws and building codes. The management agreement indemnifies the agent (holds harmless) for noncompliance on the part of the owner, although the agent is required to adhere to the law and indemnification does not excuse violations on the part of management.

The management agreement also provides for compensation to the managing agent. This is usually a percentage of the gross collections, although a set monthly fee may be specified instead. The latter may provide a minimum fee in case of an operating income shortfall or be the sole fee for managing a specific property type, such as a condominium. To be legally binding, the management agreement must be in writing and signed by both parties.

The management agreement authorizes the real estate manager to establish bank accounts for the property, collect rents and deposits, pay for approved operating expenses, and market and lease apartments. The agent is usually also authorized to hire personnel and to contract for needed services. If expenses exceed preset limits, special authorization may have to be obtained from the owner. The owner is required to provide funds for operating the property (to supplement shortfalls); carry appropriate insurance coverage on the property, identifying the agent as an additional named insured party; and indemnify the agent from specific liability. While the owner is responsible for compliance with applicable laws and regulations, the agent is required to notify the owner if any noncompliance is discovered. (The agency role will be revisited in chapter 10.)

Property owners hire real estate managers to manage the day-to-day operations of their investment properties. In addition to collecting rents, maintaining buildings and facilities, and filling vacancies, real estate managers also administer maintenance plans, hire and monitor independent contractors, and make capital improvements to the property. Property management firms routinely conduct market research and develop selling techniques for leasing agents, as well as foster good resident relations. Financial management of the property—collecting rents, paying bills, preparing operating budgets, purchasing administration and inventory control, and keeping detailed records of all these activities—is critically important to the owner. The key objective is to control costs and boost profits. The property management firm is also responsible for hiring, training, and supervising management and maintenance personnel; providing for the safety and security of those living and working at the property; and assuring compliance with federal, state, and local laws.

SUMMARY

Professional real estate managers are contracted to operate and maintain real property according to the objectives of the property owner. Specific functions include management of on-site and off-site personnel, administration of funds and bank accounts, leasing, and resident relations. The property manager's goal is to preserve and increase the value of the property under management. The extent of the management role is dictated by the form of ownership and the terms of the management agreement between the owner (principal) and the management firm (agent). The site manager is responsible for day-to-day operations of the property, including collecting rents, marketing and leasing apartments, and general administration and maintenance operations.

Although the particular responsibilities of the site manager will vary according to the size and type of property and the form of ownership, site managers generally must implement administrative policies and practices, and manage maintenance procedures, and are responsible in varying degrees for income and expense projections, staffing, marketing, leasing, building security, and risk reduction. The site manager must also be familiar with budgeting, accounting, and record keeping and be prepared to implement company policies on site. In the chapters that follow, these duties will be discussed in detail.

Key Terms

agent
corporation
manufactured housing community
partnership
planned unit development (PUD)
real estate investment trust (REIT)
sole proprietor

Key Concepts

capital appreciation
condominium ownership
cooperative ownership
management agreement
periodic return

Key Points

- What distinguishes the forms of ownership?
- What are the objectives of real estate ownership?
- What are the differences between "ownership by choice" and "ownership by circumstance?" How might these differences affect ownership goals?
- What features are used to differentiate types of residential property?
- What is a management agreement?

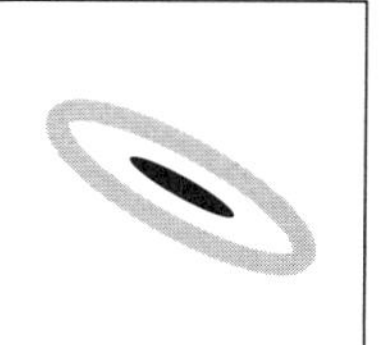

2

Site Management

Whether the property under management is a small apartment building containing only a dozen or so apartments, a large complex consisting of several hundred units in more than one building, a high-rise condominium, a manufactured housing community, or a portfolio of single-family homes, the basic responsibilities of site management are the same. What will differ are the intensity and repetition of some particular tasks, which vary according to property type and size and the expectations of the owner or the management company. The essential responsibilities of site management encompass administration, maintenance operations, personnel management, resident relations and resident retention (customer service), leasing, and marketing, all of which are interrelated and subject to overlap. Typically, these responsibilities are assigned—in part or in total—to individual site managers.

Viewed broadly, management of residential real estate affects more than the building itself. The reputation of an apartment building helps shape both the reputation and physical condition of the neighborhood and the quality of its residents' lives. (The management theory that stresses continuous improvement of services, products, and support delivered to its customers is known as Total Quality Management—TQM.) The quality of service the residents receive reflects the site manager's proficiency in planning, delegating, and coordinating management and maintenance tasks. Because residents are retained or lost on the basis of service, the site manager's actions influence vacancy, turnover, and renewal rates. He or she also influences the impression of the property and the management company by his or her dealings with potential employees, vendors, and contractors. In every aspect of his or her duties, the site manager has a real and lasting impact on all of these factors, which, in turn, have a profound impact on rental income, operating expenses, and net income. The importance of the site manager to the success of residential real estate cannot be overstated.

The success of a residential rental property is determined by its day-to-day operation and how the site manager applies his or her conceptual, technical, and interpersonal skills. Indeed, for many residents of a rental property, "landlord" may be synonymous with the site manager and the on-site staff. Whether leasing apartments, paying rent, or requesting service, residents see the site manager as a symbol of the authority of the owner and the management company. In fact, for most residents, the site manager and other on-site personnel are the only points of contact with the management company or the owner. Thus, the site manager plays an especially important role in property management.

To be successful as real estate professionals, site managers must possess certain qualities and develop specific capabilities. In particular, they must be able to manage both people and resources. This means they must have

- Good organizational and planning skills,
- Sound approaches to decision making,
- Excellent communication and time-management skills, and
- A knack for solving problems.

Because the site manager is the vital link between the management organization, site employees, and residents, as well as the vendors, outside contractors, and governmental agencies, all of these skills will be used.

THE ROLE OF THE SITE MANAGER

For the sake of discussion, the responsibilities of the site manager can be broken down into several categories:

- Administration
- Maintenance operations
- Personnel
- Customer service
- Marketing
- Representation of the management company and the owner

Although these discrete categories provide an organizational structure for this book, it must be understood that they are interconnected as part of a complex whole.

For example, in developing a marketing strategy for a property, the site manager may be involved in the planning of an advertising campaign. In addition, he or she often develops the copy, places the ad, and measures its effectiveness. Customer service as it is applied to apartment properties means developing and implementing programs whose goal is resident retention, but it also refers to resident relations in general. The administrative and financial functions are critical: The site manager typically assists in developing the annual budget for the property, collects monies, tracks income and expenses, solicits bids for jobs, approves bills for payment, and enforces resident compliance with rent payment schedules and lease provisions. Operation of the property relates to practical considerations such as maintenance and repairs in both apartments and common areas and includes communication with and supervision of the on-site staff. Guiding and organizing all of these interrelated activities are the management policies and procedures, which the site manager is responsible for implementing.

Each of these areas, individually, is essential to the central task of creating and preserving value in residential property. In reality, none of the site manager's responsibilities can be viewed individually—for example, legal issues cannot be considered independent of marketing, leasing, and collections. The site manager may perform several functions simultaneously, and all of them must be properly organized and coordinated.

Administration

Administration is the coordination, integration, and implementation of all resources—human, financial, and material—in order to make the residential property run smoothly and efficiently. Administration simply means the management actions of planning, directing, budgeting, and implementing what is necessary to achieve an organization's objectives. For the site manager, this means diligent rent collection, careful record keeping, attentive monitoring of income and expenses (and budget variances), early action regarding lease renewals, and knowledgeable handling of legal and financial matters, all of which are required for a property to generate the maximum income. Without sound judgment based on careful consideration of relevant information, a thorough understanding of the cycle of tenancy, and attention to legal and financial matters and the ultimate goals of the property owner, administration constitutes little more than paper shuffling. (Because management of human resources calls on all of the site manager's skills, most especially communication and interpersonal skills, personnel relations will be discussed separate from administration later in this chapter and at length in chapter 3.)

Planning, Budgeting, and Reporting. Planning is involved in all aspects of site management. In the administrative area, budgeting is a specific type of planning—it involves anticipating tasks and estimating income and operating costs for specific periods of time. Anticipation of lease expirations, development of work schedules, and efforts to assure that parts and supplies are readily available are also planning activities. As the person who most closely monitors the property's daily operations, the site manager is in a position to identify the property's needs and recommend their priority to the property manager. In some cases, the site manager will assist the property manager in the preparation of the annual operating budget and then monitor the income stream and allocation of expenses on a monthly basis. Regardless of his or her specific role in the budgeting process, the site manager will be working to achieve a specific income goal through scheduled rent increases, improved rent collections (reducing delinquencies and losses), and shorter turnover times.

Because he or she knows the typical expenses for the property better than anyone else, a site manager is able to identify when allocations are insufficient or expenditures are unnecessary. This knowledge comes from careful monitoring of income and expense items from month to month, which assures adherence to budget projections. When problems such as unanticipated resident turnover or unforeseen maintenance and repairs arise, the site manager notifies the property manager and may assist in modifying the budget projections accordingly as well as work to correct the problems. The site manager must also work to achieve specific income goals through increased rent, careful scheduling of operations, effective rent collections, and reduced turnover times.

Preparation of various financial, administrative, and maintenance reports for the property is another important part of site management. This may include tracking each day's receipts and expenditures as well as preparing weekly, monthly, and quarterly income and expense reports. These reports may be completed by hand or using a computer. Information that should be tracked includes rental rates and amounts collected for each apartment unit (rent roll), residents who have not paid their rent (delinquencies), and units that are not occupied (vacancies). Security deposits are recorded as monies collected from or returned to residents, and the site manager must note any deductions for repairs. Complete and up-to-date records of the move-in and move-out condition of apartments facilitates the computation of such deductions. Accurate record keeping and timely return of security deposits are important administrative, financial, and legal functions of site management. In particular, the information is vital when the collection of delinquent rent or payments for property damage is pursued in court. (These legal implications of financial administration will be detailed in chapter 10.)

Record keeping and operations are closely linked. Keeping a daily log of maintenance and repair requests and their disposition (work orders) contributes to efficient use of resources and personnel. Making sure that maintenance requests are handled promptly and correctly requires preparation of work schedules for site personnel and outside contractors. Maintaining records of purchase orders for merchandise received and services performed will also contribute to efficiency. Timely ordering and establishment of inventory controls assure adequate stocks of supplies, tools, and parts and allow service requests to be fulfilled in a reasonable amount of time. All of these actions are geared toward containing costs and increasing revenues,

Typical Site Management Reports

- Daily accounting sheet
- Rent roll
- Delinquency report
- Vacancy report
- Security deposit record
- Petty cash report
- Income and expense reports
- Work schedules
- Maintenance log
- Inventory record

thus preserving the value of the property. (Financial administration will be discussed in chapter 4.)

Leasing and Lease Renewals. Leasing agents may work exclusively at the site or come from the management company office to show apartments and acquire signed applications from prospects as well as secure signatures from existing residents for lease renewals. However, the site manager also has substantial responsibility for leasing on site, including selection of residents, approval of leases, and decisions regarding which residents should receive lease renewals at what terms. The residents who are selected (or renewed) must be able to pay their rent and have good payment records. A history of good relations with prior landlords and other residents is also important. Disruptive behavior not only detracts from the quiet enjoyment of the other residents of the community, but also has a direct impact on the financial well-being of the property—such behavior will drive away more-desirable residents. This turnover adds to operating costs and takes away from resident retention efforts. Because site managers usually request and evaluate the credit information and rental histories of applicants, they play a key role in the qualification of prospective residents. (The same type of scrutiny is important for qualifying current residents for renewal leases.)

In addition to overseeing the selection of residents, site managers prepare, process, and may even sign rental applications, leases (initial and renewal), additions to them (called addenda), and related documents. The manager's specific duties will depend on the management company's standard procedures and local law. Because marketing and leasing programs must conform with requirements of fair housing laws, uniformity and fairness in the application of policies and procedures is important for legal protection of the on-site staff, the management company, and the property owner. Thorough and well-organized records of all leases and related documents should also be maintained—both to monitor the expiration of leases in anticipation of renewal efforts and to assure legal protection for both the landlord and the residents. (Leasing will be discussed in chapter 6.)

Part of the leasing process involves monitoring the performance of leasing agents. If a particular agent's closing or renewal ratio is far below that of the others on the leasing team, the reason may be related to the agent's technique or perhaps to personal problems. In either case, the site manager should try to identify the cause of the problem and help the employee solve it. Likewise, an agent who outperforms all others may be able to provide suggestions or techniques to boost the other leasing agents' performance.

Financial and Legal Issues. Among the site manager's financial duties are collecting rents, security deposits, and other receipts (fees, assessments, service charges) and safeguarding them. Making bank deposits daily and maintaining accurate records of all revenues collected are also part of this process.

A related responsibility is implementing and enforcing the management company's collection policies. Collecting monies on time is especially important because delinquencies have legal as well as financial implications. In this area, the site manager plays a major role, monitoring the payment records of all residents and adjusting security deposit records when these funds are used to pay delinquent rent, late fees or legal fees, utilities, or maintenance and repair charges. Rent credits for prepayments, prorated payments, and concessions will also affect security deposits. Thus, keeping complete and accurate financial records (including copies of correspondence, documentation of payments and events, and photographs of physical damage) is essential. The site managers may also assist in the preparation of delinquency notices and participate in the eviction process (if that remedy becomes necessary).

Other legal issues affect the operation of residential rental properties. The site manager must be knowledgeable about in-house contracts, leases, and lease applications and the status of individual leases.

Another essential ingredient is familiarity with fair housing laws, the legalities of leasing and marketing, landlord-tenant law, and the legal requirements for notification of nonrenewal, renewal, and rent increases, as well housing codes and eviction procedures.

Many different types of laws—federal, state, and local— affect real estate management. Building and fire safety codes, landlord-tenant laws, and environmental laws are among them. Occupational safety and equal employment opportunity laws affect management's role as an employer. Fair housing laws and the Americans with Disabilities Act address issues of discrimination and accessibility. Because state and local requirements often differ from one another as well as from federal regulations, the site manager must be aware of laws at all levels. In general, complying with the most stringent requirements assures overall compliance. (Financial administration will be addressed in chapter 4 and specific legal issues will be detailed in chapter 10.)

Operations—Maintenance and Repairs

In the area of operations, the site manager's responsibilities may include establishing systems for controlling specific service requests as well as scheduling preventive and routine maintenance and then supervising the maintenance work. Prompt responses to service requests should be the goal, but follow-up by staff is necessary to assure that jobs are completed satisfactorily. Achievement of the goal will be facilitated by the establishment of specific policies and procedures and inventory controls. The site manager must set priorities and pace the work load so that both occupied and vacant units, as well as common facilities, receive needed maintenance. The management and scheduling of maintenance work also ensures efficient operations and acceptable response times. Operation of the property requires the site manager to coordinate the ordering of maintenance supplies to assure adequate inventories of tools and spare parts. All of these activities contribute to the efficient operation of the property, control or reduce costs, ensure resident satisfaction, and contribute to the property's physical integrity and financial strength.

Perhaps no single aspect of site management has greater impact than maintenance. Maintenance and repairs enhance the property's curb appeal, which attracts and retains residents whose rents establish the value of the property. Increasing maintenance efficiency and reducing maintenance costs also contributes directly to the property's net income.

Depending on the type and extent of the work done, maintenance can be characterized as preventive, corrective, emergency, cosmetic, or routine. Routine maintenance is the housekeeping activities that make a property look its best. Preventive maintenance involves anticipating problems and planning and scheduling maintenance and repairs to prolong the useful life of a property and its equipment. Corrective maintenance, on the other hand, is a response to a resident's service request or to something that has gone wrong. Emergency maintenance is anything that requires immediate attention (e.g., a ruptured water pipe or a backed-up sewer line must be addressed immediately to prevent further damage to the property or minimize potential danger to residents.) Cosmetic maintenance enhances the appearance of the property but may not contribute to its operation or preservation. Repairs that are not done can have financial as well as structural consequences. Such deferred maintenance hastens the process of deterioration, which reduces property values. Preventive maintenance can actually alleviate the need for corrective or emergency maintenance. In order to implement a preventive maintenance program, the site manager must plan ahead, prepare maintenance schedules, and follow through on them. (See chapter 8 for a detailed discussion of maintenance.)

Organization—Policies and Procedures

All foreseeable management problems should be addressed in an *operations manual* that contains the management company's policies and procedures directing all on-site activities. *Policies and procedures* facilitate both planning and execution of operations. For example, there should be employment policies to govern the hiring, training, compensation, promotion, and termination of site staff; maintenance policies and procedures that define how and when these services will be provided to residents; rental policies that address marketing, leasing, resident selection, fair housing practices, and lease renewal; and collection policies and procedures to cover the handling of rent payments, delinquencies, late fees, damage charges, and security deposits and their attendant record keeping. The manual may also address the site management office, legal issues, and other aspects of property

Components of an Operations Manual

- Company Profile and Organizational Structure
- The Site Office
- Personnel
- Collection Process and Record-Keeping Requirements
- Budgets and Operating Statements
- Purchasing and Disbursement
- Marketing
- Leasing and Rental Policies
- Move-In Procedures
- Move-Out Procedures
- Maintenance and Security
- Emergency Procedures
- Legal Procedures
- Forms

operations. An operations manual is important because it provides for continuity, fairness, and efficiency as new employees arrive and old ones leave. It also represents a statement of policy to the public and residents, which is especially important in terms of fairness, consistency, and nondiscrimination. It will foster good personnel relations because staff and residents will know what is required of them and how to fulfill these requirements from the outset. As a consequence, you will retain good employees, increase lease renewals, and retain more residents, resulting in a financially stronger property.

In addition to policies and procedures, an operations manual typically contains standard forms used by the management company. Instead of being considered rigid and final, operations manuals should be reviewed periodically and updated as existing policies and procedures—and applicable laws—are changed and new ones are adopted. Such flexibility contributes to the efficiency and productivity of the entire on-site staff.

Personnel—The On-Site Team

Depending on the management company, the site manager may actually recruit, interview, and hire site employees, or the entire process may be handled at the main office of the management company. Minimally, the site manager assists the property manager in identifying the personnel needs of the property (how many people, what skills) and may draft appropriate job descriptions for positions to be filled. Regardless of how employees are hired, their training and supervision, performance evaluations, and promotion or termination are usually the site manager's responsibility. Related administrative functions may include implementation of employment policies, assuring adherence to equal employment opportunity requirements, maintenance of payroll records, and compliance with relevant laws regarding the workplace.

The success of the property depends in large part on the creation of a motivated team whose members are enthusiastic and have a positive attitude. Delegating responsibility and providing leadership and motivation—development of a stable, goal-oriented staff—is exclusively the domain of the site manager and ultimately depends on his or her communication skills. Training and supervision of staff cannot be accomplished effectively without clear communication of expectations and understanding of what motivates employees to do their best work. In reviewing employees' performance, a site manager can determine appropriate means for rewarding good work and disciplining problem employees. (Personnel relations is the subject of the next chapter.)

Customer Service

Customer service is as much an attitude as an activity, and it starts with good working relations and open communication with residents. An apartment building may be a place of business for a property management company and an investment for an owner, but it is a resident's home. For this reason, professionalism and congeniality must coexist. Although they should demonstrate a sense of caring for residents, site managers still must apply the policies of the building fairly, firmly, and uniformly. Certainly, over time, a site manager is bound to develop likes or dislikes for individual residents, but personal feelings must not stand in the way of serving notice for a bounced check, a late rent payment, or some activity that detracts from the quiet enjoyment or safety of other residents.

Another important aspect of customer service is a timely response to all requests. It is the site manager's responsibility to assure that maintenance requests are fulfilled in a reasonable amount of time. If a request cannot be met promptly, it should be acknowledged with an indication of when the work will be done. Simple consideration will partially meet residents' expectations and increase their level of satisfaction. In the course of a typical day, any number of requests of varying degrees of urgency may be received from residents. A site manager must not only be able to solve problems as they occur, but also determine priorities.

Customer service presents dual challenges of satisfying residents and anticipating problems. Detailed written records of residents' service requests and complaints—and responses to them—help establish priorities and develop strategies for resolving ongoing problems. Repeated complaints about heat or air conditioning may indicate mechanical problems with these systems or the need to better train the people who maintain them. Only by keeping accurate records can you discern patterns and identify trouble spots that deserve additional attention.

Customer service fosters resident retention. Just as dissatisfied retail customers will shop elsewhere, dissatisfied residents will move. Residents will renew their leases only if they perceive that they are receiving value for their money—i.e., prompt, attentive service. Customer service also benefits the owner because retaining residents reduces vacancy losses and saves the costs of marketing, leasing, and preparing apartments for new occupants. (The importance of customer service to resident relations is discussed in chapter 7.)

Marketing Strategies and Resident Retention

Because the value of residential real estate is measured by its standing in a dynamic market, site managers must be aware of the factors that influence property values. They must also understand what steps they can take—both physical and financial—to maintain or increase the value of the property amid changing market forces.

Location and environmental factors determine the function and desirability of a property, which in turn affect its marketability. These factors are wide-ranging and include natural resources and their availability, climate, flood control, and technological advances related to land uses. For example, the availability and cost of fuel for heating an apartment building has a direct impact on its profitability. When fuel costs are high, the costs of maintaining the building will increase.

Faced with higher operating costs, the management company must decide when and how much to raise rents. While the goal may be to compensate for higher operating costs, the fact that rent increases affect occupancy has to be kept in mind. Too great an increase might discourage new rentals or renewals if prospective or current residents perceive the rent as too high. On the other hand, an insufficient increase will result in a financial deficit that must be met by reducing services or maintenance elsewhere in the property, a change that is also likely to result in higher resident turnover. This interconnectedness requires careful balancing of numerous factors.

Economic forces also affect the market, among them the rate of inflation, employment trends and wage rates, the availability of money and credit to borrowers, interest rates, and taxes. Local businesses support neighborhoods and shape the housing markets there. (People generally prefer to live close to where they work.) Governmental regulations affect the value of real estate holdings through zoning laws, rent controls, special use permits, credit controls, government-sponsored housing, guaranteed mortgage loans, and fiscal policy. All of these factors have an impact on renters' choices of where to live and how much rent they are willing or able to pay.

Simultaneously, social forces influence property values by altering the demand for particular types of properties and changing the composition of neighborhoods, cities, or regions. Population growth or decline, migrations from one region to another, shifts in population density, changes in family or household size, geographic distribution of social groups, and attitudes toward education and social activities are among the ways society affects real estate. In particular, changes in the demographic characteristics of a population, as well as people's attitudes and living arrangements, affect the demand for rental housing.

In a market analysis, all of these varied factors are considered. A market analysis has three components—regional analysis, neighborhood analysis, and property analysis. Examination of demographic data of the sort collected every ten years by the U.S. Bureau of the Census—age, income, sex, race, household characteristics, education, occupation—is representative of regional analysis. Neighborhood analysis is based on the properties and characteristics of the immediate surroundings, such as land-use patterns, local population (age, income, household size), and the age and condition of nearby buildings.

The characteristics of residents and occupants and, more specifically, changes in the economic conditions of the residents of a neighborhood are strong indicators of the direction in which local rents and property values are going. Finally, an evaluation of the property itself, including such locational factors as availability of parking, public transportation, schools, and shopping centers—and the neighborhood's reputation— are part of a property analysis that also looks at its physical condition and amenities and its financial status.

A properly performed market analysis will also examine the competition in the neighborhood. This should include at least three properties that are comparable to the one being evaluated in terms of size, location, amenities in individual apartments and common areas, leasing policies and procedures, and rents. All of the information gathered and studied in the market analysis is used to develop a plan for operating the property successfully and positioning it in the marketplace. (Marketing is the subject of chapter 5.)

SITE MANAGER PROFILE

The site manager's actions determine the quality of the owner's investment and its attractiveness to other potential investors. His or her contacts with the property manager, site employees, residents, and vendors have a direct impact on the property in many ways. They affect the services provided by the staff, the property's reputation as a place to live, the quality of life of the residents and site employees, and its vacancy and turnover rates. They also affect the management company's relations with vendors and contractors and the services those vendors provide. In order to do the job effectively, site managers must possess excellent management and communication skills and demonstrate leadership by their own professionalism.

Management Skills

Effective site managers bring together all the pieces of the management puzzle. They must be able to manage both people and resources. This means they must be organized and plan ahead, take into account all relevant factors when making decisions, and be able to solve problems in the midst of other activities. Management cannot be left to

Getting Organized

Distinguish Types of Tasks
- Must do—to be done immediately
- Should do—to be done quickly or as soon as possible
- Could do—to be done as time permits

Set Priorities
- Actions that will generate additional revenues
- Actions that will reduce operating expenses
- Actions that will increase resident retention
- Actions that will increase employee retention
- Actions that will enhance the physical integrity of the property

chance—it depends on planning, control, and commitment to continuous improvement. The contemporary site manager continually strives to improve the quality of service to residents while controlling operating costs. The key to successful management is an emphasis on quality at every step. This helps contain costs, retain residents, and generate more income for the owner.

Assuring the highest levels of quality requires effective *time management*—anticipating problems and taking steps to head them off before they become crises. This means setting goals, establishing priorities, and delegating tasks. Delegation of responsibility is critical because the site manager who says, "If you want something done right, do it yourself," is likely to end up exhausted and frustrated. Realistically, to assure timely completion of projects, site managers have to assign tasks to specific employees and coordinate the efforts of the entire management team. This distinguishes doing the work from managing it and the people. Effective delegation begins in the hiring process, first by clearly communicating the duties of a job and the skills required to do it, and then by hiring the person best able to do the work and contribute to the achievement of the property owner's and the management company's goals.

Interpersonal Skills

As in any business enterprise, effective management requires clear, unambiguous *communication*. The site manager's communications with everyone involved—residents and prospects, site personnel and other employees of the management company, suppliers and contractors, and the property owner, among others—are critical to the efficient operation of the property. The goals of communication include understanding and being understood by others, whether you are asking for information, giving instructions, or acknowledging achievements. Occasionally, the site manager may have to settle disputes and mediate differences between co-workers or residents. This requires gathering all the relevant information, listening to the different sides of the story, and asking appropriate questions that will shed light on the dispute and reveal its underlying causes. Communication is also essential in planning and coordinating work with others, giving and taking directions, training employees, and orienting residents.

There are two basic methods of communication—verbal and nonverbal. In turn, verbal communication can be separated into oral and written components. Oral communication often provides instantaneous feedback (conversations, dialogue). In face-to-face settings, the spoken word is accompanied by nonverbal cues—body language such as a smile, a frown, or folded arms can convey messages that reinforce what is being said or work against it. Written communication is especially useful in more formal situations, such as written notices to vacate with cause. Regardless of the method of communication, the message sent in all cases must be clear and consistent.

Clarity of oral communication relates to the speech itself and the words that are chosen. Site managers who use jargon when talking with residents are not going to communicate information to them effectively. It is always best to speak in everyday language and encourage questions to ensure that the listener understands your comments.

At the same time, you need to be aware of nonverbal communication. When a speaker's words are friendly and warm, but his or her body language is distant and defensive, the listener receives a mixed message and will not be persuaded. It is difficult to mask nonverbal cues; they are perceptible even when a speaker attempts to conceal them. The best advice is to be open, honest, and professional in communicating with employees, residents, and anyone else.

Written communication is most useful when the site manager needs to reach a large audience (e.g., the entire residential community), confirm a spoken message, or deliver a highly detailed message (as in a legal document). Planning and preparation are especially important in this type of communication. The writer should present information in a logical order and take the time to review what is written—for clarity, conciseness, and professionalism—before it is sent. Writing well means rewriting, so be prepared to make revisions that will improve the quality of your communication.

In reality, communication often breaks down, and some conditions contribute to this more than others. Communication will obviously be hindered by poor speaking and writing skills, as well as by contradictory nonverbal messages. However, communication can also be derailed by distractions—a noisy, hectic environment; poor timing (one of the parties is preoccupied with a personal problem); personal dislikes or hostility between people; poor listening skills or habits; or preconceptions held by one of the communicators. Therefore, effective communication requires taking into account the other person's perspective.

There are many ways to prevent communication breakdowns. Think about what the message is intended to convey. If it does not do so, the message should be modified. A basis in fact—rather than assumptions—strengthens the message, as does an environment free from distractions. Appropriateness of time and place are also important. An achievement or a promotion should be widely communicated; a reprimand requires privacy; other messages may demand confidentiality. It is equally important to be aware of—and try to prevent—hindrances to communication. Emotions can interfere with objectivity, and personal likes and dislikes can distort the message. In the management of residential properties, residents, on-site staff, and others must be treated impartially; professionalism demands this of the site manager regardless of his or her personal feelings. As the critical link in the management chain, the site manager must ensure that lines of communication remain open. (Communication with staff will be considered in chapter 3, and communication with residents is addressed in chapter 7.)

Professionalism

The Institute of Real Estate Management (IREM) was established in 1933 for the purpose of adopting specific ethical standards of practice for real estate management. As a result of the efforts of the fourteen founding property managers, each member firm was required to pledge itself to keep its funds separate from those of its clients, carry fidelity bonds on its employees, and in no way benefit financially from client's funds without full disclosure to and permission from the property owner.

Although the initial reason for organizing the Institute of Real Estate Management was to adopt ethical standards of practice, the property management profession has evolved and so has IREM. Because a major aspect of property management is site management of residential properties, IREM established the *ACCREDITED RESIDENTIAL MANAGER® (ARM®)* service award in 1974. The prerequisites of this award include successful course work, professional experience, and agreement to uphold the ARM Code of Ethics. (Professionalism is discussed in more detail in chapter 11.)

ETHICAL CONSIDERATIONS FOR THE PROFESSIONAL MANAGER

Many professions have codes of ethics, and real estate management is no exception. The ACCREDITED RESIDENTIAL MANAGER® (ARM®) Code of Ethics specifies acceptable behavior for professional residential managers. The Code of Ethics prohibits certain types of behavior, including disclosure of confidential information, conflicts of interest, and receipt of benefits without the full knowledge and prior consent of the individual's employer. Alleged violation of the ARM Code of Ethics can result in investigation and disciplinary action ranging from a written reprimand to suspension or expulsion.

A *code of ethics* is a morally binding authority that specifies right and wrong behavior. Violation of a specific code of ethics may carry a form of punishment (investigation and disciplinary action), but it usually does not lead to prosecution unless an existing law was also violated. For example, theft is both illegal and unethical; however, avoiding a resident to put off delivering an unpleasant message, while not illegal, would be unethical. The site manager is duty-bound by ethics to treat all residents fairly and impartially. By avoiding an unpleasant responsibility, the site manager does a disservice to the resident, the management company, and the property owner.

More to the point, a site manager who responds promptly to the

Key Actions Related to Site Management

Primary Functions
- Supervise on-site staff
- Maintain records of leasing and financial transactions
- Is responsible for all management actions on site

Adjunct Functions
- Assist property manager in hiring staff (identify personnel needs, develop job descriptions, interview candidates)
- Compile income and expense data used by property manager in preparing annual budget
- Compile market analysis data and assist in evaluating it

service requests of one resident but deliberately delays responding to the requests of others is practicing discrimination, and in doing so, the site manager violates both ethical and legal standards of behavior. Different treatment on the basis of gender, age, race, disability, religion, national origin, or familial status is unethical as well as illegal. From both an ethical and a legal perspective, it is absolutely essential for the site manager to be familiar with existing law and act to assure compliance by the on-site staff.

THE SITE MANAGER'S ROLE IN THE MANAGEMENT COMPANY

In all aspects of site management, the site manager is a representative of the management firm and the owner. While owners, accountants, architects, and contractors may determine the *potential* profitability of a rental property, the site manager's operation of the property will influence whether it realizes (or fails to realize) its potential. As the agent of the owner on the front line of management, the site manager will be accountable for everything that occurs at the site. Although not usually involved in establishing management company policies, the site manager is responsible for their implementation and enforcement and may have to modify them to meet the property's particular needs.

Effective site managers keep an eye on the details as well as the big picture. For example, evaluation of individual budget items and day-to-day activities adds perspective to the overall operations of the property and enables the manager to have a positive long-term impact on its financial condition and performance.

SUMMARY

Site managers are responsible for the day-to-day operations of residential properties. While their specific responsibilities may vary according to property size and type, the structure of the management company, and the owner's goals, certain responsibilities will be common. These include marketing and leasing, customer service and resident relations, staff supervision, administration, and operations.

The success of residential real estate depends on the site manager's management and communication skills, as well as such personal qualities as maturity, judgment, and professionalism. The site manager must be able to manage people and resources effectively, possess good organizational and time management skills, and be able to assess the relative importance of tasks in order to establish priorities.

The actions of site managers—in particular those granted the ARM® service award by IREM—are guided by a code of ethics that requires them to be professional at all times and to foster an atmosphere that assures employee and resident retention. Site management is a professional field that requires both attention to detail and a sense of the big picture. Without professionalism, neither the owner's objectives nor the satisfaction of the residents can be assured.

As a representative of the management company and the property owner, the site manager is first in line to deal with residents, site employees, vendors, and governmental agencies. The site manager works for the owner, and the principal goal of property management is to contain costs and generate income. However, this goal can only be achieved by promoting good relations with vendors and outside contractors, fostering staff loyalty, and providing excellent service to residents who will continue to call the property home.

Key Terms

ACCREDITED RESIDENTIAL MANAGER® (ARM®)
administration
code of ethics
fair housing laws

Key Concepts

communication
operations manual
policies and procedures
site management
time management

Key Points

- What are the basic responsibilities of site management?
- What qualities must a successful site manager possess?
- Why are communication and interpersonal skills critical to site management?
- How is a code of ethics similar to a law? How is it different?

3

Personnel Relations—Building an Effective Team

The success of residential real estate ultimately depends on its human component—its staff members sharing a commitment to both individual accomplishments and team goals. Starting with the recruiting process and continuing through training and supervision, personnel relations is a key component of real estate management. An apartment community that offers numerous amenities but has an unprofessional and unresponsive staff will not retain many residents beyond their initial lease terms. In turn, high resident turnover will erode the income generated by the property, increase expenses, and jeopardize the owner's investment.

The relationship between the site manager and the property manager is much like that of an orchestra conductor and a composer. The property manager—along with the owner—composes the music. The site manager is the conductor, bringing harmony by conveying the expectations of the owner and the management company to the site staff and ensuring that the entire group works together to achieve these goals.

Together, the property manager and the site manager determine the quality of the on-site staff by assessing the needs of the property, writing the job descriptions used to recruit potential employees, interviewing candidates, and making hiring decisions. Once site employees have been hired, the site manager directly supervises their work, conveying performance expectations and implementing the personnel policies of the management company. Staff efficiency and productivity depend on effective communication. Choosing responsible site employees and continually motivating them assures that the property will perform at the highest possible level.

IDENTIFYING STAFFING NEEDS

A stable, goal-oriented staff is an asset to any company. In the case of real estate management, staff members are entrusted to implement the policies of the management company, maintain the owner's property, and enter residents' apartments to make repairs. The key to having such employees is being selective in hiring them in the first place. The selection process is critical to bringing productive employees into the firm and keeping them there; the site staff represents a major investment for the management company in terms of both time and money. While the site manager must pay careful attention to all matters that concern on-site employees, recruitment is especially important because it is the starting point for building sound personnel relations and fostering employee retention.

Personnel needs depend on the age and size of the property, its population density, the number and kinds of amenities, the extensiveness of the grounds, and the owner's goals. For example, a 100-unit apartment building might require a site manager, one full-time maintenance technician, a part-time maintenance technician (depending on the property's age, turnover, and other factors), and a part-time leasing agent. If the leasing office is open more than five days a week, or during intensive lease-up, another part-time or full-time leasing agent may be required. On the other hand, a 300-unit apartment building could require a site manager, an assistant site manager, a full-time leasing agent, a maintenance supervisor, and two maintenance technicians, perhaps including an additional employee to do painting or maintain the grounds or recreational facilities.

What tasks have to be performed—and how often—will also be a determining factor. What must be done on a daily, weekly, or monthly basis? The list of site tasks should account for everything from rent col-

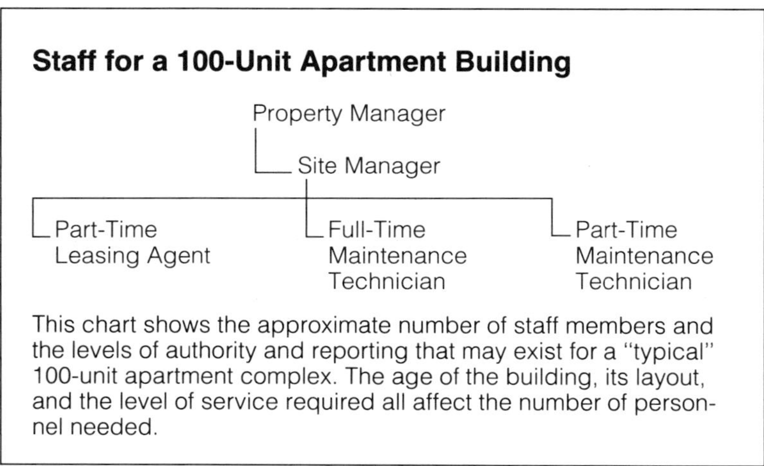

This chart shows the approximate number of staff members and the levels of authority and reporting that may exist for a "typical" 100-unit apartment complex. The age of the building, its layout, and the level of service required all affect the number of personnel needed.

lection to landscaping and may be very detailed. Much like a budget, the determination of personnel needs will include both time requirements and the amount of money needed to meet specific goals, as well as the skills and background required of the person who will perform each task. A very large property that offers numerous services and amenities will have a longer list of tasks than a smaller building that offers only basic resident services. Once all the tasks have been accounted for, they can be combined to form larger categories such as administration, leasing, and maintenance. Such function-specific categories are also useful in determining if positions should be part-time or full-time and whether outside contractors should be used instead. Advance planning and careful analysis of work flow assures that the right number of people are hired for appropriate positions from the start.

Property management requires flexibility, so no single formula for determining the size of a staff applies to all cases. A management company may employ a social director who coordinates programs throughout a property manager's entire portfolio or HVAC technicians who complement the on-site staffs of several properties. Such strategies cost less than using outside vendors and assure rapid response to the needs of any one property.

Once needs have been identified and evaluated, individual job descriptions should be developed. A carefully prepared *job description* concisely defines the tasks and requisite skills for a position. It also states who will supervise the work (the person to whom the employee will report). A job description should also specify minimum educa-

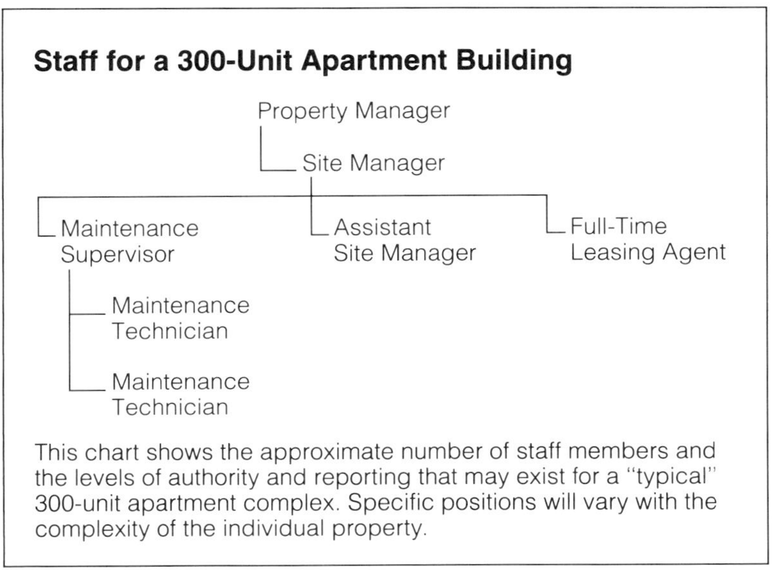

This chart shows the approximate number of staff members and the levels of authority and reporting that may exist for a "typical" 300-unit apartment complex. Specific positions will vary with the complexity of the individual property.

tional requirements and indicate whether additional qualifications (e.g., specialized technical training, licensure or certification, achievement of the ARM® service award) or a particular level of expertise (e.g., size of property, years of experience) is necessary or desirable. By thus eliminating unqualified candidates from consideration, the job description aids in the selection of qualified personnel and enables the site manager to evaluate employee performance in a meaningful way.

The language of the job description should be clear and easy to understand. It should also afford management the opportunity to expand the responsibilities of a job as needed. This is accomplished by avoiding language so specific that variations of interpretation are impossible. Inclusion of a statement such as, "Duties shall include, but not be limited to," or "Responsibilities may from time to time be changed to reflect the needs of the department or the management company," increases your freedom to assign tasks to employees. (In some unionized positions, job descriptions will be more circumscribed.) Job descriptions should never include any references to gender, age, physical ability, race, or any other characteristics that could be interpreted as discriminatory—the Americans with Disabilities Act (ADA) limits job descriptions and hiring decisions to a position's essential job functions, and civil rights laws prohibit discrimination on other bases (Equal Employment Opportunity—EEO).

In addition to helping identify the best candidates, a well-prepared job description makes clear the employer's expectations about job performance and is an essential part of job training and retraining. It can be referred to if a current employee's work has suffered and is a yardstick for measuring performance, determining pay raises, and awarding promotions. The job description also serves as a public statement of company norms, which may be useful in responding to EEO, ADA, and wrongful discharge claims if they should arise.

THE SELECTION PROCESS

The selection process is the means by which suitable job candidates are identified and eventually hired. A sound selection process brings on board employees who will remain with the company for some time, resulting in a stable, satisfied staff and an efficiently operated property. In addition, the site manager reaps personal benefits from a capable staff, including peace of mind from knowing that jobs will be done correctly and on time. The result is also good for residents, staff members, the management company, and the owner.

Once the needs of the property and the specific skills required for the position have been identified, recruitment can begin. Recruitment is intended to attract suitable job candidates to apply for the position, with the best-qualified applicants being invited to interview. Based on candidates' qualifications and successful interviews, the site manager and the property manager will make hiring decisions and fill the open position.

Recruitment—Finding the Right Person for the Job

There are several approaches to finding qualified job candidates, and each of them has benefits and drawbacks. Classified advertisements, employment agencies, and personal referrals are all directed outward. Recruiting from among current employees offers great potential with relatively little downside.

Internal Promotion. Although some believe that it doubles the cost of training because both the person promoted and his or her successor must be trained simultaneously, promotion from within re-

> **Hiring Do's and Don'ts**
>
> **DO**
> - Prepare or update job description(s)
> - Ask all candidates the same questions
> - Ask hypothetical questions to test problem-solving skills
> - Check all references
>
> **DON'T**
> - Overlook current employees who are ready for promotion
> - Prejudge candidates—keep an open mind
> - Be distracted by a charming candidate—stick to job-related issues
> - Ask personal questions that could be considered discriminatory

tains and increases the value of excellent employees. True, the initial training expense may be slightly higher, but promotion may actually be more efficient. Because the promoted employee is already familiar with the company, he or she may understand the new position quite well. This can reduce the actual training required. The promoted employee may be able to train his or her successor, thus reducing the demands on the trainee's supervisor and strengthening the sense of teamwork. Starting a newcomer in a lower-level position also provides room for individual growth within the company, which fosters loyalty and stability and offsets the need to seek future opportunities elsewhere. By offering existing employees the opportunity to remain with the company and grow professionally, internal promotion enhances the company's reputation as an employer, and that will attract other well-qualified candidates from outside the company. Thus, promotion from within becomes an additional, powerful recruiting tool.

Help-Wanted Advertisements. Newspaper ads generate quick responses, but they can yield hundreds of candidates. Because many respondents are likely to be overqualified or underqualified for the advertised position, selecting the best-qualified candidates is often time-consuming and burdensome. To expedite the screening process, the help-wanted ad should instruct respondents to submit a resume, work history, salary requirements, and other pertinent information that matches them to the position's requirements. An additional safeguard is the use of a blind box number. These are commonly offered by newspapers; they provide anonymity and help control this step by sparing employers a deluge of telephone calls and letters from hopeful candidates, which require staff time and additional expense for responses and follow-up.

As an alternative to the blind box, you may specify the hours when telephone calls will be accepted. This approach is especially useful for initial screening of candidates for jobs that require good interpersonal skills. Brief preliminary interviews can be conducted over the telephone, and based on the caller's qualifications and the outcome of the telephone interview, he or she may be invited to come to the management office and fill out an application. After the form is reviewed, the person may be called for a comprehensive interview. However, management companies differ in their approaches to hiring. If timing is critical (e.g., several employees must be hired at once for a new apartment community), it may be preferable to include a street address in the ad along with specific hours to apply. In such a situation, the management office would likely assign people to screen applicants and conduct interviews throughout the day to expedite the hiring process.

Employment Agencies. This approach can also be useful. The agency will need a detailed job description and a list of minimum qualifications. The agency screens candidates for the skills or experience necessary for the available position, and only the most qualified candidates are interviewed by the employer. Such time and work savings can be substantial, especially if the employer does not have a personnel department or if the position to be filled requires specialized skills. However, the job of agencies is "selling" job applicants to clients, and they may offer unqualified candidates merely to fill a position and collect a fee. In addition, the agency's fee, which may be the equivalent of a month's salary or a percentage of the annual salary for the position being filled, may exceed what some management companies can allocate for recruitment.

Referrals. Personal referrals from current employees of the company can be a valuable resource. Such prospects usually already know something about the company and are probably capable individuals or they would not have been referred. However, great care must be exercised when relying on personal referrals. Over time, they may tend to perpetuate a particular cultural or racial composition of the staff, which could be perceived as discriminatory. In a richly diverse cultural environment, no company can afford to do this.

Another consideration is placing close friends together on the job. This is especially problematic in a supervisor-subordinate relationship, which could pose difficulties if one of the people is disciplined or dismissed. There is also the temptation for one employee to cover up a friend's mistake or dishonesty.

Networking is yet another source of referrals. Involvement in associations and organizations—the Institute of Real Estate Management, for example—can provide many contacts that allow real estate professionals to keep up-to-date with local business activities. Often others in the field have passed up qualified job candidates because they had only one position to fill, and they may be willing to share copies of resumes they have received. Established networking relationships can help you locate the right person for a position and quickly check his or her credentials.

In addition to active recruitment, a property management firm receives many unsolicited resumes and applications. These should be reviewed when they are received, even if no positions are open, because you never know when a position may become available. Qualified applicants often make unsolicited inquiries. Resumes and applications of such people should be dated and kept on file. All who make inquiries should receive a written response, regardless of whether the resume or application will be kept. Even a rejection letter can create a favorable impression, and since the reputation of a company is its greatest asset, such a gesture of goodwill can be invaluable.

The Application Process

The hiring process for all site personnel should follow an established procedure, including the use of a standard application form. All job applicants should be evaluated consistently and objectively as a matter of fairness and to make certain that the hiring process is not discriminatory.

Application Forms and Procedures. Regardless of how prospective employees are recruited, all candidates should complete an employment application form. A standard form organizes the information needed to make hiring decisions and aids in comparing the candidates' qualifications.

An employment application (exhibit 3.1) should include spaces for the applicant's name, address, telephone number, social security

EXHIBIT 3.1

Sample Employment Application

Your interest in applying for employment is appreciated. It is our policy that all individuals applying for employment shall be treated equitably and without regard to race, color, religion, sex, national origin, ancestry, age, marital status, physical or mental handicap unrelated to ability, or unfavorable discharge from military service. Your qualifications will be reviewed in strict accordance with this policy.

Please print all information

Personal Information

Name ____________________

Address ____________________

City ____________ State ____________ Zip ____________

Home Phone ____________ Business Phone ____________

Social Security Number ____________ Are you a U.S. citizen? ____________

Employment Desired

Position ____________ Date Available ____________ Salary Desired ____________

How did you learn about the job? ____________________

List your skills and qualifications for the job ____________________

____

____

Have you ever been convicted of a crime other than a minor traffic violation?

______ If yes, please explain ____________________

Are you currently employed? ______ If so, may we contact your employer?

____

Have you ever applied
to this company before? ______ Where ____________ When ____________

Have you ever declared bankruptcy? ______ When ____________

Education

Institution	Name and Location of School	Years Attended	Date Graduated	Subjects Studied
Grammar school				
High school				
College				
Other (specify)				

Specialized training ____________________

____

____

EXHIBIT 3.1 *(continued)*

Employment History (List most recent job first.)

Employer (Name, Address, Supervisor)	Dates of Employment	Position	Salary	Reason for Leaving

Other activities—e.g., civic, athletic, trade or professional memberships; volunteer work. (Exclude organizations whose name or character indicates race, color, religion, national origin, or ancestry of its members.) ______________________

____

____

References

Name ______________________ Years known ________

Address ______________________

Business ______________________ Phone ________

Name ______________________ Years known ________

Address ______________________

Business ______________________ Phone ________

Nearest relative or person to contact in case of emergency ______________

____

Address ______________________ Phone ________

I hereby authorize all educational institutions, persons, law enforcement agencies, military services, and former employers to release information they may have about me to [*Name of Management Company*] or its agents, and release them from any liability or responsibility from doing so. I understand that any omission or false preemployment information given is reason for disqualification or dismissal, and that an offer of employment is subject to verification of employment history satisfactory to [*Name of Management Company.*]

Signature ______________________ Date ________

Do not write below this line

Interviewed by ______________________ Date ________

Remarks ______________________

____

Hired _____ Department _____ Position _____ To report _____ Salary _____ number, and citizenship status. It should also require information on educational background and relevant training as well as jobs previously held and their respective responsibilities. References from previous employers are another important consideration. The employers' names, addresses, and telephone numbers should be requested along with the names of the applicants' supervisors, the duties they performed, how long they were employed, and their rate of pay. Reasons for leaving positions can provide additional insights. Applicants should also be asked to sign a waiver authorizing the prospective employer to contact references and former employers for verification of the information on the application and to run credit and criminal background checks where applicable. This information will enable you to evaluate each candidate's qualifications objectively and identify patterns that could make you question a candidate's commitment—frequent job changes, for example.

Individual applicants should be evaluated on the basis of the skills and characteristics required for the position, as identified in the job description. The first step is to create a profile of the position that lists specific duties and the skills needed to accomplish them. This will allow comparison of each applicant's qualifications with those of the "ideal" candidate. After evaluating all the applications, the qualified candidates should be ranked and interview questions prepared. Those who are not qualified should be advised that they are not being considered further.

The Interview—The Importance of Listening

The interview may be the only opportunity to evaluate a job candidate personally and determine whether an individual is suited to a position. It may be advisable to divide the interview process into two steps. General interviews conducted over the phone or in person can be used to screen likely candidates. Those candidates who have passed the brief preliminary interviews then meet with other people in the office for more thorough interviews. Although this may add some time to the hiring process, it can be a useful way to select the best candidates from a number of applicants.

In order to get the most information in the least amount of time during the actual interview, it is essential to prepare in advance. Interview questions should be probing enough to allow you to evaluate

Key Steps in the Interview Process

- Identify objectives
- Be specific about job requirements
- Use open-ended questions: Listen to—don't talk over—candidates' responses
- Probe to get complete information: Don't leap to premature conclusions
- Answer candidates' questions

candidates without making them uncomfortable. Ideally, most of the interview questions will be open-ended and call on candidates to talk about ways they would respond to particular situations. Questions that can be answered either yes or no generally will not yield enough good information to help make informed hiring decisions.

These questions should also be related to the position to be filled. A leasing agent would not be asked to answer the same questions as a maintenance technician, or vice versa, but all candidates for a particular position should be asked the same questions. This can be done by developing a standardized interview format so that all candidates will receive equal consideration. A written list of questions also assures that nothing is left out during the interview.

Interviews should be conducted in a relaxed, private atmosphere that will foster candor. Just as yes or no questions yield only limited information, questions that are misleading may confuse applicants or detract from a friendly environment. On the other hand, questions that ask what, how, and why allow candidates to provide explanations. Open-ended questions can be used to discover how a job candidate would behave in different types of situations. The subject of the questions and the answers to them should characterize actual behavior in hypothetical situations calling for such traits as honesty, punctuality, or loyalty. In this dynamic, people-oriented field, questions that measure candidates' creativity, enthusiasm, and motivation are also informative. The following are some examples.

- What did you like most about your previous job? What did you like least?
- What did you learn from that job?
- What would you say are your strong points?

- What would you say are your weak points?
- What would be the ideal position for you? Why?
- What are your career goals for the next three years? The next five years?
- If you are hired, what kind of an employee will we get?
- What can you do that will make a difference at the property and help us achieve our goals?

Allow enough space in your interview guide to take notes about candidates' responses. (If another person is participating in the interview, you can compare notes.) Written documentation not only facilitates hiring decisions, it helps avoid problems if a decision is questioned at a later time.

Role playing is another helpful tool for assessing candidates. Role-play scenarios may be specific to a position or they can be general—a test of selling skills is appropriate for leasing agents while interpersonal skills are applicable to all on-site positions. The best approach is for the interviewer to assume the role of a protagonist (e.g., an irate resident, a prospective resident raising objections to an apartment, a co-worker), with the applicant acting out a response. Scenarios can be drawn from prior incidents at the property or purely hypothetical, but the role-play itself should have a specific objective within the interview. To explore how someone might handle a confrontation, you may want to characterize an irate resident for the candidate to calm down and assist. The cause of the upset might be a noisy neighbor, unfinished in-unit maintenance, or someone else's car in the resident's parking space. To test a candidate's selling skills, you could explore a prospective resident's objections to a particular apartment based on the lack of a separate dining room, too little closet space, or an undesirable view. An incident between co-workers would provide additional insights about a candidate's attitudes or willingness to be a team player. Different circumstances would yield different responses. The aim is to find out how (and how well) someone would fit into the established group and do the particular job.

The interview is also an opportunity to follow up on details or omissions from the application form. Asking why a person left a previous job or questioning any gaps that appear in the applicant's record will clarify his or her qualifications. Because communication is essential even at this early stage, the applicant should be given an opportunity to ask questions about the position or the company. The applicant is also trying to decide, "Do I want to work here?"

Although you will need a great deal of information, certain questions should never be asked either in the interview or on the application form. These include the candidate's age, marital status or birthplace—or native language—and whether he or she has ever been arrested (although it is legal to ask if an applicant has ever been *convicted* of a felony). Note, however, that the point about native language has differing implications: Facility in a second language relevant to the resident profile could be an advantage if not a requisite for hiring, but asking about a candidate's native language for the purpose of identifying nationality would be discriminatory. The guidelines on what can and cannot be asked in an interview or on an application form vary from state to state. Local regulations should be consulted prior to implementing a policy. In cases where federal, state, and local laws differ, it is wise to follow the ones that are most stringent. Perhaps the best rule of thumb is: If a question is directly related to the job, ask it. If not, don't ask.

Usually the top two or three job candidates are called back for a second interview. This is an opportunity to ask additional or follow-up questions that remain after the initial interview. Second interviews also provide a basis for comparing the contenders for the position. While the first interview may have covered their work history, education, and applicable skills, the second interview is an opportunity to probe the candidates' motivation and attitudes, which are critical factors in a hiring decision.

Obviously, not all candidates will be fully qualified. Those who are not selected for follow-up interviews should be notified promptly. Rejection letters should be carefully worded and provide objective reasons for not selecting the candidate. Because of the potential for legal liability, it is best if these letters come from the main office. However, if rejection letters are sent by the site manager, they should be reviewed by the property manager beforehand.

Hiring Decisions

Individual capability (aptitude), attitude, and demonstrated reliability should be the main factors in selecting a new employee. While some

What to Look for in Job Candidates

General Requirements
- People skills
- Problem-solving skills
- Communication skills
- Motivation
- Experience

Depending on the Job
- Formal education
- Technical skills
- Certification or licensing
- Computer literacy
- Writing ability
- Potential for growth

of the reasons for selecting one candidate over another are likely to be subjective (e.g., a person's conduct during an interview creates distinct impressions), any factors that could be construed as discriminatory should not enter into the decision. In site management, sound hiring decisions are based on such factors as stability, long-term patterns of professional behavior, knowledge of building type and market conditions or maintenance procedures, performance on screening tests, and favorable references and credit checks.

Prior to a formal offer of employment, it is imperative to check all the information provided, including personal (character) references. Some companies are reluctant to give negative reports on former employees, so it may be advisable to have applicants sign a separate waiver that releases previous employers from liability for information given in references. (A copy of the waiver is sent to the former employer along with the request.) The status of professional or other licenses (e.g., real estate licenses, skilled trade licenses) should be verified at this time. For security purposes, fiduciary bonds may also be required for all employees who handle money, and bonding companies typically require credit checks and police reports on applicants. This step provides additional insurance against losses. (It may be prudent to have credit checks and police reports run on all applicants, regardless of whether their jobs will require them to handle money.

EXHIBIT 3.2

Proofs of Citizenship and Employment Eligibility

Documents that establish identity AND employment eligibility
- U.S. passport
- Certificate of U.S. citizenship
- Certificate of naturalization
- Unexpired foreign passport with attached employment authorization
- Alien registration card with photograph

Documents that establish identity
- State-issued driver's license or I.D. card with a photograph or descriptive information
- U.S. military card

Documents that establish employment eligibility
- Original social security number card
- Birth certificate issued by state, county, or municipal authority
- Unexpired INS employment authorization

However, advice of legal counsel should be sought before such a procedure is implemented.) Assuming a candidate passes these last screening tests, the formal offer of employment should always be made in writing, even when an offer is made (and accepted) in person or over the telephone.

Under the *Immigration Reform and Control Act of 1986,* employers are required to verify employment eligibility. Employers often address this issue when the new employee reports for work. The law requires employees to complete U.S. Immigration and Naturalization Services (INS) Form I-9 and present proof of their identity and eligibility to work (exhibit 3.2). The Act also prohibits discrimination on the basis of national origin or citizenship in hiring, firing, recruiting, or referring for a fee, provided an individual is authorized to work in the United States. There are some exceptions to the 1986 Act. They include "casual" domestic employees whose employment is sporadic, irregular, or intermittent; independent contractors such as consultants, fee management companies, real estate agents, accountants, lawyers, and those hired through temporary employment agencies; and "grandfathered" employees—those hired prior to November 7, 1986, and in "continuing employment." It is important to understand how this law—and others—affect employers' decisions.

Avoiding Discriminatory Practices

Hiring policies and procedures set by the management company, implemented by the site manager, and followed faithfully will assure compliance with fair employment practices and equal employment opportunity laws. Nondiscrimination means that individual candidates are considered on the basis of their capabilities and not on the basis of any characteristics that might be attributed to a group. Factors such as race, age, pregnancy, religion, national origin, or disability must not enter into the hiring decision, influence compensation offered for a job, or affect employment longevity after hiring. Such discrimination is prohibited under federal civil rights laws enforced by the *Equal Employment Opportunity Commission (EEOC)* as well as by states and municipalities. Some local jurisdictions bar discrimination on the basis of marital status, sexual orientation, or other criteria.

Furthermore, the *Americans with Disabilities Act (ADA)* prohibits discrimination in job application procedures, hiring, advancement, discharge, compensation, or job training *because of an applicant's disability*. (A disability is a physical or mental impairment that substantially limits one or more of the major life functions.) A "qualified individual with a disability" is someone with a disability who can perform the essential functions of the position he or she holds or desires, with or without reasonable accommodation.

During the interview, you should avoid making assumptions about someone's needs or expressing personal comments or observations that could be considered demeaning or misleading. However, it is appropriate to ask questions about past job experience and ability to perform specific job functions. These should be asked of all applicants. In other words, disabled job candidates should not be treated differently from other prospective employees—a disability cannot be an issue in a hiring decision.

STAFF TRAINING AND SUPERVISION—PREPARING FOR SUCCESS

Orientation of new employees may be conducted at the management company's main office or on site. During the new employee orientation, the site manager should discuss the company, its history, organization, and goals, in addition to the employee's specific duties and responsibilities and the company's expectations regarding his or her performance. The new employee should also be given the information in writing. Minimally, there should be a written job description that details the duties of the position. Ideally, each newly hired employee would receive a copy of the employee manual or other written material that explains the company's policies and procedures for all aspects of employment. Orientation is also the site manager's opportunity to familiarize new employees with the firm's policies concerning resident relations and ethical practices as well as company benefits, performance reviews (how they are done and how often), and career advancement. A complete tour of the property will let you introduce the new employee to his or her co-workers as well as any residents you encounter along the way.

Communicating Expectations and Motivating Personnel

Employees have a right to know what is expected of them, and employers have an obligation to communicate expectations unequivocally. Site management jobs are very different from each other. Performance expectations should be based on the duties and responsibilities of the job and discussed at length in the employee's orientation. A leasing agent might be expected to achieve a certain number of signed leases within a defined period of time. A maintenance technician might be required to perform certain repairs within established time limits or to respond to different types of work orders in specific ways. An office assistant may have to prepare reports on a fixed schedule. In addition to communicating expectations about performance of particular tasks, certain positions demand special qualities from employees. For example, a leasing agent must be able to relate well to people, be expressive, have a good closing technique, and communicate effectively. The attributes sought in the hiring process become the measures of employee success.

Because site management is people-oriented, expectations about personal appearance and grooming should be stated to all employees. They represent the property to the residents and to the community at large, and their appearance is an important part of maintaining a professional image that reflects favorably on the property and the

EXHIBIT 3.3

Motivational Techniques for the Site Manager

- Listen to staff members' ideas and suggestions
- Acknowledge others' ideas and accomplishments
- Give positive feedback for jobs well done
- Help individuals achieve their goals
- Foster teamwork
- Clarify expectations
- Be consistent
- Be approachable—admit to being human and making mistakes
- Encourage creativity
- Discourage defensiveness
- Reward excellence

management company. Some management companies ensure this by making uniforms available to their employees (the employees are responsible for keeping them clean). Sometimes properties specify that on-site office workers must wear clothing that matches the color schemes developed for marketing campaigns. Regardless whether uniforms are required, a dress code should make clear what is unacceptable (e.g., blue jeans and tee shirts).

Motivating employees is crucial. Fostering an atmosphere in which they feel needed and valued, praising them when they do well, and helping them when they struggle are among the best motivators (exhibit 3.3). It is important to find out what will motivate each individual and use that information to guide the employee. An employee may respond to praise, challenges, or the promise of financial rewards, but not all employees will respond the same way to the same motivators. Praise may take the form of awards, contests, letters of recognition, or public acknowledgment. Additional tasks, increasing responsibility, and promotions are examples of challenges. Financial rewards may depend on position: Salary increases are most common, but commissions and bonus or incentive plans may also be used. While people seek different rewards, everyone responds favorably to involvement and participation and the feeling that they and their insights are valued. Such an atmosphere, in turn, generates new ideas that contribute to the success of the entire team.

It is important to acknowledge that employees may be experiencing personal problems. In the past, involvement in the personal problems of employees was discouraged. Domestic problems, alcoholism, or other difficulties were considered outside the realm of professional life. However, as the work force continues to shrink, companies have begun to respond differently to the personal needs of their employees. Flexible work schedules, job sharing, and day care for children are but a few of the options being explored by employers. Employees who once would have been summarily fired because of substance-abuse problems today are given the opportunity to receive counseling and keep their jobs, provided they attend sessions regularly and improve their on-the-job performance accordingly. While there is a cost—and some risk—in such a strategy, giving an employee a chance to improve his or her life at home and work represents an investment in that person, which in turn rewards the company with loyal and stable staff members. As a precaution, you may want to confer with an attorney and a risk consultant before making a final decision in such a situation.

Retaining Good Employees. A great deal of effort is invested in developing a team, and rebuilding it because of turnover is very expensive. Talented and dedicated personnel are a site manager's most valuable resource. Enabling employees to grow professionally and seek new challenges in the workplace will promote commitment and loyalty and reduce job-hopping. Communication and training help workers grow personally as the demands placed on the business increase. Employees who are encouraged to undertake new tasks and are legitimately capable of mastering the work will be increasingly productive, such that it may not be necessary to hire additional personnel. Employees also benefit if they develop more self-confidence and can base their sense of security on their own growing abilities rather than on the minimum effort their jobs might require of them. Workshops and seminars offered through associations or colleges on such topics as accounting, maintenance, human relations, interpersonal skills, and management techniques provide opportunities for both personal and professional development. Depending on the cost, the management company may pay tuition for its employees to attend courses, although the quality and relevance of course offerings should be thoroughly investigated in advance. A large staff may justify the expense of bringing programs of general interest in house (e.g., interpersonal skills, communication). Some training programs can be tailored to a particular audience, making the experience even better because it is company-specific. (Professionalism, as such, is discussed in detail in chapter 11.)

Policies and Procedures—Fairness and Consistency

The personnel policies and procedures of the management company and the site office should be detailed in an *employee handbook,* which all new staff members should receive. Employee benefits, general policies, and disciplinary rules should be included, and everything in it should be updated periodically. An employee handbook should contain the following information:

1. Information about the company, including a brief history, a statement of objectives, and an organizational chart.
2. The company's policies affecting internal and external activities such as employee attitudes, promotion from within, public relations, and ethics.
3. The general rules of employment, including hours of work, overtime pay, pay days, benefits, holidays, sick leave, personal leave, vacations, and performance evaluations.

A well-prepared employee handbook provides detailed information about employees' rights and responsibilities and gives clear guidelines on behavior and the employer's expectations (exhibit 3.4).

A comprehensive employee handbook that explains the policies and procedures of the management company and the property also discourages wrongful discharge claims by terminated employees. The employee handbook constitutes a formal written policy regarding standards of conduct—as a requirement under that policy, and in conformance with the company's specific policies and procedures regarding termination, documentation of employee performance can be used to demonstrate the validity of a dismissal.

EVALUATING PERSONNEL

Because communication is vital to efficient site operations, regular performance reviews should also be scheduled—and they should be

EXHIBIT 3.4

Typical Contents of an Employee Handbook

- Introduction and company history
- Personnel policies—hiring, promotions, transfers, discipline, grievance procedures, layoffs, termination of employment
- Compensation—wage and salary policy, exempt and nonexempt status, hours of work and work week, workday schedule, straight time pay, paydays, overtime pay, temporary rates, performance reviews
- Employee benefits—vacation, sick leave, personal leave, holidays and holiday pay, educational assistance, leave of absence, death in immediate family, jury duty, military leave of absence
- Group insurance and retirement plan—life insurance, health insurance, disability insurance, work-related illness or injuries, retirement plan
- Miscellaneous—safety and security on the job
- Employee acknowledgment—statement, signature, and date

NOTE: Usually the employee handbook is considered company property and must be returned when an employee resigns or is terminated.

conducted when promised. These sessions should be viewed as opportunities for employees to learn about their performance and address their concerns about their jobs. However, employee evaluations should be an ongoing process and not limited to formal annual or semiannual reviews. An observant site manager will monitor the performance of his or her staff continually and communicate the need for adjustments or reward outstanding work as required. When communication is fostered in the workplace, teamwork will flourish, evaluation of personnel will be spontaneous, and problems will be addressed before they become unmanageable.

Probationary Period

A probationary period of employment, during which a new employee is trained for the job and expected to become familiar with the property and its workings, may be a standard operating procedure of the property management firm. At the end of a specified period—usually three months, but sometimes longer—the employee's progress is reviewed, and the decision is made whether to continue or terminate employment. Often the employee will not receive full benefits during probation (for example, paid sick days may be limited or vacation time may not be available). Upon completion of the probationary period and favorable review, the individual becomes a "regular" employee. (The term "permanent employee" should be avoided because it has legal ramifications if an employee who is dismissed decides to pursue a wrongful discharge claim.)

Performance Review

Performance review is a useful device for encouraging employees who are doing a good job and helping those who are struggling. If the site manager has been providing regular feedback to staff members, the performance review may only be a formal confirmation of what has already been said. Performance reviews are commonly conducted once a year, although new employees are usually reviewed at the end of their first six months on the job. The early review is an opportunity for the employee and the site manager to discuss their initial employment decisions, reaffirming a good decision or choosing to go their separate ways because of a poor one.

All employees should be expected to use their skills and talents to their fullest, and everyone should be treated with respect regardless of the tasks they perform or whether their role is supervisory or subordinate. The formal review should reiterate the site manager's expectations of the employee, evaluate the employee's performance (pointing out strengths and weaknesses as appropriate), and reward good work. If an employee's performance has not met expectations, this review is an opportunity for the site manager and the employee to plan ways to identify shortcomings and their causes and to improve performance. Of course, the employee review is not a substitute for regular and continuing evaluation of performance and open communication at all times. Informal communication can be the most valuable of all. Continual feedback to all employees will reinforce desired behavior as well as reiterate the site manager's expectations.

Ongoing Communication. Communication should be an ongoing process and not limited to annual performance reviews. As a supervisor, the site manager should foster a work environment in which communication is welcome. Employees should be able to offer suggestions, comments, and constructive criticisms without fear of reprisals. In such an atmosphere, problems will surface quickly and be resolved painlessly.

The site manager might consider an "open door" policy for airing work-related and personal problems. More than merely leaving the office door open, such a policy should encourage staff members to examine their working relationships with fellow employees with openness and candor. Open communication should not be viewed solely as a means by which employees complain about the workplace or their jobs. Grievances are a natural part of life and work, and misunderstandings can result in employee dissatisfaction or loss of reliable people if their concerns are not addressed promptly and sincerely. Open communication enables people to work more efficiently. It encourages the sharing of information and ideas by inviting employees' opinions and responding to them, using new employee orientation and performance reviews as part of an ongoing communication program, and training supervisors in methods of effective communication. Open communication also improves employee morale by making the workplace atmosphere more pleasant.

Personal contact is the simplest and most effective method of fostering good employee relations. Both formal and informal meetings are useful ways to explain company policies and procedures and respond to employee concerns. Clear communication helps retain valued employees. Because employees usually rely on their co-workers for news and information about the workplace, it is important to make sure that damaging rumors based on speculation do not spread. This can be averted by responding promptly to events and explaining them fully. Being forthcoming about occurrences that affect the company is the best way to control rumors and foster goodwill among employees.

A formal communication policy might establish a number of specific vehicles for keeping staff members informed, including an employee handbook, periodic newsletters, and a company bulletin board. Such a policy is more appropriate to a large property management firm or apartment community than a small one. On a smaller property, diligent efforts to keep lines of communication open may substitute for an explicit policy. Newsletters may be replaced by written memos, personal messages, and face-to-face conversations. Of course, face-to-face conversations are a vital form of communication everywhere.

Many companies communicate with employees through periodic

newsletters, and the ease and convenience of desktop publishing make this a viable option. The writing style should be friendly and personal, and the finished product should be free from typographical and grammatical errors, which appear careless and unprofessional. A newsletter that is directed to all employees creates a sense of community and teamwork. Employees are interested in the company they work for and want to know about its successes, failures, and general business activities. Recognition of service anniversaries and promotions and news about fellow workers will add a personal touch.

Impact of Staff Turnover—Financial Costs and Management Disruption

Retention of employees not only minimizes personnel costs, it increases the value of individual employees because responsible and dedicated people remain in place. However, employee retention depends on many factors, including compensation, opportunities for advancement, a satisfying work environment, personal growth and development, and challenging work assignments.

The most obvious tangible rewards of dedicated service are pay and benefits. In order to retain employees in a competitive environment, their compensation must not only keep pace with market levels of wages and salaries, but offer them satisfaction and an incentive to strive for greater rewards. Salary adjustments based on performance evaluations should be scheduled regularly, budgeted routinely, and administered fairly. As an additional incentive, some portion of employees' compensation might be linked to the company's annual profits or the annual net income of the property.

In times of economic contraction or recession, financial rewards for a job well done may not be feasible. Instead of pay raises, providing employees with additional opportunities for training and development of new job skills may be an option. Professional growth and development can be very satisfying personally. In truth, employee job satisfaction often derives from many factors other than pay—things like interesting work, appreciation of work done, good working conditions, loyal management, and help with personal problems are very important to some individuals. Meeting these needs fosters teamwork and job satisfaction among employees.

HANDLING AND RESOLVING EMPLOYEE PROBLEMS

Good working relations with employees contribute directly to maintaining good "customer relations" with your residents and the property owner. To foster a productive and pleasant atmosphere, the site manager must be fair and impartial in all dealings with employees and respond quickly to any personnel problems that may arise. While many so-called personnel problems are less likely to occur if you follow company policies and standardize your hiring procedures, there is always some possibility that staff members will have to be disciplined or terminated. Company policies should provide for such eventualities.

Progressive Discipline

Occasionally employees will not follow standard procedures. Sometimes a staff member may be rude to a resident or a co-worker. Every situation will be different, and some will have greater potential for negative outcomes. For example, a violation of the dress code would require a different response than a discriminatory statement to a prospective resident. Site managers have to be prepared to deal with a variety of potential personnel problems.

Whatever the type, personnel problems should be addressed swiftly and decisively to make sure that they do not lead to future—and potentially more severe—incidents. Immediately upon learning about or witnessing a behavioral problem that requires action, the site manager should attempt to find out as much as possible about the incident and the circumstances surrounding it. What led to the event? What is the employee's perspective on it? All the relevant information should be written down, and the employee should be given an opportunity to explain privately what happened and why. Confidentiality is critical in all disciplinary matters, whether major or minor.

Another consideration is your personal reaction. If you are angry about an alleged case of employee misconduct, it may be wise to let 24 hours pass before confronting the employee. This will minimize the chance for prejudging the employee and allow you to approach the problem professionally. Not only might an employee be offended

Progressive Discipline

- Oral notice or warning
- Written notice or warning
- Period of Probation
- Dismissal

by a public accusation of wrongdoing, the effort to restore his or her dignity and reputation could include legal action.

Because it is costly and time-consuming to hire and train new employees, it is more desirable to eliminate the problem than to terminate the employee. Consequently, a system of progressive discipline will enable supervisors to encourage problem employees to correct their unacceptable behavior. Giving employees an opportunity to overcome difficulties rather than face immediate dismissal promotes continuity and stability of the site staff and fosters an atmosphere of fairness and a sense of support from the employer. Under a system of *progressive discipline,* employees are given "warnings" or notices regarding on-the-job problems, the number and nature of the notices depending on the severity of the problem. Minor infractions may require only a conversation about company policy and a request that the employee discontinue the behavior. If the problem persists, it may be necessary to prepare a written memorandum and place a copy of it in the employee's personnel file (i.e., put the problem "on the record"). A more severe problem may require a written memorandum with a copy to the employee's personnel file from the start. The memorandum should detail the problem and include corrective steps acceptable to both sides. After discussion, the memo should be signed by both the employee and the supervisor, and the employee should receive a copy. In some cases, particularly when an employee's conduct is an ongoing problem, it may be wise to have another supervisor in the room during the conversation, someone who can act as a witness in case of subsequent litigation.

Sometimes a period of "probation" may be required—the employee is given time in which to overcome the problem. This allows the site manager to monitor the employee's progress and improvement. If the problem is corrected before the end of the probationary period, it is appropriate to acknowledge the fact and cancel the probation in writing. However, the employee must understand the consequences of not correcting the problem within the agreed-upon period of time, which would be dismissal. Regardless of how the probation is set up, the employee should continue to receive pay and benefits during this period.

Timely attention to disciplinary problems is important for several reasons. Poor performance by one individual can directly affect the performance of the other employees; at a minimum, it is likely to lower team morale. In order to avert more serious consequences, the site manager should act immediately—and decisively—when a problem first appears. Timely action is also the only way to help employees improve. The consequences of inaction can be profound, affecting both the morale and productivity of other staff members. In addition, failure to take proper disciplinary action may fuel a wrongful discharge claim if an employee eventually has to be dismissed or result in a lawsuit initiated by an irate or dissatisfied resident.

Termination of Employment

The most extreme action is dismissal or termination. In cases of gross negligence or particularly offensive behavior, termination of employment may be the only choice. It may also be the only remaining alternative if all other means of solving a problem have been exhausted. Nonetheless, great care should be taken when recommending to the property manager that an employee be fired. Because firing an employee has both legal and social ramifications, there must be grounds for immediate dismissal.

Before an employee is dismissed, the circumstances surrounding the events or incidents that are the basis for the termination should be verified and documented—usually repetition of undesirable behavior is a prime consideration. Personnel records, especially a written record of progressive discipline, are extremely useful in this regard. Because a dismissed employee could sue the employer for damages based on discriminatory or other unfair practices, the reasons for termination should be recorded carefully. Documentation should concentrate on the work performed or not performed and not on assumptions regarding its cause (for example, *suspicion* of substance abuse).

The termination itself should be handled privately and confidentially. It should not be used as an opportunity to humiliate the employee (termination is humbling enough). The employee should be told the reasons for dismissal and informed that the decision is irreversible. All keys, pagers, and company identification cards should be returned by the employee, and vendors and suppliers should be notified that the employee is no longer with the firm. Current wages and money owed for unused vacation time or sick days—plus severance pay, if applicable—should be paid to the outgoing employee at the time of discharge, after all company equipment has been returned. If an apartment was part of the employee's compensation, giving it up must also be addressed.

While employment can be terminated for many different reasons, it is illegal to dismiss an employee for trying to form a union, filing a job safety complaint, or belonging to a particular age group, race, religion, or gender. Former employees can also challenge terminations on the basis of fairness, in which case they may claim wrongful discharge and sue their employer. Wrongful discharge suits can be divided into the following categories:

Issues of Good Faith—The employer did not satisfy its obligation to treat its employees fairly. This assumes an implied promise that neither the employer nor the employee will do anything to injure the right of the other to receive the benefits of their agreement. In this case, the agreement is the position, and terminating employment is a breach of the agreement.

Promises Made—It is important to avoid making any statements that might be interpreted as a promise of permanent employment. This includes classifying employees as permanent; instead, they should be classified as regular or, if appropriate, probationary.

The Public Good—Firing employees because of their unwillingness to lie or because they reported illegal activities (whistle blowing) violates federal laws. Other examples would be firing an employee because of time taken for jury duty or the military reserve, both of which constitute public service.

Of course, not all terminations are the result of disciplinary problems or poor performance. Sometimes employees may be laid off, or they may resign their positions to take a job elsewhere or to retire.

Layoffs. When the property income decreases or its operating expenses increase, or if vacancies are excessive, a layoff may be the only way to counter the financial shortfall. Whether permanent or temporary, a layoff can be devastating to employees and their families. The stress on those who remain on the job will increase, and because of the staff shortage, they may have to perform additional work without additional pay. The site manager in this situation also experiences anxiety. Developing positive ways to meet on-the-job challenges while preserving staff morale can be difficult, but it is especially important at these times.

Providing advance notice of an impending layoff and giving employees information that will help them file for unemployment compensation are steps that can be taken if a layoff becomes inevitable. However, the employer who must resort to a layoff has very few options for assisting the terminated employees, especially meeting their financial needs. The most valuable assistance is being direct with employees about the condition of the business, giving them as much warning as possible about the company's future and theirs, and providing them with assistance in finding new employment. The site manager may be able to contact business associates—other managers, other management companies—who may have positions available (i.e., networking). Job-seeker services and resume consultants may also be available locally.

Before giving notice to any employees, all personnel should be reviewed to preclude discrimination against any group as a result of the layoff. In real estate management, layoffs usually begin in the departments that are not directly involved in providing services to residents or property owners, and job performance and seniority often determine which employees will remain.

Resignations. Employee resignations should not be viewed as evidence of disloyalty. Often an employee will leave in order to take a position with greater responsibility or higher pay—there may be no room for upward mobility in the current job. When an employee resigns, the site manager and the individual should agree on a final workday. In general, employees are expected to give two weeks' notice prior to leaving. During this time, the outgoing employee may be responsible for training his or her successor. Regardless of who terminates the employment—or why—the site manager should talk with the departing individual. An exit interview with the employee affords an opportunity for a frank discussion of the strengths and weaknesses of the workplace and a chance to invite suggestions for making it more satisfying to work there.

ADMINISTRATIVE ISSUES

As with other aspects of site management, personnel relations also has administrative responsibilities. These may include implementing employee policies, maintaining payroll records and attending to issues related to compensation, keeping up-to-date files on current employees and retaining files for former employees, and monitoring workplace compliance with equal employment opportunity laws and the Americans with Disabilities Act (ADA). Because these functions are often performed at the management company's central office, the site manager's role may be limited.

Compensation, Benefits, and Payroll

Pay and benefits are the obvious material rewards to employees. Their administration by the site manager usually includes monitoring of hours worked and authorization of overtime pay and benefits. Payroll responsibilities might include computing deductions from employees' paychecks for social security and income taxes. However, most payroll calculations are computerized today, and site managers are rarely required to issue individual paychecks.

The reason for monitoring hours worked is set forth in the *Fair Labor Standards Act (FLSA).* Also called Wage and Hour Law, the FLSA regulates the minimum wage per hour and the maximum number of hours an employee can work per day and per week in hourly rate positions. Any time worked in excess of the maximum requires overtime pay—one and one-half times the regular rate for hours worked over 40 hours per week. In general, recruiting qualified employees in the competitive market demands paying wages that are higher than minimum wage. Other incentives and benefits may be necessary as well.

The FLSA also stipulates the circumstances under which employees are exempt from its wage and hour regulations. Among the qualifying tests are supervision of others or duties that do not require specific hourly production. Although exempt workers are not affected by the hours per day or per week maximums, their base salaries must be at least equal to what a nonexempt worker would earn at minimum wage for the maximum number of weekly hours permitted under the FLSA.

Employers in the United States are required to participate in federal programs that provide for workers who are terminated, retire, or become disabled. The *Federal Unemployment Tax Act (FUTA)* and state unemployment programs are intended to compensate employees who lose their jobs. Contributions are paid entirely by the employer at a rate based on the number of employees and the number of claims made. While the federal government collects the taxes, the funds are usually disbursed by the states. In addition, under the *Federal Insurance Contributions Act (FICA)*, employers and employees make equal contributions for social security based on the employee's income. (Payment of payroll taxes is discussed in chapter 4.)

The *Occupational Safety and Health Act of 1970 (OSHA)* requires employers to assure the workplace is free of hazards that may cause injury to employees. In addition to keeping the workplace generally clean and safe, employers are required to post a notice in a conspicuous place stating the provisions of OSHA, including employers' and employees' responsibilities, inspection and complaint procedures, and citations and penalties for violations. OSHA also requires employers to keep a log of work-related injuries and post an annual summary of them.

Most employers must also carry *workers' compensation insurance,* which provides benefits to employees who suffer work-related illnesses or injuries. Workers' compensation insurance may be purchased either through the state or from private insurance companies. Workers injured on the job can submit claims for lost wages and compensation for injuries (for example, loss of a limb). In addition to this compensation, most state workers' compensation programs provide for retraining of employees who are no longer able to perform their previous job functions because of work-related injuries or illnesses and must therefore learn a new trade or profession.

The *Consolidated Omnibus Budget Reconciliation Act of 1986 (COBRA)* allows for the extension of group health insurance coverage to employees and their dependents who would otherwise lose their coverage because of a reduction of work hours or termination for any reason other than discharge for gross misconduct. COBRA covers medical benefits through group insurance plans, HMOs, and PPOs and grants individuals the right to continue—at their own expense—the same coverage they had the day before their termination or the reduction in hours. Site managers should be aware of the notification requirements of COBRA and make all relevant material available to departing employees. (COBRA applies to virtually every private and public employer with a group health plan except the federal government, the District of Columbia, churches and synagogues, and firms with fewer than 20 employees.)

Personnel Files

The site manager may be responsible for maintaining records on current and past employees, although such files are often kept at the management company's main office. These files should be readily accessible, and the information contained in them should be complete. Typical contents include:

- Original job applications
- References that have been checked
- W-4 forms indicating personal exemptions allowed (also kept in payroll files)
- I-9 forms (proof of identity and employment eligibility)
- Insurance information
- Data related to payroll matters (salary or hourly wages, records of pay raises, additional compensation)
- Records of performance reviews
- Written records of any disciplinary action taken as well as the circumstances that led to it

The information in these files should be job-related only; no "anecdotal" information should find its way into personnel records. For example, a manager's personal opinions about an employee would not belong there. Not only may such information be inaccurate, if it is demonstrated that the information damaged the employee's reputation, there may be grounds for a libel suit. The contents of a personnel file should also be confidential, and information from it should be released only at the written direction of an employee, as when he or she seeks work elsewhere or applies for a loan. (The management company may have a standard release form for employees to sign.)

EEO and ADA Compliance

Equal employment opportunity legislation provides a legal basis for individuals to pursue the work of their choice and to seek advancement in that work subject to the limits of their qualifications, skills, and personal initiative.

Title VII of the U.S. Civil Rights Act of 1964 defines unlawful employment discrimination as:

- Failing or refusing to hire or discharging any individual, or discriminating against any individual with respect to compensation, terms, conditions, or privileges of employment because of race, color, religion, sex, or national origin; or
- Limiting, segregating, or classifying employees or applicants for employment in any way that could deprive or tend to deprive any individual of employment opportunities or otherwise adversely affect his or her status because of race, color, religion, sex, or national origin.

Title VII applies to any employer in a commercial activity with fifteen or more employees. It applies to *all* individuals, regardless of their race, sex, religion, or national origin and is enforced by the Equal Employment Opportunity Commission (EEOC).

Sexual harassment, another aspect of discrimination on the basis of sex, is also prohibited under Title VII. *Sexual harassment* is any unwelcome sexual behavior, ranging from the extremely blatant (e.g., offering a benefit such as a raise or a promotion in exchange for sex) to the more subtle behavior of interfering with an employee's work performance by creating an intimidating, hostile, or offensive atmosphere. U.S. courts have ruled that display of pornographic materials in the workplace, sexual harassment of other employees, or the presence of explicit graffiti about employees constitutes a hostile atmosphere.

Site managers should not tolerate any form of discrimination in the workplace. In addition to legal liability and expenses, a firm's reputation, morale, and productivity suffer in such an environment. Reference to applicable laws and legal counsel will help establish ap-

Key Actions Related to Personnel Relations in Site Management

Primary Functions

- Identify staffing needs in conjunction with the property manager
- Participate in recruiting, interviewing, and hiring procedures
- Oversee staff training
- Assign tasks and delegate responsibilities
- Monitor hours worked by on-site employees and submit time to payroll
- Communicate expectations and motivate personnel
- Evaluate personnel performance and conduct performance reviews

Adjunct Functions

- Maintain personnel files
- Ensure OSHA compliance—keep workplace clean and safe, post required notices
- Ensure compliance with EEO and ADA requirements
- Foster professional development of employees through work assignments and training opportunities

propriate procedures. While the EEOC has not adopted any specific record-keeping requirements for employers, any firm with 100 or more employees is required to file an information report with the EEOC and place an EEOC poster in a conspicuous location on site.

Another federal law affecting employers is the Americans with Disabilities Act (ADA) of 1990. This is a mandate to end discrimination against individuals with disabilities and bring them into the economic and social mainstream. The ADA states that an employer may not discriminate against any qualified individual with a disability with regard to any term, condition, or privilege of employment. Compliance with the ADA includes the obligation to provide reasonable accommodation to disabled employees or job candidates, which can include making facilities accessible, instituting flexible leave policies, adjusting and modifying screening tests and training materials, acquiring new or modifying existing equipment, and providing qualified readers to assist vision-impaired employees.

Other examples of reasonable accommodation are restructuring of jobs or work schedules for a disabled individual. Often such changes are minimal. Jobs may be restructured by eliminating nonessential elements, delegating assignments more appropriately, exchanging assignments with those of another employee, or redesigning work procedures. Part-time or modified work schedules may be a solution for employees who cannot work a standard schedule because they need particular medical treatments. Employees who require fully accessible public transportation that is not available at all times would also benefit from such an accommodation.

Obviously, for legal as well as moral reasons, site managers should be aware of the laws that prohibit discrimination and follow established nondiscriminatory employment policies and practices. It is the responsibility of the site manager to make certain that both EEO and ADA requirements are met at the site.

SUMMARY

The site manager plays a critical role in personnel relations. Because the on-site staff is so important to the success of a property, the selection of personnel must be undertaken with great care. The process involves planning and consideration of the property's needs and the owner's goals. Once these factors have been considered, a job description is prepared. This defines the duties and responsibilities of a position, outlines the necessary skills and background to fulfill it, and spells out what is expected of that employee.

The selection process is the means by which suitable job candidates are identified and eventually hired. Another important consideration is that new employees will become part of an established team. In order to assure stability and productivity of the team, the entire hiring process should honestly address the responsibilities and expectations of a position, and job candidates should be given every opportunity to ask questions during their interviews and otherwise.

Hiring decisions should be based on the specific skills and abilities of individual job candidates as well as their educational and employment backgrounds. Issues of age, race, religion, gender, or disability should not enter the decision-making process.

Once they are on the job, the site manager must continually communicate expectations and motivate employees. Motivation takes many forms in addition to monetary compensation. New challenges, genuine involvement, and opportunities to contribute are other rewards. Employees also deserve to receive fair and reasonable evaluation of their work—they should be rewarded for good performance and notified when their performance is poor.

The site manager's administrative responsibilities relate to payroll, reporting, and keeping records on job safety. Most on-site administrative activities supplement those of the management company. While paychecks may be prepared elsewhere, many of the payroll records originate on site. Monitoring of EEO, ADA, and OSHA compliance is more likely to be an on-site function.

The human component is the bedrock of site management. Good personnel relations will not only motivate employees to efficiency and productivity and maintain staff morale, it will foster resident retention, which contributes to the owner's income goals.

Key Terms

Americans with Disabilities Act (ADA)
Equal Employment Opportunity Commission (EEOC)
Fair Labor Standards Act (FLSA)
Federal Insurance Contributions Act (FICA)
Federal Unemployment Tax Act (FUTA)
Immigration Reform and Control Act (1986)
Occupational Safety and Health Act (OSHA)

Key Concepts

employee handbook
employee orientation
employee recruitment
employee retention
job description
performance review
probationary status
workers' compensation insurance

Key Points

- What factors are considered in determining the appropriate staff size for a property?
- What are the steps of the selection process?
- What impact does staff turnover have on the workplace in site management?
- How is progressive discipline appropriate to personnel management?
- What are the various laws that regulate employment?

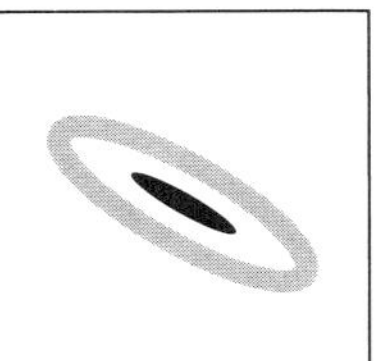

4

Financial Issues—Maximizing the Bottom Line

The goals of ownership cannot be achieved without deliberate financial administration. In fact, you will probably not have a more crucial responsibility as site manager than your handling of financial issues. Financial administration is so important because it relates to all the elements of residential site management—budgeting, collections and disbursements, personnel relations, maintenance, risk management, and legal issues—which contribute to the objective of meeting the owner's investment goals for the property.

Meeting the owner's financial goals requires development of realistic operating budgets coupled with successful efforts to meet budget projections. Market-level rents, low vacancy and rent loss, and low turnover rates will have to be achieved consistently if the property is to generate sufficient income. At the same time, operating expenses will have to be controlled without sacrificing the physical integrity of the property.

INCOME, EXPENSES, AND PROFIT

One measure of the profitability of an income-producing property is the amount of income returned to the owner. For rental real estate, this is the *cash flow* that results from its efficient operation. While the site manager is not responsible for setting the income goals of the property, his or her actions influence whether they are met. Accomplishing these goals demands an understanding of the elements of the cash flow calculation.

The Components of Cash Flow

From the start of this book, the point has been made that effective site management means striving to attain the highest possible level of income with the lowest possible level of expenses. A partial measure of a site manager's success is found in the *net operating income (NOI)* of the property. Although every factor that contributes to NOI cannot be controlled, increasing rents, reducing vacancy and collection losses, and controlling expenses will help maximize NOI.

	Gross Potential Rental Income
minus	Vacancy and Rent Loss
plus	Miscellaneous Income
equals	Effective Gross Income
minus	Operating Expenses
equals	Net Operating Income (NOI)
minus	Debt Service (principal and/or interest)
minus	Capital Expenditures (when applicable)
equals	Cash Flow

Although the site manager's involvement with financial management usually ends with the production of NOI, the owner's assessment of the property's value is usually based on cash flow. Increased NOI can enable the owner to refinance the property under more favorable terms that would lower debt service and thereby increase cash flow. Increased NOI also increases the market value of the property.

Gross Potential Rental Income. The maximum amount of income the property is capable of producing is called the gross potential rental income (also known as gross *possible* rental income). It is based on full occupancy of all the leasable space within a building at the highest possible (market) rental rates. The figure for gross potential rental income is based on the assumption that all residents pay their rents in full and on time. Gross potential rental income is a benchmark figure for the property that remains more or less constant from one month to the next—it is subject to change only if rental rates increase or decrease or if the number of units that *could* be rented varies. For example, if a basement apartment is converted to a laundry room, the gross potential rental income for the building would decline: Assuming all other factors remained constant, the laundry room would become part of the building's common area and therefore unrentable, although it would produce miscellaneous income from coin-operated equipment. On the other hand, if that same basement apartment were to be used temporarily as storage space and no physical changes were made to it, its scheduled rental income would be reduced for the duration, resulting in a lower gross potential rental income. These distinctions are important because a unit used for other purposes, even temporarily, represents an economic vacancy.

Vacancy and Rent Loss. In reality, gross potential rental income is rarely achieved. Usually one must take into account units that generate no income (vacancies) and rents not collected from residents (delinquencies). Both of these factors reduce the amount of rental income received for any given period of time.

From an accounting perspective, vacancies and rent losses are handled differently. While unpaid rent is a true loss of income, delinquent rent—whenever received—will eventually be included in the income of the property. Vacancies, on the other hand, represent a reduction in scheduled income but not outright losses. By contrast, bad debts may be written off the books.

There are two kinds of vacancies, physical and economic. *Physical vacancies* are unoccupied apartments that are available but producing no income. However, *economic vacancy* has broader implications. It includes units that are unoccupied (physical vacancies) as well as those that are leased or otherwise occupied but generate no rental income. For example, an apartment rented in July for occupancy in September is not classified as vacant, yet it will generate no income until September. Apartments that are used as models, offices, or staff apartments also constitute economic vacancies. (Some management companies provide free apartments for on-site employees, while others charge rent.) The concept of economic vacancy is more useful than physical vacancy in calculating NOI because it presents a more accurate picture of the property's financial condition. For example, the inability to increase rental rates because of economic conditions would result in a higher economic vacancy rate than the number of physical vacancies only, assuming they remain constant.

Miscellaneous Income. Any income that comes from sources other than scheduled rent—for example, coin-operated laundry equipment, vending machines, parking charges, or late fees—is called miscellaneous or *unscheduled* income.

Effective Gross Income. Effective gross income is what remains after vacancy and rent losses have been subtracted from gross potential rental income and miscellaneous income has been added to the remainder. Effective gross income is the money available to pay the expenses of the property. It should match the total amount collected (gross receipts) for the reporting period—usually a month.

Operating Expenses. Operating expenses for rental properties typically include real estate taxes, insurance premiums, utilities, payroll, maintenance and repairs, painting and redecorating, landscaping and grounds keeping, and marketing and leasing costs, as well as charges for legal, accounting, and management services, fees for licenses and permits, and administrative and office expenses. (Personal property taxes, when assessed against such things as appliances or removable fixtures at the property, are also considered an operating expense.) The site manager is expected to monitor and pace the costs of operations that are within his or her control (e.g., turnaround of vacant units) to maximize every dollar spent and every dollar saved.

Net Operating Income (NOI). NOI is what remains after operating expenses have been subtracted from effective gross income. It is a measure of the site manager's success in attaining the highest possible level of income and the lowest possible level of expenses without sacrificing the physical requirements of the property. The goal of financial administration is to maximize NOI. When operating expenses for the period exceed the available funds (effective gross income), the NOI will be negative, and the owner may have to provide funds out of pocket to cover operating expenses. While negative NOI is not desirable, it is a likely consequence during periods of transition (e.g., lease-up of a new property or rehabilitation of an existing one) when receipts and expenditures are difficult to predict accurately.

Debt Service. Debt service is the amount required to repay the mortgage loan on the property. Usually the payment includes both *principal* (an amount to pay down or *amortize* the loan) and *interest* (the cost of borrowing the money expressed as an annual percentage rate). Although debt service is a recurring expense, it is not considered an operating expense because it is not paid to maintain the property. Making debt service payments is usually the owner's responsibility, although some management agreements require the management company to pay debt service from the property's operating account. While the owner wants to be sure that the property will generate enough income to pay the mortgage and provide a satisfactory periodic return, when debt service payments exceed NOI, the result is negative cash flow. Under these circumstances, the owner will have to make up the difference out of pocket to cover the debt service payment or face foreclosure action by the lender.

Capital Expenditures. The NOI is also one of the sources of funds for capital expenditures. Capital expenditures are major amounts spent to maintain or improve the property (e.g., replacing a roof) and thereby increase its value. Such improvements to the real estate become part of the depreciable assets for income tax purposes and are not deductible as operating expenses. Funds for capital expenditures may be accumulated by setting aside a portion of the NOI generated monthly—usually in an interest-bearing account. Another source of funds is a second mortgage. Specific expenditures from these funds are planned in advance in a capital budget (discussed later in this chapter).

Cash Flow. Cash flow is what remains after debt service payments and reserve fund contributions are deducted from NOI. This represents part of the owner's profits from the investment. The owner is responsible for all applicable income taxes on the property's income.

The amount subject to income taxes will depend in part on the owner's other sources of personal income (e.g., salary, stock dividends) and deductions.

The Site Manager's Role

A property owner ordinarily has two investment goals in owning real estate. One is to generate income; the other is to preserve and increase the property's value. As a measure of periodic return, the owner seeks maximum NOI from the property because the greater the NOI, the higher the property value. While the value of real estate can be estimated in different ways, one technique is commonly used by appraisers and investors alike. It uses a capitalization rate to convert a future income stream from a property into an estimate of property value. The capitalization or "cap" rate is a percentage rate derived from the market based on recent sales of similar properties (net income divided by sale price). It is the average investor's perception of the risk of an investment and reflects the expected return from that investment.

Expressed in the following algebraic formula, property value (V) is determined by dividing NOI (I) by a *capitalization rate (R).*

$$\frac{\text{Net Operating Income (NOI)}}{\text{Capitalization Rate}} = \text{Estimated Property Value; } \frac{I}{R} = V$$

The cap rate for a particular property depends on many factors, including the property type and current market conditions (i.e., loan-to-value ratios and interest rates). Variations in the cap rate translate into dramatically different property values—value decreases as the cap rate rises, and increases as the cap rate declines. When the same cap rate is used in the comparison of similar properties in the market area, the property with the highest NOI will have the highest estimated value.

If the NOI of a property decreases and the cap rate does not change, the property value will be reduced. This is in addition to the reduction in periodic income resulting from the lower NOI. Thus, any factor that affects NOI also affects property value. For example, if the cap rate is 10 percent and the annual income of a property is $100,000, its value would be $1 million ($100,000 ÷ .10). Assuming the cap rate remains at 10 percent, if the income is reduced to $80,000, the property value will be only $800,000. On the other hand, if the income increases to $150,000, the property value will also increase—to $1,500,000.

The importance of cost savings is also magnified by the cap rate. Increasing the income a property produces by only a few thousand dollars a year has a meaningful impact on that property's value. For example, if the site manager of the property in the preceding example is able to reduce costs and increase revenues for a net gain of $5,000, the property value will increase significantly—i.e., by $50,000 (105,000 ÷ .10 = $1,050,000).

Although site managers' responsibilities in the area of financial administration can vary widely depending on the management company, the owner, and the portfolio of properties, all site managers have direct impact on the physical condition and financial status of the property, which determine its level of income and, ultimately, its value. However, property values are also influenced by many other factors, including prevailing economic conditions and neighborhood trends. While site managers directly influence a property's ability to generate income, their actions also influence neighborhoods. Owners and management companies that choose to rehabilitate buildings in economically depressed areas are working to reverse local economic trends and rebuild communities. The success of an individual property, therefore, contributes to the vitality of the entire neighborhood.

Nearly everything done on a daily basis influences the financial integrity of the property. The site manager's decisions—or lack of them—have a critical impact on the "bottom line" of a property, ranging from the potential income it can generate to what remains after expenses have been deducted from gross income. The site manager's financial responsibilities may include the following:

- Attaining high closing ratios and lease renewal rates, which reduce the expenses related to turnover, and monitoring the performance of the property in the market.
- Adhering to credit history policy and procedures within the resident selection process to assure leasing to qualified prospects.
- Collecting rent and late fees on a timely basis, reducing delinquencies and bad debts, and enforcing rent collection and eviction policies.

- Maintaining accurate financial records for inclusion in monthly reports to the owner.
- Observing and reporting trends in marketing, leasing, delinquencies, and turnover rates, as well as activities of competing properties, to ensure that the property is positioned properly in the marketplace.
- Implementing resident retention programs.
- Contributing to the efficient operation of the property through effective management, including scheduling and supervision of maintenance, applying spending controls to the operating budget and following established purchasing guidelines, and proper pacing of expenses with income.
- Maintaining accurate and complete records that will assist the property manager in preparation of the annual budget.

By anticipating problems and eliminating or mitigating their impact on the property, site managers are able to strengthen the financial condition of the properties they manage.

While maximizing NOI and property value are goals of real estate ownership, the management company benefits as well. By increasing the property's value, the management company enhances its own professional reputation, which may ultimately translate into increased referral business as well as increased management fees.

FINANCIAL ADMINISTRATION

As a site manager, you will be responsible for administering the day-to-day financial affairs of the property. Ranging from implementation of policies and procedures for collecting rents and other forms of income to maintaining records for comparison with bills before expenses are paid and assisting the property manager in the preparation of budgets, your efforts will be instrumental in achieving the owner's goals while making the property an appealing place for residents to call home.

Policies and Procedures

Site managers are responsible for enforcing the policies and procedures of the management company. In order to meet the owner's income goals, collection policies must be enforced firmly and impartially. This applies to both rents and amounts due for services. Specific policies and procedures guide the manager in making cost-effective purchases and prompt payments and establishing effective inventory controls.

Collections—the Income Side. The key to any collection procedure is timeliness. When collections are received late, a ripple effect is felt throughout the entire property. Without funds for needed repairs and maintenance, the physical condition of the property will suffer. This will hurt resident retention efforts, and the result will be a less-desirable property that struggles to compete in the marketplace. These consequences underscore the importance of making all efforts to collect rents and fees on time. (The legal implications of collections are discussed in detail in chapter 10.)

All monies collected should be recorded as soon as possible. Accuracy is of the utmost importance. Checks and money orders usually include the name of the issuer, and personal checks can serve as their own receipts. However, as a matter of standard operating procedure, written receipts should be issued for all income collected and all refundable deposits (not just cash received). Issuance of receipts may also be required by law in many states.

Because large amounts of cash present a risk (i.e., theft), it is desirable to minimize cash collections. This can be done by establishing and enforcing a policy that checks or money orders are preferred forms of payment. Note, however, that refusal to accept cash could complicate an existing delinquency or even create a new one because arranging for a cashier's check or money order is not always convenient. In addition, refusal to accept cash may be illegal in some jurisdictions. In cases of delinquency, acceptance of cash actually may be desirable to expedite collections and avert problems with checks being returned for nonsufficient funds (NSF checks).

In collections, creation of numbered triplicate receipts is advisable. The original is given to the party who made the payment, and the copies are used as internal tracking devices for accounting purposes (one for the site-office and another for the property management office). Standard receipt forms available from any office supply store will usually meet the needs of a site management office. Most of them include ample space to record not only the name of the person paying and the amount paid, but whether the payment was for rent, a security deposit, or a specific fee. There should also be spaces for the name of the resident, the apartment number, the period covered, and the signature of the person who issues the receipt. In addition, all monies collected should be recorded in a *receipts journal or ledger* that creates a cumulative record of receipts by type.

All payments from residents should be recorded in a *rent roll* (or other financial report) that lists the apartments in numerical order. Most printed forms include columns for recording residents' names, rental rates, the date of payment, the period covered, and specific types of payments. (The word "vacant" is shown in the name column for unoccupied units.) A computerized rent roll should be set up similarly. Rents and other payments are entered in the rent roll separately and totaled by category (column) and by unit (line). The sum of the column totals must equal the sum of the payment amounts to balance. The rent roll records are used to prepare monthly income reports for the owner. All payments from residents should also be recorded on individual *resident ledger* cards.

Checks received as payment should be stamped immediately for bank deposit. The stamp should read "For Deposit Only" and include the bank account number. Bank deposits should be prepared at the end of each day—more often if necessary. Checks should be listed separately and the total amount of any cash receipts should be included. Deposit forms should be filled out in triplicate (copies for the bank, the manager, and the main office), and totals should be verified with some kind of hard copy (e.g., adding machine tape, calculator or computer printout). Alternatively, the completed deposit slip can be photocopied for distribution. The deposit should be taken to the bank, preferably the same day before the bank closes. Otherwise arrangement should be made for night deposits in a bank lockbox. If large amounts of cash are involved, it may be advisable to have two people handle the deposit transaction. Having a second person review the deposit slip and accompany the deposit to the bank provides an internal security check. (Bonding of employees is covered in chapter 3, and security issues are discussed in chapter 9.)

Purchasing and Inventory Control. Purchase orders should always be completed for supplies and equipment. A properly used *purchase order* form shows the name of the vendor; the date of the order;

the kind, quantity, and price of each item or service ordered; the delivery date and terms of acceptance; and whether substitutions are allowed if the desired item is not available but a comparable version is. It also should include a notation of the name of the person placing the order. If something is purchased for a specific rental unit, the apartment number should also be shown, along with a designated work order number. Maintaining a log record of purchase orders issued (in numerical sequence) facilitates tracking of goods and services as received. Exhibit 4.1 is an example that provides a running record of purchase amounts and budget adjustments.

Purchase orders create a record of how many and how often items are ordered and are useful in monitoring inventory levels to assure adequate supplies of replacement parts. Tracking inventory through purchase orders can prevent purchasing too many or too few spare parts and supplies, both of which can be costly. Overstock represents cash that is not available for other uses, while inadequate inventory increases the expense if a staff member must purchase a single part or if a repair must be delayed.

An additional means of controlling costs is a system to verify inventory levels and track the frequency with which items are restocked. This can be as simple as a checkout list in the supply storeroom. Each item is recorded as it is received and stored (verified by cross-checking purchase orders and billing invoices) and again as it is removed from inventory (verified by cross-checking work order numbers). For either of these procedures, the inventory count is adjusted up or down accordingly. By regularly reviewing this list, you will be able to anticipate what needs to be restocked and when. Careful monitoring of inventory will allow you to quickly identify spending trends that may require budget adjustments. Whether you use a simple checklist or work with a computer, an inventory system is a cost control measure that should not be overlooked.

Payments—the Expense Side. Bills for goods and services (operating expenses) should be paid only after making certain that the correct materials have been delivered and work has been completed in accordance with specifications. Inventorying materials as they are received and inspecting all labor performed will help the site manager maintain better control over operating expenses.

The best practice is to make payments only from *invoices* and not

EXHIBIT 4.1

Sample Purchase Order Log

Purchase Order Log

Property:	Annual budget:	Month:
Account:	Monthly budget:	Page:

	Date	P.O. Number	P.O. Amount	Invoice Number	Invoice Amount	Annual Budget Remaining
Opening Balance			(Monthly Budget)			(Previous Month)
1						
Running Balance						
2						
Running Balance						
3						
Running Balance						
4						
Running Balance						
5						
Running Balance						
6						
Running Balance						
7						
Running Balance						
8						
Running Balance						
9						
Running Balance						
10						
Running Balance						
11						
Running Balance						
12						
Running Balance						
13						
Running Balance						

P.O. Monthly Total

Budget Remaining
(To Carry Forward)

Page of

This example provides spaces for budget adjustments as well as matching invoices with purchase orders. Often a handwritten list of purchase orders in numerical sequence, noting the vendor name and the date, will provide sufficient data for matching invoices to purchase orders at the site.

from statements of account. Invoices are usually for a single order, and they should clearly show a purchase order number and state the terms of payment. Unless otherwise stated, normal terms of payment are "Net 30 Days" from the date of the invoice; bills due at the end of the month may be marked simply "E.O.M." Sometimes a discount is allowed: "2% 10th" means a 2-percent discount may be taken if payment is made by the tenth of the month; "2% 10 Days" means the discount can be taken if payment is made within ten days of the invoice date.

Before payment is authorized, all incoming bills should be carefully reviewed to be sure that the correct items and quantities were received and that they show the correct property account. Packing lists and bills of lading should be checked against original purchase orders at delivery and against the invoice at the time of payment. Any discrepancies should be reconciled before payment is made. Some management companies may require a copy of the purchase order to be attached to the invoice for ease of verification.

Statements of account should also be scrutinized. Careful review will determine whether any entries for amounts due are for items that have already been paid and what remains to be paid. Any discrepancies should be clarified with the vendor. If necessary, request a duplicate invoice that displays the purchase order number, quantity and description of items purchased, unit prices, and total costs.

Systematizing the payment process makes a great deal of sense. In some offices, a rubber stamp is used to indicate the date received. However, most record-keeping requirements will be satisfied if the person opening the mail writes the date of receipt on the face of the invoice. Then, bills can be accumulated in a file folder for payment at a later date. (Some businesses make it a practice to pay bills only once a month, and they notify their regular vendors of this.) Paying bills in one or more large batches may be efficient, but this practice can lead to penalties for late payments or forfeiture of early-payment discounts. Even at one and two percent of invoice amounts, these savings add up over time. Therefore, bills should be organized for payment so that all discounts will be taken appropriately and on time. This is especially important if bills are received and paid throughout the month.

Any time set aside for paying bills is a good opportunity to check whether other recurring payments (e.g., real estate taxes, mortgage, insurance premiums) are also due. Payroll checks that are handled on site can be made out at the same time. You can use a "tickler" file to remind yourself of recurring expenses that are not necessarily invoiced. This may consist of notes on a monthly calendar or a series of 3 x 5-inch file cards organized by months (or even by weeks) or a computer programmed with the coded information.

All payments should be made by check and recorded in check number order. No payments should be made in cash unless absolutely necessary, in which case a signed receipt should always be obtained. In general, cash-on-delivery (COD) purchases should be avoided. Use of numbered purchase orders and work orders is preferred because they assure accurate and consistent record keeping and facilitate budget reconciliation. They also reduce the likelihood of payments being missed.

The exception to this payment rule is the use of *petty cash.* There can be some cash available in the site management office, but the amount should be as low as possible while remaining practical. Petty cash is used to purchase postage stamps and occasional office supplies, pay for postage due, make change, or refund coins lost in vending machines. One person should be assigned to keep track of amounts paid out and added to the fund. Use of a cumulative log to record payment amounts and appropriate account codes is recommended. Requiring personnel to initial their pay-outs assures that the source of any discrepancies can be readily identified.

Paid bills and check stubs are used to record payments in the *disbursements journal or ledger.* The check number, date paid, recipient, item or service purchased, account code (if any), and the dollar amount should also be noted in the check register. A purchase order number should be recorded when applicable. If an invoice covers a specific time period or an expense is related to a specific rental unit, these facts should be noted as well. It is also important to indicate when a partial payment is made.

The payment amount is listed twice—in one column to indicate the check amount and in a second column to indicate the type of expense. If an invoice covers two different types of accountable expenses, the amounts should be entered separately. For example, charges for advertising in the Yellow Pages may be included in a regular telephone bill; the record of payment to the telephone company should separate telephone utility charges and advertising expenses. Each expense column and the payment amount column should be totaled.

The sum of all the expense columns should equal the total for the check amount column. The entries in the disbursements journal are both a cumulative record of payments over time and a resource for estimating future expenses for the annual budget.

Paid invoices may be filed in alphabetical order by vendor and separated according to month and year of payment, or they can be filed by category—e.g., property tax, insurance, utilities, painting and redecorating. It is important to be able to retrieve these records because property managers often request duplicate copies of invoices—one for inclusion in the monthly report to the owner and another for management records.

Payroll. Employees should be paid at set intervals. Weekly and monthly pay periods represent extremes of frequency. Biweekly (twenty-six times a year) or twice monthly (twenty-four times a year) payroll cycles are generally more efficient.

Site managers' responsibilities vary with respect to payroll. One management company may require the site manager merely to record employee time and report it to the main office, while another may expect the site manager to calculate wages and withholdings or even issue paychecks. In general, site managers have more limited payroll responsibilities; nevertheless, a basic understanding of the payroll function is important.

In order to comply with the withholding and reporting requirements established by law, accurate records must be maintained for each employee. Monies withheld from employees' wages must be reported to federal and state governments according to a specified schedule, and federal income taxes that have been withheld from employee salaries must be deposited with the federal government on a regular basis. The same is true of state and local income taxes. The amount of taxes withheld determines whether deposits must be made quarterly, monthly, or more often. The taxes are due the government when the wages are paid.

In addition, the employer pays an amount equivalent to the social security and medicare tax withheld from the employee's wages under the Federal Insurance Contributions Act (FICA), and both amounts must be included in the federal tax deposits. An Employer's Quarterly Federal Tax Return (Form 941) must be filed with the federal government. These forms are usually received from the government in advance of the due date. (Federal income tax rates and payment requirements are outlined in *Circular E, Employer's Tax Guide* published by the Internal Revenue Service and revised annually.)

Federal unemployment tax (FUTA) may be paid quarterly or annually and is reported on an Employer's Annual Federal Unemployment Tax Return (Form 940). The FUTA tax rate, published in the annual IRS *Circular E,* is applied to individual employees' wages up to a certain dollar level. This is a tax on the employer and cannot be deducted from employees' wages.

Some states require employers to pay a percentage equivalent of each employee's wages to the state on a regular schedule. The funds are held in an account for the employer and used to provide unemployment compensation for terminated employees. The state determines how much an employer pays, and the amount may be increased or decreased, depending on the number of claims against the employer's account. The standard form used to notify the employer of specific changes should be kept with the payroll accounting records so that whoever prepares the payroll will be aware of new calculations.

Federal unemployment tax must be paid regardless of whether one is required to contribute to a state fund. However, amounts paid to state unemployment funds may be credited toward FUTA totals, up to a certain percentage of employees' wages. Most unemployment benefits are administered at the state level.

Understanding and Using Budgets

Budgets are the working tools of management. A *budget* is an itemized estimate of income and expenses for the future. It is used to establish the priority of spending based on the income the property is expected to produce and the expenses it is expected to incur in achieving the owner's investment objectives. The budget will be used throughout the year, and comparison to actual income and expenses reveals how well the property is performing and how accurate the forecasts were. When variances occur, or when unforeseen circumstances arise, the budget may have to be adjusted. Variances may also indicate problems that need attention (e.g., an undiscovered water leak that has caused an increase in the water bill).

Types of Budgets. There are several types of budgets that are typically used in real estate management. An *operating budget* is prepared

EXHIBIT 4.2

Major Expense Categories Common to Annual Operating Budgets

Real Estate Tax
Insurance
Utilities (electricity, fuel oil, gas, water, sewer)
Rubbish Removal
Maintenance and Repair (including supplies)
Interior Painting and Decorating
Landscaping (often including exterior grounds keeping, interior plant rentals)
Recreational Facilities (operations and maintenance)
Payroll
Management Fee
Advertising and Promotion
Legal Expenses
Office Expenses (office supplies, postage, stationary, telephone)
Security

Depending on the size of the property, many major categories may be subdivided into individual line items. For some properties, there may not be a payroll category as such—maintenance personnel expenses, for example, would be included in the overall maintenance category.

---

annually. It commonly includes projections for gross potential rental income, vacancy and rent losses, and miscellaneous income (these adjustments yield an estimate of effective gross income), as well as major—and sometimes minor—categories of expenses. (Exhibit 4.2 lists the major categories.) Expenses are totaled and deducted from effective gross income to estimate NOI. Usually prepared on the basis of income and expense data from previous years and cost estimates from vendors, this *annual budget* projects the entire year's income and expenses, the latter broken down by category (e.g., insurance, utilities, rubbish removal, advertising and promotion). It should also take into account any departures from normal operations that are anticipated for the coming year (e.g., temporarily high vacancies because of remodeling).

If unanticipated expenses arise, the budget is a tool for identifying alternative sources of funds to pay them. For example, if the winter is unusually cold, not only will fuel consumption exceed projections, but increased market demand for fuel may lead to price increases. In that situation, a site manager will likely be asked to review the budget and identify specific expenditures that can be postponed or canceled, offsetting the higher fuel costs. If alternatives sources cannot be found in the budget, it may be necessary to draw on reserve funds, or raise rents, or ask the owner to provide the needed funds.

Although the annual budget serves as a point of reference for the owner and the manager, actual income and expenses can differ significantly from projections as the year progresses. To compensate for such differences, sometimes property managers prepare quarterly (or even monthly) revised budgets that reflect adjustments to the original projections contained in the annual budget. These budgets tend to be much more accurate because they are not projected as far into the future, and they can more readily reflect seasonal variances in income and expenses. Nevertheless, it is not sufficient merely to change an amount budgeted for a particular item. A variance may indicate a problem (such as the leak mentioned earlier), or it might point toward an error in judgment during the preparation of the original budget that will need to be investigated, addressed, and (one hopes) corrected.

While an operating budget would include expenses for normal repairs within the category of maintenance (e.g., repair of a furnace or patching the roof), a *capital budget* is an estimate of the costs and timing of major improvements or replacements and should reflect specific long-range plans for the property. Replacement of a furnace is much more expensive than mere repairs and would require a major capital investment. Such improvements constitute depreciable assets, and a percentage of their cost would be tax deductible in successive years (as "depreciation").

Accumulation of reserve funds for such capital expenditures is another important consideration. The capital budget determines how much must be set aside as reserve funds on a regular basis. In principle the cost of an improvement can simply be divided by the number of months before the improvement will be made. If funds are to be accumulated over a period of years, however, *inflation* must also be considered. If the interest earned on the reserve funds is not substantially higher than the rate of inflation, the accumulated funds will not cover the actual cost of the improvement. Furthermore, increases in the costs of materials may exceed the inflation rate, in which case larger monthly reserve installments may be necessary to assure a reasonable match between the amount accumulated and the ultimate cost.

Budget Preparation. Each line item in the annual budget requires one or more specific calculations. Gross potential rental income is estimated by multiplying the numbers of apartments (by type) by the applicable monthly rental rates and then by the number of months the rates are in effect. (Rent increases and the dates they are implemented will affect the total for the year.)

An estimate of income lost due to vacancies or other factors should be calculated as well. Often a fixed percentage rate is applied to the total projected income to account for vacancy and rent losses. However, it is also necessary to consider any income lost because of rent concessions made to secure leases. Although they may be necessary because of market conditions, such concessions reduce both the total rent collected for a specific apartment and the NOI for the property. Because NOI is the basis for calculating property value, rent concessions also lower the property value.

Miscellaneous income should also be projected. This requires awareness of all sources and payments, particularly as they may vary. For example, if a concessionaire collects money from coin laundry equipment or vending machines, the property's portion might be received quarterly or every other month, and amounts may not be equal. Often such income is estimated solely from prior years' receipts or adjusted for the new year based on projected occupancy and vacancy rates.

Gross potential rental income must be adjusted for vacancy and rent losses (deducted) and miscellaneous income (added) to estimate effective gross income for the year. Effective gross income is the estimated amount of money that will be available to pay for operating and nonoperating expenses as well as provide income to the owner.

Operating expenses consist of two types: fixed and variable. Line items with fixed costs are relatively straightforward to estimate based on previous years' costs or contractual arrangements—e.g., landscaping, security, and pool service. Variable costs, however, are more difficult to project because they depend on other factors. For example, estimates for heat and air conditioning are subject to rate changes and seasonal variations in energy consumption, neither of which can be predicted with absolute certainty. Other costs are completely unanticipated; for example, a water-line break or a freeze that damages trees and plantings. Even some fixed-cost items may require revision. Heavy snowfall in October could exhaust an entire budget allocation for snow removal by December, in which case snow removal costs for January through March—in some areas, through April—would have to be met from other sources.

A budget should be as accurate as possible, but it must also be realistic. You should be able to justify each line item, both income and expense, and show your calculations. (Amounts should be shown in whole dollars.) Past years' accounting records are excellent sources to consult when identifying specific types and amounts of expenses, assuming these figures do not include abnormal or one-time expenditures. In developing a first-time budget for a new apartment community, it may be possible to consult managers of other nearby apartment properties about types and amounts of expenditures. Another potential resource is published data, such as the annual experience exchange report published by the Institute of Real Estate Management—*Income/Expense Analysis: Conventional Apartments.*

Because revenue is collected and expenses are paid on a monthly basis, the amounts for the different categories in the annual budget may be distributed across the twelve months of the year to facilitate comparison and reporting. However, monthly allocations for expenses should be estimated with great care. Some budget items may be the same every month, in which case the total projected for the year can be divided by twelve to yield the monthly amount. On the other hand, management fees or other items based on a percentage of revenue may fluctuate as rental income varies. Still other line items are paid on a different schedule or apply for only part of the year. Real estate taxes may be paid twice a year—not necessarily at exact six-month intervals—and insurance premiums may be paid annually or semiannually. However, money for these expenses is often allocated in equal monthly amounts to assure accrual of the full amount and minimize periodic variances. Funds may be allocated for grounds keeping in the warmer months and for snow removal in the colder ones, and these amounts may vary. (In some areas, snow removal is a major expense for as much as half of the year.) Allocations for advertising expenses may also vary from month to month, depending on the period when the greatest leasing activity is anticipated, while advertising for a new development or a newly rehabilitated property may require budgeting money and monitoring expenditures on a weekly basis. It is also important to remember that utility rates can vary with the season, and bills for them are paid after consumption. Appropriate monthly allocations will minimize variances.

Budget Variances. Actual income and expenses will differ from the amounts budgeted for most items, and significant variances month-to-month and year-to-date will have to be explained to the property owner. (Company policy likely will set parameters that define when variances require explanation—e.g., a 5-percent differential.) Variances should be reported as both a dollar amount and a percentage of the budget allocation, identified with an "F" when they are favorable (higher income or lower expense) or a "U" when they are unfavorable (lower income or higher expense). Because budgets are usually prepared annually, unforeseen events can have an impact on actual financial results during the course of the budget year. Exhibit 4.3 shows a representative variance analysis.

The variance analysis should be accompanied by a narrative report that explains the reasons for significant variances from budget (e.g., lower fuel costs because of a mild winter). Knowing the reasons for budget variances enables the owner and the property manager to determine the accuracy of current budget projections, develop more realistic budgets in the future, and adjust policies and procedures to bring expenses back in line with the budget (i.e., next year's budgeted fuel costs could be reduced by implementing energy-conservation measures). The narrative explanation also helps the manager build a case for future capital expenditures, if needed.

Maximizing Income and Controlling Expenses

The first step toward maximizing income is to keep rents as high as possible (what the market will accept) while keeping vacancy rates and rent losses as low as possible. There are several ways a site manager can do this. You must be aware of market conditions and other factors that will affect rents, vacancies, and delinquencies. If local conditions include overbuilding of apartments, vacancy rates will eventually increase. This requires constant monitoring of local rental conditions and your property's position in the market. A critical component of this is pacing rent increases with market conditions. For example, if demand is strong for one-bedroom apartments but not for three-bedroom apartments, rent increases would be greater for apartments with one-bedroom. Other steps need to be taken concurrently. Stronger policies and procedures for qualifying prospective residents will help reduce delinquencies and premature breaking of leases. Shortening the grace period and raising late fees will deter delinquencies. Improving closing and renewal techniques will reduce turnover costs and increase a property's income. A more efficient maintenance schedule

EXHIBIT 4.3

Sample Budget Variance Analysis (Simplified)

	CURRENT MONTH (August)					YEAR-TO-DATE				
			Variance					Variance		
	Budget	**Actual**	**$**		**%**	**Budget**	**Actual**	**$**		**%**
Revenue	12,000	12,444	444	F	3.7	96,000	97,250	1,250	F	1.3
Management Fee	(600)	(628)	28	U	4.7	(4,800)	(4,780)	20	F	0.4
Personnel	(1,200)	(1,305)	105	U	8.8	(9,600)	(9,820)	220	U	2.3
Utilities	(600)	(640)	40	U	6.7	(4,800)	(5,100)	300	U	6.3
Insurance	(120)	(120)	—		—	(960)	(960)	—		—
Taxes	(1,200)	(1,200)	—		—	(9,600)	(9,600)	—		—
Maintenance	(600)	(585)	15	F	2.5	(4,800)	(4,615)	185	F	3.9
Variable	(600)	(624)	24	U	4.0	(4,800)	(4,997)	197	U	4.1
Total Expenses	(4,920)	(5,102)	182	U	3.7	(39,360)	(39,872)	512	U	1.3
NOI	7,080	7,342	262	F	3.7	56,640	57,378	738	F	1.3
Debt Service	(3,458)	(3,458)	—		—	(27,664)	(27,664)	—		—
Cash Flow	3,622	3,884	262	F	7.2	28,976	29,714	738	F	2.5

In calculating percentage variances, the absolute difference between budget and actual is divided by the budgeted amount. An "F" indicates a variance in the owner's favor; "U" indicates an unfavorable variance. (For example, \$12,444 − \$12,000 = \$444 (F); \$444 ÷ \$12,000 = 3.7 percent.) Percentages have been rounded off.

The management fees indicated here are *not* intended as a guideline for compensation. All fees are negotiable and should compensate the duties and responsibilities involved. "Variable" expenses in this example account for small amounts that would not be itemized individually. In general, the example is intended solely to represent the format of a variance analysis.

will mean vacant units are rent-ready sooner. Quality service delivered promptly and courteously to residents will encourage renewals. In addition, you can strengthen your marketing position by shopping your competition to identify factors that make your apartment community competitive and attractive to prospective residents. (Market analysis is addressed in chapter 5.)

A site manager's performance is measurable in terms of signed leases and maximum collections. Lease renewal is also very important. Because it is more cost-effective to retain good residents than to replace them, the importance of personal contact cannot be overemphasized. Resident retention efforts begin the first time a prospect enters the site office. Every contact and exchange becomes part of the resident's history, for good or bad. It is person-to-person interaction that brings residents to a property in the first place, and a personal touch is necessary to keep them there. Announcing renewal offers 60 to 90 days before leases expire, explaining to residents why rent increases are necessary, providing residents with information on the costs of moving, pointing out the services and amenities your property offers that competitors do not, and delivering renewal leases personally will greatly increase the likelihood of renewals. (Resident relations is the subject of chapter 7.)

In a soft market when rent increases are not feasible and concessions are being offered to woo residents, renewal takes on added importance. Flexibility in lease terms can be useful in retaining residents. For example, offering a resident the opportunity to renew at the same rent for the first six months and a higher rate for the remaining six months of the new lease term may keep an apartment occupied and generate greater resident loyalty. Another approach is to add an amenity to the apartment unit, such as a ceiling fan or a microwave oven. This can mean higher rent when the market improves, and, unlike a rent concession or rate reduction, the investment can be recouped because the item remains in place and adds value to the apartment.

Because it is not always possible to retain good residents, every effort should be made to minimize the period of vacancy when they choose not to renew. This can be accomplished by scheduling new residents' leases to begin as soon as possible after the previous occupants move out. (This will entail tightening the maintenance and unit preparation schedules.) Encouraging new residents to move in early—e.g., by offering to prorate rent to accommodate a mid-month move-in—can reduce the costs of economic vacancy. Of course, residency standards should not be compromised. (Leasing and lease renewal are discussed in more detail in chapter 6, and resident retention in discussed in chapter 7.)

Among your most important responsibilities as site manager are aggressive marketing and prompt and decisive action in addressing delinquencies. This includes careful qualification of all rental applicants before a lease is offered—you can avert problems by not renting to potentially troublesome residents. (Contacting previous landlords and scrutiny of credit bureau reports should be part of the qualification procedure.) Furthermore, the lease should clearly define residents' responsibilities and the consequences of late payment—i.e., late fees, notices of delinquency, and eviction for nonpayment. (The related legal proceedings are covered in chapter 10.) You should make every effort to collect rent before it becomes past due. This will require calling residents about late rent or visiting them at home in the evenings or on weekends. Reliance on written notices alone will not be enough. By following consistent policies and practices in all aspects of leasing and rent collection, you can reduce losses and maximize income.

Just as it is important to manage collections effectively, controlling expenses is the key to maximizing the bottom line—NOI. Several steps can be taken to reduce or control operating expenses:

- Costs for materials can be controlled by establishing accounts at supply houses that have the best prices and the most extensive inventory. Not only does this reduce costs, it saves travel time and associated labor costs. Bulk purchases of commonly used parts and supplies can also reduce the cost per item.
- Annual review of supply houses will ensure good quality and selection at competitive prices.
- Implementing tighter inventory controls will reduce waste and ensure efficient use of existing stock.
- Negotiation of all service contracts with a focus on economies of scale is another way to lower costs. For example, having one landscape contractor take care of two or more properties may result in lower service fees for both.
- Implementing preventive maintenance procedures means problems will be addressed before they become more costly.

- Low-cost energy conservation measures—e.g., additional insulation, weatherstripping, energy-efficient light bulbs—can significantly reduce utility costs,

Even small measures like calling to find out whether an item is in stock or using a fax machine to place orders from supply houses can reduce labor costs and generate sizeable savings over the course of a year.

Accounting and Record Keeping

A properly labeled set of financial records is an absolute necessity in real estate management. Some or all of the record keeping for a particular property will be the site manager's responsibility. When information is readily available, it is easier to isolate and address problems as they arise. Financial records may be maintained as paper copies or stored in a computer. If a computer is used, be sure to make backup copies of everything on a routine basis (on floppy disk) and check that this is being done by everyone. Retaining a hard copy is a further precaution against accidentally erasing information.

Minimally, three major categories of files are required: rental records, income and expense information, and financial reports. Exhibit 4.4 shows the various types of financial records, how they are usually filed, and how long they should be retained. Additional files should be created as necessary or appropriate for the size of the apartment community, the range of amenities and management services provided, and the reporting requirements of the management company or the property owner.

Accounting is a process in which financial records are created, administered, and used for analysis. It incorporates various procedures that control the handling of money when it is received and paid out and the methods by which these transactions are recorded and reported. *Cash-basis accounting* records income as it is received and payments as they are made. *Accrual-basis accounting* is more complex, recording income when it is earned and expenses when they are incurred, regardless of when they are received or paid. A *mixed cash-accrual system* may also be used. For example, monthly receipts and disbursements might be accounted on a cash basis, while payments made semiannually (e.g., real estate taxes or insurance premiums) or annually may be accounted on an accrual basis so as not to distort NOI

EXHIBIT 4.4

Files for Financial Management

The series of files shown here pertains to financial reporting and accounting only. Items in the first group are rental records; the second group comprise expense and payment records, and the last are financial reports.

Item	How Filed	For How Long
Rent roll	By month	4 years
Receipts journal	By date	4 years
Rental ledger	By unit, in 3 sections: paid, unpaid, vacant	4 years
Delinquency reports	By date	4 years
Bank accounts	By account number and date	7 years
Checks	By account number and statement period	7 years
Cash disbursements journal	By date	4 years
Purchase orders	Numerically	4 years
Paid invoices	Alphabetical by vendor*	4 years
Receiving documents	Alphabetical by vendor*	4 years
Unpaid invoices	Alphabetical by vendor	4 years
Annual income tax returns	By year	7 years†
Annual financial statements	By year	Indefinitely
Payroll tax reports	By date and type of tax paid	7 years†
Current budget	By month	7 years

*Can be filed by expense categories (i.e., taxes, utilities, maintenance and repair).

†Generally, these are private records retained by the owner. If they are kept by the management company, the location would be the main office (not the site office).

Most of these types of records would be maintained in the management company office rather than on site. Many are likely to be generated and stored in a computer. Retention periods are guidelines only—retention of some types of records is prescribed by law. Company policy will likely stipulate where and how long specific records are to be maintained in "active" files and/or in storage.

from month to month. Standard forms available from office supply stores will usually meet the accounting needs of an on-site management office using a cash accounting system (e.g., ledgers, columnar pads). However, many property management firms develop their own forms or formats to assure uniformity of recording and reporting financial information, both to the owner and within the company. In some instances, the property owner's forms and/or accounting system may have to be used to assure consistent reporting across his or her portfolio of investment properties.

Chart of Accounts. Regardless of the types of forms used, it is a sound business practice to establish a chart of accounts that assigns a specific account code or number to each type of income and expense so that related items can be categorized systematically. Use of account codes assists in tracking expenses because it assures that recurring items are always treated the same way. This in turn aids future projections as accumulated information in specific categories becomes the basis for preparing the next year's budget.

Charts of accounts can be set up in many different ways. Items of income and expense may be listed alphabetically and numbered sequentially on that basis. Alternatively, major categories of expense (e.g., taxes and insurance, utilities, maintenance, administrative) may be subdivided by function to account for recurring items, and they may be ordered to reflect frequency (most often to least often). Exhibit 4.5 shows a representative assortment of items in a chart of accounts. In such a system, account codes (numbers) and entries can be added (or deleted) within categories without displacing the major-frequency items. However, the particulars regarding the organization and classification of the accounts themselves are not nearly as important as the way the chart of accounts is used. Consistent usage assures accuracy over the long term.

Reporting to the Owner—Manager-Owner Interaction

Having an accounting system in place enables the management company to prepare reports that summarize the financial condition of the apartment community for the owner. Because such reports exist to satisfy the accounting needs of the recipients, the format and level of detail in these reports may vary. The site manager collects information used to compile these reports and may assist the property manager in assembling the data; however, site managers usually have limited contact with owners.

The owner is usually sent a monthly report of financial activity. This report includes information regarding income, expenses, and cash flow. Some types of data may be detailed on the respective

EXHIBIT 4.5

Sample Chart of Accounts

RECEIPTS

Rental Income
Security Deposit Forfeit
Nonrefundable Fees
Other Income
Refundable Security Deposits

DISBURSEMENTS

Taxes and Insurance
Property Tax
Personal Property Tax
Sales Tax
Insurance

Utilities
Electricity
Gas or Oil
Heating
Sewer
Rubbish Removal

Personnel Expenses
Payroll (wages)
Payroll Taxes
Unemployment Benefits
Workers' Compensation

Maintenance and Repairs
Air Conditioning
Appliances
Carpentry
Lock/Key Repair/Replacement
Electrical
Plumbing
Water Heater
Heating
Other Interior
Exterior

Painting and Redecorating
Painting
Cleaning
Carpet Shampooing

Services
Gardening/Landscaping
Pest Control
Security
Snow Removal

Recreational Facilities
Recreation Room
Pool
Exercise Room

Advertising and Public Relations
Advertising
Leasing Commissions
Signage

Professional Services
Accounting Fees
Legal Fees
Property Management Fees

Administrative
Business License Fees and Permits
Deposit Refunds
Postage/Printing

Finance Expenditures
Principal/Interest on 1st Mortgage
Principal/Interest on 2d Mortgage
Late Fees

Capital Expenditures
Exterior Painting
Parking Lots
Fencing
Exterior Replacement
Roof
Landscaping
Carpet and Tile Replacement
Drapery and Blind Replacement
Appliance Replacement

Owner Disbursements

Typical Reports to Owners

- Summary of Operations (narrative)
- Income and Expense Statement
- Budget Variance Analysis
- Rent Roll
- Vacancy Report
- Delinquency Report
- Check Disbursement or Check Register Report

NOTE: If a separate record of security deposits or miscellaneous income is maintained, copies of these may be included in the owner's report as necessary or appropriate.

recording forms (e.g., rent roll, delinquency report). A *vacancy report* (also sometimes called an *occupancy report*) indicates changes in the number of occupied units (move-ins and move-outs) in addition to specific information on vacant units (unit number, type, and size; length of vacancy); there may even be notes about unit features and amenities and color schemes.

The *income statement* summarizes the receipts (collections) and expenses (disbursements) for the period. Revenue from all sources, including rents, nonrefundable fees, and miscellaneous income, is listed first and totaled. Next, current operating expenses may be itemized for major categories (e.g., utilities, maintenance and repairs, staff

EXHIBIT 4.5 *(continued)*

This list represents a fairly complete itemization of income and expense categories—the availability and use of computers and spreadsheet software make detailed tracking possible and relatively easy. Whether a chart of accounts is created in such detail depends on the record-keeping needs of the management company and the property owner.

Regardless of category names and break downs, usual practice is to assign a number to each item. For example, income categories may be numbered in the 100 series, operating expenses in the 200 series, debt service in the 300 series, and so on. In a more detailed chart of accounts, the utilities category might be 800 and each separate expense item numbered in series—801, 802, etc. The chart of accounts facilitates monitoring of individual items of income and expense and preparation of the annual operating budget—major categories or individual line items and their respective numbers should be shown in the budget as well. Consistent use precludes error and maximizes efficiency.

EXHIBIT 4.6

Sample Statement of Income (Simplified)

August 31, This Year

	Current Month	%	Year-to-Date	%
Revenues	$12,444.00	100.0	$97,250.00	100.0
Expenses	(5,102.00)	(41.0)	(39,872.00)	(41.0)
NOI	7,342.00	59.0	57,378.00	59.0
Debt Service	(3,458.00)	(27.8)	(27,664.00)	(28.4)
Cash Flow	$3,884.00	31.2	29,714.00	30.6

All items are compared as a percent of revenue.

Revenues and Expenses in this report are actual monies collected and paid out (consistent with the example in exhibit 4.3).

salaries, advertising, and management fees) and totaled. Inclusion of account numbers for income and expense items will facilitate comparison to budget projections. Total operating expenses are subtracted from total income to yield NOI. If the owner pays debt service directly, the report will conclude with NOI. If the management company pays debt service, the amount will be deducted from NOI along with any capital expenditures or reserve allocations to determine cash flow. Cash flow is the item of greatest interest to both owner and manager. A simplified income statement is shown in exhibit 4.6.

Actual figures for income and expenses are also compared to budget projections for the month and for the year-to-date as part of the report (see exhibit 4.3 and related discussion earlier in this chapter). This is an important step because it includes cumulative totals and documents the impact of favorable or unfavorable variances over the longer term. An expense overage in one month may be made up at a later date and thus have negligible impact on the annual NOI. Such a variance may be avoidable in the future by allocating monthly amounts more carefully or improving overall performance. On the other hand, an unexpected vacancy that extends over several months will have significant impact on NOI for the period it exists and for the year.

The full report should include a narrative description of each of the forms and statements and an explanation of any specific differences from expected occurrences or variances from budget projections. This is often presented first, followed by the various report

Key Actions Related to Financial Issues in Site Management

Primary Functions
- Lease apartments at competitive rents
- Implement rent collection policies
- Track delinquencies and vacancies
- Monitor and control operating expenses
- Monitor inventory levels
- Maintain site records of receipts, expenditures, purchases, and inventory

Adjunct Functions
- Collect income and expense data for budgeting
- Analyze income and expense data sources for budgeting
- Recommend budget amounts for line items
- Review income and expense reports to analyze variances from budget
- Explain budget variances
- Recommend strategies to increase income and control expenses
- Authorize payment of expenses, including payroll

forms in sequence. Remember that not all variances are negative. The narrative summary is an opportunity to highlight successes as well as shortcomings and make suggestions for improvements.

A more comprehensive financial analysis may be done periodically by the management company or its accountants (at least once a year). A *balance sheet* showing assets and liabilities (rather than income and expenses) is prepared to indicate the financial condition of the apartment community at a specific point in time. All cash in current bank accounts plus the current value of depreciable property and equipment (reflecting accumulated depreciation) constitute the assets of the property. Long-term debt (e.g., mortgage balance), accrued wages and related taxes, security deposits payable, and accrued expenses (accounts payable) constitute its liabilities. The difference between assets and liabilities represents the owner's *equity* in the property.

SUMMARY

The success of a residential rental property is measured by the net income it generates. As site manager, your decisions have a direct impact on the property's success in terms of meeting the owner's investment goals and the management company's requirements. Conscientious collection of rents and other income, effective control of expenses, and accurate and complete record keeping will all contribute to these goals.

Financial management of a property involves establishing thorough and accurate records for the property and for each individual unit or resident. Every dollar of income or expense must be accounted for and categorized based on its source or destination. The records you maintain will form the basis for reports to the owner and future years' budget projections. By maximizing NOI through efficient site management and minimizing variances between actual and budgeted income and expenses, *you* determine the financial success of the property.

Key Terms

accrual-basis accounting
balance sheet
cash-basis accounting
debt service
effective gross income
gross potential rental income
income statement
net operating income (NOI)
reserve account
vacancy and rent loss

Key Concepts

annual budget
budget variance analysis
capital expenditures
capitalization (cap) rate
cash flow
chart of accounts
economic vacancy
miscellaneous (unscheduled) income
physical vacancy

Key Points

- How do actions by the site manager affect property value?
- How is NOI derived from gross potential rental income?
- Why is a budget an important management tool?
- What is the difference between an operating and a capital budget?
- How are budget variances evaluated?
- How does cash-basis accounting differ from accrual-basis accounting?
- What types of information are reported to the owner?

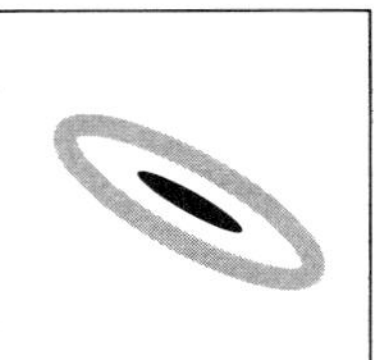

5

Marketing the Property

Marketing is the process of promoting goods and services for sale. The classic components of marketing are the Four Ps: product, price, place, and promotion—selection and development of the *product,* determination of *price,* selection and design of distribution channels *(place),* and all aspects of generating or enhancing demand for the product, including advertising *(promotion).* In real estate management, the product is housing—be it an apartment, a single-family home, a condominium unit, etc. The price is the rent a resident will pay to live there, and the place is where it is located. Promotion is what is done to attract prospective residents to the property, convince them of the value of living there, and induce them to become—and remain—residents.

What distinguishes the marketing of real estate from the marketing of other types of products and services is the fact that real estate is immovable. An apartment's appeal depends on its location, which cannot be changed—potential customers (prospective renters) must be attracted to the property to see the apartment.

Another factor that distinguishes real estate from other products and services is the degree of difficulty involved in altering it to meet market demands. Specific features of a property determine its market niche and the number of potential residents to whom it will appeal. If a property is old or in poor condition, major renovation may be necessary before it can be marketed to a particular population of prospective residents, especially if it is situated in a keenly competitive market. Such change will require expenditure of considerable time, effort, and money.

Everyone involved in marketing and leasing activities—from the property manager to the site manager to the leasing agents—has to understand the property's features (its strengths and weaknesses) and locational factors before a particular market can be targeted and a marketing campaign can be developed. If the property's features are not properly related to the target market, both time and money will be misspent. Careful study of the market will reduce the time and money spent to achieve specific leasing goals.

Those who market rental housing must understand the local housing market before they can develop and implement a specific marketing plan. It is also important to measure the effectiveness of the marketing effort. The site manager's specific contributions to the marketing effort are likely to be quite varied. Whether you will participate in every phase of the marketing process or have a more limited role, you should understand what each activity involves and how it fits into the overall operation of the property.

UNDERSTANDING THE MARKET

The primary factor that limits the potential market for a particular property is its *location*. Rental housing generally attracts prospective residents from the surrounding neighborhood or region because they are tied to the community through area schools, places of employment, shopping, recreational facilities, and other such considerations. By contrast, a time-share condominium located in a popular resort area may attract residents from the entire country or even from other parts of the world.

The demographic characteristics of the *population* of potential residents are also considerations. People's ages, incomes, occupations, and lifestyles, as well as the size of their households, determine how different *property types* appeal to them. Apartments, townhouses, and

Factors Affecting Apartment Markets

- Location
- Population of potential renters
- General economic conditions
- Property type
- Apartment size and layout
- Rent, deposits, and fees
- Services and amenities

single-family homes all possess unique characteristics that make them particularly appealing to certain prospective residents. Marketing efforts directed to the wrong market segment will not be as successful as those that are carefully targeted.

Both *apartment size* and *layout*—the number of rooms and how they are arranged—also limit a property's market. Small studio apartments are not marketed to the same audience or in the same way as those with one or two (or three) bedrooms. The number of people in a household and their income generally define the size, layout, and location of their desired living quarters.

The *rental price* also limits the market for a property. The prospective resident being targeted must be both able and willing to pay the rent and the required deposits, fees, and utilities. In-unit and property *amenities* (microwave ovens, fireplaces; swimming pools, recreation facilities) as well as the quality of the *services* provided are other factors that define a property's market—residents with higher incomes generally expect more amenities and services (they can afford to pay higher rents to obtain them). Thus, marketing depends on numerous factors, many of them reinforcing each other.

Evaluating the Market

Because the value of a property is established in a dynamic market, real estate management professionals have to understand the various forces that influence the property and property values. These include physical or environmental factors, economic activities and trends, governmental regulations and actions, and social standards. Physical and economic factors affect the neighborhood and the region in which the property is located. If a property is well maintained, but the neighborhood around it declines, fewer and fewer people will want to live there. By the same token, rehabilitation of an apartment property may stimulate economic and social renewal for the surrounding neighborhood. Economic and social forces shape demand, making particular property types more or less desirable. Changing governmental regulations influence who lives where—apartment communities that were once exclusively occupied by adults are now rented to families with children. Examples of *physical forces,* which may be created by either nature or society, include availability of natural resources, climate and topography, soil fertility, flood control and soil conservation measures, natural disasters such as hurricanes or earthquakes, and technological advances affecting land uses. Among the numerous *economic forces* are worker productivity measured as Gross Domestic Product, employment and unemployment trends and wage levels, affordability of homeownership, the availability of credit, price levels, and the rate of inflation, interest rates, and tax burdens.

In addition, *governmental regulatory factors* can exert considerable influence. Zoning laws, building codes (e.g., fire and life-safety requirements), environmental regulations, rent controls, national defense measures, special use permits, and landlord-tenant laws determine land uses, set standards for housing construction and maintenance, and regulate rental rates among other efforts. Housing subsidies, guaranteed mortgage loans, credit controls, and monetary policies, including all forms of taxation, are also ways government affects the use of real estate.

The influence of *social forces* can also be seen. These factors include population growth, decline, or stability; shifts in population density; changes in household and family size and formation; prevailing moral codes; changing geographical distribution of social groups; attitudes toward education and social activities; and current thinking about architectural design. The real estate manager must consider all of these factors when preparing a *market analysis* because the property is fixed in its environment even though that environment may change from year to year.

Market analysis has three components—regional analysis, neighborhood analysis, and property analysis. Each takes into account a specific geographic area and has a particular focus. The first looks at the larger geographic area and its economy. The second focuses on the immediate surroundings of a property. The last examines the property itself and how it compares to its competition—properties that are

Components of a Market Analysis

Regional analysis
- Demographic profile—age, income, household size
- Economy—types of business and industry, business climate, availability of capital
- Transportation—roads, rail and bus routes
- State and local government—structure, regulation, and taxation
- Educational institutions—colleges, universities

Neighborhood analysis
- Geographic boundaries
- Population characteristics
- Economic elements—employment opportunities
- Local schools
- Locational factors
- Property types
- Use patterns
- Rents, deposits, and fees
- Competition

Property analysis
- Building location
- Building size and unit types
- Building condition
- Curb appeal
- Features and attractiveness of units
- Amenities and services
- Financial integrity
- Current occupancy level
- Resident profile
- Management, including site staff
- Health, safety, and environmental compliance

similar in size and layout and appeal to the same market segment. The information gathered in a market analysis will be used to determine the property's market position, establish rents, and identify the best marketing strategy to maximize the return on the owner's investment and increase the property's value. The market analysis will reveal the property's strengths and weaknesses and suggest ways to make the most of its assets (and minimize its liabilities) to make it more competitive.

Regional Analysis. General economic conditions and population characteristics, as well as geographic features of the area surrounding the property, are outlined in a regional analysis. These factors affect the demand for space in a particular apartment building and can determine the economic well-being of the property and others surrounding it.

Consumers create demand, and this gives real estate its value. To evaluate demand for a property, the real estate manager gathers and analyzes information about the general characteristics of the region, including historical data and growth projections for the region's population *(demographic profile),* its businesses and industries, public improvements and facilities, transportation and traffic conditions, the educational system, and regional tourism and recreation. The manager looks for trends that signal future growth and opportunity, little or no change in current conditions, or eventual decline. Because governmental regulation and taxation and the social climate of a region also affect the value of real estate, the manager must carefully analyze these aspects as well.

Much of the data used in regional analysis comes from statistical compilations available from the federal government (Department of Commerce, Bureau of the Census; Department of Labor, Bureau of Labor Statistics; and Department of Housing and Urban Development). Commercial firms often collect and consolidate regional statistics compiled by the U.S. government. Professional associations (Institute of Real Estate Management, National Apartment Association) are also potential resources. However, the most valuable information can usually be found within the region itself, through state and local governmental agencies, public utilities, financial institutions, colleges and universities, chambers of commerce, and local economic development agencies. Local newspapers and magazines periodically survey their readers and the results of their research often include consumer demographic data.

As with any statistical information, the limitations of the data should be kept in mind. In order to be useful, information must be current; the validity of numerical data declines with age. Information on communities with fast growth or slow growth will be less accurate than that on communities with steady, predictable growth. Sample size is also important—the sample must be large enough to allow reliable statistical generalizations to be made; too small a sample may yield biased results. The source of the information should be considered as well. Data reported by local chambers of commerce may be more promotional than factual because their aim is to make their communities appealing, not necessarily to provide unbiased information.

Neighborhood Analysis. The next level of analysis is an in-depth study of the area around the property. The objective of a neighborhood analysis is to discern its relevant attributes, characterize its population and its economic base, and determine the dominant property types. Factors such as family size, age groups, ethnic composition, income levels, local schools, and types of businesses are part of what characterize a neighborhood. Because this study is usually focused on the immediate surroundings, it may seem more important than the regional analysis; however, without a thorough regional analysis, the neighborhood analysis may be too optimistic or too pessimistic. A particular neighborhood may flourish despite a sagging regional economy, or it may lag behind regional trends.

The first step in this analysis is to determine the boundaries of the neighborhood. For a particular property, the neighborhood may comprise only a few nearby buildings or an area of many square blocks. Neighborhood boundaries often are natural or constructed barriers that separate areas having similar populations or land uses. Rivers, lakes, ravines, interstate highways, railroad tracks, parks, and streets are examples. Sometimes neighborhood boundaries are not easily determined. You may have to gather information from many different sources (municipal and county governments, local utility companies, newspaper reports, the local library, the school board, welfare agencies) in order to map a neighborhood precisely.

Once the boundaries of the neighborhood have been defined, the real estate manager looks for trends in the data and estimates their impact. A neighborhood is not a static environment. Neighborhood conditions change, and one of the central tasks of market analysis is determining why the changes are taking place and how they will affect your property. Changing numbers of individuals in different age and income groups and changes in household size indicate population shifts—as a result, studio apartments may become less desirable than two-bedroom two-bathroom units. Fluctuating real estate sales prices and rental rates indicate changing demand and other economic forces—a lack of new construction of multifamily housing may indicate the unavailability of financing. Differences in types of property development (new versus renovated; commercial versus residential),

Factors Affecting Location Quality

- Accessibility of highways (entrance and exit ramps)
- Accessibility of major roads
- Availability of mass transit (nearby stops)
- Proximity to schools and colleges
- Availability of employment locally
- Proximity to convenience store or center
- Proximity to neighborhood shopping center or supermarket
- Proximity to regional mall or major shopping center
- Proximity to central business district
- Proximity to parks, sports, and fitness centers; recreational facilities
- Availability of cultural activities and entertainment centers
- Reputation of the neighborhood
- Reputations and conditions of areas surrounding the neighborhood
- Numbers of crimes against people
- Numbers of crimes against property
- Availability of police, fire, and emergency medical services
- Availability of social services (government and human services centers)

changes in land value and use, and vacancy rates indicate additional economic forces are at work.

A physical inspection of the neighborhood is essential. The manager wants to know the character of a neighborhood as well as its general appearance and which of its features favor the property being analyzed or work against it. The location and quality of schools, location of places of worship, accessibility of shopping and recreational facilities, and availability of public transportation are important factors. The ratio of residential to commercial to industrial properties must also be considered. Is the neighborhood balanced? Are there discernible trends in the growth of one sector versus another (e.g., industrialization or commercialization of a residential neighborhood)? An apartment building surrounded by industrial buildings is an indication that such changes are taking place. Features that favor the property and its neighborhood should be stressed in the marketing campaign. At the same time, negative features of the neighborhood have to be recognized, regardless of whether they can be remedied. A strategy must be established so the on-site staff can discuss the positive and negative aspects of the neighborhood in a productive manner.

Life Cycle of a Neighborhood

- Development
- Maturity
- Decline
- Blight
- Rehabilitation

Another consideration is its place in the *neighborhood life cycle.* Over time, neighborhoods pass through several evolutionary stages, including development, maturity, decline, blight, and rehabilitation. During the development stage, new buildings are completed rapidly to house the new residents who wish to live in an attractive and prosperous area, and real estate prices increase steadily. Eventually, as the rate of immigration and the volume of available housing stabilize, a neighborhood enters a period of maturity during which real estate prices level off and reach equilibrium. Gradually, as other neighborhoods are developed, the appeal of the mature neighborhood fades, and people begin to move out. In the ensuing period of decline, properties gradually lose their value as the neighborhood becomes less attractive to residents and investors alike. At the depths of its decline, a neighborhood is said to have entered a period of blight—vacancies are at their highest levels, property conditions physically at their worst, and property values at their lowest, and vacant buildings and unimproved lots may be common. A neighborhood may remain blighted for a long time, and deteriorated buildings may be abandoned or demolished. However, as some properties decline in value, they represent bargains for investors, and the neighborhood may enter a period of rehabilitation, during which investors purchase financially and physically distressed properties and rejuvenate them. The goal of rehabilitation is to restore specific properties and, in so doing, restore a neighborhood to its former (or better) condition.

If the results of the neighborhood analysis seem incomplete or uncertain, further investigation will be necessary. A manager would be unwise to predict a change in a community's land values from a single statistic. Careful interpretation of facts is essential to an accurate market analysis. For example, population growth often indicates prosperity for a neighborhood, but the circumstances of that growth are also important. Large construction projects may create new jobs for communities—both temporary and permanent. When construction is complete, however, transient construction workers will move on, reducing both the number of jobs and the population in the area—the result can be an overbuilt market. To be accurate, a market study should be based on post-construction population and employment figures. In order to know whether conditions are improving, staying the same, or declining, the manager will have to monitor current trends. The more that is known about a neighborhood, the better. Evaluating a trend outside its context can result in miscalculation and financial loss. The best neighborhood study is one that is updated regularly.

Property Analysis. A property analysis includes the results of a careful and thorough inspection of the building (literally from the roof down) along with a description of its rental space and common areas, basic architectural design, overall physical condition, and factors related to its recent operation. A property analysis should be able to answer the following questions about its characteristics and components.

- *Building size*—How many units does the building contain? What are the sizes of the units, and how many rooms do they each have? What is the unit mix?
- *Individual units*—How attractive is the rental space (layout, exposure, view, features, age and condition of fixtures and appliances)? How large are the different unit types? Will they appeal to prospective residents?
- *Condition*—What is the physical condition of the building? Has it been well maintained? Can obsolescence—both deferred maintenance and out-of-date design—be corrected?
- *Common areas*—What is the condition of the heavily used elements (floors, floor coverings, lobbies, entry halls, stairways, storage areas, laundry rooms)? Are common areas being maximized (e.g., well-organized storage facilities, appealing and efficient laundry room)?
- *Curb appeal*—How desirable is the property from the standpoint of appearance (visual impression, age, style, grounds, layout, approaches, public space)? How attractive and effective is the signage?
- *Building-to-land ratio*—What is the relationship between the

building and the land on which it is located (parking, current zoning)? Can the land be used more efficiently?
- *Compliance status*—Is there any evidence of violations of health, safety, or environmental standards?
- *Current management*—What are the current standards of building management? What policies and procedures are in effect for resident selection and resident retention, rent collection, maintenance, purchasing control, administration, and hiring and training of personnel?
- *Staff*—How is the property currently staffed? What are staff attitudes, capabilities, training, and goals? Is the staff neat and professional in its appearance and conduct?
- *Occupancy*—What has been the historical occupancy level and what are the current levels for different unit types?
- *Financial integrity*—How much income does the property generate? Are expenses high or low compared to competing properties? What is its level of debt?

The property analysis tells you about the current status of the property as well as what kinds of changes *must* be made to make it more rentable, *should* be made to make it more competitive, and *could* be made to make it the most desirable place to live in the neighborhood. The comparative costs of such changes will determine what will be done and how soon.

All told, the property analysis tells you about the subject property, its competition, and where it fits in the current rental marketplace. It also tells you about the quality of the housing you are offering right now, as well as the deferred maintenance and obsolescence that exist and the property's financial condition (income and expenses), and it should include a profile of your current residents). (The resident profile is addressed later in this chapter.)

Evaluating the Competition. Having determined the physical and financial strengths and weaknesses of the managed property, the next task is to learn how it compares with its competition. A major part of this is learning what competing properties "do right" or "do wrong" in appealing to the target market. You should also observe the techniques of competing leasing agents so you can evaluate their strengths and weaknesses in comparison to the staff at your property.

Knowing what local residents consider important and what makes some properties more appealing than others, real estate managers can position a property to its best competitive advantage. In general, the following factors should be considered.

- The numbers and types of units available within the area.
- The average age and character of the buildings in which they are located—building condition, curb appeal, caliber of maintenance.
- Features and fixtures that are similar in most units within the market—layout, numbers of rooms, room sizes, specific appliances.
- Amenities and services offered at each of the properties.
- The current rent for an average unit (monthly and on a square-foot basis) as well as deposits and fees; lease terms and rent concessions offered to renters.
- The occupancy level of all units of a given type; the occupancy level of units in the market that are superior, average, and inferior.
- Rental rates and occupancy levels in recent years and trends for each.
- The quality of the staff and services at competing properties.

In comparing properties, one should consider how the rent and occupancy trends of various unit types compare with real estate market trends in general; how vacant units in the area compare to those in your property in regard to size, age, condition, amenities, and rents; and, based on the results of the neighborhood analysis, whether the demand for your property warrants an increase or decrease in rental rates.

An excellent way to compare properties effectively is to categorize the features of the building and its competitors using a market survey form, sometimes called a *rental grid.* The purpose is to show whether a feature at the property is as good as that of its competition and how much rent that feature is worth. The typical components of a rental grid are listed in exhibit 5.1.

Using a grid format allows feature-by-feature evaluation of competing properties. The categories for comparison are listed in the left-hand column; the column next to it is used to evaluate the property

EXHIBIT 5.1

Typical Components of a Rental Grid

- Property
- Location rating
- Age
- Total units
- Occupancy (%)
- Overall condition
- Curb appeal
- Security deposit ($)
- Pets allowed?
- Pet deposit ($)
- Apartment rents ($) and size (square feet)
  —Efficiency
  —One-bedroom
  —Two-bedroom
- Rent per square foot
- Rent concessions
- Appliances
- Air conditioning (in unit/central)
- Number of bathrooms
- Drapes/blinds
- Fireplace (gas/wood)
- Microwave
- Laundry room or washer/dryer in unit
- Utilities
- Parking (garage, covered, open)
- Security
- Swimming pool
- Recreational facilities

When a grid format is used, the presence of features may be indicated by yes or no, and such factors as location and condition may be rated as excellent (E), good (G), fair (F), or poor (P). Some or all utilities may be included in the rent or paid by the resident directly; the distinction is important, as utilities paid by the landord can be a strong marketing motivator. Utilities are usually indicated as follows: gas (G), electricity (E), water (W), sewer (S), heat (H). Because different types of units often differ in their features as well as their sizes and rents, separate comparisons should be made for different unit types (e.g., efficiency, one bedroom, two bedroom).

Resident Profile

- Average income and income range
- Average age and age range
- Typical occupations
- Location of employment
- Number of people in household
- Education level achieved
- Locations and types of previous residences
- Interests and hobbies

that is the subject of the analysis, and subsequent columns to the right are devoted to each of its competitors. In its simplest form, the presence or absence of features may be noted along with specific facts regarding rents, fees, and concessions. Sometimes a qualitative rating scale—i.e., excellent, good, fair, or poor—may be used. Such a rating system facilitates assessment of the relative strengths and weaknesses among the properties, allowing the analyst to make judgments about the overall value and appeal of the subject property and its various competitors. Ultimately, these kinds of information may be used in determining rental rates for the subject property as it is positioned in the marketplace.

Resident Profile. Effective marketing requires knowledge of your current residents. Existing residents represent your current market and could, presumably, be representative of prospective (future) residents. By gathering information on their ages, household income, education, occupation, household composition (number of children and their ages), pets, travel time to work, and interests, you will be able to develop a profile of your current residents. The *resident profile* is a marketing resource. It enables you and your staff to direct the leasing efforts for the property toward the specific type of resident you seek, bearing in mind that you must comply with fair housing laws.

Several sources of information can be used to create a resident profile, including rental applications, information reported when residents are qualified, and periodic surveys of current occupants. Residents who have renewed their leases should be surveyed at the time of renewal to update rental records and find out why they stayed. Exhibit 5.2 contains questions typically asked in a resident survey.

EXHIBIT 5.2

Sample Resident Survey

We appreciate your assistance in completing this form. It will enable us to serve you better. Please submit one form for each adult member of the household.

1. What is your occupation? ______
2. Where are you employed? ______
3. What is your employer's address? ______
4. What is your mode of transportation to work?
   ______ Bus
   ______ Train
   ______ Car
   ______ Walk
   ______ Other
5. What is your average travel time to work? ______
6. What is your age?
   ______ 18–25
   ______ 26–35
   ______ 36–45
   ______ 46–55
   ______ Over 55
7. How long have you lived here? ______
8. What type of unit do you occupy? ______ Unit number ______
9. How many are in your household? ______
10. Tell us about your interests and hobbies. ______
    ______
11. Please rank the following features from 1 to 10, with the most important feature as number 1.
    ______ Location
    ______ Access to transportation
    ______ Access to schools
    ______ Access to shopping
    ______ Access to recreational facilities
    ______ Apartment layout
    ______ Apartment amenities
    ______ Laundry room
    ______ Bike room
    ______ Rent
12. Do you have any additional comments you would like to share? ______
    ______
    ______

Please return this form to the rental office.
Thank you.

Signature (optional) ______ Date ______

The profile of current residents will enable you to determine whether they (and others matching the profile) will be able to support the property in the near and distant future. For properties that are financially secure and for which no changes are anticipated, the current resident profile may correspond to future plans. For a property that will be rehabilitated or upgraded, however, an entirely new resident profile may be sought based on higher income being needed to pay a higher rent.

DEVELOPING A MARKETING PLAN

A *marketing plan* consists of strategies for attracting prospective residents and retaining current ones, specific goals to be achieved and a time frame for their accomplishment, and a budget to accomplish them. If a marketing plan is to be effective, it must promote the best (most marketable) features of the property and present them in ways most likely to reach the targeted group of prospective residents. A thorough analysis of the marketplace, including the subject property, is the first step in developing a marketing plan. The next step is to identify what changes need to be made at the subject property, from financial to physical, to enhance its marketability. The ultimate goal of the marketing plan is to make consumers (the market of prospective residents) aware of the property, its availability, and the advantages it offers over the competition. This is achieved by using appropriate marketing techniques and media and careful positioning of the property.

Budgeting for Marketing

Customarily, marketing budgets for apartments have been approached as either percentages of gross income devoted to advertising (based on income-expense surveys) or specific dollar amounts based on anticipated apartment turnover. Some owners and real estate managers may budget what they think they can afford; others base their decisions on what they thing their competition is spending. The process of arriving at an appropriate marketing budget is more complicated than merely establishing a subjective (and often arbitrary) figure for what might be necessary. Both the costs that are likely to be incurred for specific promotions and the potential availability of funds to pay for them have to be considered. Ultimately, the dollars made available and spent on marketing will depend on the owner's goals for the property in terms of expected levels of occupancy and rental income. The amount of money an owner or property manager allocates to the marketing budget will differ from one property to another. Regardless of the number of vacancies or the amount of money available for marketing, the real estate manager must be selective in spending these funds in order to best achieve the goals of attracting and retaining residents. Clearly, the marketing budget for the lease-up of a newly developed apartment property will be very different from that for an established apartment community that must address periodic turnover.

Careful thought must be given to exactly what the budgeted dollars are expected to buy. What kinds of costs might be incurred for different marketing activities, how successful they are expected to be, how effectively they fulfill the owner's goals, and whether they are affordable must be known in advance. Many people in the apartment industry spend both money and energy merely turning over one resident after another. Although it is important to attract new residents, this approach is, by itself, very reckless. Concentrating efforts and devoting resources to retaining residents who already live in the property should always be a major consideration, especially in times of economic downturn or overbuilding.

Marketing Techniques

Once the marketing budget is in place, plans can be made for using the money most effectively. The best practice is to prepare a definitive marketing plan that states how much money will be allocated for advertising and promotion, when and where specific ads will be placed, and how the results will be measured. In addition to advertising as such, the plan should include public relations considerations. The specific features of the property and the profile of the most likely residents—i.e., the results of the market analysis—will determine the contents of your promotional messages and the best media to deliver them. Each medium has advantages and disadvantages related to its relative cost and the audience it reaches. Marketing materials and promotional campaigns must also comply with fair housing laws.

Apartment Marketing Methods

- Signage
- Newspaper advertising (classified, display)
- Apartment guides
- Brochures
- Other promotional materials (flyers, mailers, postcards)
- Personal referrals
- Locator services
- Broadcast advertising (television, radio)
- Public relations (press releases, newsletters)

Signage. Signage is probably the most important marketing tool because it is the first thing prospects see. As such, it is the basic real estate marketing tool. In a well-planned marketing campaign, the visual themes established by signage will be used throughout the property. These themes include color, logo, lettering, and whatever message is conveyed by the marketing program.

Every property should display a sign that identifies the site. It may also show the name of the management company and should tell where to obtain rental information—minimally, a telephone number. The sign itself should be tasteful and not detract from the visual appeal of the property. The color, size, and location of the sign are critical factors. People should be able to read it from the street. Well-designed signage can enhance the prestige of a building. In addition, on-site signage—in particular, monument signs—is durable (i.e., has a long life expectancy) and requires only minimal maintenance. Because signage is often regulated by the municipality, local requirements should be investigated before committing to particular signage on site.

While good signage is critical, it is not sufficient on its own to market apartments because only people passing the building will respond to it. More than likely, anyone who does respond to on-site signage is already a strong prospect because of having seen—and been impressed by—the property. Other uses of signage include directional signs that point out visitor parking and the leasing office on the property. How much signage is needed and whether it is to be permanent (a monument sign) or temporary (a banner) are considerations for the marketing budget and the marketing plan. Despite the importance and prominence of signage, effective marketing requires use of other vehicles as well.

Advertising Media. Newspaper advertising is very cost-effective because a newspaper is read by a high percentage of the population of a given area. Newspapers offer several formats for advertising rental apartments. *Classified advertising,* which usually occupies its own section of the newspaper, is the most common medium for advertising apartments for rent. The content of a classified ad should be clear and straightforward. It should include the location of the property, the type of unit, the rent, any special features, a phone number to call, and a fair housing statement.

Classified ads are relatively inexpensive to place, and they reach a wide audience. Because many people consult them, they are a very effective way to advertise apartments, especially when only one unit is currently available, although large apartment communities with numerous available apartments often benefit from continual advertising. Inclusion of the rent allows the prospect to determine whether he or she can afford it and serves minimally as a prescreening measure. Another prescreening measure is a statement whether or not pets are acceptable. The primary disadvantage of newspaper advertisements is that their wide reach means large numbers of prospects will be attracted to the property, any of whom are likely to be unqualified (or disinterested once they see the location). The result can be hours spent dealing with these people at the expense of serving qualified prospects.

Display advertising, on the other hand, is larger and more expensive. While classified ads are intended to relate pertinent information as efficiently as possible, display ads often combine theme and imagery with information about available apartments. The graphic arts component is crucial. The image of display advertising should be consistent with the overall image of the property (signage, color, themes, logos).

Display ads are often used to promote newly developed or renovated properties, during initial lease-up or when large numbers of units of the same or different types are available, although classified ads are also useful in these situations. The content of display ads may be more generalized—i.e., characterization of the property as a whole, the range of available units and rents, and amenities of the apartments and common facilities. They are used primarily to invite prospects to visit the property rather than to lease a specific apartment.

In addition to classified and display ads, newspapers with large circulations occasionally publish special real estate sections that include information on properties, developers, and management companies. They are often presented in a magazine or tabloid format and their appeal is strong; however, their effectiveness—advertising in these sections is likely to be general rather than specific—must be considered in light of their cost, which is considerably higher than advertising in local apartment guides. *Apartment guides* are magazine-like compilations of apartment rental advertising. They are published periodically (generally monthly or bimonthly) and distributed free of charge to prospects. Such guides serve much the same function as a locator service, except that the resident deals directly with the advertiser, and the landlord pays no fee apart from the cost of designing and placing the ad.

Apartment guide advertising can be as effective as (and often more effective than) classified ads in newspapers. Not only is the apartment guide more cost effective because it allows more copy space for the development of themes and inclusion of photographs, maps and other images, but it is better at reaching a target market because of more specific distribution within particular neighborhoods. In addition, apartment guides often have professional staffs who can assist in development and design of advertising as well as provide shopping reports and leasing and marketing training programs for leasing agents.

Brochures are highly detailed pieces of advertising. They are often printed in color on glossy paper and may include sample floor plans of units as well as information about the property and the surrounding community. The visual image presented in brochures and other printed promotional materials (color, logo, theme, graphics, typeface) should be consistent with that of any outdoor signs and display advertisements in use. Brochures can be given to prospects during their visit to the leasing office—to serve as a guide and reminder of what they see on their tour of the property. Brochures are also suitable for mailing to people who make telephone or written inquiries. They are often a component of direct mail campaigns and are very useful in promoting properties, especially those that are brand new or recently renovated.

Brochures can be affordable or very expensive, depending on your design and budget. The quality of the paper (weight, glossy finish), the size and number of pages, and the use of two or more colors, as well as the quantity printed, will determine the actual price. Regardless of budget, brochures should be designed to be useful for as long as possible. In order to do this, a design that allows information on rents to be updated periodically is advisable. One way to do this is to leave blank spaces after the unit types and write in their current rents as needed. Alternatively, printed labels with unit types and rents can be affixed to brochures. A more satisfying—and less unsightly—approach is to indicate an approximate starting rent (e.g., one-bedroom apartments from $575). Another option is to include a separate up-to-date price sheet with the brochure. If a leasing agent quotes a rental rate to a prospect, both the quote and the date through which it is effective should be written on the brochure. This reduces the opportunity for confusion if the prospect comes back at a later date and deals with a different leasing agent.

In addition to brochures, other promotional materials include *flyers, mailers,* and *postcards.* Like brochures, these media can be used in direct mail campaigns and promotion of new properties. They can be produced by photocopying (colored paper or card stock can be used), which allows flexibility and is more economical than printing brochures. These types of promotional materials can be designed and produced in limited quantities for specific marketing campaigns, while brochures, which must be printed in large quantities to justify design costs and color printing, are used for more general marketing purposes.

Personal *referrals* are an excellent source of prospects based on word-of-mouth advertising. Satisfied residents can be encouraged to refer their friends and associates to the property by establishing a referral program that offers some form of compensation to the resident whose referral results in a signed lease. Referral incentives may consist of cash payments, rental discounts, or improvements to the current resident's apartment (e.g., installation of a ceiling fan or new wallpaper). In some states, paying residents for referrals is illegal (they do not hold brokers' licenses), so alternative incentives may have to be developed.

While rental discounts as incentives may seem attractive, they can be problematic. Offering a rental discount to a resident who has a poor payment history may be counterproductive in two ways: The persons referred by that resident may also have trouble paying rent, and any rent concession granted to the current resident will further reduce the effective rent derived from his or her unit. This, in turn, reduces NOI and the value of the property. Indirect incentives such as a new appliance or other amenity are preferable because they have no impact on the effective rent of the unit. Furthermore, the amenity becomes an effective adjunct marketing tool because it remains in the unit after the current resident leaves, making the unit more appealing. It also justifies a higher rent for that unit.

Locator services are another means of identifying prospects. Their sole objective is to match prospective residents with available rental units. They often help people who are relocating to an area, although many people use them to find an apartment quickly even when they are only moving within a city. By providing a centralized listing of available apartments by location, unit type, and rent, locator services save prospective renters the effort of scanning classified ads and calling to set up appointments. They are usually able to find a number of units that fit a prospect's needs in a short time (e.g., several two-bedroom apartments in a certain neighborhood close to public transportation). In addition to showing apartments, some locator services can be contracted to refer prospects to the property, shop the competition, conduct marketing studies, train leasing personnel, or even carry out entire marketing and leasing programs tailored to specific properties on behalf of the management company.

Locator services charge a fee—typically a percentage of the first month's rent—that is often paid by the owner of the property rather than the resident, although in some situations the resident may pay it. The question of who pays the fee is an important one that requires careful consideration. Dealing with a locator service that charges the prospect has the potential to reduce the volume of traffic to your property. Another consideration is whether the locator service charges *both* the prospect and the property owner. This should be disclosed at the outset. The specific fee—or a schedule of fees—should be stated in the contract between the management company and the locator service. Thus, listing with a locator service would be an item to include in the budget for advertising.

When contracting a locator service, several points must be kept in mind. Many states require that people performing such services hold real estate licenses. If that is the case in your state, the contract should require verification of licensing of services personnel. The contract should state that the service is to use the management company's rental application and lease forms and that management company approval is necessary before a lease is signed. Because key control is so important, locator services should not receive master keys, and the contract should state that the locator service assumes responsibility for lost keys and locksmith charges if rekeying becomes necessary. In addition, the locator service should have proper workers' compensation insurance as well as non-owned automobile coverage for members of its staff who visit your property. (Insurance issues are discussed in chapter 9.) The contract should also state that the locator service will comply with fair housing requirements.

Broadcast advertising is occasionally used to promote new residential properties. Because both production and air-time costs of *television* advertising are high, this form is used infrequently in marketing rental apartments. The costs of advertising on cable-access channels may be lower than on network television, and cable television can target specific markets based on the programming of a particular channel; however, cable television is not available in all markets.

An alternative is *radio* advertising, which is much less expensive than television in terms of both production and air-time costs. Radio is especially useful in advertising an open house at a property—these events tend to draw large numbers of prospective residents. One seeming advantage of both radio and television is that they reach very large audiences, but such wide geographic coverage can be disadvantageous if it exceeds the market for your property. If a radio station is heard throughout a large metropolitan area or across a significant portion of a state, the owner's advertising dollars are probably paying to reach many people who would not respond to the advertisement even if they were looking for new homes. In addition, it is difficult to match your resident profile with a television or radio station's audience, and most people try to live relatively close to where they work.

Billboards can be effective for announcing the location, types of units, and projected occupancy date of newly opened properties. They generally are used to depict a theme on a larger-than-life scale based on the desired resident profile. However, billboard advertising has a number of drawbacks. Often the advertiser has little or no control over where ads will appear, and the location of a billboard and its relation to traffic is critical. The higher the traffic count, the more desirable the location and the higher the cost. In addition, billboards often have negative connotations, and their availability is sometimes limited (they are illegal in some communities).

Public Relations (PR). Purchased advertising is not the only way to promote your property. *Public relations* is a form of communication that is used primarily for image building. It tends to deal with issues rather than specific products or services. One of the most common forms of public relations is *press releases,* which can be a cost-effective means of reaching a wide audience. Although press releases are usually prepared by property managers, site managers should understand their uses. Press releases sent to the business or real estate editors of local newspapers and broadcast media can lead to rental inquiries at virtually no cost. Many editors rely on press releases and photographs to fill space in their publications; when they are used, they serve as "free" advertising. Even so, press releases should not be used in the place of paid advertising because they will not lease units directly, and there are never any guarantees that they will be used.

Press releases should be short and to the point—one page is the preferred length, although a maximum of two double-spaced pages may be sent. They should contain the name and phone number of a person to contact at the top of the page, and the first paragraph should contain all the relevant information (who, what, when, where, and why). In addition, the subject should be a legitimate news item, not an advertisement of apartments for rent at the property. Items that could be used in a public relations campaign include the hiring and internal promotion of management personnel, "grand opening" of a new property, or reopening after a rehabilitation. Other good subjects for press releases are professional achievements of site staff members, an award recently received by a member of the staff or a resident, or completion of a community service project in which both residents and staff participated. Public relations derives its credibility from the fact that it is *not* advertising, which gives it the appearance of impartiality and spontaneity. Because the management firm's "public" includes its residents and outside contractors and vendors, sending copies of press releases and periodic *newsletters* to all of these individuals can help strengthen existing relationships. In addition to attracting new residents, press releases are a means of promoting new or expanded services to current ones. Newsletters serve the same purpose.

Aside from these public relations efforts, a property's public image is also affected by the site personnel and their attitudes, the appearance of the property—i.e., its curb appeal—and the environment in the site office. Personnel should conduct themselves in a professional manner, the property should be free of unsightly litter, and the site office should always be neat and well-organized. Responsibility for establishing and maintaining good public relations ultimately rests with the people who work at the property. The best public relations is creating a sense of home for residents. The result will be retention of residents and positive word-of-mouth advertising—residents will renew their leases and refer their friends to the property.

Fair Housing Considerations. A variety of federal laws, state statutes, and local ordinances prohibit discrimination against certain "protected classes" in multifamily housing. This is an important consideration in marketing. Discrimination on the basis of race, color, national origin, religion, or sex or because of physical or mental disability or familial status (children under 18 living with parents or legal guardians, pregnant women, or people seeking custody of children under age 18) is expressly forbidden under federal law. Under state or local laws, protected classes may be extended to include people who are unmarried, receive public assistance, or have certain lifestyles or sexual preferences. To assure compliance with fair housing laws, all rental policies for the property should be reviewed and approved by legal counsel, and all prospects, applicants, and residents should be treated fairly and consistently. This is largely the domain of the site manager and the on-site staff.

However you decide to market your property, whether it is undergoing initial lease-up or you are merely seeking residents to fill turnover vacancies, you must satisfy affirmative marketing regulations. This means that prospective residents who can be identified as members of any protected class as defined by federal, state, or local fair housing law cannot be subjected to discrimination in rental housing. There are two types of discrimination:

1. *Different treatment* occurs when members of protected classes are treated differently than others who are not members of that class, and
2. *Different impact* results when prospects are treated equally, but the impact of the treatment is different because of an individual's minority status.

Charging a higher security deposit or a higher rental rate is an example of different treatment. If a disabled person does not have the same access as someone who is not disabled, the result is different impact. (More information on fair housing laws is provided in chapter 10.)

Fair housing laws are quite comprehensive and prohibit a wide range of discriminatory conduct:

- Advertising or other promotional materials that express (or imply) exclusion of protected classes. Photographs used in advertisements should be representative of the population of the community at large and not just a particular group within it—i.e., convey an image of equal housing opportunity.
- Misrepresentation of the availability (or unavailability) of an apartment based on a prospect's membership in a protected class.
- Refusal to rent an apartment because of an applicant's minority status.
- Applying more burdensome qualification criteria to minority applicants.
- Dealing with prospects in a manner that is intended to maintain the segregated character of an apartment community—i.e., *steering*.
- Discrimination in the terms, conditions, or privileges of residency based on an individual's minority status.
- Discrimination in the use of facilities (including limitations on the use of common-area facilities) because of a person's minority status.
- Discrimination in the application of eviction policies based on minority status.

Regardless of how particular policies or guidelines are stated, if they result in a disproportionate number of applicants from protected classes being rejected or if they are applied in a manner that excludes specific individuals, they are discriminatory. That is why it is imperative to review the property's rental policies and practices periodically and check with legal counsel as necessary or appropriate to assure compliance with applicable fair housing laws. The best approach is to make sure that all prospects are shown all available apartments they are qualified to rent. Resident selection criteria should be applied uniformly and without exception, and residents should be treated consistently with regard to rent collections, service requests, and lease renewals.

Violation of fair housing laws can result in civil lawsuits, with the possibility of punitive damages being assessed as well. Fines for violating fair housing laws can be quite heavy. Claimants may be awarded actual damages, damages for pain and suffering, punitive damages, attorneys' fees and court costs, and civil penalties. These direct costs do not include damage to the reputation of the management company, the property, and you as the site manager if fair housing laws are violated—the indirect costs can be irretrievable.

What should you do to avoid claims of discrimination? You can begin by scrutinizing the content of your advertising. Words have implications, and some specific words can create problems. For example, it is illegal to advertise "seniors welcome" or "adults only" unless the property complies with very stringent statutory requirements. (Housing for the elderly was defined in chapter 1.) Be certain that practices and attitudes throughout your site office are not discriminatory. Nondiscrimination in housing—initially, during tenancy, and at lease renewal—encompasses marketing and advertising programs, apartment showings, and applicant screening procedures, as well as acceptance and subsequent treatment of residents who belong to protected classes.

All prospects and residents should be treated respectfully, and all site personnel should conduct themselves in a professional manner. The best practice is to show all prospects the same apartments for the unit type or types desired—you should not try to decide whether a prospect would be "comfortable" living at the property or "steer" him or her to a certain section of it. If you offer one prospect a soft drink or coffee, offer all prospects soft drinks or coffee. Be aware of how you treat prospects and residents, and treat them all the same way because inconsistency of treatment has legal implications.

The Marketing Campaign

The process of bringing together the demographic factors identified in the market analysis, the profile of current residents, the economic conditions of the region and the neighborhood, and information about the subject property as well as competitors' rents, vacancies, and marketing strategies is called *positioning* the property. The marketing campaign should be designed to target people whom the property can realistically attract as residents. Rents should be set competitively based on the kind of building, the units being leased, the amenities offered, and the comparative appeal of the property. Ideally, the marketing campaign should be based on a unifying theme that carries through to signs, logos, brochures, and advertising. The campaign should be designed to attract prospective residents and retain current ones who match the target profile, although it should not be so specific that it turns away other qualified prospects. Advertising and public relations, as well as the media in which they are presented, are key components of a marketing campaign.

Opening New Properties. Marketing efforts for new properties stress the rapid leasing of large numbers of units under specific time constraints. Unlike the marketing of existing properties, which responds to turnover of established units, new properties pose special challenges for site managers and leasing agents. Usually, marketing new properties involves comprehensive planning that begins months in advance of the opening. The efforts of all on-site personnel must be carefully coordinated, from arranging for the release of new units for occupancy and monitoring move-in schedules to cleaning models and leased apartments prior to move-in, assuring a smooth move-in process, and identifying and solving problems as they arise.

There is an element of trial and error that accompanies the lease-up period. If leasing goals are not being met, marketing strategies may have to be reevaluated. For example, prospective residents may react differently than expected and favor one apartment type over another. They may want to pay less for a one-bedroom apartment and be willing to pay more for a two-bedroom unit. If this occurs, you and the leasing personnel must respond accordingly. Not only would you adjust the rent on the more desirable unit, but the weaknesses of the other unit type must be ascertained to determine what can be done to increase its appeal to prospective residents.

There is also a heightened sense of urgency during lease-up. Because of the high level of activity, on-site personnel will probably work longer hours, and additional people may have to be hired on a temporary basis to expedite the leasing efforts and facilitate move-ins. Lease-up is usually monitored very closely to allow for these kinds of adjustments; a weekly reporting schedule is typical, although daily reports may be required as well. The budget for marketing a new property will be proportionately much larger than that for addressing turnover at an established property of the same size. Also during this period of intensive activity, review and adjustment of the marketing budget will probably be more frequent than monthly.

Resident Retention. The success of a marketing program is measured in terms of the number of prospects who sign leases, the cost to reach each prospect, the duration of each vacancy, the value of concessions (if granted), and conversion ratios. However, a successful marketing campaign will be meaningless if residents do not renew their leases. Under these circumstances, the energies of the entire staff (management, leasing agents, maintenance technicians) will be consumed with turning over apartments. Occupancy rates are based not only on attracting new residents, but on retaining existing ones. Marketing success depends on the level and quality of service provided to residents by the maintenance staff, courtesy and promptness in responding to service requests, and the general atmosphere fostered by the site manager. Service is the key to resident retention. Without such attention to retaining good residents, the turnover rate will increase and the property's income will suffer.

A survey of current residents, as in exhibit 5.2, will tell you what brought them to the property in the first place and what factors compel them to stay. Similarly, an exit survey (exhibit 5.3) can be used to find out the reasons residents choose not to renew their leases. Using the results to correct shortcomings of the property can mean higher resident retention rates in the future. (Resident retention is discussed in more detail in chapter 7.)

Dealing with a Soft Market. The real estate market is cyclic in nature, reflecting changes in *supply and demand.* Rents tend to be fairly stable when supply and demand are in equilibrium, but when the demand for rental housing exceeds the available supply, those units that are available can command higher rents. On the other hand, in a market where supply exceeds demand (a renters' market), it can be difficult or impossible to raise rents or even to maintain them at current levels. A market is *overbuilt* when the supply of rental units far exceeds demand for them; this is also referred to as a *soft market.*

A number of factors contribute to this phenomenon. At the time when an apartment community is conceived and financing is obtained, market conditions may favor new development. However, the time between the date of a loan commitment and the completion of

EXHIBIT 5.3

Sample Exit Survey

Please take a few minutes to complete this survey. It will help us do our jobs better.

Apartment # ______ Address ________________ Date ____________

1. Why did you select our apartments as a place to live?
   ______ Convenience
   ______ Best value
   ______ Social amenities
   ______ Architectural design
   ______ View
   ______ Other
2. Would you consider living here again? ______ Yes ______ No
   Recommend it to your friends? ______ Yes ______ No
   Why or why not? ____________________________
3. Do you believe your apartment was a good value for the rent you paid?
   ______ Yes ______ No Please comment ____________________
4. Please evaluate the following:

	Excellent	Satisfactory	Poor
Efficiency of the staff	______	______	______
Courtesy of the staff	______	______	______
Housekeeping of the apartment community	______	______	______
Heating and air conditioning	______	______	______
Maintenance of the grounds	______	______	______

5. Do you consider the swimming pool an asset?
   ______ Yes ______ No
   Why or why not? ____________________________
6. Is public transportation convenient and accessible? ______ Yes ______ No
7. Why did you leave?
   ______ To rent another apartment
   ______ To buy a house
   ______ Leaving town
   ______ Other
   If you are renting another apartment, please explain: ____________________
   ____
8. Other comments and suggestions: ____________________________
   ____
   ____

Thank you for your help.

Signature (optional) ______________________ Date ____________

NOTE: The content of an exit survey should be specific to the property. Parking might be a consideration instead of access to transportation, and there might be other facilities in addition to or instead of a swimming pool.

To improve responses from vacating residents, you may want to include a stamped envelope addressed to the management company along with the exit survey.

construction is so long—sometimes several years—that the market can change drastically by the time a new community is ready for occupancy. The result may be a market-wide excess of rentable space. If several new apartment communities open in the same area at the same time, the problem of oversupply will take even longer to overcome.

Other considerations are population shifts, changes in the job market (e.g., major employers leaving the region and not being replaced), and a lack of consumer confidence. When unemployment rates are high, affordability is an issue. Often residents will compensate by moving to smaller apartments. Others may choose to share an apartment (take in a roommate) or even return home to live with their families, further reducing apartment occupancy. On the other hand, when interest rates for home mortgages are low, homeownership can be very attractive compared to apartment rentals, creating additional competition for residents. Several clear signs can indicate that a market is becoming soft:

- Declining traffic—smaller numbers of prospects in general.
- Declining prospect quality—fewer prospects qualifying to become residents.
- Lower conversion ratios—fewer prospects becoming residents.
- Longer turnover times—units vacant longer between residents.
- Increasing numbers of evictions for nonpayment of rent—more rents paid late or not at all.
- Increasing numbers of "skips"—more residents abandoning their leases.
- Diminishing renewals—an increase in month-to-month occupancy.
- Increasingly generous leasing incentives and reductions in rent and security deposits required to compete effectively.

High vacancy rates often accompany a poor economy and a large amount of new competitive space. In such situations, it is common to offer concessions—e.g., a period of free rent as a marketing incentive. However, these incentives may be ill-advised. Such concessions are costly for an owner to make because the reduction in NOI reduces cash flow and can lower the property value over the long term. Nevertheless, in a soft market where competitors are offering rent-free periods, concessions may not be a matter of choice.

Offering an incoming resident a period of free rent technically reduces the amount of income derived from the unit—one month rent free means rent will be collected for only eleven months on a one-year lease. However, the impact of this concession on property value and long-term income may not be as great as a straightforward reduction of the rent, provided the unit is priced competitively. If the rental rate is lowered, not only is the total rent collected over the full term of the lease reduced, but a subsequent rent increase will still leave the unit's rate below where it should be. It could take several years to recover the rent lost from a rate reduction. When a financial concession seems necessary, the owner and the manager must strive to minimize the negative effects of the concession on NOI. Often real estate managers will devise policies whereby residents are offered free rent for the last month of the year to guarantee that they will not break their leases prematurely.

A soft market demands extra efforts in all areas of site management. All forms of advertising will have to be reevaluated and public relations efforts increased. The competition must be monitored more closely—often on a weekly basis. The appeal of your property must be increased, and there must be renewed focus on resident retention. Increasing the appeal of the property could involve landscaping, exterior painting, or adding features such a ceiling fans or microwaves to vacant units. Focusing on resident retention entails improving services to residents, responding to maintenance requests in a more timely manner, and doing the job right the first time. Renewal incentives may be necessary. These can range from a discount on one-month's rent to painting or redecorating one room or the whole apartment. Often the concession will be tied to an extended lease term to slow the turnover. Alternatively, a lease might be renewed without a rent increase.

Employee performance may have to be improved, and this may require investment in educational seminars to develop their leasing or communication skills. However demanding these efforts may seem, they are necessary to meet the challenges posed by a soft market. Professional managers recognize the benefit of maintaining the property and being responsive to residents. Finally, the site manager has the additional challenge of making sure staff morale does not flag during a soft market.

MEASURING MARKETING EFFECTIVENESS

Marketing effectiveness is measured in terms of how many prospects come to the property, how many of those prospects become residents, how long a particular unit remains vacant, and the advertising cost per signed lease. Obviously, a property that is fully leased—with no move-outs expected—does not need to advertise in the same way as a new property. However, this may not be a realistic situation. In most large buildings there is continual turnover and, therefore, continual advertising is a necessity.

All promotional efforts should be monitored to measure their effectiveness. By cataloging the source of each business contact, you can identify the advertising and public relations activities that are most successful. To accomplish this, leasing agents should ask prospective residents why they chose to consider the property. A *traffic report* (exhibit 5.4) is commonly used to record this information. It is also used to track the number of inquiries over a certain period of time, what types of apartments prospects are interested in, what promotional vehicles attracted their attention, and the outcomes (appointments, showings, signed leases). It is also important to learn why prospects decide *not* to rent. By evaluating traffic reports, you can determine the effectiveness of different marketing techniques and advertising media. The most effective approaches are the ones that produce the largest number of qualified prospects who sign leases and accomplish this at the lowest cost per prospect in the shortest period of time. Activities and media that are successful should be continued; those that are not should be modified or eliminated.

The amount of advertising required depends in part on your location. A property in a prominent location may have enough walk-in traffic that little or no advertising is needed (in this case, signage would be emphasized), while one in a less-conspicuous location may need a great deal of advertising to generate even a minimum of traffic. There is no set rule about how much advertising is necessary. However, advertising is best thought of as an investment, with advertising expenses considered in terms of the cost to convert prospects into residents. If you spend $120 for a classified advertisement to fill a single vacancy and ten prospects respond to the advertisement, the $120 investment would translate into a cost of $12 per prospect. Now

EXHIBIT 5.4

Sample Traffic Report

Weekly Traffic Report

Week of ____________

Property ____________ Prepared by ____________

	Mon.	Tues.	Wed.	Thurs.	Fri.	Sat.	Sun.	Total	Total Rented
Nature of Inquiry									
Telephone call									
Visitor									
Time of Inquiry									
Morning (before noon)									
Afternoon (noon to 5 p.m.)									
Evening (after 5 p.m.)									
Referred By									
Large newspaper display ad									
Classified ad									
Billboard									
Drive-by									
Telephone directory									
Word of mouth									
Direct mail									
Locator service									
Television									
Radio									
Housing authorities									
Type Desired									
One-bedroom									
Two-bedroom									
Three-bedroom									
Four-bedroom									
Furnished									
Unfurnished									
Reasons for Not Renting									
Rent too high									
Security deposit too high									
Undesirable product									
Undesirable prospect									
Other									

Key Actions Related to Marketing in Site Management

Primary Functions
- Gather market information about the neighborhood and the property
- Shop the competition
- Compile resident profile
- Supervise leasing agents
- Conduct surveys of current and prospective residents
- Implement resident retention and lease renewal programs
- Measure results of marketing techniques to evaluate their effectiveness

Adjunct Functions
- Assist property manager in analyzing the market study
- Assist property manager in developing a marketing plan and budget
- Assist property manager in coordinating lease-up efforts during openings of new properties
- Contribute to specific advertising campaigns (write ad copy, suggest where to advertise, write press releases)
- Monitor marketing campaigns for fair housing compliance

suppose two of the ten are qualified and willing to sign a lease for the unit at $600 per month. If one prospect signs the lease and the other commits to signing a lease for the next available apartment, the *conversion ratio* is 2:10, a rather modest 20 percent, and the cost of the advertisement translates to $60 per signed lease. (On a larger scale—e.g., multiple vacancies—a 20-percent conversion ratio is not very high. If such performance continued, all aspects of the marketing program—advertising, product, staff conduct, closing techniques—would

EXHIBIT 5.4 *(continued)*

The *Total* column is the total number of inquiries—the volume of traffic for the period; the *Total Rented* column shows how many leases resulted in the same period. Comparison of the two columns yields *conversion ratios* for inquiries to rentals (for the first two categories) and provides a measure of the effectiveness of the different advertising media.

Adapted with permission of the publisher from Barbara Kamanitz Holland, *Managing Single-Family Homes* (Chicago: Institute of Real Estate Management, 1987).

have to be evaluated.) The cost of the ad, the chosen medium (the newspaper classified section), and the amount of time before a new resident is actually found must also be evaluated in relation to the conversion ratio to measure the overall effectiveness of the particular marketing effort.

Another common means of tracking marketing results is a rental inquiry form or *prospect card.* (This will be discussed in detail in chapter 6.) Such a record of prospects can be a resource for future use if other units become available right away. A prospect list can make additional advertising unnecessary, but its useful life is very short. Most potential residents with an urgent need for an apartment will usually sign a lease within 30–60 days of beginning their search.

The most that can be expected of advertising and other promotional efforts is that they will generate prospects. Prospects become residents only after visiting a property. Ultimately, staff members who show apartments to prospects must persuade them that a particular unit is the best value to accommodate their needs. This requires development of selling skills and closing techniques. (Sales techniques are discussed in chapter 6.)

SUMMARY

Because apartment properties exist in competitive markets, it is necessary to distinguish one property from another in the eyes of the consumer. Marketing is the effort to introduce consumers—prospective renters—to the merits of your rental housing using advertising, public relations, and selling techniques. Resident retention efforts are an extension of marketing and should begin as soon as prospects sign leases.

Evaluations of the market and the property form the basis for a comprehensive marketing plan. Depending on the owner's expectations, the specific situation of the property, and the budget allocated to marketing, a marketing campaign is developed to target a specific resident profile. The resident profile is based on various characteristics of the population of likely occupants of the property, including income and household size, as well as the profile of current residents at your own and competing properties.

A marketing campaign may include advertising the property using media that will reach the target audience, attracting drive-by prospects with the property's curb appeal and signage, and inspiring current residents to refer others to the property by word-of-mouth. Resident retention, which reduces turnover costs and increases NOI, is itself another effective marketing tool and requires the concerted efforts of the entire on-site team.

Marketing is only the beginning, however. While marketing introduces prospective residents to the property, the critical test is the actual conversion of prospects into residents. Leasing will be explored in the next chapter.

Key Terms

advertising
classified advertising
competition
conversion ratio
display advertising
marketing
marketing plan
traffic report

Key Concepts

curb appeal
demographic profile
market analysis
neighborhood analysis
positioning (in the market)
property analysis
public relations
regional analysis
resident profile

Key Points

- What are the components of a market analysis?
- How is a neighborhood analysis different from a regional analysis?
- Why evaluate the competition?
- What steps are taken when developing a marketing plan?
- Why is a marketing budget important to the marketing plan?
- How does fair housing law affect marketing activities?
- What are the advantages and disadvantages of different advertising media?
- Why is resident retention important to marketing?
- How does a site manager measure the effectiveness of a marketing campaign?

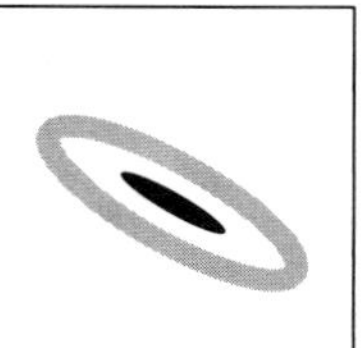

6

Leasing—The Foundation of Residential Management

Marketing sets the stage for the leasing of apartments. While marketing efforts attract prospective residents to the property, leasing is the process of converting prospects into residents. Of course, it is not sufficient merely to fill apartments, nor is it that simple. Rather, the process involves convincing a prospective resident of the merits of a particular apartment and making sure he or she is qualified in terms of the owner's standards before a lease is signed. Leasing is the foundation for real estate management, whether you manage a large high-rise apartment complex, a relatively small garden complex, or a portfolio of single-family homes.

THE IMPACT OF FAIR HOUSING LAWS

The legal implications of leasing are profound. Because of this, specific leasing procedures should be developed and followed consistently so that no prospect is ever treated differently than any others.

Equal treatment is mandated under the provisions of Title VIII of the Civil Rights Act of 1968, which prohibits housing discrimination on the basis of race, color, religion, national origin, or sex. The *Fair Housing Amendments Act of 1988* further prohibits discrimination on the basis of familial status (children) or mental or physical disability. The intent of the fair housing laws is to give every person an *equal opportunity* to live where he or she desires. (Discriminatory marketing practices were discussed in chapter 5.)

For the sake of both fairness and legality, it is important to maintain consistency in all phases of the relationship with prospects and residents. To maintain such consistency, all employees should receive thorough training in fair housing practices, and all policies should be clearly stated in writing. For example, if income level compared to rent is an important selection criterion, the formula to calculate the ratio of rent to income should be standardized, documented, and applied to all applicants. Because fair housing laws are subject to change, particularly as states and local jurisdictions enact their own rules, the most stringent law in place is the one that must be complied with (state, county, and municipal codes can supersede federal acts). Consultation with an attorney and reading on the subject of fair housing are two ways to keep yourself—and your staff—informed about these important laws.

Interpretation of fair housing laws has been very strict, partly because very few people tell prospects they are unwelcome specifically because of their race or another factor. Discrimination need not be blatant to be real; even an unwitting breach of the law can result in a discrimination lawsuit, an event that can end a career and result in a substantial monetary fine. One of the most common discriminatory practices is *steering*. A prospect who inquires about an available apartment may be dissuaded from living at a particular site, encouraged to look elsewhere, or shown only apartments within a certain section of the complex, creating a segregated environment. An applicant from whom vacancies are hidden is also a victim of steering.

The management company should make its policy of nondiscrimination clear to prospective residents and staff members alike. This should be communicated by displaying a U.S. Department of Housing and Urban Development (HUD) fair housing poster in the leasing office. It is unfortunate, but some owners may imply that they would like the management company to discriminate against certain groups of people. They might say, "Don't rent to the wrong type, okay?" or be even more subtle. If you encounter any hint that a discriminatory leasing policy is desired or preferred, refer the matter to the property manager.

Just as it is essential to be explicit about the management company's policy of nondiscrimination, it is imperative to take strong action to prevent discriminatory practices. Discriminatory behavior by on-site employees should be met with swift action—this means firing employees whose behavior is discriminatory. If you engage in discriminatory behavior, regardless of whether the owner pressures you to do so, *you* are liable under the law, and you put both your own and your firm's professional reputations at stake. If someone you employ engages in discriminatory behavior, the ramifications are equally serious.

THE LEASING OFFICE

A neat, well-organized office will allow staff members to function efficiently, and that will create a positive first impression for prospects. Because the leasing office is usually the first place prospects visit, it should convey a professional image. There may not be a separate leasing office; in many cases, the leasing office may be part of the site manager's apartment. This merely reflects the economic reality that it is not always possible or practical to maintain a separate leasing office.

Whether the leasing office is located in the site manager's apartment or is part of a larger on-site management office, prospect cards, rental applications, leases, lease riders (specific additional terms), copies of the "house rules," and any adjunct materials such as brochures should be readily available. Having all materials necessary to the leasing process close at hand not only makes the job easier, it demonstrates professionalism to prospects. A leasing agent who fumbles to collect needed materials or fails to bring the right keys to show an apartment will be less effective than one who is able to complete the leasing process quickly and allow prospects to go about their other business.

Conversely, piles of papers, dirty walls or fixtures, inadequate lighting, poorly coordinated furniture, and unpleasant smells will create an unfavorable impression. A cluttered office can be remedied by installing shelving or file cabinets. The work environment can be improved overall by painting walls in light or bright colors, hanging new wallpaper, shampooing the carpet regularly, washing windows and glass doors, and refraining from smoking. This will not only improve the appearance of an existing space but also keep it fresh and appealing. Prospects who find the leasing office inviting will be more inclined to stay and sign a lease.

Staff appearance and conduct complete the image of professionalism. Achieving this may require establishment of a comprehensive dress code, which can help maintain an appropriate atmosphere. At the very least, all personnel who work in the leasing office should be required to dress in a manner appropriate to their professional status and a business environment. However, leasing personnel might be encouraged to wear clothing or accessories that complement color schemes in the rental office or building logo.

Even more important are staff attitudes and demeanor. Leasing professionals should be cordial and outgoing and strive to represent the property and the management company in the best possible way. (You should seek out such characteristics when hiring leasing personnel.) Because a negative first impression can result in the loss of a leasing opportunity, the importance of starting the relationship with prospects on the right foot cannot be overemphasized.

Making Appointments

Whether they make initial contacts with prospects by phone or in person, staff members should be friendly and helpful and project self-confidence. An approach that conveys energy and enthusiasm should be encouraged. Personnel assigned to answer the telephone should be trained to identify themselves and the apartment community first, then ask for callers' names and follow with the question, "How may I help you?"

You and your leasing staff should show genuine interest in prospects and give them your undivided attention. The initial telephone contact is very important because it is the beginning of the leasing effort and the first chance to screen prospects. It is also an opportunity to identify prospects' needs and desires as well as determine how well your property will meet them. The latter can be done by asking the caller some basic questions:

- What size apartment are you looking for?
- What range of rent do you want to pay?
- How many people will occupy the apartment?
- Do you have a pet?
- When do you need the apartment?

Of course, the answers to these and other questions will probably prompt additional questions. For example, if a prospect responds that he or she has a pet, it is appropriate to ask what kind of pet and how large. If the caller has a large dog and your property has a "no pets" policy, there may be no point in making an appointment to visit your property. (A creative site manager might refer the prospect to another property in the management company's portfolio that accepts pets.) On the other hand, if the prospect needs a two-bedroom apartment immediately and you have several available in his or her price range, a showing can be scheduled at the caller's earliest convenience.

Asking questions will help guide the conversation in a direction that will reflect the strengths of the property and inspire interest in seeing it. However, leasing agents have to maintain a delicate balance: They should provide enough information to generate interest in visiting the property, but not so much information that prospects feel they can visit other properties first and make comparisons later. Describe what makes your property unique and catalog the outstanding features of the desired unit. Then invite the caller to visit the property. Be sure to ask for the prospect's name and telephone number, and try to make a firm appointment for a showing. Once you agree on a time, give clear directions to your property, and thank the person for calling.

Just as these elements are essential to successful telephone contacts, you also have to remember what *not* to do.

- Don't let the phone ring more than three times.
- Don't mumble the property name or speak unclearly.
- Don't fail to identify yourself.
- Don't act as if a caller is inconveniencing you.
- Don't put the caller on hold without asking permission and waiting for it to be granted.

Always be prepared. These initial telephone contacts are ideal opportunities to learn more about prospects. Taking notes on a *prospect card* will not only provide a written record of the call, but also help you better meet prospects' needs when you show them apartments. If callers ask for information you do not have, tell them you will find out and call them back.

Prospects who arrive in person should be shown the same courtesies. As soon as prospects enter the leasing office, they should be acknowledged, made to feel comfortable, and invited to complete a prospect card. Often it is more desirable to have a leasing agent fill out a prospect card in the course of the conversation. This allows the leasing agent to begin developing a rapport with the prospect while essential information is being written down. It is important to get as much information as possible, even though a prospect may be anxious to tour the property or see the apartment. If a prospect seems uncooperative or in a hurry, you might say, "This information will help me find the right apartment for you more quickly."

Completing the Prospect Card. The information noted on the prospect card will enable the interviewer to identify the units that will most likely appeal to particular prospects. The card should have spaces for the prospect's name, address, and phone number, preferred rent, a desired move-in date, and the number of occupants, as well as any preferences for features or amenities if they are mentioned. It is also a good idea to note the name of the leasing agent who originally spoke with the prospect. Sometimes the original agent is not able to meet a visiting prospect in person, or someone else may have to handle a follow-up visit.

There should also be space on the prospect card to record the date and results of the showing or follow-up attempts. A section for comments on the blank back of the card can be used for taking notes about which units were shown, what appealed to the prospect during the tour, and any objections the prospect raised. (The example in exhibit 6.1 has spaces for all these kinds of information.) An effective prospect card can tell you when to follow up with prospects and how to concentrate on the strongest sources of your prospect traffic, as well as identify peak periods for showings. It also becomes an excellent resource and reference on where your prospects live and work and why particular prospects did not move into your apartment community.

EXHIBIT 6.1

Sample Prospect Card

Prospect Card

Date ______________________ Call __________ Walk In __________
Name ____
Address ____
Home Phone ________________ Work Phone ________________
Desired Unit ____
Requested Rent ($) ____________ Desired Move-In Date ____________
Number of occupants __________________________________

Unit(s) Shown __________________ Quoted Rent ____________
Reason Moving ______________________________________
How did prospect learn about us? (signs, advertising, other) ____________
Taken by __________________ Follow-Up Remarks ____________
____

This example, while representative, is more likely to be filled out by the leasing agent or other interviewer. A card to be filled out by the prospect might be more "user friendly" if some of the items are presented as questions. For example: What size apartment are you seeking? How may people will be living there? When do you want to move in?

Prospect cards can provide valuable marketing information regarding the effectiveness of specific advertising—i.e., whether you are reaching the target market. By including the question, "How did you learn about us?" on the card, and listing the items you want to track—newspapers, outdoor signs, drive-by, resident referral—you can determine the source of the traffic. Prospects' home addresses will tell you what geographic areas your advertising has reached. If you are planning an open house or large-scale promotion of a property, this information, along with a zip code breakdown of qualified prospects, will help you plan a targeted mailing list. If you notice that several prospects work for the same company, you can familiarize yourself with the firm and mail appropriate announcements and leasing information to this key employer (as a service to its employees).

Information from unqualified prospects can be useful, too. For example, if you manage a no-pets community and pet owners are consistently responding to your outdoor sign, you might want to consider revising the sign or the policy. If many prospects who discovered your community through a newspaper ad cannot afford your rent, it is time to redesign the ad to appeal to a more appropriate audience or advertise in a vehicle that serves a more affluent segment of the population. Simply including the rent or rental range in your advertisements may minimize the problem of unqualified prospects.

Regardless of who fills out the card, the leasing agent should quickly review the general information about the prospect and what he or she is seeking. This information should guide the selection of apartments to be shown and details to be pointed out to the prospect. (Take the prospect card with you for the showing—that way the prospect will know it was filled out for a reason.) Open-ended questions directed to the prospect will help the agent narrow the choices to better meet a particular renter's needs and desires.

The remainder of this chapter will focus on the specific steps in the leasing process. However, not all prospects will decide to become residents immediately, and the prospect card serves as a record of efforts to follow up with interested prospects until a firm decision (yes or no) has been reached. If a prospect does not complete a lease application after a showing, timely and appropriate follow-up is imperative. Prospects who are excited about your community and expect to make a decision within a day or two should be contacted the next day. Prospects who are mildly interested and hoping to decide on an apartment within four or five days should be called within 24–48 hours. Those who are interested but have no immediate time constraint should be called back within 72 hours. If prospects show no more immediate interest, additional follow-up calls can be made at weekly intervals. However, for those who seem to be "window shoppers" or you are sure are not interested in the property, a thank-you note should be sent within 72 hours. This is more than a courtesy; even a prospect who does not rent now may call back in the future or, perhaps, provide you with a referral. Certainly your courtesy will be remembered as a gesture of good will.

Showing Apartments

The showing will determine whether prospects will be converted into residents when they visit your apartment community. A tour of the apartment community should point out its features—e.g., recreational facilities, amenities, the model apartment—preferably before individual apartments are shown. This assures that prospects take note of them. (When the apartment is shown first, prospects tend to pay less attention to the property as a whole, or its features may be ignored altogether.) Throughout the tour of the property and the apartment, the leasing agent should explain how different features will benefit the prospect (e.g., efficiency, convenience, aesthetics). Asking prospects open-ended questions as you go along will involve them in the leasing process.

The tour should highlight the property's strengths and show it in the best possible light. Apartments that are damaged or in need of cleaning or painting, as well as common areas that need cleaning or repair, should be excluded from the tour. Anything unsightly will erode a prospect's confidence in the property and the management company. More to the point, maintenance and repairs should be done promptly, not only to correct these situations so you do not have to avoid any areas during the tour, but also to preserve the property's value. Because current residents will also see these problems areas, prompt repairs are important from a renewal perspective as well.

Model Apartments. Model apartments can be effective marketing and leasing tools, but they are not necessary or appropriate in all circumstances. Models are most often created for brand-new or recently rehabilitated buildings where lease-up usually begins while the property is still undergoing construction. Because the most desirable apartments are the easiest ones to lease, it is often a good idea to decorate a less-desirable unit as a model. This allows you to demonstrate what can be done to overcome perceived disadvantages. Models should be easily accessible from the leasing office—especially for prospects with disabilities—and their location should provide an opportunity to show the property's amenities.

Models should be cleaned and inspected regularly to make sure they look (and smell) their best. Decorations should be tasteful, accentuating the best features of a unit and its layout. The furnishings should reflect the income level of the target market and be appropriate for the size of the unit. Heavy, dark-colored furniture makes rooms appear smaller; lighter colors and smaller pieces create a spacious feeling. Plants, books, and photos will make a unit look "lived-in" and enhance its appeal to prospects. While in the model, you may want to discuss prospects' needs and impressions or begin to close a lease.

When showing the model, allow prospects to enter first. This will enable you to observe their reactions to it. Their body language may be positive or negative, and from it you can gauge the best approach to showing and closing. It is a good idea to carry a tape measure or have one in the model in case prospects wish to note room dimensions for comparison to the size of their furniture. Taking the measurements will give you an opportunity to work together, which will give the prospect a sense of participation rather than being a mere observer during the showing.

In our daily lives, decisions are often made at the kitchen or dining room table. A similar approach can be used when visiting a model apartment by having all the leasing materials ready and having prospects sit at a table to discuss the benefits of an apartment and its community. The desired atmosphere influences even the choice of a table—a round one will be more inviting than a rectangular one because there is no "head."

Because models do not generate income directly, they are usually omitted in smaller buildings or when demand is high, and prospects are shown only vacant apartments. Whether a property has models or not will depend on local market conditions as well as the property's performance within the market and is not a reflection of the professional atmosphere at the property.

Available Vacancies. Any showing of apartments should include a visit to the available vacancy. If several apartments are vacant, the first one you show should come as close as possible to fulfilling the prospect's stated parameters of unit size and desired rent. Others can be shown as well, especially if the conversation with the prospect indicates that additional features or fixtures are being sought.

Each vacant unit you show is an opportunity to relate apartment features and amenities to the prospect's specific needs and desires. Your goal is to establish in prospects' minds how they will benefit from living in a particular apartment by matching its features to their requirements; this step is essential to "selling" the apartment and demonstrates the importance of reviewing prospect cards. For example, someone who seeks spacious closets should be shown all of the walk-in closets and storage space in an apartment as well as any locker space available. Other examples of features commonly found in modern apartments—and their benefits—are listed below.

- Frost-free refrigerators or self-cleaning ovens are easy to maintain.
- Microwave ovens, garbage disposals, dishwashers, or in-unit washers and dryers offer convenience.
- Attractive and convenient on-site laundry facilities save trips to a coin laundry off site.
- Cable television provides additional entertainment choices.
- Wall-to-wall carpeting helps minimize noise; vinyl flooring is easy to maintain.
- Air conditioning provides added comfort.
- Ceiling fans add comfort and save on heating and air-conditioning costs.
- A patio or balcony creates an outdoor extension of an apartment.

All of these are examples of features that can be "sold" to prospects in terms of time and convenience. On the other hand, a spectacular view needs no explanation.

Often prospects will raise objections because a particular unit does not appeal to them or seems expensive, or they may not be ready to sign a lease. Most objections can be overcome if an effort is made to explore them and address them head on. For example, an objection to a particular color of carpet may disappear if the prospect can be shown how it will complement a variety of furniture colors and patterns. Showing another apartment with a different color carpet is another option. Concerns about the rent being high can be addressed by explaining what the rent includes—e.g., prompt service provided by a well-trained professional staff—and cataloging how your amenities are different from or better than those of your competition. If a prospect thinks the rooms are too small, you can ask about the furniture sizes and relate them to room dimensions. Scale drawings of apartment floor plans also help prospects visualize the use of space within apartments.

Objections are your opportunity to reassure prospective residents that your property is the place for them to make their home. To do this successfully, you will have to maintain an ongoing dialogue—

listen carefully to what prospects say and respond to their verbal and nonverbal communications. It is essential to address their likes and dislikes and try to find solutions to their perceived problems. There is more to selling apartments than pointing out features and benefits and overcoming prospects' objections. Prospects are also likely to be interested in the neighborhood and will ask about schools, banks, restaurants, shopping, public transportation, health clubs, and other aspects of the surrounding area. The site manager and the leasing agents should be thoroughly familiar with these elements of the neighborhood so they can answer specific questions.

Closing

The culmination of the leasing effort is the invitation to fill out a rental application. This is the goal of all that has gone before—i.e., the *closing.* There are many approaches to closing, and each is appropriate to given situations and types of salespeople. Often, an assertive closing technique is necessary. However, your closing should be natural and suited to your personality. While the closing may recapitulate everything you have talked about and shown to the prospect, at a minimum, it should highlight all of the tangible and intangible features of the property.

One approach to closing is to conclude the tour with an oral review of what the apartment and the property offer the prospect. This type of summary closing is based on answers to specific questions the prospect may have raised or the leasing agent might have anticipated. Prospects' needs and desires should be restated in terms of how the apartments they were shown fulfill their wants and needs—i.e., how they will benefit personally. The goal is to convince prospects that they need look no further.

Extremely indecisive prospects may need help in making the decision to rent. Repeated reassurance that the apartment they saw fits their expressed needs may be enough. Sometimes additional probing is needed to uncover a critical deciding factor. Continually summarizing the features and benefits of a particular unit should ultimately reassure the prospect that a decision to live in your community is the right one. Asking prospects what else you can do to help them select an apartment is also appropriate. If a prospect seems ready to leave without completing a rental application, ask if there is something wrong with the property or the apartments they were shown. Ask what improvements can be made. Even if this approach does not persuade the prospect to rent, perhaps you will at least learn of a particular problem that needs to be remedied.

If a prospect seems genuinely interested but is unable to make a decision, you might try to create a sense of urgency. A need to act swiftly may sway the prospect to make an immediate commitment. If management is planning to raise the rent, you can let the prospect know that the rent will be higher after a certain date. If only a few units are available and interest has been strong, you can try to convince the prospect to act now—while there is still a choice of locations—because these particular units are not expected to remain vacant for long. You might offer to hold an apartment for a brief period (a few hours or overnight), in which case the prospect should be asked to leave a nominal deposit, perhaps $50, which will be refunded if he or she decides not to complete an application. Alternatively, you might offer to repeat the tour and review its features and benefits.

Bear in mind that a high-pressure approach can backfire and alienate the prospective resident. Saying things like, "It's your only chance," or "This is the last unit of this type" sounds pushy, regardless of whether it is true. Such statements also set up the prospect for disappointment or dissatisfaction if the result is not absolutely perfect. Because people are very sensitive about their homes, the closing, like the rest of the leasing effort, should be courteous and respectful—i.e., handled in a professional manner. Often all that is needed is for the leasing agent to be alert to cues from the prospect. One of the simplest and most effective closings is: "Let's go back to the leasing office and fill out the rental application now."

Although you may be uncomfortable with the idea of closing the deal, prospects expect it. People rarely visit apartments for the fun of it; they are looking for new homes. Because of this, the closing should be a natural culmination of your marketing and leasing efforts. At a minimum, the prospect should be asked to complete a lease application. Leasing an apartment is, after all, the reason the prospect came to the property.

Rent Concessions. Rent concessions can be a short term solution to converting prospects into residents. In fact, they may be a necessity in a soft market. However, their use should be approached with caution. As noted in chapter 4, such concessions as free rent can be very costly. In particular, they reduce NOI and property value. When rental income is reduced, the services that attracted residents to the property in the first place may have to be reduced. Thus begins a downward spiral in which more and larger concessions must be granted to attract new residents and retain existing ones, and further erosion of the property's financial condition may lead to sacrifice of still more services.

The best practice is to provide excellent service; make only promises you can keep, and keep the promises you make. Good service leads to satisfied residents who renew their leases. Better still, they will tell their friends what a pleasure it is to live in your property. Such word-of-mouth advertising cannot be surpassed.

Completing the Rental Application

Once a prospect has made the decision to rent from you, a *rental application form* should be completed by every person of legal age who will live in the apartment. (A rental application is a legal document signed by every adult applicant and countersigned by appropriate on-site staff.) Often application forms are available with a built-in duplicate copy (with or without carbon paper) so applicants can have a copy. Use of a standard form assures consistent collection of the same kinds of information from all applicants and fosters uniformity of processing. (Consistency is a key to compliance with fair housing laws.)

The information commonly requested on a rental application is listed in exhibit 6.2. Both for reasons of fairness and to minimize liability, no one should ever be denied the opportunity to complete an application, regardless of whether it appears that a particular prospect will meet the management company's resident selection standards. Resident qualification criteria should be a part of the property's operations manual.

A standard rental application form usually includes a statement that the prospect, by signing the form, grants the management company permission to verify the information provided. Management companies generally hire credit bureaus to conduct the financial in-

EXHIBIT 6.2

Rental Application Information

Property/Lease Information

- The space to be rented (street address and apartment number)
- Duration of the lease term (if applicant is approved)
- Rental rate (dollars per month)
- Amount of security deposit and other deposits or nonrefundable charges

Applicant Information—Personal

- Name(s) and social security number(s) of principal applicant and all adults who will sign the lease
- Name(s) of all other occupants, including minor children
- Driver's license numbers of all adult occupants and automobile license numbers along with make, model, and year of all vehicles
- Description of any pets, if allowed (some management companies require a photo)

Applicant Residency Information

- *Current* address and phone number of applicant(s)
- Name and phone number of current landlord; address, if different from applicant's
- Duration of current tenancy
- Amount of rent paid
- Reason for leaving
- The same information for *prior* residence

Applicant Employment Information

- *Current* place of employment (company name, address, and phone number), job title, years with company, immediate supervisor, and salary
- Same information for *prior* employer

Applicant Financial Status

- Institution names and account numbers for bank savings and checking accounts, credit cards or charge accounts, automobile or other outstanding loans

---

vestigation of an applicant. Not only does this limit the liability of a management company if an applicant is rejected (responsibility for the accuracy of information is partially shifted to a third party), but a credit bureau has better access to confidential information. Reputable organizations know precisely what to ask without inadvertently requesting information that cannot be released. However the information is to be acquired, the *Fair Credit Reporting Act* requires that the prospect must

EXHIBIT 6.2 ***(continued)***

Other Information

- Identification of any requisite deposits or fees to be paid at the time the application is completed (e.g., for processing a credit check) and whether they are refundable
- A statement of authenticity of information and authorization of the landlord to verify it with a credit bureau; if the information is found to be not valid, the landlord may reject the application
- Applicant signature(s)
- Spaces for the date and signatures of staff who process the application

NOTE: While it is reasonable to request all of this information and more, it is important to realize that all blanks will not be completely filled by every applicant. Those who do not drive, or who drive but do not own an automobile, will leave some spaces blank. If applicants have had the same residence or employer for more than two years, information from prior sources may not be necessary or it may be difficult to verify.

The leasing agent or the site manager should review the information with the applicant and fill in any blanks or clarify something that is hard to read. The agent should remind the prospect that the application is a legal document. It is appropriate to have each adult complete a separate application form. This will facilitate the verification process, especially if the applicants have separate credit histories.

In signing the application, the prospect authorizes current and former landlords to provide information and agrees to hold them harmless (release them from liability) for information provided in support of the application. Signing the application also represents agreement to enter into a lease if the application is approved.

---

be advised that his or her credit is being checked. The applicant must understand that the management company has established specific qualification criteria and that he or she is responsible for providing complete and accurate information. (Providing false information is grounds for denial of a lease—or eviction if the falsification is discovered during tenancy.)

In some areas, it is customary to charge a nonrefundable application and administration fee, which is used to cover the costs of verifying information on the lease application, including a credit check. A security deposit may be collected in full or in part when the rental application is signed. If the deposit is not paid in full with the application, the balance should be due when the lease is signed or when the first month's rent is collected prior to occupancy.

Once a rental application or lease has been signed, if a resident does not move in, it may be permissible to retain all or part of the security deposit, but this depends on the circumstances, the language of the application or lease, and local practice. (This should be referred to legal counsel; it may be a matter of local landlord-tenant law and company policy and should be stated on the rental application form or the lease agreement.) If an applicant does not qualify, the security deposit should be returned along with any prepaid rent. (Note that the security deposit should be separate from any nonrefundable fee.)

ADMINISTRATIVE MATTERS

A site manager's administrative responsibilities in the area of leasing include qualifying applicants; completing and recording leases; collecting application fees, security deposits, and the first month's rent; monitoring move-in and move-out procedures; and processing lease renewal paperwork. Making a list of items related to leasing and move-in, and following this checklist, will facilitate lease administration.

Qualification of Applicants

Before a prospect can be accepted as a resident, he or she must be *qualified.* Minimally, this will entail answering the following questions.

- Does the prospect have sufficient resources to pay the unit rent as well as his or her other financial obligations?
- Will he or she pay the rent on time?
- Will he or she fulfill the obligations of the lease agreement?
- Will he or she respect the privacy and property of the other residents?
- Will he or she maintain the unit?

When evaluating employment and income information provided by applicants, you should consider the length of time a worker has been in a position with a company, the amount earned, and the frequency with which it is paid. While these factors may not qualify or disqualify a prospect individually, taken together they can be a good indicator of personal financial strength.

- *Length of service*—The longer someone has been in a position, the more likely it is that the employer and employee are mutually satisfied with each other's performance, increasing the likelihood of the prospect's job security.
- *Amount of income*—The amount of rent as a percentage of the prospect's wages or salary is often used to estimate the ability to pay rent. However, the prospect should be asked about other sources of income as well as current obligations. Auto loans and credit card payments can consume a large portion of someone's income and make it more difficult to pay rent on time. Many companies establish a rent-to-income ratio as part of their resident selection criteria.
- *Frequency of payment*—Knowing how often the prospect is paid can be helpful in predicting the timeliness of rent payments. Wages paid monthly may require careful budgeting to meet specific payments while wages paid weekly may mean more than one paycheck will be needed for the rent.

Review of these factors may cast a favorable light on a particular prospect, but none of them indicates whether he or she manages money wisely. Just as it is important to verify sufficient income, it is also important to check the applicant's record of loan and revolving credit payments. Regular and timely payments demonstrate responsibility and the ability to manage money.

Regardless of whether an individual is accepted or rejected, you should notify the applicant promptly when the decision is made. If rejection is based on credit history, and the applicant asks why or challenges it, he or she should be referred to the credit bureau or to the management company's main office if a credit bureau is not used. Written records of the disposition of all rental applications should be retained for an appropriate period because sometimes a rejected prospect will pursue the matter on the basis of discrimination. (Exhibit 6.3 provides an example of such a written record.)

EXHIBIT 6.3

Sample Application Follow-up Form

Property Address ______________________
Applicant ______________________ Date __________

1. Rental Reference, Current
   Name of Reference __________ Phone __________
   Is rent paid promptly? __________ Amount of rent __________
   Period of tenancy __________ Has lease expired? __________
   Has required notice been given? __________
   Do you recommend as a resident? __________
   Was applicant ever a nuisance? __________
2. Rental Reference, Past
   Name of Reference __________ Phone __________
   Was rent paid promptly? __________ Amount of rent __________
   Period of tenancy __________
   Do you recommend as a resident? __________
   Was applicant ever a nuisance? __________
   In what condition were the leased premises left? __________
3. Credit Verification
   Name of credit agency __________ Phone __________
   Credit rating of applicant __________
4. Employment Verification
   Name of Reference __________ Phone __________
   Length of service __________ Salary verified at $ __________
5. Household expenses/income ratio __________

Comments

Verified by ______________________ Date __________
Application ________ Accepted ________ Rejected
Reasons for decision ______________________

It is important to obtain telephone confirmation from the applicant's current landlord that he or she pays the rent on time and does not currently owe the landlord any money. You also want to know if the past lease has expired or if the applicant is still liable for future payments. If the applicant has broken the lease, find out why. Applicants with no previous rental experience, limited credit histories, or marginal credit ratings may need a qualified co-signer to guarantee their performance of the lease terms. As an alternative, they may be asked to pay the first and last months' rent *in advance,* along with the security deposit. Similarly, applicants who are retired may or may not have a "credit history" if they pay cash for all of their expenses. For such retirees, income from pensions, social security, and savings or investments should be verifiable.

While financial investigation of all applicants is critical, it is also important to verify that they will be good neighbors and treat the property with care. One way to do this is to ask their current landlords whether the applicants have been the sources of complaints about noise or other disturbances where they currently live, but this information will be more difficult to obtain than financial records. The definitive sources are applicants' *previous* landlords. While you can ask about a prospect's rental payment record and respect for neighbors and the property, a current landlord's comments should be interpreted with care. A current landlord may speak highly of an applicant even if he or she has not been an ideal resident; facilitating someone's move to another property is one way to assure that a troublesome resident will soon be gone. Information from the current landlord should confirm what you learn from the applicant's previous landlord. This is especially important if someone is moving after only one year. Because the prior landlord no longer has to deal with your prospect, he or she may be more frank. If there were problems between your prospect and his or her previous landlord, you may wish to discuss the circumstances with the applicant. The landlord's observations may be ill-founded, and the applicant's perspective will help you determine whether he or she is, indeed, qualified to lease an apartment at your property. Often a previous landlord will be more willing to respond to a written inquiry that includes a copy of the signed rental application form indicating that the applicant holds him or her harmless.

The verification data are used to determine whether or not to offer an applicant a lease. Even though most apartment residents in the United States pay rent from their wages or salary, an individual's ability to pay is more than a matter of rent as a percentage of income. People do not usually use savings or proceeds from investments for this purpose—for many renters these "extra" sources of funds simply do not exist. If a resident, roommate, or spouse loses his or her job, savings may not be sufficient to meet living expenses for an extended period. In times of financial difficulty, food, medicine, and clothing may take precedence over rent payments.

In addition to sources and amounts of income, past payment records, and the level of indebtedness—the main factors in determining prospects' ability to pay rent—the amount of money available for rent is also affected by the size of a household and the number of its members who are employed. When there are two or more roommates, problems arise when one leaves the apartment. Their lease applications may have been approved on the basis of all the roommates' incomes, and the departure of one means those who remain have to make up the balance of the rent or find another roommate. The incidence of default can be quite high in these situations.

It is likewise difficult to predict how long a prospect may be a resident. However, those whose records indicate prior long-term occupancies are probably likely to reside at a new location for a long time as well. Although most people dislike moving, turnover in residential properties is common. It is precisely because frequent turnover reduces the property's income and increases costs for cleaning, repair, and leasing that long-term residents are desired.

Security Deposit Administration

Residents are required to provide a guarantee of their performance of the terms and conditions of the lease—assurance that they will meet the requirements for payment of rent, preservation of the property, etc. Usually, this takes the form of a refundable *security deposit.* Security deposits differ from one community to another and by building type. A large single-family home with numerous features and amenities may command the equivalent of more than one month's rent as security deposit while a studio apartment may require substantially less. In either case, a security deposit different from the monthly rental amount will preclude its being used for the last month's rent.

Many states regulate the way security deposits are held, and some require landlords to deposit them in a trust or *escrow* account or in a separate bank account maintained exclusively for security deposits. (Depending on state law, security deposits may not be *commingled* with other funds.) Some states do not require security deposits be held in separate accounts—they may be deposited in property operating accounts, and as long as residents who are eligible receive their security deposits within a prescribed period of time, the landlord will have satisfied the law.

If all of the lease obligations have been met, the security deposit is ultimately returned in full to the resident. However, all or part of a security deposit may be retained to pay for property damage that exceeds normal or expected *wear and tear* or to compensate the owner for any outstanding amounts owed by the resident (e.g., rent, late charges, assessed damages). If a security deposit is being retained or only part of it is being returned, most states require landlords to provide an itemized statement of account to residents within a certain period of time. If this requirement is not met, the landlord can face monetary penalties and be required to return all of the resident's security deposit as well as pay damages to the resident.

Some states require that landlords pay interest on security deposits, and if the amount of interest exceeds $10, the management company is required to issue an IRS Form 1099 along with the returned security deposit. Many states with this requirement also stipulate that in order for a resident to receive interest, he or she must pay the rent on time and not owe the landlord any money for damage to the premises.

A statement of the condition of the unit at the beginning of the tenancy will facilitate the calculation of any deductions from the security deposit to defray the costs of replacements or repairs. Use of a standardized move-in/move-out inspection form is recommended. The example shown in exhibit 6.4 includes space to record cleaning and repair costs.

The disposition of security deposits is, perhaps, the most sensitive issue in the landlord-tenant relationship. It is a common reason for complaints to state and local agencies. Indeed, many renters count on the return of security deposits to pay moving costs, future security deposits, and rent payments. Delaying the return of security deposits may well damage a former resident's credit rating, which has its own repercussions. Because of this, any charges assessed against the security deposit should be explained clearly, and the remainder should be returned to the departing resident promptly. (The legalities of security deposits detailed in chapter 10.)

In addition to the security deposit, some management companies require a key deposit, which is refunded when all of the keys are returned at the end of the tenancy. If pets are permitted, it is advisable to collect a separate pet deposit, which is additional security provided by the resident to defray the costs of cleaning and repairing the apart-

EXHIBIT 6.4

Sample Move-In/Move-Out Inspection Form

Property ______________________ Unit ________

Date ____________ Inspected by ______________________

Area/Item	Move-in condition			Move-out condition			Remarks
Living Room and Dining Room	Good	Fair	Poor	Good	Fair	Poor	
Doors and Locks							
Floors and Baseboards							
Walls and Ceilings							
Windows and Drapes							
Electrical Fixtures							
Electrical Switches, Outlets							
Closets							
Kitchen							
Doors and Locks							
Floors and Baseboards							
Walls and Ceilings							
Electrical Fixtures							
Electrical Switches, Outlets							
Range and Refrigerator							
Sink							
Cabinets							
Bedroom(s)							
Doors and Locks							
Floors and Baseboards							
Walls and Ceilings							
Electrical Fixtures							
Electrical Switches, Outlets							
Windows and Drapes							
Closets							

ment after a pet owner moves out. (Lease clauses related to pets will be discussed in chapter 10.)

There are also a number of states that recognize a nonrefundable cleaning fee, which helps absorb part of the expense of making an apartment ready for occupancy. Under such an arrangement, the only

EXHIBIT 6.4 *(continued)*

Area/Item	Move-in condition			Move-out condition			Remarks
Bathroom(s)	Good	Fair	Poor	Good	Fair	Poor	
Doors and Locks							
Floors and Baseboards							
Walls and Ceilings							
Windows and Drapes							
Shower							
Lavatory and Tub							
Faucets							
Toilet							
Electrical Fixtures							
Electrical Switches, Outlets							
Closet							
Towel Rack							

Resident's signature **Date** **Owner's agent** **Date**

Properly completed, this form is a record of the unit's condition before and after occupancy and can serve as part of the documentation (for the departing resident) of charges against the security deposit.

way a security deposit can be used to defray cleaning costs is if the cost of the damage exceeds the nonrefundable cleaning fee paid to the landlord.

The Lease Agreement

A *lease* is a contractual agreement made between a landlord (the owner or *lessor*) and a tenant (the resident or *lessee*) for the use or possession of rental housing (the *premises*) for a specific time in exchange for a *consideration*—i.e., rent. (The word tenant is used here in the context of landlord-tenant law; otherwise, apartment occupants are preferably referred to as residents throughout this book. A lease may be referred to as a *rental agreement* in other contexts for the same reason.) The following are the principal contents of a residential lease.

- *The parties*—The names of the landlord and the tenant. The property manager or the site manager may sign the lease as an agent of the owner. Both landlord and tenant must sign the lease to validate it.
- *Description of the leased premises*—The apartment number and address of the building. This information must be accurate. Any inaccuracies in the lease will be held in favor of the tenant if a dispute must be settled in court.
- *Lease term*—The duration of the lease (including the commencement and termination dates) and any specific provisions related to renewal or cancellation.
- *Rent*—The amount of rent to be paid each period and the date it is due. Rent is usually paid monthly and due on the first of the month. Nonpayment of rent is cause for termination of the lease.
- *Use of the premises*—Inherent in the lease agreement is a specific use of the space (living quarters), and any other use may be cause for termination of the lease.

Leases usually also detail the rights and obligations of the parties with respect to their relationship to each other (as landlord and tenant) and to the property. Of particular concern are the responsibilities to pay specific utilities and to maintain the property and the leased space. The amount and conditions for return of any required security deposit are also stated. In general, a lease guarantees the owner that there will be no financial loss because of an unexpected vacancy—it assures the owner that the space will remain occupied for a certain period of time and that a certain amount of income can be anticipated for that period. (The tenant is obligated to pay the rent regardless of whether the apartment is occupied.) The lease also guarantees the tenant possession of the space for the duration of the lease at a set rental rate; it requires the landlord to maintain the habitability of the premises and guarantees the tenant quiet enjoyment (without interference by the landlord). The tenant, in turn, has an obligation to respect the right to quiet enjoyment of his or her neighbors.

Good management practice requires a written lease. Because an oral agreement is difficult to substantiate legally in the event of a dispute, most states require a written lease if the term is one year or longer. A written lease reduces or eliminates misunderstandings between landlord and tenant. New tenants should be asked if they have read the lease and understand it; many leases include such a statement above the place for the tenant's signature. Any provisions that are unclear should be explained, with the understanding that the agent is not an attorney and that the tenant is free to seek legal counsel before signing the lease agreement. An additional safeguard for both the landlord and the tenant is requiring residents to initial key lease provisions such as those concerning timely rent payment, late fees, security deposit refund procedures, renter's insurance, and pets. (Specific lease clauses and related issues are discussed in depth in chapter 10.)

Move-in Procedures. *Move-in* is another chance to present the apartment, the property, and the management to new residents in the best possible light. The site manager should take this opportunity to inspect the apartment with the new resident, and any unfinished maintenance or needed improvements should be noted on a move-in/move-out inspection form (as in exhibit 6.4). The form should be signed by both the resident and a representative of the management company and retained for comparison with the apartment's condition when the resident moves out. If the apartment is inspected before the move-in, it is a good idea to provide residents with a form for listing items that need repair. (Exhibit 6.5 is an example.) Ideally, there should be no repairs to do; if there are, management should be prepared to deal with them quickly. Because first impressions are very important, the form should be returned within a week of move-in, and maintenance and repair should be scheduled as soon as possible thereafter.

During orientation, you should also go over the rules and regulations of the property with new residents and have them sign a statement acknowledging their understanding of the policies and procedures. This action will demonstrate the seriousness of the "house rules" and strengthen your position if a resident later persists in violating the rules. (House rules are usually attached to the lease as an addendum and are therefore part of the legal contract between the landlord and tenant.)

Either during orientation or shortly after their arrival, new residents should be asked to complete a move-in questionnaire. This should address the resident's impressions of the apartment, the community, and the staff. In fact, combining a move-in questionnaire and

EXHIBIT 6.5

Sample Resident's Move-In Report

Welcome to your new home. We have made every effort to prepare your apartment for occupancy. If we have overlooked anything or something needs maintenance or repair, please take a few minutes over the next few days to complete this form and return it to the office within a week, and we will make an appointment with you to address any problems.

Name ____________ Apt. # ______ Home phone ____________
Work phone ________________ Date form returned ____________

1. ________________________________
2. ________________________________
3. ________________________________
4. ________________________________
5. ________________________________
6. ________________________________
7. ________________________________
8. ________________________________
9. ________________________________
10. ________________________________

This type of form can be combined with general survey questions about why the resident chose this apartment, where he or she lived before, etc. Such a move-in survey can be correlated with information on the prospect card and rental application to determine the effectiveness of the marketing program as well as begin to measure a particular resident's satisfaction.

a service request form can establish a positive relationship from the start and foster resident retention.

Lease Renewal

Lease renewal contributes to the property's NOI for several reasons.

- It eliminates the rent loss due to vacancy that occurs when a new resident does not move in immediately after the previous one moves out.
- It saves the marketing expense of finding a new resident.
- It usually costs less to "improve" an apartment for a resident in place than to prepare the space for a new resident.
- It saves the time and cost of qualifying a new resident—the current resident is already a known quantity (payment history, degree of respect for the property and other residents).

Leasing and Move-In Procedures

- Complete application.
- Set up resident files.
- Complete credit check and other verifications.
- Notify prospect of approval or rejection.
- Assign apartment and remove from vacancy report.
- Schedule move-in date.
- Notify maintenance and repair staff of leasing of apartment.
- Make appointment for signing lease.
- Prepare lease.
- Prepare welcome package and orientation information.
- Transfer utilities.
- Have keys ready.
- Conduct final inspection of completed work within the apartment.
- Conduct move-in inspection with resident (signed by both resident and owner's agent) or ask resident to complete a defects report.
- Collect rent, security deposit, and other monies.
- Sign lease and give copy to resident.
- Complete orientation, including house rules and regulations.
- Give keys to resident.

In its simplest form, the renewal effort may comprise little more than sending a resident a new lease that reflects the new term and adjusted rent. This is usually done 30–90 days before expiration of the current lease. However, merely sending a new lease does nothing to retain residents. A silently dissatisfied resident may simply move out when the notice of a rent increase is received.

Lease renewal should consist of at least three steps: Contact the resident personally, send a lease or notice of extension, and follow up to discuss the renewal particulars. In some cases, material incentives may be necessary to assure lease renewals. Offering to repaint a resident's apartment or hang new wall paper sends a message that the resident's business is appreciated and may stimulate an early decision to stay. (Resident retention is discussed in more detail in chapter 7, and the legalities of lease renewal are covered in chapter 10.)

Despite your best efforts, some residents will not renew their leases. Residents may move for a variety of reasons not necessarily related to the apartment, the staff, or the property. For example, a resident may buy a house or have to relocate because of a job transfer.

Move-Out and Apartment Turnover Procedures

- Receive and acknowledge notice to vacate.
- Schedule move-out inspection with resident.
- Update vacancy reports.
- Verify rent roll changes.
- Notify main office of move-out.
- Pre-inspect apartment.
- Schedule turnover work.
- Schedule showings.
- Complete move-out inspection with resident.
- Compute costs of cleaning or repairs, if applicable.
- Collect keys.
- Remove resident's name from mail box and building directory.
- Refund security deposit or send proper notification that refund has been forfeited partially or completely.

Sometimes residents move because of changes in their domestic situations (marriage, childbirth, separation, divorce) or simply because their leases have expired and they prefer different surroundings. Whatever the reason, move-outs create demands that will affect the stability of the property both immediately and in the future. To assure that all the details are attended to, it is a good idea to develop a list of move-out or apartment turnover procedures.

Move-Out Procedures. If residents are leaving simply because the lease has expired and they want to move on, the move-out procedure should not be difficult. There are three basic conditions to be met:

1. *Notice of intent to vacate*—Depending on state and local requirements under landlord-tenant law, it may be necessary for the landlord to notify residents in advance—generally, at least 30 days before their leases expire. Most leases require that residents provide written notice of their intent *not* to renew within a similar time frame. (If a resident indicates his or her intent to move in person or over the phone, you should ask for written confirmation.) You can then provide a written statement explaining the resident's responsibilities, management's procedures for showing the unit, and the requirements for cleaning

Key Actions Related to Leasing in Site Management

Primary Functions
- Administer leasing office procedures
  - —Making appointments with prospects
  - —Showing apartments
  - —Completing applications
- Verify application data
- Collect rent, security deposits, and other applicable fees
- Sign legal documents, including lease agreement and addenda
- Conduct move-in and move-out inspections
- Monitor fair housing compliance

Adjunct Functions
- Make sure vacant units are rent-ready
- Administer security deposit funds

and inspection that must be met to assure return of the security deposit. The form should also explain the legal ramifications of failure to vacate the premises, which is especially important when an apartment is rerented and the previous tenant continues to occupy it.

2. *Move-out inspection*—The move-out inspection should be conducted after residents have vacated the apartment. Its purpose is to document the condition of the apartment and determine what repairs (if any) have to be made before the next residents move in. Based on this inspection, you should calculate the amount of the security deposit to be returned to the resident.

   Using the same form you completed when the resident moved in will facilitate an accurate assessment. In addition, review of the maintenance and repair records for the apartment will help determine any damage that is the resident's responsibility. To avoid disputes about the apartment's condition and the charges for cleaning or repairs, the inspection should be conducted in the presence of the resident.

   The inspection form should have spaces to list cleaning requirements, note any damages in excess of ordinary wear and tear, and record the number of keys returned. Both you and the resident should sign and date the form. The resident should receive an accounting that includes charges for maintenance and cleaning deducted from the security deposit, accumulated interest (if required by law), and the amount being returned. This information, along with any rent or late fees due, may be included in the move-out inspection report (if the departing resident is to receive a copy) or provided separately.

3. *Regain possession*—You must determine the exact date the resident will move out of the apartment and be on hand to collect keys and regain possession of the apartment. For security reasons, locks should be changed *after* an occupant moves out; this may be required by state or local law.

After an apartment is vacated, it must be prepared for a new resident. Provided all the appropriate move-out procedures have been followed and the departing resident has left the unit in good condition, turnaround can be straightforward and the apartment can be placed on the market immediately so it can begin producing income as soon as it is rented. If residents are being evicted or seek to terminate the lease early, however, the procedure can be considerably more stressful and will demand more attention. (These issues have legal consequences and are discussed in more detail in chapter 10.)

SUMMARY

Once marketing has attracted likely prospects to the property, leasing is an effort to convert them into residents. Starting with the initial contact, leasing efforts are directed toward convincing prospective residents that they should make a particular property their home. Whether the contact is made by a leasing agent or the site manager, over the telephone or in person, all reasonable efforts must be made to obtain the qualified prospect's signature on a rental application and, ultimately, on a lease.

All leasing activities must comply with fair housing laws. Prospects' financial resources and past behavior as tenants are evaluated as part of the resident selection process. If prospects are able to pay the rent, have established patterns of timely payments, and demonstrated respect for other residents and an owners' property, they should be qualified to lease an apartment at your property.

Leasing success is the result of intelligent marketing campaigns, efficient operation of the leasing office, well-honed selling skills, and effective closing techniques. Once prospects become residents, your focus should be on retaining them.

Renewing the leases of established residents is far more cost-effective than repeated efforts to sign leases with new ones. Lease renewal efforts begin as soon as new residents take possession of their apartments. Attention to residents' needs and requests, a professional approach, and personal respect are key ingredients in convincing them to stay beyond the initial lease term.

Key Terms

credit bureau
escrow account
lease
model apartment
prospect card
steering
turnover

Key Concepts

closing
concessions
fair housing
lease renewal
overcoming objections
qualification of prospects
security deposit
wear and tear

Key Points

- How is the prospect card used in leasing?
- What are the steps in showing an apartment?
- How are various closing techniques applied in different situations?
- What are the criteria for resident selection?
- What are the principle contents of the lease?
- What is the function of move-in and move-out inspections?
- Why is lease renewal desirable?

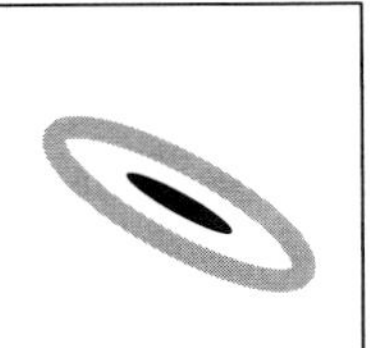

7

Resident Relations

All the interactions between residents and site personnel form the foundation of resident relations. As site manager, your goal is to create satisfied customers who will not only renew their leases, but will refer their friends and acquaintances to the property by word of mouth. Without sustained efforts to foster good resident relations, maintenance requests can take on negative overtones, and every encounter with residents has the potential to become needlessly unpleasant. As a result, vacancy rates will increase as lease renewals and resident referrals diminish, and the NOI and value of the property will suffer.

In addition to the impact on the property's financial integrity, resident relations represents one of the most enjoyable aspects of site management. Dealing with residents is not just about resolving disputes or responding to maintenance requests—although these are part of a site manager's daily activities. Encounters with residents are also opportunities to form and strengthen relationships. If you predicate resident relations solely on the resolution of problems, you will not be prepared to like your residents, and site managers should like working with people because that is the basis of real estate management.

THE IMPORTANCE OF COMMUNICATION

Most people take for granted that they can communicate effectively when, in fact, everyone would benefit if their communication skills were improved. Although individual capacity for communication varies from one person to another, everyone has the potential to be an effective communicator. In resident relations, the site manager's communication skills and those of the staff members he or she trains are critical and cannot be taken for granted.

Your success as a communicator depends on the ability to determine and address the information needs of different people and choose the means of communication most appropriate to the people and the situation. There must also be a good fit between your personality and the manner in which you are trying to communicate. If you are not comfortable, it will show, and that will compromise the effectiveness of your message. To a large extent, site managers must communicate effectively regardless of any personal discomfort.

As site manager, you are responsible for essential communication with residents, vendors, outside contractors, on-site employees, and other management personnel. Your communication must be direct, honest, impartial, and balanced, whether it is written or oral, in person or over the telephone. A large part of communication is determining the best manner and medium to achieve a specific goal. With experience and practice, you will know when it is appropriate to speak to someone in person or when a letter is more suitable.

Objectives of Communication

Communication has four basic objectives.

1. Being understood—presenting facts, intentions, feelings, or perceptions to someone so he or she knows exactly what is meant.
2. Gaining acceptance—convincing people to agree about a particular point.
3. Accomplishing something—convincing people to act because they understand why something is important and what role they have in accomplishing it.

Role of Communication in Resident Relations

- Presenting and receiving information
- Planning and coordinating work of on-site employees, outside contractors, and vendors
- Solving problems
- Attracting prospects and leasing apartments
- Increasing resident retention
- Creating a positive public image

4. Understanding others—learning what other people think or believe about a particular situation.

These basic objectives make it clear why communication is so important to business activities in general and site management in particular. Success in communicating with residents, site employees, and others in the management firm requires that all parties to the communication understand each other; this, in turn, requires a basis of understanding each other's point of view. Effective communication enables the entire staff to do their jobs right the first time, thereby saving resources (time, money, labor), meeting high performance standards, and increasing resident satisfaction.

Ideally, all communication would be straightforward and complete—messages and intentions would be understood, and tasks would be accomplished with a minimum of confusion. In reality, however, communication can fail for a variety of reasons. Consider the following factors, which can be obstacles to successful communication.

- *Timing*—Is the person able to listen? Is the setting too noisy? Are too many other activities competing for attention? Is it close to lunchtime or the end of the day? Is a person currently in the right frame of mind to listen?
- *Personal feelings*—Strong feelings of personal animosity will close channels of communication or color messages negatively. Someone who is upset about a personal problem may be preoccupied and unwilling or unable to listen carefully or take action. Likewise, people who feel threatened will hear a distorted message.

These kinds of obstacles can be overcome by considering your prior experience with a particular person and how the two of you have communicated in the past. What can you learn from those past communications to help you now? If a situation is so difficult that you seriously doubt your own ability to handle it in an evenhanded manner, it may be necessary to ask someone else to deal with a resident. However, you should be careful not to create excuses every time an unpleasant situation arises because, as site manager, handling them is one of your responsibilities.

- *Insufficient explanations*—No one can do a job properly with incomplete or inaccurate information. When communicating instructions, stop and consider whether *you* understand exactly how to approach a particular task: Think about what you want to say before saying it. The components of your message should be organized in a logical sequence, separating the important from the unimportant. It helps to keep the goal of the activity in mind. If you understand a process completely and are able to answer how and why it should be done, it will be easier for you to explain the procedure to someone else. Using specialized language should be avoided as well: Professional jargon—or colloquial slang—can easily be misinterpreted or misunderstood.

  There is also a danger of providing too much information, which can be very confusing. Too much detail may not expedite a project; in fact, it may delay it. One key to effective site management is determining what is important and what is not.

  Another common management error is being in too great a hurry to move on to another project and overlooking important factors in a current one. Under these circumstances, employees may be reluctant to ask questions (even though they do not fully understand something) because you seem "too busy." Fostering an environment in which questions are not only tolerated, but encouraged, will result in greater productivity and create a friendly, supportive work environment.

- *The number of people involved*—The greater the number of people the communication must pass through, the more likely the original message will be distorted. Remember that a story changes with each retelling: By virtue of being passed from one person to another, details are lost or exaggerated, and what began as an interesting or amusing account can become unbelievable. The same thing can happen to relatively straightforward instructions or business communications. To combat this, written instructions should be used to back up and reinforce directions being given orally. Writing out the instructions will also enhance your own understanding, provide a ready reference for you and others, and increase the likelihood that a task will be done right the first time.

- *Failure to consider other points of view*—People will not listen if they think their ideas are not being given a fair hearing. They will also be less likely to honor requests made of them. Therefore, the insights and experiences of other team members should be taken into account—they may have a better idea. Residents' insights are valuable, too.

  Preconceived notions are another component of this obstacle to communication. Whether they center on the belief that someone's insights are irrelevant or are simply a failure to pay attention to the message, preconceptions should be set aside.

In this age of litigation, communication also has a legal aspect. To protect themselves, the management company, and the owner from liability, site managers should always strive to communicate clearly while bearing in mind the legal ramifications of what they are saying. Words should be chosen carefully, and all form letters should be approved before they are sent out. Such precautions can avert problems and legal fees at very little initial cost.

Although obstacles can arise in all forms of communication, they are critical in the context of oral presentation, where success is based on the recognition that communication is a two-way process. Dialogue—i.e., *feedback*—is especially important. A listener's apparent boredom, irritation, or confusion suggests that you have failed to communicate, while nods of agreement or understanding generally indicate success. Such visual cues not only signal whether you are being heard and how your message is being received, they also provide an opportunity to modify your presentation to make it successful.

Miscommunication can also be the result of two people discussing a problem at different levels. This can occur easily in real estate management. For site managers, apartments are economic units in business transactions—an objective point of view. For residents, however, apartments are their homes—a subjective and often emotionally charged point of view. Because of these differing perspectives, taking a technical approach to a problem or quoting landlord-tenant law will probably only alienate a resident, while a more empathetic approach or a show of appreciation for a resident's situation is more likely to be successful.

Another form of miscommunication is misunderstanding, which is usually the result of faulty or incomplete communication. This can often be traced to carelessness, forgetfulness, or personality differences. While none of these sources of miscommunication can be eliminated altogether, understanding them will help you overcome some of their effects and improve the quality of your own communication.

One obstacle to communication that can be eliminated is carelessness. Carelessness is often the result of being pressed for time. The result is poorly planned messages that have to be reconsidered and repeated. A hectic schedule that leaves little time for preparation can also overwhelm one's memory. These types of problems can be avoided by simply taking the time to do it right in the first place. Because miscommunication of instructions can be a source of serious problems, it is a good idea to write down important tasks and points you want to remember beforehand. The same applies to any oral presentation. You should also carefully evaluate whether written communication would be more effective and, ultimately, less time-consuming.

Elimination of obstacles requires consideration of how people interact in general. Friction can occur between people no matter how fond they are of each other. It is natural to develop likes and dislikes, and personal preferences can facilitate communication or impede it. Because they deal with people so frequently, site managers need to be aware of their own feelings and, as much as possible, prevent those feelings from interfering with their communications and their professionalism.

Communication Techniques

As was briefly discussed in chapter 2, there are two basic methods of communication—verbal and nonverbal. *Verbal communication* relies on the spoken or written word, while *nonverbal communication* takes the form of visual and audible cues. For example, a frown that creeps across your face while you are speaking implies negativity, and

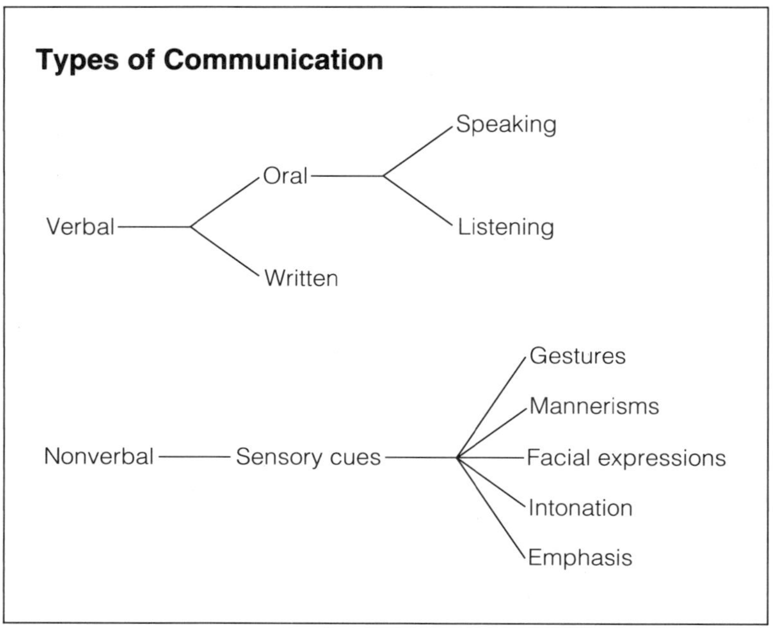

that can carry through to your voice. Folded arms may signal defensiveness, while rapid movements convey excitement. Sitting behind a large desk sends a clear message that you want to maintain a distance from the other person, just as sitting side-by-side on a couch implies a desire to be more personable (formal versus informal).

Verbal and nonverbal communication can work together or be at odds with each other. A smile will reinforce the positive message of a cheery "hello." However, if the same greeting is delivered through clenched teeth or with a barely disguised look of disappointment, your words will be contradicted, resulting in a confusing message.

Speaking. The primary rule of speaking is to express yourself as clearly as possible. Failure to consider the content of your message and how it relates to the composition of your audience can have adverse effects. In any spoken communication, there are numerous potential obstacles to understanding. These include the use of jargon, assumptions about the subject or the audience, a poor (or inappropriate) choice of words, and the speaker's attitude.

Like most professions, real estate management has its own specialized *jargon*. While this facilitates communication within the profession, it can seem like a foreign language to others. Some people use jargon because they think it makes them appear intelligent and more important. Ironically, people outside the profession are likely to tune you out if they cannot understand you. This is particularly true of your residents. Rather than giving you an "edge" in a discussion, jargon can alienate your listeners and damage relationships by creating the illusion that you are on the "inside" and they are on the "outside."

People have different viewpoints, backgrounds, personal interests, educations, and experiences and, therefore, different levels of understanding. Your choice of words and your manner of presentation are important components of successful communication. Remember, anything that can be interpreted in more than one way probably will be.

Context is also an important consideration. An opinion or a judgment based on bits and pieces of information—without knowledge of prior events or understanding of the subject—will create problems. By providing your audience with enough background so that listeners can understand your point and your purpose, you are more likely to be successful in communicating your message. If you are asking residents to do—or not do—something, they should be told why, as well as what and how and when.

The *attitude* of the speaker is critical to successful communication. Projection of any kind of negative attitude has the potential to create serious problems. A commanding attitude can intimidate listeners. Sarcasm intended to be funny may be misunderstood or misinterpreted, and a know-it-all attitude will discourage dialogue, especially if your intent is to invite suggestions or recommendations. By contrast, a positive attitude—cheerfulness and enthusiasm—makes communication flow more freely and openly.

Nonverbal Cues. Nonverbal communication may take any number of forms—a frown, a look of fear or puzzlement, a smile of joy, physical distance. Posture and gestures send messages, both positive and negative, such that others' nonverbal cues also require interpretation. Meanings vary from culture to culture, from situation to situation, and some reactions may appear very similar despite profoundly different meanings (e.g., a startled look can mean fear, or it may mean surprise).

Listening. Listening is just as important to successful communication as are speaking and writing, perhaps more so. Probably the most common source of miscommunication is emphasis on being understood at the expense of understanding. Just as you must make sure that the message you *send* is clear, you must also be certain that you *receive* information correctly. In residential management, failure to listen to residents leads to misunderstandings, missteps, and missed opportunities. Attentiveness can prevent potentially unpleasant situations from occurring and help overcome those that already have.

Studies have shown that nearly half of the time spent communicating is devoted to listening, but that most people do not listen well. This is because few people have ever really learned *how* to listen. They believe communication is the responsibility of the speaker rather than a process in which both speaker and listener must participate actively. The characteristics of poor and good listeners are a study in contrasts.

Poor listeners tend to be judgmental—often they assume a subject is boring because they know nothing about it. On the other hand, good listeners tend to reserve judgment until they thoroughly understand the message. While a poor listener may place more emphasis on appearance and delivery than on the content of the speaker's message, a good listener expects something from every encounter.

Poor listeners are often overcome by their emotions, reacting to words or intonations without understanding the point of what is being said. They tend to concentrate on how something is said or think of rebuttals instead of paying attention to the conversation. Inflexibility and aversion to other points of view are also part of the mind-set of poor listeners. They are easily distracted and often merely pretend to pay attention. A good listener prepares to listen and asks questions to clarify points. Good listeners sort through the message to identify important points and disregard extraneous information. (Some attributes characteristic of good listeners are presented in exhibit 7.1.)

Given the numerous points at which communication can break down, efforts to sustain and enhance communication are especially important. During a conversation with a resident, if there is anything you are uncertain about, you can rephrase what you have heard and ask the speaker if you correctly understand what he or she is saying. Repeating basic points and verifying the message received will enable

EXHIBIT 7.1

Characteristics of a Good Listener

- Listens to the whole message, including the specific points the speaker is trying to make.
- Thinks about the speaker, not himself or herself.
- Pays attention to what is being said.
- Maintains eye contact.
- Does not interrupt.
- Asks questions when appropriate.
- Is open to other points of view.
- Shares impressions with the speaker to confirm the message.
- Does not let personal beliefs or feelings interfere with listening to the message and understanding it.

you to respond appropriately to a situation the first time. You should use the same active approach when the situation is reversed and you are the speaker—your listener may be passive, and you will need to know that you have been understood.

Written Communication. Because it lacks the benefit of immediate feedback, written communication relies heavily on clarity of expression, both in choice of words and in presentation. Letters or notices directed to residents will have to be prepared quite frequently, but the same ground rules apply to anything you write. The following are guidelines for effective written communication.

- *Present information in a logical sequence.* If you are writing about several kinds of issues, it may be helpful to organize them by type (e.g., group maintenance issues together). On the other hand, some topics may lend themselves better to a chronological sequence. What occurred first? Then what happened? How are the events related? The tone for the entire communication is set in the first lines, so they are a very important factor in determining how readers will respond.
- *Communicate clearly and directly.* Extremely complicated sentences or very specialized language can make an already complicated issue even more difficult to understand. A simply phrased, direct letter or memo will be more effective than a complex,

obscure one. Writing a good letter is much like working with building blocks—a strong foundation is needed and each piece must reinforce the others to keep the structure from collapsing on itself.

- *Consider your readers' perspective.* If you are addressing residents about their failure to uphold their responsibilities, it is better to phrase your request for compliance as a reminder of existing policy (or an addendum to policy) than as an accusation. For example, if there have been problems with the laundry room, an angry letter to all residents will only alienate many of them; it is better to remind them of the existing laundry room policy and the importance of courtesy for all residents. (Whenever possible, it is better to direct these types of letters toward the actual offenders rather than all of the residents, most of whom may, in fact, be in compliance with the policies. Sending generic letters of this type to the resident population as a whole may be perceived as insulting and degrading.) If you are angry over a particular situation, sitting down and writing an angry letter may make you feel better immediately, but you should leave it in your desk overnight; reread it the next day—and revise it appropriately. Your goal should be to resolve the situation productively, not escalate an already hostile situation.
- *Review your writing carefully.* Check the accuracy of the information, and make sure there are no grammatical, punctuation, or spelling errors (they make your writing appear sloppy and imply carelessness). To be absolutely certain, have someone else proofread your work. Another reader is more likely to catch a mistake or a breakdown in logic. Another tactic is to read the document aloud and ask yourself how you would respond to it. Often the tone of a letter will sabotage its goal by generating a negative reaction rather than a positive response.
- *Practice writing.* There is no substitute for practice. You can also learn a great deal about good writing by reading books on all subjects, not just communication. In addition, many community colleges and extension campuses of state universities offer courses in business writing that will strengthen writing skills.

It may also be beneficial to collect samples of letters that apply to common situations and share them with your staff as training tools.

These letters may be kept in folders, organized by subject, to provide examples of both good and bad writing. The file should be reviewed periodically and the samples updated as appropriate.

Communication is relevant to marketing, leasing, maintenance, and lease renewal, all of which are components of resident relations. The key to successful communication, regardless of mode, is knowing your audience and considering what they need (or expect) from you. This is critical to understanding what you intend to communicate. Every member of the on-site team needs to be involved because all of their efforts are related to the marketing, leasing, and maintenance of the property, which are the heart of resident retention.

INTERACTING WITH RESIDENTS

Contact with residents takes many forms and extends into all areas of site management. Because of this fact, cordiality and professionalism should be everyone's watchwords. Usually, contacts with residents are conducted without incident. Nevertheless, the potential ramifications of negative encounters demand extra effort on everyone's part to ensure that interactions with residents are as positive and productive as possible.

Personal Contacts

Personal contacts with residents take place every day in real estate management. Whether the contact is an initial telephone inquiry about a rental, move-in or move-out activities, or lease renewal, you *will* have to deal with residents one-on-one. Some situations can be decidedly unpleasant, especially when they are related to unsatisfactory maintenance, delinquencies, or problems with other residents. Most often, however, interactions with residents are neutral or enjoyable and can be handled routinely. Your goals should be to communicate information clearly and accurately and to establish a dialogue in which residents can also share information with you.

Telephone Conversations. Whether the subject is a prospect's needs or a resident's service request, telephone conversations are an

Points of Interaction with Residents

Specific Transactions
- Move-in
- Orientation
- Provision of services (e.g., maintenance)
- Lease renewal
- Move-out
- Personal contacts (telephone and in person)

Written Communications
- Residents' handbook
- Newsletters
- Bulletin boards
- Personal letters and group notices

important part of resident relations. Starting with the greeting and carrying over to the tone and content of the conversation itself, telephone contacts are extremely sophisticated forms of communication; as such, they should not be treated lightly or dismissed out of hand.

Phone manners should be friendly and confident. Callers should never be made to feel that they are inconveniencing you; they should be treated as though they are the most important people in the world. As much as possible, your greetings should always be cheerful and enthusiastic. An abrupt or disinterested telephone greeting has a very different impact than one that conveys a sincere desire to be of service: In the first instance, the caller will perceive the person who answers the telephone as someone who would rather be doing something else, while an upbeat telephone manner will imply genuine interest and enthusiasm.

The greeting itself should convey information, identifying the company and the person who answered the phone. The tone should be friendly and helpful, communicating a desire to be of service: "Hello, ABC Management. This is Bill. How may I help you?" is a good example. The greeting should also be sincere—callers can easily identify insincerity, and the negative impact on resident relations is immeasurable.

Friendliness can easily be projected if you smile when you answer the telephone. You will be amazed at the difference between a greeting with a smile and one without. Callers will notice the difference, too. How you handle telephone calls should serve as an example for others on your staff. A mirror and a tape recorder will help you—and the other staff members—practice your telephone technique. Practice will also help keep your greetings fresh.

For all its convenience and importance, however, there is a tendency to rely on the telephone too much. While a telephone call is an ideal way to communicate quickly, it is not suitable for resolving conflicts or discussing important details. In such situations, there is no substitute for face-to-face conversation. The telephone can also be a hindrance during those times when the site office is short-staffed or especially busy because callers can be shortchanged by not receiving the attention they deserve. Often it is a good idea to ask callers if you can return their calls later when you will be able to devote your complete attention to their questions or concerns. Sometimes it is more appropriate to schedule a meeting one-on-one or with a group to clear the air. Trying to balance everyone's needs and desires simultaneously will only increase the likelihood of dissatisfaction—and miscommunication—along the way.

Orientation. Orientation is your opportunity to familiarize new residents with the property and the rules and regulations—to inform them of what they can expect from you and what you expect of them. This is the time to explain policies and procedures, revisit the on-site facilities, and review the features and operation of equipment in their apartment. You should also explain the landlord's and the resident's responsibilities under the lease and provide information on emergency procedures. When difficulties arise, it is often because people are uninformed; they cannot evaluate a situation fairly if they lack all the facts. A well-conducted resident orientation helps avoid these problems.

Ideally, the orientation should be conducted by the site manager, and all occupants of the apartment should be present. Ample time should be scheduled —at least one-half hour, preferably *before* residents move in or as soon after move-in as possible. Site managers should establish a rapport and try to make new residents feel comfortable and welcome in their new homes. However, because of prior commitments, this may not always be possible, so the assistant site manager should be prepared to conduct move-in orientations. Because of residents' schedules, you may have to be flexible and schedule a repeat performance to assure that everyone in a household receives all the information.

The orientation is also an opportunity for you to impress upon newcomers their rights and responsibilities as residents and for them to ask questions. However, while it is important to be businesslike so that all important issues are covered, it is just as important to make new residents feel at home, confirming their decision to live at the property.

The following are among the items that *could* be included in an orientation.

- Residents' and landlord's obligations under the lease
- Rent payment (preferably by check)
- Late fees
- Renters' insurance (building owner's insurance does not cover residents' possessions)
- Subletting (landlord approval required)
- Security deposit refunds (move-in/move-out inspections document conditions and resident charges)
- Pet policies
- Rules and regulations
- Operating hours (office, laundry room, recreational facilities)
- Maintenance and repairs (maintenance request procedures, filter changes, smoke alarm batteries, pest control, and other services)
- Care and cleaning of the apartment
- Lost keys
- Policies and procedures for inspection of the apartment
- Operation of appliances in the unit
- Energy conservation
- Complaint and grievance procedures
- Other contents of the residents' handbook

Although orientation is a very important and serious part of the landlord-tenant relationship, it does not have to be grave. You can show your interest in the lives of new residents by asking if they have any questions or talking about their move-in plans. Let them know that you care. (Providing coloring books and crayons or videos for residents' children during orientation or the leasing presentation is a good way to keep youngsters occupied and allow the parents to concentrate on the business at hand.)

Move-in. The site manager should inspect the apartment with the new resident before the first box of possessions crosses the threshold. The best approach is to use a specific move-in checklist and have residents sign and date it afterward (see exhibit 6.4). Any problems identified at this time should be rectified as soon as possible. A properly documented move-in inspection will establish the condition of the unit for comparison at move-out. This will expedite return of the security deposit at the end of the lease term and foster goodwill among residents throughout the period of occupancy. (Formal inspection of the unit interior will be discussed in chapter 8.)

Lease Renewal. Resident retention represents a way to reap the benefits of open communication and diligent service. Lease renewals are desirable because they reduce vacancy-related rent losses, save marketing funds, minimize the need for improvements as part of the turnover process, and save the time and expense of qualifying new residents. Although renewal efforts can be as simple as sending a resident a new lease 30–90 days before the current one expires, there is more to lease renewal than this. (Specific notice requirements are contained in applicable landlord-tenant law for each state.) In reality, resident retention efforts must be nurtured throughout the term of the lease—not relegated to the final month or two before a lease expires. Because of this, a strategic approach to lease renewal is necessary.

The single greatest incentive for residents to renew their leases is continued value and excellent customer service. Residents are motivated by the security of guaranteed rent for a fixed period of time. If they believe they are receiving good value for their money and being treated well, they will be more inclined to renew their leases.

The bottom line on lease renewals is demonstrating how much residents are valued, and superior service is the best "thank you." Providing the best service to residents requires sustained commitment on the part of all site personnel. This begins with hiring people who will make an appropriate commitment and take their jobs seriously. Lines of communication between residents and management personnel must be developed and kept open. Service can always be improved somewhere, somehow, so that realistic lease renewal and resident retention goals can be achieved.

Move-out. Residents move out for many reasons that are not related to the performance of the management staff. Employment promotions, transfers, or terminations; home purchases; and a desire for new surroundings are all legitimate reasons to move. So are changes in their personal lives—roommate problems, economic difficulties that force a resident to return home to live with parents, marriage, childbirth, separation, divorce. It is very important to attend to property concerns during move-out, and it is to everyone's advantage (owner, management company, and resident alike) for the premises to be in the best possible condition at the end of the tenancy. In most cases, adequate planning and appropriately enforced policies will ensure this. (See chapter 6 for a complete discussion.)

A major concern for departing residents is loss of their security deposits. While a security deposit may not represent a great deal of money in absolute terms, most residents consider it a sizable sum. Tension may be high for departing residents who now face the added expenses of the move—a new security deposit, utility deposits or transfer fees, or closing costs on a home purchase—as well as the anxiety brought on by a change in surroundings. Most residents are well aware of security deposit "horror stories" in which unethical landlords have refused to refund deposits because of exaggerated charges for damage or for cleaning and repairs. You can overcome these concerns by scrupulous documentation of the conditions of apartments prior to move-in and at move-out and by explaining at the outset what is required to ensure full refund of security deposits.

Resident relations does not stop when a resident vacates an apartment. If residents believe they have been treated unfairly, especially with regard to security deposits, they will go out of their way to tell others about their experience. No community can afford this negative publicity or a bad reputation—in the long run, it will have an adverse effect on the owner's financial situation. Ideally, every resident who departs should leave "in style," with good feelings about the time spent living in your community. That is the next best thing to resident retention. (Move-in and move-out procedures were detailed in chapter 6.)

The Residents' Handbook

A *residents' handbook* is minimally a compilation of "house rules" and other information apartment occupants need for ready reference. All newcomers should receive a copy of the residents' handbook when they sign their leases. (It is a good practice to review this handbook personally with each resident during orientation.) Such a handbook will inform residents of some of their rights and responsibilities. It should also summarize some of the more basic lease provisions (e.g., when rent is due) as well as management's policies regarding use of the facilities at the site (swimming pool, exercise room, laundry room), residents' responsibilities for their pets (if appropriate), and requests for maintenance or other services. Inclusion of acceptable and prohibited behaviors should help prevent carelessness and subsequent property damage. However, residents will be more responsive to positive statements that invite their compliance—for example: "Please let us know if there is a problem," rather than a series of admonitions such as "Do not do . . . ."

A good handbook will answer many questions new residents may have and can supplement the information provided to them during orientation, such as instructions for using their appliances or important telephone numbers. (Exhibit 7.2 identifies typical contents of a residents' handbook.) Usually such a handbook is compact—a few sheets stapled together—but an attractively produced packet of useful information, regardless of the specific contents, will be more readily received and used. The handbook should be organized logically for easy reference, and it should be updated periodically to keep residents informed of any changes to property policies and procedures. In such cases, it is best to reprint and replace the whole handbook rather than expect residents to replace one or a few pages.

Other Interactions

There will be many, less formal, opportunities to interact with residents, and there are different ways you can communicate information to them quickly. From the perspective of resident relations, seemingly minor, informal interactions are perhaps the most important of all because they take place constantly.

EXHIBIT 7.2

Information Commonly Provided in a Residents' Handbook

- Office hours of the management company; number to call in case of problems
- When rent is due, how payment is to be made, and where to mail payments; how late payments are handled (late fees)
- Procedures for requesting maintenance
- Landlord's right to enter the premises in emergencies and otherwise; obligation to notify residents before doing so
- Emergency telephone numbers (site manager, police, fire department, ambulance)—place on first or last page for easy reference
- Emergency procedures (how to report an emergency, location of fire exits, evacuation routes)—place on first or last page for easy reference
- Insurance residents are expected or required to carry
- Guest occupancy guidelines (for visitors and persons not named on the lease)
- Residents' responsibility for their visitors
- Residents' responsibility for replacing light bulbs and smoke detector batteries, keeping their apartments clean
- Description of appliances, how they work, and how to take care of them properly
- Trash (when and where picked up; size and type of bags or containers to use; separation of recyclables if required)
- Lockout procedures, including any charges to let residents in
- Charges for replacement of lost keys
- Parking (assignment of spaces)
- Pets (whether and what kinds are allowed; residents' responsibilities)
- Furnishings (any limitations or special permission for large or heavy pieces such as waterbeds)
- Noise policies (noises must be contained within apartments out of consideration for others)
- Any other prohibitions (e.g., storage of objects on balconies)
- Use of pool, laundry room, and other amenities
- Where to direct questions about subletting or other changes to the lease agreement
- Lease renewal procedures
- Requirement for written notice of intent to vacate (to be given 30–60 days before lease expiration or as prescribed by the lease)
- Security deposits (purpose, conditions for return, clean-up and repair charges; deductions for cleaning and damage in excess of normal wear and tear)
- Move-in and move-out inspections (unit to be left in original rental condition, excepting normal wear and tear; basis for deductions from security deposits)
- Community information (availability/accessibility/telephone numbers of transportation, shopping, entertainment, schools, churches, synagogues, social services)

Good relations with residents are often fostered by attention to little details that mean a great deal to people in general. Simply remembering residents' names—and addressing them by name when you see them—creates tremendous good will. By the same token, asking about important events in their lives (births, graduations, marriages) signals interest in them as people and not just as rent checks. Hosting social gatherings also creates a genuine sense of community among residents. Many apartment communities have community affairs or social directors on staff; they may be responsible for implementing and coordinating resident retention programs by way of community activities such as neighborhood watches and community-wide parties and get-togethers. In addition to making residents feel at home, such personal touches make your job more satisfying.

A *bulletin board* is an effective way to communicate general information that is not imperative for all residents to know. Often located in a laundry room, mail room, or recreation room, a bulletin board can be used to announce social events. Enabling residents to use bulletin boards to share information among themselves fosters a sense of community. However, material placed on bulletin boards should be approved by the site manager and then kept current. Copies on instructional bulletin boards should be replaced when they become tattered.

Newsletters are an excellent way to communicate personal news about residents (promotions, births, weddings) as well as supplement management-specific information and introduce new staff members. Newsletters are the number one way to communicate with residents about social events and important dates and remind them of policies and procedures. Newsletters give you the opportunity to reinforce lease renewal and resident referral programs or promote new enhancements and amenities at the community, which, in turn, influence resident retention. Another important factor is the degree of control offered by newsletters. While no one can make sure that all residents look at—much less read—a bulletin board, you can at least make sure that a copy of the newsletter is delivered to every apartment.

While it is very important to make residents feel comfortable, the limits of the relationship between management and residents must also be recognized. Residential management is unique in that the relationship concerns people's homes, but it is still a business relationship. For this reason, personal attachments to residents must not be allowed to interfere with your professional responsibilities. Good resident relations means treating *all* residents fairly, consistently, and firmly.

HANDLING SITUATIONS EFFECTIVELY

The way specific situations are handled is the true test of a site manager's effectiveness. While few people have problems dealing with others when tensions are absent, difficult situations challenge everyone. Unless service requests and resident complaints are handled promptly and appropriately, residents will not renew their leases, and the momentum of your resident retention efforts will be reduced if not lost.

Maintenance and Other Services

Because residents require a variety of services, residential properties are labor-intensive operations. The most common services are related in some way to maintenance of the property and the individual rental units. Difficulty opening doors or locks, leaky toilets, problems with heat or air conditioning, and appliance malfunctions are the types of problems residents bring to the attention of management. They are also the reasons for many resident complaints and move-outs.

Maintenance Requests. Rather than formally request service through the site office, residents often direct their service requests to the first staff member they see—regardless of whether that person is a maintenance technician. Such indirect requests can have several negative repercussions. A member of the staff may simply forget the request was made, which could lead to poor opinions of management and greater potential for liability. Also, informal service requests may not reflect the priorities formulated in the maintenance plan, so evaluating staff performance may be difficult—a maintenance technician may have responded to six service requests in a single day when you thought that there were only three. (These points will be discussed in detail in chapter 8.)

Effective maintenance service is the best way to satisfy residents, but a maintenance program can only be as effective as the system for receiving and processing service requests. In order to manage service

Residents' Complaints

- Complaints about their apartments
- Complaints about the property
- Complaints about other residents
- Complaints about the staff
- Complaints about policies and procedures
- Complaints about rent increases
- Complaints about other apartments and other people in the neighborhood

requests, the site manager must develop and implement a means of channeling them to the appropriate on-site person. This depends on communication with residents and staff. Not only should there be a standard procedure for initiating service requests, but all residents should be made aware of it.

Resident Complaints. Despite the best efforts to satisfy service requests and provide for residents' needs, there will undoubtedly be resident complaints. Rather than being viewed as exclusively negative, resident complaints should be seen as opportunities to correct problems and build even better resident relations.

In all cases, complaints should receive timely and professional responses. A timely response to a complaint strengthens resident relations, while improper attention—or outright inattention—can only sow the seeds of dissatisfaction. If residents think their concerns are being ignored, even the most conscientious of them might withhold their rent or vacate the premises. This is why it is so important for all on-site employees to be trained to listen to residents and to take appropriate steps to address their complaints. While a standard policy can guide your handling of resident complaints as a general rule, specific kinds of complaints will have to be dealt with in specific ways. (The related concept of constructive eviction—breach of the landlord's obligation to make necessary repairs—will be discussed in chapter 10.)

From both a liability and a customer service perspective, it is essential to have written records of all complaints. Whether you manage one building or several, it is difficult to keep track of the details of each and every resident complaint unless it is written down. A *com-*

plaint log kept in the site office can be used to record the substance of each complaint, the date and time it was received, who made it, and how it was resolved.

If a complaint is about an emergency situation—a threat to life, health, or safety—the response should be immediate. You should find out whether the police, fire department, or emergency medical services have been notified (when necessary), and if not, do so yourself—right away. If the situation is less urgent, it is best to obtain all of the necessary information before you formulate a response. While the kinds of complaints will vary, most residents' complaints are related to their apartments, the property as a whole, and their fellow residents.

Complaints about Their Apartments. These range from minor annoyances to genuine emergencies. Responses to life-threatening or property-damaging situations should be immediate. If a situation is not an emergency, a response should be made within 24 hours. It is important to distinguish between what residents consider an emergency and what management will respond to as an emergency. Both residents and staff members need to understand the differences. A dripping faucet or a "running" toilet makes an irritating noise, but unless a clogged drain accompanies either problem, there is no immediate danger or potential for damage—such repairs can be made within 24 hours or the next business day, either of which is a reasonable response time to a resident request. A lack of heat on a frigid night, on the other hand, warrants an emergency service call and an immediate response. (Chapter 8 addresses maintenance, and chapter 9 covers emergency procedures.)

Complaints about the Property. Complaints about the appearance of the property, the quality and frequency of interior and exterior maintenance and repairs, or management services in general are warning signs. They indicate resident dissatisfaction, and ignoring them can have a serious impact on occupancy rates and the financial integrity of the property. Whenever residents lodge such complaints, the situation should be investigated promptly and corrected quickly. Your attention to complaints will not only impress residents who make them, but demonstrate to other residents—who probably observed the same situation but did not complain—that you and your staff care and are responsive.

Complaints about Other Residents. Living in close proximity can generate tensions as neighbors impinge on one another. Specific complaints may relate to noise (loud music, shouting or fights), unleashed pets, unsupervised children, strange hours (late night comings and goings), or concerns about illegal activities (prostitution, drug dealing). In every instance, you should let the complaining resident know that the situation will be investigated thoroughly. It should be possible to handle most such problems by talking with the resident about whom the complaint was made or contacting the appropriate authorities. Once the situation has been investigated, the resident who lodged the complaint should be informed about whether and how the situation was resolved.

If a resident complains about a potentially dangerous situation (e.g., a violent fight), ask if the police have been called; if not, do so yourself—immediately. Domestic situations of this type can be very dangerous and are best left to the proper authorities. Police should also be notified of actual and suspected illegal activities. Often these can be handled confidentially until or unless a formal complaint must be made.

Complaints about loud music, on the other hand, can be addressed more directly by the site manager or building security personnel. The noisy resident should be told that there have been complaints and asked politely to turn down the volume. *(Regardless of the cause of the complaint, do not identify the source.)* Afterward, you should advise the complainer about the action you have taken. If these types of problems persist, more forceful action may be appropriate, including written notice to cease the offending behavior or vacate the apartment.

Other Specific Complaints. These include complaints about policies and procedures (including rent increases), the staff, and the neighborhood. Often complaints about policies and procedures can be very informative because a policy may have been implemented without considering the extent of its potential ramifications. In some cases, this may mean reevaluating a policy or procedure and making appropriate adjustments. Often the best tactic is to explain the reasoning behind a policy or procedure or the basis for a rent increase; this involves relating the policy to the resident. By explaining that a change is related to safety or required by the insurance company, you will impress upon residents that a particular policy or procedure is not intended to take away what they consider to be rights. For example, a swimming pool may be closed after 10:00 P.M. to reduce accidents and injuries, not to deprive residents of the right to use it.

With regard to rent increases, residents should be told in general terms how operating costs have increased, relating this fact to their daily lives. If residents recently experienced an increase in their electric bills, you can explain that the community experienced the same increase.

Complaints about staff members must be handled discreetly, and all relevant information should be collected and verified before you act. (Chapter 3 discussed approaches to employee problems.) With regard to the neighborhood, communication with other real estate managers and local authorities is a good starting point in responding to your residents' concerns.

Confrontations

Because people's feelings about their apartments are so personal, site managers are sometimes confronted by an angry resident. In such a situation, you may be attempting to communicate with someone who is too upset to respond—frustration has overcome the resident's patience, and anger is guiding his or her conduct. Any objection or argument will only fuel the person's frustration. When this occurs, remember that your primary responsibility is to ensure communication and provide a professional response. In order to do this, you will have to calm the resident so you can understand the situation and take steps to resolve it.

Interrupting the person will probably not have a calming effect; in fact, it can make the situation worse. If the resident is standing, offer him or her a seat. Often, asking how you can help and allowing the resident to reply without interruption helps defuse a tense situation. Angry people tend to speak quickly, so you may have to ask someone to slow down so you can make notes of the relevant points. This has several benefits. It will force the person to be more rational as well as

Dealing with Confrontation

- Express desire to help
- Calm the person down
- Listen, don't argue or debate the issue
- Investigate
- Respond to problem with positive decision or action
- Follow through
- Above all, remain calm and professional

demonstrate your desire to be helpful. It will also have a calming effect on the person. After you finish writing, the main points should be read back, asking the resident if you have all the information.

Demonstrating your interest in understanding and resolving a situation is not the same as committing immediately to a particular approach. It may be wisest to ask the resident for some time to investigate a problem further before you address it or to enlist the assistance of a supervisor or specialist. This may mean setting a specific date and time to meet or talk again with the person about the problem. It is important to keep this promise; telling a resident that you will look into a problem and then not following through will only increase that person's hostility.

It may not always be possible to calm a person who is upset and abusive. If that is the case, tell the resident you are willing and anxious to help but unable to do so until he or she can communicate the problem effectively and in a civilized manner. It goes without saying that swearing and threats are unacceptable behaviors, and you are within your rights to refuse to discuss the matter further until the person calms down. However strong the temptation, you should not lower yourself to the same level as an abusive resident. If the resident is unwilling to moderate his or her behavior, it is appropriate for you to say, "I think it is best if we discuss the subject later," and simply hang up the telephone or leave the room. If the situation appears very volatile, you may have to ask the resident to leave or have him or her escorted out of the office by security personnel or the police. However, this approach would almost certainly escalate the conflict, so judgment must be exercised. As soon as you can reasonably do so, invite the resident to meet with you to discuss the problem. This can be handled with a phone call or personal note. By writing a letter to the resident, you may be able to better communicate the problem by summarizing the events in the quiet of your office and offering a range of possible solutions both of you can discuss. Above all, you must resist the temptation to respond rudely; it is important to maintain your composure and professional attitude—even when others do not.

Tenant Associations

Real estate managers' opinions of formal organizations of residents, called *tenant associations,* vary greatly. Some managers consider them objectionable and try to ignore or neutralize them; others view them as valid organizations that must be recognized. Regardless of individual managers' opinions, the management company should have an official policy regarding tenant associations. Whether the policy is to recognize them or not, tenant associations should not be regarded as a branch of management, and the members should not be considered employees of the property. At most, an association representative might be consulted, but only in an advisory capacity. The representative would have neither decision-making authority nor official responsibility.

If the policy of your management company is to *not* recognize a tenant association, you may not want to meet with representatives of the association as a group. However, it is appropriate to meet with *individual residents* to discuss their specific grievances. If a problem is severe enough to warrant a group discussion, management should schedule its own general meeting of all residents—without consulting the association. In doing so, management will control the time, the place, and, most importantly, the agenda of the discussion.

Recognition of associations should not change the way management responds to grievances: As with individual complaints, problems should be discussed and solutions to legitimate grievances should be sought. Recognition of a tenant association is not the same as considering it a bargaining entity. This point should be made clear to all residents.

Usually, the existence of an association can be traced to legitimate complaints about the property, such as health and safety concerns or inadequate service, so it should not be dismissed out of hand. However, the formation of a tenant association can usually be averted if you have a strong resident relations program. This translates into prompt responses to service requests, thorough and competent maintenance of the property, and consistent and fair treatment of all residents. By the same token, tenant associations should not be viewed negatively in every case; they can be a positive force in solving problems at the property, increasing security, reducing theft and property destruction, and establishing a genuine sense of community. [NOTE: The preceding comments relate to for-profit privately owned housing. Condominiums, cooperatives, and government-assisted properties often have extensive resident involvement in their management, including resident committees with decision-making authority.]

RESIDENT RETENTION

The best way to retain residents is to provide quality housing at competitive rents with courteous, prompt, and professional service. This requires a long-term commitment to continuous improvement. An ongoing resident retention program creates a positive feeling among the residents about the property and its management and provides avenues for solving minor problems before they become major issues. Every time a resident moves out, the owner incurs expenses to renovate, advertise, and lease the unit—not to mention the loss of rental income for the duration of the vacancy. By providing incentives for residents to stay, owners can avoid or postpone these costs. Bear in mind, too, that older properties may need renovation to stay competitive and hold their place in the leasing market, and even new buildings can have high vacancy rates. No matter the age or target market of the property, elevating your own standards—and those of the entire staff—is key to successful resident retention.

A sound resident retention program is an acknowledgment that it is not enough to begin paying attention to residents just before their leases expire. Quality service should be provided all year long. Site managers need to be aware that residents are concerned about such things as building appearance, responsiveness to service requests, and overall atmosphere. Achieving resident satisfaction requires planning and commitment to high-quality service. The following questions can guide the development of a comprehensive resident retention plan:

- How can the current level of service quality be improved?
- What level of service are we willing to provide?
- How will we know when quality is excellent, good, or poor?

Key Actions Related to Resident Relations in Site Management

- Deal with residents in a personal and professional manner
- Communicate management policies and procedures effectively
- Conduct move-in and move-out inspections
- Process service requests
- Handle resident complaints
- Implement lease renewal strategies
- Implement resident retention programs

- What is acceptable behavior on the part of the on-site team?
- Who will be responsible for training, development, and follow-up?

Each resident has unique needs, and housing is only one of them. Understanding what your residents need and want requires special skills, including the ability to listen, observe, and develop a plan that takes into account residents' desires, the property's needs, and the owner's expectations. Most residents' needs include comfort, peace of mind, a perception of getting excellent value for their money, and being treated respectfully and fairly.

To be successful, resident retention programs depend on frequent communication to create a positive impression that the owner and management company care about their residents. This means responding to residents' requests promptly, maintaining the property, and keeping lines of communication with residents open. All levels of the property staff need to be aware of the importance of resident relations. Every encounter with a resident is critical. The person who answers incoming telephone calls must understand the responsibility of being the first person to represent the property to a caller. Residents and others should be glad they were able to speak to an amiable person who is demonstrably willing to answer their questions and respond to their complaints.

As a site manager, you need to make yourself available to residents directly. Your sensitivity in this area not only assures resident satisfaction, but also contributes to the financial performance and success of the property. It is wise to view every contact with residents as an indirect approach to renewal of their leases. While the site manager is ultimately responsible for ensuring that residents are treated well, others on the staff also have a role to play. Maintenance personnel have to understand that it does not matter how well a mechanical problem was fixed if the resident is not satisfied or was in some way offended. People in the office have to understand that a single accounting error or an inappropriate comment can destroy a long-term relationship with a resident. Leasing agents have to recognize the need to sell quality and lifestyle as well as an apartment. Resident retention demands an ongoing commitment on the part of all those involved—i.e., every member of the on-site staff. Before a resident's needs can be satisfied, they must be known.

SUMMARY

Good resident relations depend on understanding the importance and objectives of communication. It requires the on-site staff to identify when communication is breaking down and find ways to respond appropriately to different situations.

Communication is dynamic—it involves speaking *and* listening, writing *and* understanding. Because of this dynamism, improving one's communication skills requires a genuine commitment to reflection on what is being said or written, evaluation of how information is being presented and how it might be perceived, and consideration of how the presentation can be improved.

Good resident relations depends on clear communication and consistent and fair treatment of all residents. By stating management policies, a residents' handbook can contribute substantially to this goal. It can also be one of the main resources for answering residents' questions about their homes and providing procedures to assist residents with different types of problems they may encounter.

The site manager and other staff members will have countless opportunities to interact with residents. These include marketing and leasing to prospects, responding to residents' service requests, and dealing with their complaints. Communication and so-called people skills are requisite qualifications for all site personnel. Specific training and good skills will facilitate communication and help avert confrontation. The goal is a level of resident satisfaction that will foster resident retention.

Key Terms

feedback
resident complaint
residents' handbook
service request
tenant association

Key Concepts

move-in orientation
nonverbal communication
resident relations
resident retention
verbal communication

Key Points

- What are the objectives of communication?
- What are the barriers to communication? How can they be overcome?
- How are verbal and nonverbal communication related?
- What types of things do residents most often complain about?
- How should a site manager deal with confrontation?
- Why is resident relations so important?

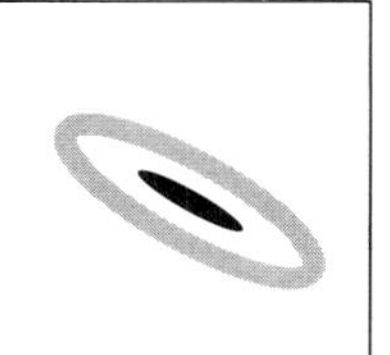

8

Maintenance

A new residential property is a beautiful sight. The grounds and the building exterior are neat and attractive. The same is true of the interior. From the elevators to the laundry facilities to the individual apartments, the entire property is handsome and inviting. However, with time and use, the physical appearance of a property gradually declines. Potholes develop in parking lots, paint fades and peels, woodwork becomes scarred, and carpets show signs of wear. Left alone, minor eyesores could become structural problems, threatening the integrity of the building and perhaps even rendering it uninhabitable.

The ramifications can be serious, even if there is only nominal physical deterioration of the exterior. When a property's curb appeal begins to suffer, the effectiveness of marketing efforts is diminished. Based on appearance alone, a building can acquire a negative reputation, which is then passed from current residents to prospective residents by word of mouth. Such problems can be averted by making needed repairs promptly and maintaining the entire property in the best possible physical condition.

UNDERSTANDING THE IMPORTANCE OF MAINTENANCE—PHYSICAL AND FINANCIAL BENEFITS

Maintenance is the process of keeping a property in an existing state or preserving it from physical deterioration. Just as neighborhoods pass through "life cycles" (discussed in chapter 5), buildings have their own life cycles that are related to the inevitable process of wearing out. Maintenance is work done to prevent or retard this process by promptly repairing or replacing worn components with comparable or improved ones.

Maintenance is a dynamic process with consequences that affect many areas of real estate management. The property management company, the property manager, the site manager and on-site staff, and the owner are judged by the physical appearance of a property: It will either welcome prospects or turn them away, and it plays a role in current residents' decisions about renewing their leases. Ultimately, the financial condition of the property is seriously affected—for better or worse—by the lack of maintenance. For example, a major roof leak could prevent one or more apartments from being rented. The building's condition also determines the basis of insurance premiums and affects the owner's ability to refinance the property.

Everything in the property you manage will need some type of maintenance at some time, whether it involves cleaning, painting, repair, or replacement. From the hallway carpeting to the landscaping surrounding your building, a comprehensive maintenance plan will enhance its appearance and reduce operating costs. It will also establish and perpetuate high standards of comfort and safety for the residents and improve the efficiency and morale of the site staff. Maintenance planning will also have a positive effect on the attitudes of residents, who tend to mirror the attitude of management—if management does not care, neither will the residents.

The quality of maintenance also has a profound impact on the quality of resident relations. As pointed out in chapter 7, most complaints from residents concern maintenance-related issues—poor maintenance, inadequate heat or air conditioning, the quality of service in general—reflecting perceptions of management's responsiveness to service requests and the attitudes of site personnel who receive them. A well-planned maintenance program will eliminate most—if not all—of these kinds of complaints.

The Dynamics of Maintenance—A Comparison

Sound Maintenance and Service

An attractive property with apartments in good physical condition

↓

Higher closing ratios, more rentals to generate operating funds

↓

Responsiveness to residents' needs

↓

Satisfied residents and higher renewal rates

↓

Few vacancies—Less turnover and lower operating costs

Poor Maintenance and Service

A less attractive property/apartments, some units unrentable

↓

Fewer rentals to generate operating funds

↓

Inadequate service

↓

Dissatisfied residents and fewer renewals

↓

Increased vacancies—Greater turnover, higher operating costs

Types of Maintenance

Because real estate is a depreciating asset, steps must be taken to arrest the natural process of deterioration that takes place over its life span. Maintenance is perhaps the most important means of doing this. In real estate management, maintenance constitutes a sizable investment of time, labor, and money. Analysis of costs over the life of a building has revealed that the original design and construction account for only about 25 percent of the total while the remaining 75 percent is for

Objectives of Maintenance

- Optimal functioning of the property
- Reduced operating costs
- Extension of useful life of equipment
- Resident satisfaction
- Increased resident retention
- Maximized property income and value

maintenance. Therefore, one of the most important jobs for real estate managers is stabilizing or reducing these costs while at the same time guaranteeing the highest maintenance standards attainable.

Maintenance is more complicated than merely painting and repairing. Six types of maintenance can be identified—preventive, corrective, routine, emergency, cosmetic, and deferred. The first three are the heart and soul of a comprehensive maintenance plan; the remainder reflect its implementation. To help you understand this differentiation, each of them will be explained in its turn.

Preventive Maintenance. *Preventive maintenance* comprises periodic inspections and scheduled maintenance and repairs intended to prolong the operating life of a property and the equipment installed there. Preventive maintenance is the basis of a comprehensive maintenance program. The key to successful preventive maintenance is careful allocation of time and labor and a pacing of operating expenses over a given period of time. The goal is to minimize breakdowns and preclude the need for corrective and emergency maintenance and repairs. Preventive maintenance is the most important type of maintenance and requires the greatest attention to planning, which includes:

1. Periodically inspecting the property, anticipating needs, and being concerned about quality;
2. Preparing work schedules;
3. Conducting maintenance on a regular basis;
4. Implementing inventory controls; and
5. Addressing problems that arise despite preventive maintenance—to prevent them from becoming worse and costing more to repair later.

Types of Maintenance

- Preventive Maintenance
- Corrective Maintenance
- Routine or Custodial Maintenance
- Emergency Maintenance
- Cosmetic Maintenance
- Deferred Maintenance

Preventive maintenance also extends the operating life of equipment and components. For example, changing air-conditioner filters on a regular basis is simple and relatively inexpensive, yet not doing it has far-reaching implications. Dirty filters make the equipment work harder and wear out faster: More electricity is used to produce the same amount of cooling; this leads to wide temperature fluctuations and excessive running of mechanical equipment that shortens its life. Replacing filters maximizes the life of the equipment and reduces utility costs, which can be an added incentive for renewal if residents pay for their own air conditioning. Changing filters takes less time than repair or replacement of the equipment itself; it also lowers related maintenance and material costs and reduces energy consumption. There are many examples of preventive maintenance, including these:

- Cleaning equipment and components
- Lubricating motors
- Replacing belts on mechanical equipment
- Cleaning flues and vents
- Cleaning drain traps
- Cleaning common areas according to a predetermined schedule
- Using washable paint on walls and other surfaces
- Pruning trees and shrubs
- Fertilizing lawns
- Exterminating pests

As an added bonus, advance planning of maintenance tasks and adherence to a specific schedule mean maintenance personnel can work more efficiently, and the need for emergency repairs can be minimized. Regular scheduling also makes maintenance and repair costs more predictable.

Performing preventive maintenance as a part of apartment turnover reduces scheduling difficulties once apartment units are occupied, thus saving significant amounts of time. Finding small problems before they become larger and more costly frees maintenance technicians for other activities. Preventive maintenance also reduces operating expenses, thereby increasing the property's NOI.

Corrective Maintenance. Unlike preventive maintenance, which is intended to anticipate problems and minimize breakdowns, *corrective maintenance* is done after something has gone wrong, in response to a resident's request for service, or when an inspection uncovers a problem. No matter how comprehensive the preventive maintenance program, even the best-maintained equipment will break down once in a while. Plumbing that leaks, appliances that do not work, electrical malfunctions, and resident misuse of appliances and amenities are common reasons for service requests. Although corrective maintenance is a normal part of any maintenance program, the need for much of it can be minimized by attention to preventive maintenance, staff training, and resident orientation.

Routine Maintenance. *Routine maintenance*, also called *custodial or janitorial maintenance,* is the day-to-day upkeep of the property. It includes mopping and waxing floors, washing windows, polishing fixtures, and generally keeping the interior and exterior of a building clean and presentable. These routine activities are essential to preserving the appearance and value of the property. Routine maintenance offers other benefits, as well. These include the increased sense of security that results from having clean, bright lights; the lessened potential for pest problems when trash bin areas are well-tended and free of litter; and the extension of carpet life by regular cleaning.

Emergency Maintenance. Any unscheduled maintenance that must be done immediately to prevent further property damage or minimize danger to people (e.g., a gas leak, a broken glass door) is considered *emergency maintenance.* While such work cannot be preplanned, a sound preventive maintenance program can safeguard against some types of emergencies arising and minimize the costs of responding when they do occur. When emergency maintenance is needed, the response should be swift and decisive. Proper training of maintenance personnel in handling different types of emergency situations will assure that this is done. (Emergency procedures for responding to catastrophic events such as a fire or flood should be addressed in an operations manual; these are discussed in chapter 9.)

Cosmetic Maintenance. As the name implies, *cosmetic maintenance* is intended to improve or enhance the appearance of the property or individual apartments. Examples of cosmetic maintenance include painting (or repainting) to change a color scheme, redecorating apartments, or replacing drapes with vertical blinds. While not essential to operations or the functioning of equipment, this type of maintenance nonetheless reaps financial rewards. By increasing the aesthetic appeal of the property, you will also attract rental prospects and retain current residents within your defined market niche. A property that is continually becoming a more-desirable place to live will support optimum rents and have fewer vacancies, which will increase both the income of the property and its value.

Deferred Maintenance. In the course of scheduling maintenance activities, some work may be postponed because of money or time constraints or seasonal considerations (e.g., waiting until spring to repave a parking lot). However, *deferred maintenance* can also be a sign of careless or poor management, and it can be quite costly. As an example of the latter, delaying minor but necessary roof repairs can lead to more extensive damage that requires replacement of the roof (a capital expenditure). If damaged shingles are not replaced, the roof can begin to leak, weakening and ruining the ceilings in apartments on one or more levels. As a result, not only will the roof have to be repaired (or replaced), but repairs to the damaged ceilings can be extremely costly, especially if water damages support structures. In addition, there is potential for loss of rental income while the building is repaired. In this case, a simple roof repair, costing at most a few hundred dollars, could prevent the expenditure of thousands of dollars for repairs to the roof and other parts of the building.

On the other hand, maintenance may be "deferred" by choice: Sometimes it is necessary to schedule a series of tasks to expedite completion of all of them, or you may need someone with technical skill or specific equipment to make a particular repair. Timing is often an important consideration in making repairs economically as well as efficiently. As an example, if the wood trim around an entry door is cracked, and a contractor has been hired to paint all the exterior trim three months from now, you might want to wait until then to repair the trim. Waiting to paint stairwells until all the interior hallways are scheduled to be painted in the near future is another example. The distinction between delaying a task until an optimal time and neglecting it altogether is an important one—while both are considered deferred maintenance, only one will benefit the property.

As site manager, you will have a key role in determining which maintenance tasks will be deferred and which will be done right away. In doing so, you should consider the effects of a deferment on the property's operations and your residents' safety and satisfaction. Although a particular decision may be economically sound, it could be *perceived* by residents as neglect and, thus, have unintended negative consequences. From an investment standpoint, what may seem too expensive in the near term will, in fact, enhance the value of the property in the long term.

Setting Maintenance Goals for the Management Team

Maintenance is an important component of management's efforts to achieve the owner's goals for his or her real estate investment. A comprehensive maintenance program should set clear, reasonable, and measurable goals, such as the following:

- To maintain an established standard at which systems and equipment in the building will function.
- To be able to prepare a vacant apartment for occupancy within a certain amount of time.
- To maintain established standards of cleanliness throughout the common areas of the building.
- To respond to residents' service requests within a prescribed period after they are received.
- To reduce the number of return calls for the same maintenance problem.
- To reduce the number of emergency repair calls.

Functional standards relate to preventive maintenance—things like periodically inspecting apartments for signs of water leaks, checking gutters for clogging, and monitoring the coolant pressure in air conditioning (HVAC) equipment. For the latter, the goal might be to have no breakdowns in HVAC equipment within a specific period; the measure would be whether or not the goal was met.

Response times can be related to acknowledgment of service requests, appropriate scheduling, and speed of completion. While all requests should be acknowledged as quickly as possible, scheduling of different types of work may depend on the urgency of a needed repair, the maintenance schedule already in place, and the availability of parts (or supplies) and someone to do the work.

An overriding consideration, always, is cost. In budgeting for maintenance, records from past years are used to project spending along with known or anticipated future expenditures. Some caution should be exercised when using past years' records. They may not be accurate in general, or they may reflect years when maintenance was extraordinary—or minimal—and should not be averaged into a budget. While specific data are invaluable, their interpretation demands careful judgment. Based on their past experiences at the property, the on-site staff can help determine whether records for particular years reflect what can be expected for future years.

Because a goal of good management is containment of costs, there are likely to be dollar limits on some types of maintenance expenditures (on a per-square-foot or per-unit basis), and these can contribute to decisions to defer maintenance. Cost is also a consideration in determining urgency (routine versus emergency) as well as categorizing specific tasks as major or minor repairs.

DEVELOPING A MAINTENANCE PROGRAM

Although maintenance goals guide its development, the substance of the maintenance program will be the variety of specific tasks to be performed at the property and a schedule for reasonably accomplishing them. The maintenance requirements of a particular property will depend on its age, condition, size, location, and complexity as well as the number of occupants and the frequency of turnover. These factors also affect staffing (see chapter 3), scheduling of routine and preventive maintenance, and responses to specific service requests.

The benefits of a well-planned maintenance program are numerous. As site manager, you will be made aware of the progress of all projects and tasks. The staff will perform their assignments well because they know their work will be observed and that you care about its quality. Residents will take note of the staff's efforts and your concern about the property and take pride in living there.

Scheduling Maintenance Work

The scheduling of maintenance work is one of the site manager's primary responsibilities, and it may include direct supervision of the work. At a large property, however, the site manager may determine maintenance goals with a maintenance supervisor who has direct responsibility for supervising an on-site maintenance staff. In such situations, the site manager commonly holds weekly—or even daily—meetings with the maintenance supervisor to discuss the property's needs. For example, the site manager will inform the maintenance supervisor that five units have to be prepared for leasing or move-in by a certain date, and it is the maintenance supervisor's responsibility to see that this is done. In determining which vacant units should be made available for marketing, it is important for the maintenance supervisor to weigh the relative ease—and costs—of making different units rent-ready and balance that information against the site manager's assessment of the relative marketability of individual apartments. While the site manager is responsible for setting priorities, in conjunction with the main office, the maintenance supervisor's perspective is an invaluable part of the decision-making process.

When determining what maintenance work must be done, and when, site managers rely on numerous sources of information, including the following:

- Property inspections
- Maintenance specifications for components of the property supplied by the manufacturers
- Preventive maintenance schedules for the property
- Requirements or standards set by the property manager, the owner, or various governmental agencies

- Requests from residents
- Unexpected emergencies
- Projects designed to enhance the property

The potential liability risk associated with a condition is also a consideration.

Regardless of how need is determined, all maintenance and repairs (except for emergency work) should be scheduled in advance. Therefore, time management is the most crucial aspect of a maintenance program. To make sure that maintenance is carried out as efficiently as possible, all maintenance work should be scheduled using both long-range and daily plans that reflect the property's maintenance priorities. Preventive maintenance and servicing can be scheduled in advance on an annual basis and broken down by months (i.e., semiannual and quarterly repetitions of tasks would be scheduled at six-month and three-month intervals, respectively). Other periodic maintenance—including some of the routine janitorial tasks—can be scheduled on a monthly basis indicating the week or the day of the week when the work will be done. Both of these schedules must accommodate the daily, repetitive tasks.

Each day's work should be scheduled the day before at the latest, and the scheduling should be reasonably flexible so that service requests and emergencies can be accommodated. Such an approach will allow you to balance regularly scheduled work with newly discovered needs from inspection reports, as well as handle special projects and turn around vacant units. Use of a *tickler file* for scheduling such occasional maintenance tasks as periodic greasing, oiling, and cleaning (often based on manufacturers' suggested service intervals) will help assure that nothing is overlooked—even during unanticipated hectic periods. Whether you use a year-long calendar or a personal computer as such a reminder, key maintenance tasks should be noted at appropriate intervals.

Although some work may take precedence over routine maintenance, which can be rescheduled, routine tasks should be accomplished as nearly on schedule as possible so as not to create a backlog of maintenance and repair work. Obviously, emergencies have to be addressed regardless of other work scheduled. The most workable plans and schedules set deadlines that are attainable. It is always advisable to seek input from your staff regarding scheduling. Those who will do the work are often the most knowledgeable about time requirements and whether a maintenance schedule is realistic.

Determining How Maintenance Is to Be Done—Considering Alternatives

As noted in chapter 2, there should be an operations manual for the property that spells out the management company's *standard operating procedures (SOP)*—the policies and procedures that apply to the management of the property, including maintenance. The manual should also contain the forms and checklists that will expedite the work. (Alternatively, a maintenance manual may be separate from an operations manual.) In explaining how specific tasks are to be performed, the manual should identify requisite skills or stipulate whether site personnel or contract laborers are to be used. Because labor constitutes about 80 percent of maintenance costs, supervision of maintenance technicians is an important duty. Unfortunately, some people consider looking for the lowest price on parts to be effective maintenance management when their time would be better spent managing the labor.

Doing an effective job requires careful analysis of what needs to be done, by whom, and when. The people doing the work must be properly trained and motivated, and their work must be monitored. It is also important to determine the scope of each project (the types of tools and equipment needed, parts that are needed and their availability) and arrange for access to the apartment or other areas.

The size of the maintenance staff and the skills needed to perform specific tasks will determine the site manager's approach to maintenance. You will have to decide not only what will be most efficient, keeping in mind the immediate economic costs, but whether the assignment will be an opportunity for an employee to develop professionally and experience job satisfaction. By developing job descriptions initially, you will have a clear idea of the skills needed when people are hired, and both you and the employee will understand what the job requires—i.e., the performance expectations of the job will be clearly defined. (The importance of job descriptions was explained in chapter 3.)

Site Employees versus Contract Workers. The choice between using site personnel and contracting for maintenance services will depend on many factors, including how often a particular job should be done; how long each task should take; whether specialized training, licensing, or certification is required; and whether specialized tools and equipment are needed. Contracted maintenance services may be desirable for any or all of the following reasons:

- Site staff already have a full workload.
- The job requires specific licensing from local, state, and/or federal agencies.
- Servicing of equipment not performed by a certified contractor may void warranties or insurance coverage.
- A contractor's greater technical expertise may translate into greater efficiency and lower costs.
- A contractor has more specialized workers.
- A contractor has more specific insurance.
- The contractor deals with details of payroll, union negotiations, and training.
- The contractor handles scheduling and monitoring of the work.
- The contractor often can purchase parts or supplies more efficiently and more economically.

These are all compelling reasons for using contractors to perform certain site maintenance tasks. However, there are also drawbacks to having contractors work on the property, and they must be considered as well.

- Cost—contractors frequently charge high hourly rates; they may also mark up the cost of parts and supplies that could be purchased directly from the supplier for less.
- Quality of work—it is difficult to monitor and assure the contracted job will be done right the first time.
- Corrections or changes—if follow-up work is required, getting a contractor to correct problems can be difficult.
- Scheduling—a contractor's schedule may not be optimal for your property. Also, if the job was awarded at an agreed-to price, the contractor may not be motivated to stay on schedule.
- Flexibility—contractors may not be as flexible in meeting changing conditions at the property (i.e, addressing new problems or emergencies).

- Personnel—selection and direction of personnel are not under the site manager's control.

The decision to use outside contractors requires careful consideration. Management companies frequently have policies regarding specific types of jobs that are always, sometimes, or never awarded to contractors. Whenever possible, contracts should stipulate "caps"—limits for time and materials that are not to be exceeded.

Maintenance typically performed by contractors includes servicing of heating, ventilating, and air-conditioning (HVAC) equipment, elevators, swimming pools, and coin-operated laundry equipment. While some types of electrical and plumbing work can be performed by unlicensed laborers, wiring and pipes may have to be installed and connected to main lines by licensed contractors. It is generally not cost-effective to have skilled tradespeople on staff or to own (or lease) heavy equipment that will not be in constant use. These are the most common reasons for contracting certain services—e.g., waste disposal (trash removal and recycling pickup), snow removal, parking lot patching and striping, exterminating (pest control), window cleaning, exterior painting, and major landscaping.

Service Contracts. Whenever contractors are to be used, it is imperative to choose them carefully and negotiate good contracts. While a site manager's participation in negotiations and the selection process may be limited, he or she will undoubtedly be involved in the on-site administration of the contract and monitoring of the project's progress. Whatever his or her role, the site manager should have an opportunity to identify the service needed at the property—perhaps suggesting contractors to be considered or some of the specifics to be covered in the contract—and become familiar in advance with the contract arrangements and how they are to be administered.

Usually, *specifications* outlining the particulars of a job (types of tasks, quality of materials, etc.) are established by the property manager or others at the management company (in conjunction with information and recommendations from the on-site staff), and these are submitted to qualified contractors who are asked to *bid* on the work—i.e., present an estimate of time and costs for materials and labor, or quote a fee for a period or for each time a service is provided. Having several contractors submit bids will allow a choice based on cost, or speed, or both, that will provide the best-quality service at the lowest possible cost. When a contractor is selected, the written agreement should spell out in detail:

- What work is to be done (procedures)
- What materials will be used
- When the work is to be performed and completed (schedule or deadline)
- Who will do the work (if special skill or a license is required)
- How much the work will cost, perhaps limited by a "cap"
- Who provides materials (parts, supplies)
- Who provides specialized equipment (if needed)
- Where and when bills are to be submitted and terms of payment
- The types and amounts of liability (personal injury and property damage) and worker's compensation insurance carried by the contractor and the name and telephone number of the contractor's insurance companies and agents
- A warranty for work performed and a stipulation for withholding funds to assure satisfactory completion of the job
- A nonperformance clause and/or escape clause to provide for termination of the contracted services

For work that must be done by licensed or certified professionals, proof of the contractor's qualifications should be required (copies of licenses or certificates issued to them). All contractors and subcontractors should be bonded against mishaps or nonpayment of their suppliers or labor (performance and payment bonds). A contractor's employees and suppliers who are not paid can file a *mechanic's lien* against the property for the value of their labor or materials; such a lien could create problems for the property owner in obtaining financing or refinancing or selling the property. When specialized or heavy-duty equipment will be needed, documentation of accessibility and availability is a prudent request. Whether particular equipment is owned or leased may also be a consideration, because default of a loan or lease could preclude fulfillment of the agreement with you.

The contract should also specify who is responsible for obtaining permits (if they are required); usually this is the contractor's role. (Except for rehabilitation or new construction, the need for architectural or engineering drawings will be minimal; if they are needed, a licensed professional may have to prepare or approve them.) Contingency provisions for weather- or illness-related delays are usually not addressed in maintenance or service contracts because work is scheduled on a repeat basis and some flexibility is allowable.

Finally, all such contracts should be drafted properly to assure that they will minimize the risk of liability to the property, its ownership, and the management company. Certificates of insurance should be required as proof of the types and quality of the contractor's coverage. Minimum levels of coverage for liability, property damage, and workers' compensation may be stipulated, and identification of the manager or management company—or the property owner—as additional named insured parties should be required.

Contracts for services are likely to be issued in the name of the property or its ownership, even though they may be signed by the property manager or an officer of the management company as the owner's agent. If you sign contracts as the owner's agent, it is wise to sign your name and write "as authorized agent for the owner" beside it. All contracts should be reviewed by legal counsel before being accepted and signed, and a copy of the signed contract should be kept in the on-site files as a working reference.

Responding to Service Requests

Whether residents' requests for maintenance and other types of service are made by phone, in person, or in writing, the person who receives them should be trained to collect all relevant information. Residents should be discouraged from simply telling a maintenance technician about a needed repair during an encounter in the hall. Nor is it fair for them to expect maintenance technicians to interrupt scheduled tasks and thus delay work for other residents who are waiting their turn. So that site personnel can respond to service requests promptly, there should be a standard procedure for submitting and responding to service requests. Clear communication of service requests will foster good resident relations and facilitate record keeping. Furthermore, a standard service request policy allows the site staff to do their jobs in the best way possible and helps the site manager coordinate the activities of all site personnel.

The residents' handbook should outline the services policy, state the office hours for accepting requests, and indicate the availability

EXHIBIT 8.1

Resident Handbook—Sample Procedure for Service Requests

All service requests should be directed to the management office, preferably during office hours. A service request form can be completed in person or by a staff member (over the phone using a work order form). To help us provide better service to you, requests should be stated as clearly and completely as possible. Our goal is to respond to your request within 24 hours if possible. When work cannot be scheduled that quickly, we will explain why the delay is necessary and when you can expect the work to be completed. Every effort will be made to perform the requested service as soon as possible.

To help us monitor the quality of the service we are providing, a service request "report card" will be left with you after the work has been done. Please complete this questionnaire, grading the quality and timeliness of the service and commenting as appropriate.

In case of an emergency, please call the management office immediately. If the office is closed, call the emergency service number listed in this handbook. Examples of emergencies are:

- Fire or smoke (call fire department first)
- Security problem (e.g., door that will not shut, broken window or lock)
- No electricity, heat, or air conditioning
- Leaky plumbing (a broken pipe or overflowing toilet)
- A blocked drain or backed up sewer
- An odor of gas
- Failure of an appliance
- A nonworking elevator

This procedure is intended to ensure fast, courteous, and efficient service. If you have any questions regarding this policy, please call the site manager.

NOTE: Power outages and telephone service disruptions should be reported directly to the respective utilities, although the management will appreciate receiving such information. Gas leaks should be reported to the utility company immediately; the management company should be notified afterward.

---

of service at night, on weekends, and during holidays (exhibit 8.1 is an example). It should also include an emergency telephone number to call when the site office is closed. Residents should be asked to make requests according to the standard procedure using a service request form.

Once requests are received, residents should be advised when they can expect the work to be done. Responding to all service requests within 24 hours should be the maintenance standard, but previously scheduled work, emergencies, or a need for special parts may sometimes preclude the achievement of this goal. If a request cannot be fulfilled within your established time frame, it is imperative that someone—the site manager or the maintenance supervisor—let the resident know when the work will, in fact, be done. This is not only courteous, but will strengthen resident relations.

Providing a standard *service request form* for residents' use will facilitate the process. The form should include spaces for the following information.

- Resident's name, apartment number, and telephone numbers at work and at home
- The date and time of the request
- Authorization to enter the apartment in the resident's absence (including a signature)
- The location of the problem within the apartment (e.g., the master bathroom)
- An accurate and complete description of the work being requested
- Any relevant additional information (such as the presence of a pet, which should be kept in a room separate from where the service will be provided)
- Approval by the site manager or maintenance supervisor (signature)

It is a good idea to include spaces for indicating when a request was received, if and when it was acknowledged, when the work is to be scheduled, and its priority. An example is provided in exhibit 8.2.

Use of a standard form will facilitate maintenance record keeping and ensure employee accountability. When personal or telephone requests are received, the employee who takes the request should complete a work order form at once and note how the request was received (this is a separate form that will be discussed later in the chapter). Employees as well as residents should be required to follow the established procedure, and both should be reminded, as necessary, that indirect requests are not acceptable because maintenance at the site is scheduled in advance.

Because changes to and service needs of individual units will vary over time, it is wise to establish a file for each unit to document pertinent information and record specific maintenance performed. The file for each unit should include the following information:

- Appliance serial numbers and model numbers; colors, purchase dates, and warranty periods
- Plumbing fixture manufacturer, style, and color
- Cabinet and other hardware design
- Whether drapes or blinds were provided, the unit leased as furnished or unfurnished
- When the apartment was last cleaned, carpet was last shampooed
- Color scheme (if more than one is used on the property); dates when painted or wallpapered; installation dates of carpet or tile
- Unique characteristics of the unit (e.g., a fireplace)
- Dates and types of maintenance or service performed, especially repetitions
- Resident billing for damage (copies of letters or invoices—these charges should also be recorded in the resident's ledger)

Having this information at your disposal will expedite responses to residents' service requests and facilitate implementation of inventory controls.

Maintenance Record Keeping

Regularly scheduled items, especially preventive maintenance procedures, may follow a checklist of tasks, in which case the completed checklist with notes and recommendations (dated and signed by the individual worker) becomes the work record. However, a work order system is the most efficient way to handle service provided to residents. Every resident request should result in preparation of a *work order* (exhibit 8.3). The completed work order form indicates what is to be done, when it should be completed, and who will do the work. It is the maintenance record of the response to a service request.

All maintenance assignments should be entered in a *maintenance log or ledger* (exhibit 8.4) that serves as a cumulative record. It can be written by hand or, commonly today, entered in a computer. The log is used to record specific tasks, their locations, and the time required to complete them, along with the name of the worker and the date. A

EXHIBIT 8.2

Sample Service Request Form

Maintenance Service Request

Date ______________________ Time ______________

Resident's Name ______________________ Apartment ______________

Telephone: Work ______________________ Home ______________

Service Needed ____

____

____

May we enter the apartment in your absence? _____ Yes _____ No

Resident's signature ______________________ Date and Time ______________

Site manager's signature ______________________ Date ______________

Office Use Only Priority (circle) Urgent Routine Preventive

This type of form is typical of those used when residents are asked to make service requests in writing. The information is then used to prepare a specific work order (see exhibit 8.3). To reduce the amount of paper work and minimize the possibility of errors in interpretation or performance of the work, the service request form may be expanded to include information about parts, scheduling, and actual work done, including a place for the maintenance technician to sign it, thus combining the incoming request with the work order.

This form may also function as a resident retention tool: Providing residents with a number of service request forms during orientation underscores the importance of service and provides a clear medium for communicating service requests.

maintenance log becomes a record of all maintenance work done for the property as a whole and in the individual units—a ready resource for information on the frequency of common maintenance tasks, time requirements, and costs, all of which are important in preparing budgets and analyzing budget variances. A maintenance log also allows the site manager to evaluate the performance of maintenance technicians. It can also have legal implications—because some tasks will be related to compliance with building code requirements or environmental regulations, the log may document work sufficiently to overcome claims of constructive eviction. (This topic is discussed in chapter 10.)

Many formal and informal maintenance and repair record-keeping systems are used in site management. In one system, the work order

EXHIBIT 8.3

Sample Work Order Form

Maintenance Work Order

Work Order Number ______ Date ________________ Time ________________
Resident's Name ______________________ Apartment ________________
Home Phone ______________________ Work Phone ________________
Apartment Type __________ Location of Repair ______________________
Pet ______________________ Location in Unit ______________________
Permission to enter in resident's absence Yes ________ No ________

Maintenance required ____
____
____
Maintenance performed ____
____
____
Materials used ____
____
____
Maintenance performed by ____
Time Required ____________________ Cost of Labor ________________
Cost of Materials ______________________ Total cost ________________

Charge to Resident ______________________ Reason ________________
Unable to complete because ____
____

This type of form is completed by a staff member who receives a service request by phone (or transfers information from a service request form). Work order forms are often set up to create several copies at once (with or without carbon paper). Preferably, three copies of the form should be made—one for the on-site general maintenance file (backup for maintenance log), one for the resident's file, and one for the resident. Although a copy of each work order may be sent to the management company office, the volume of paper could become a burden. Usually, a summary report is sent in each week or each month. The work order number and costs may also be recorded on the resident's ledger. (Some management companies use a combined service request/work order form as noted in exhibit 8.2.)

EXHIBIT 8.4

Sample Maintenance Log

No.	Work Order No.	Apt. No.	Resident Name	Work To Be Done	Written		Com-pleted*	Cost	Taken By
					Time	Date			
1									
2									
3									
4									
5									
6									
7									
8									
9									
10									
11									
12									
13									
14									
15									
16									
17									

*Enter date completed or new work order number if more work to be done.

The information displayed here is usually sufficient for most purposes; however, columns may be added to track other details (e.g., purchase orders or inventory) or to indicate a need to schedule follow-up.

form includes an original and two or more copies; one copy may be kept at the site office while the remainder are given to the maintenance technician who fills in the particulars of timing and costs and returns the form to the site office when the work has been completed. Service requests, the maintenance log, and the unit maintenance record are prepared separately. Another, more sophisticated, system combines the service request with the work order in a one-write system that creates a maintenance log record and a unit maintenance record at the same time. In this system, a multipart form records the service requested by the resident and enables the maintenance technician to note when the task has been completed, including time and costs. Each type of information is recorded only once, but there are separate copies for all the different files.

MAINTENANCE PROCEDURES—THE SITE MANAGER'S ROLE

The site manager's role in maintenance will vary. If a property is large enough to require a staff of maintenance technicians, there will often be a maintenance supervisor who coordinates the work and reports to the site manager. In the absence of a maintenance supervisor, the site manager usually coordinates and supervises the work of maintenance personnel directly. When there are no maintenance personnel on site, various maintenance tasks and repairs may be contracted individually, and these arrangements may be with skilled tradespeople (e.g., a plumber) who provide a specific service "on call" or for specific services to be performed on a fixed schedule. In such situations, the site manager will still have specific responsibilities (i.e., oversight and approval of the work so the contractor can be paid—or called back if necessary).

Depending on the size of the property and the number of employees, a site manager may not be required to perform specific tasks related to maintenance—even daily inspections may be delegated to others. However, a site manager should inspect the entire property at least twice a month, if not every week. Major inspections are often conducted by or under the supervision of the property manager; however, the site manager should become familiar with and knowledgeable about the operation and maintenance of equipment and systems and their various controls. Without such knowledge, he or she cannot effectively participate in property inspections or supervise the work of maintenance personnel or evaluate their job performance.

The pivotal nature of inspections cannot be overemphasized. The results of a thorough property inspection will enable you to determine whether the property can capture optimal rents in its present condition. They will also affect budget allocations for the property—information from the inspection will help the property manager formulate the budget and anticipate necessary expenditures for maintenance and repairs. In particular, the inspection may reveal a need for maintenance that requires expenditures in excess of the amount budgeted.

Insurance coverage and premium rates are also affected by the condition of the property. Insurance premiums may be increased because of the presence of potential hazards such as uneven sidewalks or loose handrails. Liability can be reduced by making sure that (1) lighting is properly placed and illumination is adequate; (2) parking areas and driveways have appropriate caution signs and properly marked speed bumps; (3) potential trip and fall hazards are eliminated; and (4) proper fencing (with gates) is installed around a swimming pool. (These are considerations of risk management, which will be discussed in detail in chapter 9.)

Inspection and Maintenance of the Property

Property inspections are conducted for several reasons. Other than gathering information for specific purposes (budgeting, marketing, insurance coverage, energy conservation), the primary purpose of inspection is to determine the need for maintenance. Through regular inspections, you will be able to anticipate problems and address them promptly, reducing the extent of and expenditures for maintenance. They are the key to effective preventive maintenance. Inspections also enable the site manager and the maintenance personnel to learn the features of the property and help them determine the best approach to maintaining it in as good condition as possible. The result will be increased resident satisfaction and higher renewal rates as they see quick responses to real or potential maintenance problems.

Because of their immediate impact on the marketing and leasing programs, inspections should be conducted from the viewpoint of a visitor or prospective resident. The focus should be on the property's curb appeal—i.e., the aesthetic impact on visitors, prospective renters, and current residents—evaluating the use and effectiveness of graphics and signage, and the image created by the overall appearance of the property. This means the following areas will have to be scrutinized on a daily basis.

- Approaches to the property
- Landscaping
- Entrances and lobbies
- Site offices and model apartments
- Elevators and public halls
- Recreational facilities, clubhouses, parking lots or garages
- Balconies and/or patios of occupied apartments
- Interiors of rent-ready apartments

The best way to stay ahead of problems is to walk the entire property every day, preferably early in the morning before you open the site office. This will minimize distractions and enable you to notice details you might miss when you are preoccupied with other daily responsibilities.

Always use an *inspection checklist* to assure that everything is inspected properly. Use of a standard inspection report form will not only facilitate the inspection process and your communication of the findings to the maintenance staff, the property manager, and the owner, but also allow you to develop a cumulative record of the condition of the property. The completed form documents the particular inspection and facilitates scheduling of needed work and estimating costs for purposes of budgeting or cost-benefit analysis. Exhibit 8.5 lists the items commonly included in a general property inspection.

Your inspection of the building will be more efficient if you work from top to bottom and take all necessary keys with you. Ride the elevator to the roof and then walk down from floor to floor using the stairwell. If your property has several elevators and more than one stairwell, use different ones each time you inspect the property. The process of walking down through the building gives you an opportunity to inspect fire doors and assess the general condition of the stairwells. It may be wisest to plan a series of alternate routes to assure that all features of the property are inspected periodically and no single item is omitted repeatedly.

EXHIBIT 8.5

Components of an Apartment Complex Inspection Checklist

General Grounds
Overall Impression—Curb Appeal
Signage
Entry Gates
Landscaping
Shrubs and Flowers
Driveways
Walkways
Parking Areas
Trash Containers

Building Appearance
Overall Impression
Exterior Siding—Paint
Exterior Trim
Foundations and Caulking
Roof Flashing Vents
Gutters and Downspouts
Exterior Doors and Windows
Window Screens
Building Entry
Mail Boxes
Stairs and Railings
Balconies
Patio Fences
Light Fixtures and Lighting
Building Numbers

Site Office
Outside Appearance
Inside Appearance
Flooring or Carpeting
Walls and Ceilings
Windows
Office Neatness
Bathrooms
Storage Areas

Recreation Room
Outside Appearance
Inside Appearance
Flooring or Carpeting
Walls and Ceilings
Windows
Bathrooms
Furniture
Equipment
Vending Machines
Signage

Playground Area
Grounds
Equipment
Fence
Signage
Trash Containers

Swimming Pool Area
Fence
Gates and Locks
Safety Equipment
Signage
Water Condition
Walks and Decks
Furniture
Bathrooms/Showers
Trash Containers

Laundry Rooms
General Appearance
Trash Containers
Floors
Walls and Ceilings
Windows
Equipment
Vending Machines
Signage

Usually inspection forms are set up as grids with the checklist items at the left and blank columns to the right, minimally one to record the *condition* and another to indicate *action* to be taken. The form should also include spaces to identify the building or property, the date of the inspection, and a signature. Depending on the space available—and established procedure—the person

Often the size or newness of a property may preclude an examination of all features every time an inspection is done. Maximum coverage can be achieved by establishing an agenda for each week so that key items are inspected at least once a month. Other areas, such as occupied apartments, are inspected less frequently (e.g., semiannually or annually). One such approach might be the following.

Week 1—the exterior of the building, including the grounds and recreational facilities;

Week 2—the interior of the building, including the lobby, elevators, stairwells and hallways, laundry rooms, and other common areas;

Week 3—mechanical equipment, storage and work areas, model apartments, and vacant units being prepared for showing; and

Week 4—interiors of occupied units, including and especially work done in response to service requests.

Each week's work might include follow-up on tasks scheduled from the previous week's inspections. During lease-up or other periods of intensive marketing of large numbers of apartments, more frequent inspections of model apartments and vacant units will be needed to assure the best appearance when they are shown. In addition, the grounds and common areas should be inspected frequently to assure that a favorable first impression is made. Inspection reports should

EXHIBIT 8.5 ***(continued)***

conducting the inspection may be able to make detailed notes or merely indicate (with abbreviations or symbols) whether an item is satisfactory or needs work. Ideally, an inspection report form will be easy to fill out and easy to interpret when completed, and it will provide a useful long-term record of a particular inspection.

The items on an inspection form should reflect the specific features and equipment of the property where it is used. It should provide an appropriate level of detail as well (e.g., specific types of signage—exit, warning, use limitations—would be identified for the respective areas). The categories of items listed here are related to the building exterior and common areas. Mechanical systems and equipment are not addressed, but they would be an important component of a larger-scale property inspection. Usually a separate checklist is used when apartment interiors are inspected, and it, too, should be tailored to the property.

EXHIBIT 8.6

Typical Schedule for Recurring Maintenance Tasks

Project	Frequency
Patch parking lot	Yearly
Touch-up exterior paint	Twice a year
Clean gutters and downspouts	After heavy rains or quarterly
Prune shrubbery	Twice a year
Vacuum swimming pool	Daily in season*
Clean windows	Twice a year
Inspect and test fire equipment	Four times a year†
Recharge fire extinguishers	Twice a year
Inspect common area lighting	Weekly
Clean or replace HVAC filters	Monthly*
Inspect and oil exhaust fans	Four times a year
Wax lobby floors	Four times a year
Touch-up interior paint	As needed

*Climatic conditions will dictate maintenance of HVAC equipment and frequency for cleaning the swimming pool. In some locales, visits by an exterminator would be scheduled regularly.

†The local fire inspector should be consulted regarding fire safety requirements and recharging of fire extinguishers.

In use, this type of general schedule may be set up as a columnar form, including a column for scheduling the work in specific weeks or months. The frequencies listed are suggested minimums.

also note any maintenance that has been deferred (i.e., as future projects). Exhibit 8.6 lists various maintenance tasks and how often they are usually performed.

For optimum visibility, it makes sense to conduct inspections during daytime hours, although occasional night inspections offer an opportunity to observe employees on the late shift and evaluate the effectiveness of lighting and security. Conducting inspections at different times will allow you to observe whether work is being done as scheduled or only in anticipation of inspections. Such unannounced inspections will not be a "surprise" if you let people know that you intend to do this. Alert to the possibility of an unscheduled inspection "at any time," people are more likely to keep their assigned work up to date.

To expand on this overview, the following sections outline the types of tasks that are typically performed as part of the maintenance of various components of a residential property, including what to look for during regular inspections.

The Grounds—Curb Appeal. Because it is an important part of people's first impression of the property, the exterior inspection should include the *signage*: All signs should be well-maintained and easily readable. The information should be current and correct, and the presentation should be consistent in style and wording. Above all, signs must be visible. This is very important from a safety as well as a marketing perspective. Signage also affects current residents' perceptions of where they live.

Another important consideration is *landscaping*. To enhance the appearance of the property, it must be well-designed and well-maintained. Plant colors and sizes should be balanced so they are visually pleasing. To remain attractive, plants must be watered properly and their condition should be monitored—look for signs of blight or insect infestation. Trees and tall shrubs should be properly trimmed—trees should not lean against buildings; shrubbery should not overhang sidewalks. If there is a lawn, it should be free of brown or yellow spots and bald patches. If foot traffic has worn a path in an area of the lawn, installation of stepping stones in the area may be an attractive alternative to trying to restore the grass; another approach is to plant bushes that will act as a barrier to foot traffic.

The *driveway and parking lot* should be free of litter, and parking spaces should be indicated clearly. Stripes should be repainted periodically—the frequency will depend on climate and wear. Any parking structures (garages or carports) should be kept in good repair. Parking areas reserved for vehicles belonging to disabled residents must be designed in compliance with the Americans with Disabilities Act (ADA) and clearly marked. The ADA also requires ramps with railings for use by disabled residents; in addition to railings, materials that will prevent slipping can be applied to steps. If parking spaces, carports, or garages are assigned to residents, make sure the numbers or letters are large, clear, and visible. (For security purposes, parking space numbers should be different from apartment numbers.) Fire zones and "no parking zones"—as well as spaces reserved for prospects and visitors—should also be clearly marked and parking restrictions should be enforced. (It may be necessary or desirable to paint the curbing in restricted areas; city ordinances may specify this.)

The back of property should not be neglected. It should be free of litter, and fences, gates, locks, trash bin enclosures, and lighting in this area should be inspected daily.

Apart from problems with the features of the property, inspections are likely to reveal such negative image builders as abandoned vehicles, graffiti, and incidents of vandalism. These must be dealt with appropriately. Building policies should prohibit residents from working on their cars in the parking lot. Not only does it create a negative image, but automotive oils and solvents damage asphalt paving and create environmental hazards, and cars on jacks pose serious safety hazards. Graffiti should be removed or obliterated immediately (depending on the surface finish, professional cleaning may be required). Taking photographs of the graffiti prior to its removal is advisable. The pictures could prove useful to the police, especially if gangs are involved in such vandalism. Damage resulting from vandalism should be repaired promptly; local authorities should be brought in to discover the source and prosecute the offenders, if necessary.

The Exterior of the Building. The building should be inspected for any structural defects (cracks, leaks, shifts in horizontal or vertical alignments, etc.) as well as to determine the need for cleaning or painting. Examples of what to look for include cracks in walls; loose mortar between bricks or stones; separation from the wall or other damage to gutters and downspouts; any damage to roofs, including flashing and shingles; and the surface condition of finishing materials (paint, composition siding, or applied metal or stone surfaces). Exterior lighting fixtures should be in good working order.

Structural damage usually results from settling, deferred maintenance, or being struck by trees, fallen branches, or other large objects or wind-borne debris. Wood requires special care and fairly frequent painting. If wood has begun to rot, it should be replaced as soon as possible.

Roofs bear the full brunt of the natural elements in general, and extreme temperature fluctuations take a particularly heavy toll. Because of the potential for damage, roofs should be inspected at least semiannually and after heavy storms. This inspection should be done by a qualified independent roofing consultant and include careful examination of the condition of flashing, gravel, shingles, and joints. Even small defects may result in leaks that can cause major damage to the interior of the building. Any air-conditioning (or other) equipment installed on the roof adds to the potential for problems. Also to be noted and addressed are any animal nests or litter on the roof—birds and squirrels are known to build their homes in the eaves of buildings, damaging the roof in the process.

Exterior Maintenance. Regarding the exterior of the building and the surrounding grounds, maintenance tasks will follow directly from the property inspection. Parking facilities require regular sweeping, and surfaces have to be repaired, sealed, and restriped. Specific requirements will depend on the type of parking facility—carport, open space, or enclosed garage. Carports need to be thoroughly inspected for structural damage—the supports are especially susceptible to being hit by vehicles. Speed bumps should be readily visible (reflective paint can be used), and any cracks in the concrete or asphalt should be patched to prevent further damage. Light bulbs must be replaced periodically to assure optimum illumination.

The grounds should be well-tended during the growing season. Gardens or flower beds will look much better if they are free of weeds, and the lawn should be mowed on a regular basis. Shrubbery not only looks better when it is pruned regularly, but actually thrives when dead or dying branches are removed. Trees and shrubs can be damaged by too little or too much water, lawn care chemicals (fertilizers, pesticides) applied incorrectly, and repeated freeze-thaw cycles in winter.

While hoses and sprinklers are generally satisfactory for watering restricted areas, a built-in sprinkling system may be a better choice for larger areas or year-round watering. The advantages of a built-in system are that maintenance technicians do not have to tend hoses and sprinklers. Also, watering can be done at night, although this may contribute to root rot when temperatures are cooler.

Whatever the type of watering system, a key question will be how much—how often—to water lawns and shrubbery. Frequency of watering will depend on the needs of grass and particular plants, the season, and the climate. Local ordinances may restrict watering, so this aspect should not be overlooked. Your local gardening store or nursery can recommend fertilizer types (liquid versus granular), amounts, and timing of applications. Otherwise, agricultural extension service personnel (affiliated with state universities) and books on horticulture can help you determine the best way to care for plants and lawns.

Ideally, the layout of your landscaping will facilitate cutting with a tractor and trimming with a mower. Grass should be cut once a week during early spring, then every 10–14 days in late spring, summer, and fall, depending on the local climate. In some places, lawns should be cut weekly regardless. Areas along sidewalks and around buildings and trees should be edged and trimmed regularly—a detail that improves the property's appearance in general. Good lawn care also minimizes weed growth; when a herbicide must be used, choose one that will kill the kinds of weeds in your lawn. (Often fertilizers and weed killers can be combined and applied simultaneously.) Proper care of trees includes pruning, spraying to prevent diseases, and mulching.

When there is an expansive lawn, it may be possible to establish a play area for residents' children. This opportunity also comes with some caution. Play equipment must be checked periodically to assure that it is firmly anchored and there are no loose parts. There should be no sharp edges, which are potential hazards. Some equipment may need preventive maintenance in the form of oiling or painting. Play areas need regular cleaning—the area should be kept free of broken glass, sharp sticks, and other items that might injure children. Installation of sandboxes should be considered carefully because they tend to become large "litter boxes" for cats. Surrounding the play area with a fence is a good precaution, especially if it is near the street. The fence should be inspected regularly for holes or missing sections that children could pass through. In general, it is prudent to contact your insurance agent or risk management consultant for guidelines on minimizing liability in the play area.

The exterior of the building also requires specific maintenance. Wall surfaces, lights, and signs should be kept clean. Burned-out bulbs should be replaced as soon as they are discovered—long-life energy-efficient bulbs will reduce maintenance work and lighting costs. Occasional touch-up painting may also be necessary; metallic and stone finishes require professional cleaning.

Depending on climate and construction materials, more extensive maintenance may be needed to prevent deterioration or restore damaged areas of building exteriors. Cycles of freezing and thawing, settling of the building, and vibration (trucks on the roadway, nearby railroad tracks) cause cracks in the mortar of masonry structures. Because of this, the mortar must be replaced periodically (a procedure called tuck-pointing) to prevent further degradation and structural damage. Wood surfaces (e.g., doors and doorframes) are also subject to cracking and decay; areas with blistered or peeled paint should be sanded before repainting.

Inspection of building foundations may reveal cracks, water penetration, or settling of the building. To prevent further deterioration, these types of problems should be corrected as soon as they are discovered. Depending on the severity, consultation with a structural engineer may be necessary or appropriate. However, relatively minor problems may be correctable by rearranging a sprinkling system or applying a sealant to foundation walls to retard seepage.

Some areas need mostly custodial maintenance. The frequency of cleaning will be dictated by the location (i.e., visibility) and volume of traffic in the area. Windows on the ground floor of a building will be cleaned more often than those above ground. Upper-story windows may be cleaned only twice a year because of the difficulty and expense. (Often this is done by professional window washers.) Windows and glass doors in the lobby or entryway may have to be cleaned several times a day.

Windows often have moving parts, which have to be maintained. Older buildings may have double-hung windows with rope (sash cord) and counterweight systems. Over time, the sash cords fray or break and the weights may become detached, and screens may become broken, torn, or bent. These types of repairs become repetitious, but they can ordinarily be completed on site by a maintenance technician. There may be separate storm windows and screens that must be installed and removed seasonally; in more modern buildings, they may only have to be shifted up or down in their respective tracks. Modern, doubled-paned windows—installed as replacements—are far more energy efficient in all seasons and require less maintenance. In some buildings, windows may have crank mechanisms for opening and closing, or they may slide horizontally in parallel tracks; these should require less maintenance in general.

Aside from routine cleaning and maintenance of these building components, the most common problem is cracked or broken windows. For the sake of both security and safety, broken windows and window locks should be repaired as soon as they are discovered.

Landlords can be held liable for injuries or losses suffered by residents because intruders were able to gain access through broken windows, doors, or locks.

The Interior of the Building. The entrances, lobby and common areas, recreational facilities, stairwells and public corridors, elevators, and security systems require daily inspection. Damage to floor and wall coverings, inadequate lighting, and litter will be among the most obvious problems. You should also look for evidence of vandalism (broken door locks) or signs of infestation by insects, rodents, or other creatures (nests, droppings, chew marks).

Interior walls require frequent inspection. Handprints and smudges can usually be washed off. However, cracks in the plaster and chips and nicks in the paint are common occurrences. Frequent repainting can be precluded by finishing interior walls with washable paint or wall coverings. Nicks, especially on corners, will require patching as well as touch-up painting. It is a good idea to have a supply of matching paint on hand for this purpose. The paint manufacturer, number, and color should be kept on file in case you need to order more. (All paint used on site must be lead free. See the discussion of hazardous materials later in this chapter.)

Common areas such as the lobby and corridors require daily attention. Because these areas are the showcase of the apartment community, they need special care to look their very best at all times. Floors should be damp-mopped daily and scrubbed and waxed on a regular schedule. Runners or mats may be laid down to protect floor surfaces and prevent slip-and-fall accidents. Depending on the type of material, these may require minimal maintenance or frequent repair.

Carpeting should be vacuumed every day. Areas of heavy soil (due to weather or spills) can be spot cleaned as needed. Regular shampooing is a must to keep carpets fresh and prevent damage to the fibers. At a large property, it may be more economical to purchase cleaning equipment and chemicals and have site personnel do the work. However, carpet cleaning is another service that is frequently contracted.

The mail box area will require daily attention to prevent accumulation of discarded "junk" mail. There should be a separate mailbox for each unit identified with the resident's name and apartment number. (Security issues related to mailboxes and building directories will be discussed in chapter 9.) A rack may be used for holding magazines, books, and packages that are too large for the mailboxes. Alternatively, a table or shelves might be provided. A drawback of leaving packages in the open, however, is the possibility of theft. At some properties, a staff member will accept packages and notify residents to collect them. This additional service is one residents will appreciate. The U.S. postal service may recommend installation of a locked box for bulky mail and packages—the resident is left a key for access to the lockbox; after retrieving his or her mail, the lockbox key is left behind.

Mechanical Systems. Periodic inspections of mechanical areas—condition and operation of equipment—are a mandatory component of preventive maintenance. Dirty systems account for a large percentage of mechanical problems (decreased efficiency) and equipment failures. Boiler rooms, elevator pits, and any other place where mechanical equipment is located should be kept clean and free of debris because of the potential fire hazard. (Proper fire extinguishing equipment should be in place and operational; this should be verified as part of regular inspections.) Cleanliness and neatness also reduce the likelihood of someone being injured. In particular, furnaces should be inspected thoroughly because repairs are costly and breakdowns inconvenience residents. Elevators are required to be inspected and certified by local authorities—in addition to any inspections by site personnel.

Regular inspections of storage areas should be a part of the overall maintenance program as well. Tools and supplies should be stored in an orderly fashion (organized and clearly marked) once they have been entered in the parts and equipment inventory. Inspections of storage rooms should include the lighting in work areas, and the inventory record should be checked against the actual stock of parts and supplies. Potential hazards (sharp objects, obstacles) should be eliminated.

In the interest of fire safety, all fire-related equipment and systems should be inspected regularly and tested as appropriate. Sprinkler systems, panic bars, fire extinguishers, and fire and smoke alarms must be operational at all times. Specific components require special attention:

- Fire extinguishers have to be recharged periodically, usually twice a year.

- Fire hoses are subject to mildew and rot, which weaken their walls and could cause them to break in the event of a fire.
- Hoses and their plumbing connections have to be checked.
- Fire doors must not be propped open; keeping them closed prevents fire from spreading.
- Fire lanes must be well-marked and kept clear at all times (no parking).
- Evacuation routes must be clearly marked with appropriate signage.

State and local authorities regulate fire safety standards, and information on specific requirements is available from local fire departments (see also chapter 9).

Maintenance of Mechanical Equipment. Air conditioners, boilers, water heaters, elevators, and any electrical equipment on the property may require specialized service to assure efficient operation of equipment and make repairs when they are needed. While it may be profitable to train site personnel to care for these types of equipment, maintenance of some mechanical equipment requires special tools, specific training and certification, or both. This is true of elevators and HVAC equipment.

Because elevator maintenance requires specific training and specialized tools, this work should only be done by a certified contractor who can keep elevators operating at peak efficiency and time them to handle the volume of traffic in the building. (This may be necessary under the manufacturer's warranty.) However, the on-site staff can complete some elevator maintenance. Lights, fans, and the emergency telephone system must be routinely inspected. In addition, elevator cars must be kept free from litter, dirt, and graffiti.

Maintenance of HVAC systems also requires specialized training. Although most routine preventive maintenance tasks may be performed by site personnel—e.g., cleaning or replacing filters, checking circuit breakers and thermostats, lubricating moving parts in a pulley system, monitoring thermostat settings—repairs and other HVAC maintenance can be contracted to certified HVAC technicians. Regulation and programming of the equipment and seasonal start-up and shutdown are usually included in the contracted work unless the size of the property (or the management company's portfolio) justifies employing an HVAC technician.

Work on electrical wiring may have to be approved or performed by a licensed electrician, but minor electrical repairs (e.g., replacing switches and outlets) can usually be done by properly trained site personnel. Site personnel should also know the telephone number of the local utility company and where transformers and switchboxes are located, including the location of the main shutoff switch, and circumstances for shutting down the building's electrical supply.

Plumbing is another area where site personnel can perform many tasks on their own. They should be able to inspect plumbing, clear drains, and replace washers, but a licensed plumber should perform any major repairs or replacements. All maintenance employees should know the location of the main water shutoff valve and when it should be used.

Unlike plumbing or simple electrical work, any work on gas lines should be done by utility company personnel. Leaking gas should be a checklist item for inspections, but if a leak is discovered, the appropriate action is to initiate the prescribed emergency procedure and notify the utility of the problem.

In addition to inspections, regularly scheduled maintenance, and planning by the staff, the importance of resident involvement should not be underestimated. If residents know the location of circuit breakers, they can check them before calling in a maintenance request. A monthly newsletter is a good way to educate residents about simple maintenance tips and energy-saving measures—i.e., things they can do themselves.

Maintenance of Facilities and Amenities. Staff should be trained in the care of any equipment or facilities located in the property's recreational areas. This might include ping-pong or pool tables and accessories or chairs and tables for arts and crafts. Perhaps the most common recreational facility is a *swimming pool.* Swimming pools are time consuming from a maintenance perspective because they require continual maintenance during the months they are in use and may need more extensive care at start-up and closure. Routine pool maintenance includes keeping the pool area clean and attractive. State and local public health laws usually require periodic testing of water quality and monitoring of chlorine levels (or other treatment chemicals). Pool cleaning and maintenance can be contracted or performed by management company staff. This involves regular inspections of the pool area and related fixtures and furnishings and

Maintenance Tasks Site Personnel Can Perform

Plumbing—Licensed plumbers must perform more involved tasks such as replacing an entire water-supply system or working on lines in walls, headers, and between the building and the city service. However, on-site personnel can replace stems and seals in faucets; replace handles and accessories in kitchens and bathrooms; inspect, clean, and replace sink traps and seals; replace all parts of the water closet, including the wax seal at the base. In addition, site personnel can rod out clogged lines within apartment units.

Electrical—Connections to main lines and other types of work on electrical systems usually have to be performed (or inspected) by a licensed electrician. However, properly trained on-site maintenance technicians can replace electrical switches, outlets, and light fixtures.

Heating, Ventilating, and Air Conditioning—While on-site technicians are not responsible for repairs to sealed systems, they can inspect and change filters, replace thermostats, and diagnose problems in the system.

Pool maintenance—State and local laws may require maintenance by certified personnel; however, on-site maintenance personnel can check pump pressure and pH and chlorine levels as well as inspect and clean the area around the pool.

Elevators—Elevator maintenance and repairs require specialized training, and this equipment is usually serviced by licensed contractors. However, site personnel can monitor the water level in elevator pits (this is very important because many locales require excess water to be removed). The U.S. Environmental Protection Agency (EPA) specifies techniques for removal and disposal of such water, and usually this is done by automatic pumps. However, if the pump fails, it must be repaired or replaced promptly. In addition, on-site maintenance technicians are responsible for monitoring ventilation of elevator areas.

collecting water samples for testing. Jacuzzis or saunas are similarly challenging.

General maintenance of the area around the pool, which includes cleaning of tile surfaces, ladders, diving boards, and slides, can be performed by site personnel. The deck around the pool should be hosed down frequently to keep dirt from entering the pool and damaging the filtration equipment. If the pool volume is not maintained automatically, water must be added occasionally to replace what is lost by evaporation and splashing. Locker rooms and showers will also have to be cleaned and disinfected frequently. During the off season or when the pool is out of service, pool furnishings (lounges, tables, umbrellas) should be stored in a secure place. Enforcement of pool rules will facilitate maintenance, minimize problems, and assure residents' continued enjoyment of the pool.

Laundry rooms should be kept bright and clean. Because they are heavy traffic areas, daily or more frequent inspections and cleaning will probably be necessary. This should include emptying of dryer filters, thorough sweeping to remove lint and other debris, wiping or washing the outsides of machines, and emptying waste receptacles. Sinks should also be cleaned.

As long as the equipment is in good working order, residents take laundry facilities for granted; however, when equipment breaks down, residents can get quite upset. Broken washers and dryers should be repaired as soon as possible. Until the work is done, a sign should be posted identifying which machine is out of order. To minimize the inconvenience, residents should be encouraged to notify the site office as soon as they discover a machine out of order. Because of the potential damage to the property, any sign of leaks or flooding from laundry equipment should be investigated immediately.

Servicing of washing machines and dryers is typically contracted out, whether the equipment is purchased outright or leased by the property owner. Often the equipment is owned by a concessionaire whose contractual arrangements include responsibility for servicing and repairs as well as payment of a percentage of the collection income to the management company (as miscellaneous income to the property). Apart from litter and equipment breakdowns, laundry room security is a major issue (coin box breakins) and should be checked as part of the inspection procedure.

Individual Apartments. Inspection of the interior of the building should include the individual apartments, but this is not always practical when a unit is occupied. (Vacant units will be inspected repeatedly as part of the turnover process.) The need for periodic inspections of occupied units should be stated in the residents' handbook and the lease. These are opportunities to note the condition of each apartment and its installed equipment and to determine the need for specific repairs and replacement. Some types of work may be required under manufacturers' warranties or established service contracts. Your observations may also suggest a need for a visit by an exterminator. Inspections of occupied units will also help you to determine whether a lease should be renewed—you may have second thoughts about renewing the leases of residents who have damaged their units, are poor housekeepers, or keep unauthorized pets.

Residents should always be given advance notice of such inspections. This is more than a mere courtesy; the lease requires it as part of the landlord's right of access, and landlord-tenant law may state a specific procedure and minimum period of advance notice. (The respective rights and responsibilities of landlords and residents are discussed in detail in chapter 10.) Unit inspections are especially important because residents may be unaware of potential problems or fail to request needed repairs until a problem has become burdensome. Examples include leaking faucets and constantly "running" toilets, which increase water consumption and utility costs.

Maintenance inside individual units is generally done in response to service requests from residents. Otherwise, such work will depend on scheduled inspections once or twice a year. During a service call, a maintenance technician may discover a different problem and fix it then or arrange with the resident to do the work later. Taking a few extra minutes during the service call may mean finding out about additional problems, but this can save hours in the long run. Because the results benefit everyone, maintenance personnel should be encouraged to look out for conditions requiring maintenance and repairs while they are visiting residents' apartments. Whatever the situation, the additional work should be recorded in the maintenance log.

A preventive maintenance program for unit interiors is beneficial to everyone involved. Periodic replacement of washers and valve seats in faucets will prevent leaks from developing. Caulking around sinks and tubs needs to be replaced periodically, not only to improve the physical appearance of kitchens and bathrooms, but to prevent seepage that can damage walls and floors. If individual apartments have their own heating or air conditioning units, residents must be educated to clean or change filters periodically, or on-site staff should do this for all units monthly, semiannually, or annually (depending on local conditions). Clean filters are necessary for maximum efficiency, and not doing this could jeopardize or invalidate a manufacturer's warranty. Residents may need to be reminded to change filters in in-unit air conditioners and furnaces, in which case it will probably be advisable to stock appropriate filters and distribute them to residents. Alternatively, having staff attend to this not only ensures that it is done, but also provides an opportunity to monitor residents' care of the equipment. It also demonstrates that management is conscientious, which generates good will on the part of residents.

The best preventive maintenance is to instruct residents in the proper use and care of all the appliances in their apartments—this should be part of new resident orientation. The manufacturers' instructions can be left in the unit, or you can use them to create your own instruction booklet. If instruction manuals are difficult to follow, a few tips or pointers as part of the residents' handbook may be an appropriate alternative.

Other Considerations

Though they are frequently overlooked, energy conservation and recycling are also components of maintenance. These activities not only help to conserve natural resources, but also contribute to the economic well-being of the property and to civic responsibility. Because hazardous materials may be components of buildings or other mechanical systems, they are also a maintenance consideration.

Energy Conservation. *Energy conservation* can be as simple as cleaning dirty light fixtures and caulking around windows to better retain heat. Replacing inefficient fixtures can lower costs by five to ten percent (a 34-watt fluorescent bulb uses less electricity than a 40-watt incandescent bulb and produces virtually the same amount of light). While such a substitution has a high initial cost, the investment will be recovered quickly because fluorescent bulbs last ten times longer than incandescent bulbs and use only one quarter the electricity. Installation of inexpensive weatherstripping around doors and windows can result in substantial energy savings over the course of a year. When in-unit appliances have to be replaced, more energy-efficient models should be selected.

Waste Disposal and Recycling. In many areas of the United States, *recycling*—the collection and reuse of waste materials in the manufacture of new products—is mandatory. This means residents

Examples of No-Cost/Low-Cost Measures to Conserve Energy and Reduce Operating Costs

General Considerations

- Collect energy consumption information from the utility companies (water, gas, and electric included) and review usage bills. Note changes in consumption that are not related to weather conditions. Investigate to determine if there is a leak or other problem in the equipment or in the building.
- Evaluate options such as new technologies and compare fuel consumption levels, especially when equipment replacement or repair is required.
- Before replacing appliances, investigate comparative efficiency ratings (in consumer buying guides) and select items that use less electricity.

Specific Actions

- During property inspections, look for broken windows, cracked weather stripping, loose caulking, or open windows in areas that are heated or air-conditioned. Replace broken or damaged windows, weather stripping, and caulking.
- Insulate water heaters and exposed pipes.
- Replace HVAC filters regularly.
- Lower the temperature setting on thermostats in the winter; set thermostats higher in the summer.
- Replace high-wattage bulbs with lower-wattage fluorescent or energy-saving bulbs whenever possible. (Fixtures with opaque glass appear brighter if nonfrosted bulbs are used.)
- Consider replacing fixtures to use more energy-efficient bulbs (halogen, sodium vapor), particularly for exterior lighting.
- Clean fixtures and bulbs regularly.
- Turn off lights when they are not needed (e.g, in supply rooms that are entered infrequently), but be careful not to reduce illumination where it is needed for security.
- Consider replacing standard light switches with timed-dial switches for some interior areas.
- Control exterior lighting with timers or photoelectric cells, but remember that periodic adjustments will be necessary to accommodate seasonal changes.
- Use "task lighting" in workspaces rather than illuminate an entire area.
- To minimize wasted water, install flow-control devices in shower heads; fix leaking faucets and other plumbing fixtures; when toilets are being replaced, install water-saver models.
- Design or redesign landscaping to require only minimal watering. Match plantings with the climate and natural vegetation, and use mulches to retain water. Monitor watering methodology for waste, and set hoses to avoid runoff. Monitor sprinkler systems for proper timing and leaks.

No-Cost/Low-Cost Measures (*continued*)

Ways Residents Can Conserve Energy and Save Money
- Keep refrigerators full.
- Use lower-wattage light bulbs.
- Turn off lights when rooms are not being used.
- If heat or air conditioning is individually controlled, adjust thermostat settings when occupants are away.
- Arrange furniture and drapes so they do not obstruct vents, radiators, or baseboard heaters.

must be taught how to dispose of their garbage and what to do with recyclable materials. The trash pickup schedule and bagging requirements should be included in the resident handbook and orientation, along with instructions for separating recyclable materials. (Different colored bins for different types of recyclables will help residents sort materials.) This information can be reiterated in resident newsletters.

Depending on local facilities and practices, recyclable materials may be collected by your waste disposal contractor. Usually such arrangements require separation of specific categories of materials: newsprint, other paper stocks, ferrous and nonferrous metals (i.e., iron or steel from aluminum), plastics (by type), glass (by color). Because these materials are reused in manufacturing processes, and therefore have a market value, it may be worthwhile to explore separate arrangements for collection—and sale—of recyclables. The most advantageous arrangement is one in which the property derives income from the sale of recyclable materials, but this requires a large volume of recyclables and, therefore, a large amount of storage space.

To minimize spillage and prevent indiscriminate dumping, there should be a number of trash receptacles placed in convenient locations, including the laundry room. All such receptacles should be cleaned and deodorized regularly to eliminate unpleasant odors, prevent infestation by vermin, and reduce health risks. (The large dumpsters provided by the disposal service should be reasonably clean and odor-free when they are left by the vendor.) Any spillage should be picked up on a regular basis to eliminate the unsightly and unsanitary spread of rubbish by the wind.

A recycling program offers several benefits. Recycling reduces the trash disposed at landfills and thus has a positive effect on the environ-

Developing a Recycling Program

Preliminary Considerations

- What types of materials are acceptable?
- What kinds of services are offered?
- How much material (minimum weight or volume) is required for pick up?
- How often are recyclables picked up?
- Are collection containers provided?
- Where will recycling containers be placed?
- Is separation of recyclables required?
- What financial arrangements are possible (income from sale of recyclables versus payment for their removal)?
- What contractual arrangements are offered?

Planning Steps

- Contact several reputable waste haulers or recyclers in your area.
- Ask them for information and cost (or payment) estimates.
- Identify the types of waste generated on site.
- Ask employees and residents to separate recyclables from other waste.
- Decide how materials will be collected and stored.
- Educate employees and residents about recycling procedures.
- Publicize the project and encourage maximum participation.

ment. In some areas, waste disposal costs may be reduced because of the lower volume of trash. Note, however, that removal of recyclables by a waste handler may increase waste disposal costs because of the need for extra collection containers and additional trips.

Despite their benefits, extra effort is needed to establish recycling programs in rental communities. Separation of recyclables is a learned habit, and the process can be inconvenient for participants. Mandatory recycling is already in place in many areas, however, and continued movement in this direction appears certain. In general, the more convenient the program, the greater the participation. The keys to success are ease of collection and timeliness of removal along with reminders to participants that reinforce positive behaviors and make it as simple as possible for residents (and employees) to recycle wastes.

The goals of a recycling program and the means of achieving them may be established by the management company and the property owner, but specific implementation will be the domain of the site manager. Primary considerations will be the need to separate recyclables by type, the volume of materials likely to accumulate, and the location of collection containers. Specific costs must be evaluated as well as potential savings (purchase or rental of containers, compactors, or other equipment compared to reductions in disposal costs based on a smaller volume of waste).

Educating residents about the recycling program is a key responsibility of the site manager. Scheduling meetings with residents to discuss recycling programs will not only increase their awareness, but also provide opportunities to answer their questions. In large residential developments, centralized collection is most efficient, although this may pose logistical problems where residents are used to more convenient disposal procedures. Residents should be required to separate their recyclables by type—e.g., glass, paper, plastic. Depending on the size of the community, residents may be asked to take their separated wastes to appropriate receptacles or set them out for pick up by property maintenance personnel or waste disposal employees. The following are guidelines for separating recyclables.

- *Glass*—separate by color (green, brown, clear).
- *Aluminum*—soda cans may have to be crushed. Foil, pie plates, and other aluminum materials may or may not be included.
- *Plastics*—sort by type: PET (soda bottles made of polyethylene terephthalate) have a number 1 inside the recycling logo; HDPE (milk jugs and detergent bottles made of high-density polyethylene) have a number 2. Some recyclers accept only one of these, and other types of plastic may or may not be accepted.
- *Newspapers*—usually newspaper only (no inserts, magazines, or "slick" advertisements). The agency you select may do this separating for you.
- *High-grade paper*—computer paper, stationary, and other office papers.

Packaging materials are primary collection targets. While paper labels usually can remain in place, metal and plastic caps must be removed, and all containers must be free of food stuffs, which breed vermin. Because waste handlers may pick up trash and recyclables separately, unsightly overflow may be less of a problem than with ordinary trash service, even if pick ups are less frequent.

Hazardous Materials. The site manager should be aware of the presence of hazardous materials and know how to deal with them. Not only can some materials be dangerous to residents and site employees, but their mere presence can lower property values—even when there is no immediate danger.

Liability for hazardous materials is considerable and always of concern to real estate managers. In residential buildings, the primary concerns are asbestos, polychlorinated biphenyls (PCBs), chlorofluorocarbons (CFCs), lead-based paint, formaldehyde gas, and radon gas.

- *Asbestos* was once used widely in construction for insulation and fireproofing. It is a problem only when it is *friable* (crumbling into small particles or fibers); airborne asbestos fibers can cause asbestosis or lung cancer. The presence of asbestos-containing materials can be remedied either by *abatement* (removal) or *containment.* Either procedure should be done only by an appropriately licensed contractor.
- *Polychlorinated biphenyls (PCBs),* used as heat transfer agents in electrical transformers, are essentially harmless if undisturbed. However, if a transformer leaks, burns, or explodes, lethal dioxin gas may be released. Leaking transformers must be disposed in licensed locations by authorized waste handlers. Property owners are liable for any PCB contamination even after a leaking transformer has been removed. (Transformers may be owned by the electrical utility, which is responsible for their maintenance.)
- *Chlorofluorocarbons (CFCs)* are used as refrigerants in air conditioners, refrigerators, and freezers, where they remain in liquid form in enclosed systems. (They are readily vaporized to gaseous form in the environment, however.) As a result of international environmental agreements, CFC production is to be cut in half by 1995 and completely eliminated by the year 2000, and substitutes are already available. (This is being done because CFCs have been implicated in global warming and ozone depletion.)
- *Lead-based paint,* once commonly used, was banned in 1978. However, older structures may still contain some. Lead is especially hazardous to children who may accidentally ingest it. Because it is most dangerous in flake or dust form, containment is

> **Key Actions Related to Maintenance in Site Management**
>
> **Primary Functions**
> - Implement maintenance plan and maintenance standards
> - Make sure service requests receive timely, effective responses
> - Keep records of maintenance performed
> - Inspect the property and recommend maintenance actions
> - Supervise maintenance personnel
> - Oversee energy conservation and recycling efforts
>
> **Adjunct Functions**
> - Contribute to decisions on maintenance standards
> - Assist property manager in developing maintenance budget
> - Work with property manager in soliciting bids for contract work
> - Oversee work by independent contractors

often the best solution. This should be performed by specialists trained in lead abatement and containment. (Beginning in 1995, all owners of buildings constructed before 1978 will have to notify new renters about the presence of lead-based paint.)

- *Formaldehyde gas* may be emitted by foam insulation and pressed wood products (particle board). Although the gas will eventually dissipate, increased ventilation or removal of formaldehyde-containing material may be necessary.
- *Radon,* a colorless and odorless gas that occurs naturally as a by-product of the radioactive decay of radium and uranium, tends to collect in the lower levels of energy-efficient buildings (insulation limits the flow of air from inside to outside). This is a greater problem in buildings with slab foundations than those with basements. Contractors deal with radon by either sealing foundations or installing fans to ventilate the building.

Another potential problem is contamination of groundwater due to leakage from underground fuel tanks. Leaking underground storage tanks (LUSTs) have spurred regulations that require inspection and testing of tanks still in use and repair or replacement of those that are leaking. Tanks that are no longer used may remain in place if filled with an inert material; otherwise they must be removed. The regional office of the U.S. Environmental Protection Agency (EPA) should be contacted regarding procedures for dealing with these types of environmental concerns if there is a tank on a property you manage. State and local environmental laws may be more stringent than the federal regulations, in which case the former will prevail.

SUMMARY

Maintenance is perhaps the most important component of real estate management. Without a well-organized and carefully executed maintenance plan, the physical integrity of the property will suffer, operating costs will rise, residents will complain, and leases will not be renewed. As a result, the owner's return on the investment will decline, reducing the property value.

Maintenance takes several forms: preventive, corrective, routine, emergency, and cosmetic. Deferred maintenance may be symptomatic of other problems. As site manager, you are responsible for planning when and how to implement the maintenance plan developed at the direction of the property manager to meet the maintenance needs of the property.

Implementation of the maintenance plan requires competent planning and administration—bringing together people, time, money, and materials; investigating alternative approaches; establishing service policies, scheduling work appropriately, and communicating with residents and staff.

Specific maintenance tasks follow from inspections of the exterior and interior of the building, the facilities and amenities at the property, the mechanical equipment in place, and the interiors of individual apartments. Meeting the challenges of maintaining each of these areas requires knowledge and judgment and making decisions about how best to meet management goals. As a site manager, you should have a broad understanding of the importance of maintenance and its impact on prospective and current residents and effect on the job satisfaction of site employees. There is also the need to comply with building codes and other local requirements regarding equipment.

Finally, it is important that you recognize the impact of economic demands and governmental regulations regarding energy conservation and waste disposal and recycling, which are also part of the maintenance of a residential property.

Key Terms

corrective maintenance
cosmetic maintenance
emergency maintenance
maintenance log
routine maintenance
service request
work order

Key Concepts

contract workers
deferred maintenance
energy conservation
maintenance plan
preventive maintenance
property inspection
recycling

Key Points

- What is the relationship between maintenance and prospective renters and current residents?
- Why is preventive maintenance so important to effective real estate management?
- What is deferred maintenance? Why does it exist?
- What are the advantages and disadvantages of using outside service contractors for maintenance tasks?
- What role does property inspection play in the development of a maintenance plan?
- Why are energy conservation and recycling important?
- What kinds of hazardous materials are likely to be found at a residential property and why are they problematic?

9

Risk Management

Risk exists in many areas of residential real estate management. It can take the form of a safety risk (worn stair treads that create a slip and fall hazard), a security risk (a broken door lock), an emergency risk (fire or flood), or a liability risk (a management error such as wrongful eviction that raises the possibility of litigation). Because of this, one of the most important components of real estate management is the management of risk. Risk itself is uncertainty, and risk management is an effort to deal with the many uncertainties that exist at a property by understanding their nature and likelihood of occurring. Before you can address different types of risk and their management, it is important to understand the general notion of liability.

LIABILITY ISSUES IN RESIDENTIAL MANAGEMENT

The concept of *liability* (the legal obligation to do—or refrain from doing—something) is very important to an understanding of risk management. In the past under common law, a landlord was not liable to tenants who were injured on leased premises. The doctrine of *ca-*

veat emptor (let the buyer beware) did not hold the landlord responsible for the care of the tenant or anyone else on the premises. At the same time, landlords did not have the right to enter the leased premises—or the obligation to make repairs to it—during the lease term.

Under modern law, however, the landlord is not immune from liability. In fact, the potential for liability as it applies to apartment owners and managers has grown tremendously in recent years. Many liability lawsuits are based on a resident's claim that the landlord (the property owner or manager) failed to take sufficient precautions in regard to security or safety (e.g., burglary in an apartment, a fall in the common area). The explosion of litigation has also been fueled by some residents' belief that property owners and management companies have virtually unlimited financial resources (the "deep pockets" theory).

Owners and managers can defend themselves by showing that they have made a "reasonable" effort to provide a safe and secure environment for residents. *Reasonable care* is a product of several factors. These include determining whether the harm could have been foreseen, whether there is a connection between the injury and the landlord's actions (or inaction) and the seriousness of the landlord's conduct, whether there is a policy of preventing future harm, how substantial the burden is on the landlord, and the availability and cost of insurance for the risk.

Liability is not borne solely by the landlord, however. In some states, the principal of *contributory negligence* applies to questions of liability. This places a certain amount of responsibility on the resident. For example, the landlord's liability may be ameliorated if a resident who fell down a flight of stairs was found to have been intoxicated at the time of the accident, even if a step was defective when the accident occurred. This is based on the notion that the resident bears partial responsibility for his or her actions. In such cases, a court will assign only a percentage of the responsibility—and costs—to the landlord.

In tort cases involving landlord liability for injury or damage occurring at a property, it is the tenant's (plaintiff's) responsibility to prove duty, breach, foreseeability, and the link between the landlord's (defendant's) actions or inaction and the injury. However, this does not make the landlord any less responsible for exercising reasonable care to prevent foreseeable injuries when he or she knows or should know about dangers at the property (or in the neighborhood).

In determining what constitutes a "reasonable" effort, the *degree of risk* must be considered. Greater risks call for more precautions. For example, the level of security that is reasonable will differ from one neighborhood to another, depending on their relative crime rates. The reasonableness of efforts is also a factor of urgency. If a stair tread is damaged, its repair would take priority over repairing a malfunctioning dishwasher. This is so because the stair tread creates a safety risk while, at worst, the unavailability of a kitchen appliance will be an inconvenience—it poses no particular "risk."

In evaluating risks and liability, the standard of reasonable care also reflects what is provided by other, similar buildings in your neighborhood. If all apartment properties in your neighborhood provide 24-hour guards, then guards would probably be considered part of the accepted "ordinary" (reasonable) care provided in your neighborhood.

Because of the possibility of severe financial penalties for failing to make reasonable efforts, a careful review of your property's operating manuals, policies and procedures, and emergency manuals is necessary. In litigation, a plaintiff's attorney will seek to demonstrate either that existing policies and procedures were inadequate or that the defendant failed to follow those that are in place. Therefore, establishing comprehensive policies and following them carefully is essential.

TYPES OF RISKS—PEOPLE AND PROPERTY

There are many types of risks. Whether the issue is safety, security, emergency, or liability, the job of the site manager is to assist in gathering the information needed to determine whether the risk of property damage, personal injury, or liability exceeds the benefit associated with retaining the risk-producing condition; this is done through the inspection and reporting process. The property manager, together with the property owner, determines whether liability exceeds risk. In some cases, this is rather simple. A broken stair rail offers no benefits and, in fact, constitutes a serious hazard. It should be repaired or replaced immediately as a matter of basic maintenance. Assessing the risk related to a swimming pool, however, is not quite so straightforward. Indeed, a pool poses certain hazards, including death by drowning or injury from falling, but these risks must be considered in light of the benefits a pool offers, including its attractiveness to prospects and its enjoyment by existing residents. In residential site management, risk takes several basic forms:

- Safety risk—wet or newly waxed floors are slippery surfaces.
- Security risk—a door that does not lock or cannot be closed completely provides access for intruders.
- Emergency risk—fires and weather hazards cause property damage and injure or kill people. (Emergencies can be man-made or natural.)
- Liability risk—discriminatory leasing or hiring policies and practices create the potential for lawsuits.

Each of these types of risk will be discussed in turn.

Safety Risks

A key component of risk management is the implementation of safety programs. A safety program's specific goals should include injury prevention, damage control, compliance with applicable laws and regulations, and liability reduction. For these goals to be achieved, safety programs must not only take into account many potential situations, but also include comprehensive efforts to educate employees and residents about their own responsibilities. This should include steps they can take to minimize exposure to risks. As site manager, your efforts are especially important. Involvement in activities such as community watch programs and cooperation with local authorities can help make the property—and the neighborhood—a safer place.

Of all approaches to risk management, prevention is the most effective way to reduce safety risks. Although risks cannot be eliminated altogether, they can be controlled, within limits. Because of this, prevention should be a central theme in any employee or resident education program. Before a risk can be reduced, it must be acknowledged, and this is the purpose of education. Simply following directions, using safety equipment, not taking shortcuts, and reporting problems as soon as they become evident are virtually cost-free ways of reducing risk.

While brochures and other educational materials can be developed at the management company or by the site manager, there is no substitute for widely available materials produced by agencies and authorities within a community. For example, local fire departments usually have booklets designed specifically for apartment residents. These should be reviewed with new residents during their orientation. (Resident orientation is discussed in chapter 7.)

Resident materials should cover safe housekeeping and storage of cleaning supplies, emergency procedures, and the locations of fire extinguishers and emergency utility shutoffs. A diagram of the property that shows the locations of emergency exits should also be included. A page listing regular and emergency telephone numbers for police and fire departments, hospitals, poison control centers, and utilities, as well as the site office and the management company—including a 24-hour telephone number for emergency maintenance and repairs—should also be part of the package. These kinds of information should be part of the residents' handbook when one is used.

Programs involving professional speakers (police officers or representatives of community groups) are also beneficial because they can provide residents with timely information about personal safety and loss prevention. Often these types of programs can be tailored to meet your residents' specific needs and supplemented by including information about safety programs in a resident newsletter.

Other basic measures include posting "No Parking" signs in fire lanes as well as "Slow" or "Caution" signs in pedestrian walkways or areas where children play. (Playgrounds need specific attention as outlined in the accompanying box.) "Speed limit" signs should be installed on the property, too; a 5 or 10 mile-per-hour speed limit is customary for driveways and parking lots.

Regular inspections of the property should be a central part of any safety program. As a part of the regular maintenance inspection process, you should make sure that proper fire extinguishing equipment is installed and in good working order (e.g., sprinkler system, fire extinguishers, fire hoses). In most places, maintenance of fire equipment is regulated by the municipality. Inspection and servicing of this equipment must be performed by licensed professionals at specific intervals, and the inspection dates are noted on attached tags. Emergency lighting and generating equipment should also be kept in good working order. In all cases, the property should be in compliance with federal, state, and local safety requirements regarding installation of smoke detectors, placement of fire extinguishing equipment, enclosure of swimming pools, etc.

Tips for Making Playgrounds Safer

- Situate playgrounds away from vehicular traffic.
- Enclose the area with a fence.
- Use shock-absorbing surfaces.
- Install equipment properly.
- Make sure installed equipment is safe.
- Keep the entire area free of debris.
- Maintain the playground and equipment.
- Require parents to supervise their children.
- Make sure the property's insurance coverage is adequate.

The workplace also raises certain safety concerns, and there are several steps that can be taken to keep it safe.

- Train staff to *prevent* accidents.
  —Safety training programs are a good idea; the Occupational Safety and Health Act (OSHA) at the federal level and some state laws require training and periodic safety inspections and may even mandate explicit safety plans. (OSHA was discussed in chapter 3.)
- Teach staff the differences between safe and unsafe work practices.
  —Proper use of tools and equipment.
  —Proper handling and storage of cleaners, solvents, and other chemicals used on site.
  —Ways to organize storage rooms for safe use.
  —Use of safety equipment appropriate to the task (goggles, gloves, support devices, etc.).
- Bring in professionals from your workers' compensation insurance carrier (or state administrator's office) to conduct seminars on injury prevention.
- Conduct regular safety inspections in work areas.
- Have first aid supplies handy and know how to use them.

Security Risks

Because it raises so many liability issues, *security* is a very sensitive subject in real estate management. The desire for "security" on the part of residents is universal, but in residential management, security must be a cooperative effort involving building management, residents, local police, and other authorities. Because good security practices are in everyone's best interests, specific management policies and procedures must be established—and enforced—as part of a security program.

Any security program depends in large part on establishing lines of communication. This means relating information to residents and staff about what constitutes an appropriate safety measure. (Appropriateness will vary with the situation and setting.) There are also specific legal requirements that must be satisfied. For example, local codes may require certain safeguards (e.g., a particular type of door lock, buzzer systems for locked lobbies, bars on ground-level windows, emergency lighting).

The security measures in use at similar properties in the neighborhood will shape residents' expectations about "normal" security practices and procedures. From a marketing perspective, it can be costly to be out of step with local practices regarding provision of security. Without comparable security precautions, prospects may perceive a property as less desirable. Failure to provide comparable security also raises a potential liability risk because a lack of security precautions could lead to accusations of *failure to take "ordinary" precautions*. Specific security precautions include the following:

- Check daily to make sure all vacant units, storage areas, and the site office are properly secured.
- Keep existing security devices or systems functioning properly.
- Repair or replace damaged devices immediately.
- Respond quickly to resident-reported problems.
- Perform regular security inspections to uncover problems.

Clearly, then, an important part of risk management is simple—but consistent—preventive measures (e.g., educating, monitoring, repairing, enforcing)

In determining whether or not to *add* security measures, the following factors should be considered.

- Effectiveness—Does it work fairly easily? Is it superior to what is in current use?

- Cost—Is the initial expense justified? Will it translate into lower insurance premiums? What is the cost to maintain it?
- Quality—How long has it been in the marketplace? What kind of service or support can you expect once the system is installed?
- Ease of use for residents—Is it something residents can assume responsibility for?
- Possible liabilities that may be created—How will it affect residents' perceptions and expectations? Will security really be increased, or will it be reduced?
- Possible impact on marketing and resident retention—Will it add to the appeal for new residents and help retain current ones? Does it yield a marketing advantage over the competition?

Whatever the extent of security practices in your building, from a marketing as well as a liability standpoint, established measures usually should be retained, unless a better alternative can be found. Not only do residents come to expect what you already have in place, but the management company may be legally responsible for continuing existing measures or providing suitable substitutes. This could mean retaining doormen or security patrols once they have been established or providing a comparable service if anything is changed. Of course, security can be as much perception as reality. The most extensive security measures available will be useless if residents fail to lock their doors or do not keep lights on to ward off intruders.

When implementing a security program, real estate managers have to keep in mind that they also have a duty to the property owner to make security measures as efficient and effective as possible. If a specific security measure is no longer cost effective and a better alternative is available, managers have an obligation to the owner to make the change. This could become a sore point among residents, who may perceive the change as a reduction in security. The appropriate response in such circumstances is to explain to them that the change represents an alternative approach, not a reduction in security.

Specific Security Measures. There are several elements that are fairly typical of building security and can be applied in nearly every case. The most straightforward—and probably the most effective—component of any security program is limiting access to the inside of

Keeping the Apartment Community Secure

- Provide dead bolt locks on all doors—bolts should minimally have two-inch "throws."
- Provide locks on all windows and sliding glass doors. Install safety "pins" on sliding glass doors.
- Provide adequate lighting throughout the property, including the parking lot and along walkways.
- Limit access to the property with fencing.
- Provide alarms for individual units. The costs of installation and monitoring can be offset with slight increases in rents or by offering the alarm as an option available for a monthly fee. (If residents decline the offer, they should be required to sign a statement indicating they were offered an alarm and refused it.)

the building. Simply put, keeping out people who do not belong there dramatically reduces the likelihood of danger. Many home invasions, burglaries, rapes, and assaults result from lapses of personal security, which could have been prevented. Educating residents, their children, and guests about not letting strangers into the building in the first place can significantly reduce problems. This should be emphasized in the orientation of new residents, incorporated in resident handbooks, and reiterated periodically in newsletters and notices on bulletin boards. The most important security measure of all is *prevention,* and this requires training and education of residents.

Because some people will go to great lengths to circumvent security measures, additional precautions must be taken. Doors must be sturdily constructed and securely installed. Heavy-duty locks on exterior doors are an additional safeguard. Metal guard plates can be added to strengthen doors and protect against kick-ins. Hinges should be mounted on the insides of doors to prevent would-be intruders from gaining entry by merely taking a door off its hinges. Inexpensive measures such as installing mirrors in elevators and emergency alarms in laundry rooms or clubhouses can also increase security.

Keys present their own security issues. There is potential for liability if keys are retained by former residents or staff or if locks are not changed when residents move out. (Changing locks may be required by local law.) Individual residents should be required to sign a key receipt when they move in (exhibit 9.1) and to return *all* keys related to their occupancy when they move out.

EXHIBIT 9.1

Sample Key Receipt

Key Receipt

Property ______________________________

Resident ______________________________

Unit ______________ Phone number ______________

The undersigned acknowledges receipt of the following keys:

Number of Keys		Serial Numbers
__________	Apartment	__________
__________	Exterior Door	__________
__________	Mailbox	__________
__________		__________
__________		__________

Resident's Signature ______________ Date ______________

Site Manager's Signature ______________ Date ______________

NOTE: Although there is space for only one resident to sign the forrn, signatures should be obtained for every person who signs the lease.

At the same time, residential landlords must have access to rented apartments in emergencies, which raises the specter of a security risk from multiple copies of individual keys or so-called master keys. Master keys offer their own advantages and disadvantages: They save time in emergencies, but they are easily duplicated, and if the master is lost, rekeying multiple locks for a new master is costly. To avert such problems, *key control* is essential.

- Keep records of keys issued to residents and staff.
- Consider arranging to have "extra" keys yourself rather than permitting residents to duplicate theirs. (Separate duplicate keys—i.e., no master—pose other security challenges.)
- Do not let others "borrow" a master key. Always accompany the person and retain possession of the master.
- Always store master or duplicate keys in a locked cabinet, out-of-sight of visitors.
- Limit who has access to the "key box" (e.g., only the site manager and the maintenance supervisor).
- Always have keys signed "out" when employees or contractors

start work and signed "in" before they leave. Do not provide contractors with keys to occupied apartments; instead, on-site personnel should admit them. As an additional precaution, make and retain photocopies of contractors' drivers licenses.

- Limit the number of people who have master keys—i.e., only certain staff members—and make sure the keys bear no identification of the property.
- Never label keys with unit numbers or names; use "blind" codes that are recorded in a secure place separate from the keys.

Beyond the most fundamental security measures (locks and keys), additional steps can be taken to provide for building security.

Deadbolt locks and peepholes (door viewers) are necessary for personal protection. Their attraction is that they are relatively inexpensive and easy to install. Peepholes should give a wide-angle view (180 degrees); they can be installed lower on doors to maximize useability for children or disabled individuals or two peepholes can be installed at different heights to accommodate taller and shorter residents.

Good lighting is essential both inside and outside the building. Lighting should be installed wherever people typically walk at night (walkways, parking lots, building entrances). Not only should an entire area be illuminated, but lights should be placed so they make it difficult for intruders to hide in shadows. As an added precaution, you should check to make sure new hiding places have not been created when lights are on. Mirrors, windows, and additional lighting can be installed to eliminate bind spots and increase visibility. Because lighting levels will change over time—light intensity diminishes as bulbs age and dirt accumulates on fixtures—it is important to change bulbs and clean fixtures regularly (see chapter 8).

While lighting will serve as a deterrent to would-be intruders, lights must be on to be effective. A mechanical timing devise can be set to turn lights on and off at fixed intervals. However, it will have to be reset at the change of seasons or after a power failure. An alternative is a photosensitive device that regulates exterior lighting based on the amount of natural light. Such devices must be located precisely to maximize their control function. Motion sensors that turn on lights may also be considered. Whatever the lighting system, regular inspections are key to ensuring that all lights are working properly.

As to individual units, residents should be encouraged to use a timer to turn lights on and off when they are not at home. A radio left on adds to the impression of occupancy and will help discourage potential criminal activity.

Security Guards. Although using guards to provide security is an option, there is some controversy over their use on residential properties. Not only are guards expensive, but their presence can give the impression that the property is inherently unsafe. Because of the sensitivity of this issue, employment of security guards should be considered carefully; if they are used, they should be present without being oppressive.

When security guards are used, the people hired should be carefully screened and specially trained. Guards require close guidance and monitoring. Establishing a schedule to assure that the entire property is patrolled and that predetermined locations (e.g., locks and fenced areas, vacant units, models, office and storage areas) are checked periodically will facilitate this process. As an added precaution, the routes and times of the guards' movements should be varied, and they should be provided with a means of communicating with each other.

In order to be effective, guards need to understand the property and its problems. For example, if there have been burglaries in the neighborhood—or at the property—the guards should be made aware of this. They should also know the layout of the property and the locations of system controls (e.g., shutoff valves, electrical junction boxes). One of your responsibilities as site manager is to tour the property with the guards, pointing out areas of concern and suggesting things to look for. Most important, you should make sure they understand their role and their responsibilities.

It is also important to provide security guards with a list of the telephone numbers of the property management staff, maintenance and repair personnel, and other emergency contacts. They should also have a current list of residents and their apartment numbers. This will enable the guards to verify the identities of visitors to the property. In addition, you should have telephone numbers for each of the security guards and for the company if an outside service is used.

The decision to use security guards means a choice must be made between contracting for this service and using in-house personnel. Each of these options has certain advantages and disadvantages. Many states require that those who work as guards complete a certain level of training, hold a license, and carry special insurance; a contracted service usually employs trained personnel and provides its own insurance for liability. The contractor also arranges for replacement personnel in case a guard becomes ill or leaves the job. However, these advantages may be outweighed by other considerations. Contracted services can be more expensive than in-house personnel, and the management company has less direct control over the quality of the personnel and their scheduling. To minimize problems, the security contract should stipulate certain standards—for example, it may specify that guards must have worked at similar properties, been employed by the security firm for a certain period of time, and completed a training program.

In general, contracted security personnel will be less familiar with the property, although this can be remedied by providing "orientation" information to the contractor, incorporating scheduling and personnel selection criteria into the contract, and requiring regular assignment of the same people to the property. Even so, management will still have to monitor the security service, and you may have to experiment with different companies to obtain the service desired. Perhaps the greatest benefit provided by contracted service is that it partially insulates the property from liability.

Employing in-house security personnel, on the other hand, may be less expensive than a contracted service, and the management company will have complete control over the quality of personnel and their scheduling. These security personnel may already be familiar with the property and your residents—as your employees, it is easier to make sure they receive an appropriate orientation. Among the disadvantages of providing security in house, however, is the fact that management has all the responsibility for their training and direct supervision, which can increase liability and insurance costs. Because management companies are not in the specific business of providing security, it may be difficult to find reliable personnel. Also, back-up support is less readily available than with a contracted service.

Regardless of how the service is provided, once you use security guards, you have implied to residents that it is part of what they receive in return for their rent, and canceling such a service raises issues of liability between landlord and tenant.

In the final analysis, the most important element of building se-

EXHIBIT 9.2

Sample Guidelines for Providing Security

- Have someone else teach your residents about security, self defense, drugs, and burglary protection. The police are security experts; residential managers are not.
- Encourage residents to participate in neighborhood or apartment watch groups.
- Initiate a watch group for the property.
- Instruct residents on when and how to report any trouble or suspicions to management.
- Educate residents in personal security habits:
  —Always look through the peephole before answering your door.
  —Never let a stranger into the building.
  —Cancel all deliveries when you are going to be away.

Security guidelines should be included in the resident handbook and in a letter sent to all newcomers. Periodically, they should be reiterated in the resident newsletter as a reminder.

curity is resident education and cooperation. Residents have a vested interest in their own security, so it is important to incorporate security devices that are "resident-driven." This means giving residents the means to take responsibility for their own security whenever possible. You will also need to educate residents about security and provide guidelines for them to follow. Because prevention is so important to personal and property security, the simple precautions outlined in exhibit 9.2 may make many other kinds of security measures unnecessary or, at least, increase the effectiveness of existing security because of resident support and cooperation.

Security in the Site Office. Whether the site office is separate or combined with a model apartment or the site manager's residence, security should be a top priority. One of the site manager's major responsibilities is to safeguard the owner's funds and personal property at the site. Fiscal problems can be averted by establishing policies and procedures for handling rent payments and other receipts, especially payments made in cash. All cash and checks should be locked away out of sight at all times until they are deposited. This is best done by using a safe with a slit for depositing sealed envelopes containing cash. On especially large properties, this may be done in conjunction with an armored car transfer service. The appropriateness of this latter strategy will depend on the amount of cash on hand; many properties do not generate enough cash on a regular basis to make it worthwhile.

To minimize the opportunity for theft, residents should be encouraged to make all payments via check or money order. This will minimize the amount of cash on site. (No-cash policies were discussed in chapter 5.) Checks and cash should be deposited daily. Night deposits to a bank lockbox may be necessary to minimize cash on hand. It is also a good precaution to limit the number of people assigned responsibility for handling funds. Requiring written documentation of transactions (signed by the responsible employee, noting the date and time) helps determine who is responsible if money is missing. A policy of always giving numbered receipts for all monies collected—especially cash—and keeping a copy of the receipt in the office provides additional safeguards. The amounts indicated on the receipts should match the payments required on their respective leases and the amounts recorded in residents' ledgers, all of which should agree with the amount of money (cash, checks) collected.

Records are another security issue at the site office. Not only is the information contained in office records personal and confidential, but the agency relationship specifies that you are responsible for safeguarding it. Moreover, if an intruder gains access to information about residents, serious liability issues can be raised, especially if an intruder harms a resident. Records should be kept in locked cabinets. If your office has a computer system, provisions should be made for backup of records and software. An alarm system monitored by a security company that will notify the police of a break-in at the site office is a fairly inexpensive safeguard and should be seriously considered.

Emergency Risks

A site manager may encounter an emergency situation at any time. Some emergencies are life-threatening; others are not. Some are only remotely possible, while others are very likely. Examples of emergencies include fire, natural disasters (earthquake, hurricane, tornado), and man-made situations such as criminal incidents, bomb threats, and civil disorders. Other emergencies that pose less serious risks include equipment breakdowns (lack of heat in the winter or air conditioning in the summer) and elevator problems in a high-rise building. Whatever the situation, the site manager's primary duties are the same—to protect the lives of residents, guests, and employees and to protect the owner's investment from further damage.

Factors that affect risk exposure and contribute to potential emergencies should be identified so they can be addressed appropriately. Location, geography, and climate; building code requirements; construction materials; the availability of emergency support from within the community; employee training and ability to assist in emergencies (e.g., CPR training); and the resident profile of a particular building should all be considered in developing responses to emergencies.

Location, geography, and climate are important because different areas of the United States are subject to different hazards. For example, the Plains are subject to tornadoes, while the East Coast and the Gulf states experience hurricanes. Areas around rivers are susceptible to flooding, and most parts of the West Coast are at risk for earthquakes. Exceptionally heavy snowfall—even in the northern states, which are better prepared for winter weather—and summer heat and drought will tax local facilities and building systems.

Fire risks demand systematic preparation. Local ordinances dictate the nature and extent of directional signage and display of the building address (for fire department access). Fire safety codes dictate the number and placement (location, height) of pull alarms, fire extinguishers, and fire hoses as well as requirements for smoke detectors and fire drills. In most jurisdictions, sprinkler systems are mandated in buildings over a certain size or height.

Construction materials determine the nature and extent of fire risk at a property. For example, masonry is much less susceptible to fire than frame construction. Roofing materials are an especially important consideration because some may be petroleum-based, making them highly flammable and therefore more potentially dangerous than other materials available. In an emergency, a building's size and number of occupants will affect the methods of communication, the designation of evacuation routes, the scheduling of staff on site, and the options available for handling a specific situation.

You will also need to consider the special needs of your residents. The resident profile can be used to identify individuals who require assistance—elderly residents, children, individuals with disabilities, and pet owners will need special attention. The locations of their units should be marked on a map of the apartment community, and those who will be responsible for directing an evacuation (including the local fire department) should have copies of this information.

Because preparation is so important, a key part of site management is development of an emergency response plan. A detailed description of the property that includes the locations of emergency equipment and utility controls (shut-offs), accurate inspection records, and comprehensive resident files is the foundation of the planning process. A file or folder of first aid and related information is an essential component. You will also need to assemble, install, and maintain appropriate emergency equipment. The following items should be part of an emergency "kit."

- Industrial flashlights and batteries
- First aid supplies and instructions
- Blankets and fresh water
- Communication devices, such as cellular telephones
- Battery-operated radios
- Rope, shovels, and a ladder

Other items should be added as the need is determined.

Emergency Procedures. A good plan will include establishment of emergency response teams. You will need to assign individuals to be team captains and conduct periodic practice drills. Local authorities can help you develop a formal evacuation plan; local agencies (e.g., the Red Cross) can assist with follow-up. You will need a list of emergency phone numbers, including those of management personnel, site security, residents and staff who are able to perform CPR, local authorities (fire and police departments), hospitals and trauma centers, emergency support services, governmental agencies (e.g., the Federal Emergency Management Agency—FEMA), private social services (e.g., the Red Cross and the Salvation Army), and individual residents.

In an emergency, site employees and residents need to know whom to call. Communication about emergency situations usually follows a set procedure, alerting individuals in order of a "chain of command"—typically:

- Site manager
- Fire or police department or other authorities
- Maintenance staff

- Property manager and management company
- Insurance company (contacted by property manager or owner)

These procedures should be followed in emergencies that do not threaten life (e.g., broken pipes); however, in life-threatening situations, the priority should be to notify the fire department or police immediately. Whatever the situation, you and your staff should be familiar with your company's policies and procedures for dealing with emergency situations.

All told, the site manager's role in handling emergencies includes educating the residents beforehand and seeing to it that all procedures are followed. You will need to explain potential dangers to residents and define their responsibilities. It is also important to provide instruction regarding the formal evacuation plan so residents will know what to do in an emergency. This information should be provided in both the employee manual and the resident handbook. A sample plan can be outlined as follows:

- Remain calm.
- Follow procedures outlined in the emergency procedures handbook (exhibit 9.3).
- Refer to the emergency book and phone list.
- Call the proper authorities (police, fire department) and allow them to take over when they arrive; be present to answer any questions.
- Alert your emergency team (have a communication system established for contacting them quickly).
- Call support personnel and others who must be contacted (e.g., property manager, owner, insurance company, contractors, etc.).
- Contact residents.
- Look after residents' needs.
- Follow prescribed reporting procedures.
- After the emergency, follow the "postemergency" procedures that are in place.
- Secure the property from further damage.
- Follow the insurance carrier's requirements for reporting.
- Cooperate with insurance company representatives.
- Clean up the damage when instructed to do so by the property manager, authorities, or insurance company.

EXHIBIT 9.3

Sample Emergency Procedures for Employees and Residents

Fire Prevention

- Notify the building management immediately if you discover a fire hazard.
- Do not overload electrical outlets.
- Repair or replace any defective electrical appliances.
- Do not store flammable items near furnaces, water heaters, or any heat-producing appliances.
- Do not use an oven or stove to heat your apartment.
- Do not smoke in bed or when drowsy.
- Use only large, deep ashtrays. Do not empty them into wastebaskets without dowsing them with water.
- Do not wear loose clothing when cooking.
- Always check to see that all burners are shut off after using the stove and oven. Check to see if the pilot lights on gas appliances remain lit.
- Keep smoke detectors in working order. Test detectors and replace batteries regularly.
- Keep matches and lighters well out of the reach of children.
- If your home has a fireplace, always use a firescreen and make sure flue and chimney are cleaned and checked regularly. The flue should be in the open position before starting a fire. Make sure ashes are cold before disposing of them.
- Keep supplemental heating devices away from any flammable materials.
- Keep all appliances (e.g., televisions, stereos, washers and dryers) away from walls so they do not overheat.
- Establish escape routes to use in the event of an emergency.
- If you have a disability that could hinder your evacuating your apartment, let the site manager know about it.

In Case of Fire

- Call the fire department before attempting to extinguish the fire yourself.
- Do not use water on a grease or electrical fire.
- Do not panic. If you must evacuate the building, do so in an orderly manner.
- Follow the instructions of emergency personnel.
- Do not use elevators. Proceed down stairs in a single-file line.
- If you are near the fire, stay close to walls and feel doors before attempting to open them. If you feel heat, do not open the door, but use an alternate escape route.
- Stay low. Smoke and gases rise, and cleaner air will be nearer the floor.
- After leaving the building, move away and allow fire fighters access.
- Never re-enter a burning building.
- If you are unable to escape from a room, block openings around doors and vents with wet towels, rags, rugs, or clothing. Call for help if a phone is available.
- If possible, and if no smoke is coming in, open a window and wave something to draw attention to yourself.
- If your clothing catches fire, stop, drop, and roll.

EXHIBIT 9.3 *(continued)*

Medical Emergencies

- Gather as much information about the situation as possible.
- See that appropriate emergency personnel are contacted immediately.
- Remain calm and try to help the victim relax.
- Loosen the victim's clothing if breathing appears to be obstructed.
- Do not attempt to move the victim, as this may make injuries worse.
- Keep the victim warm and comfortable and remain with him or her until help arrives.
- Do not attempt to administer first aid unless you are certified in first aid or cardiopulmonary resuscitation (CPR).

Severe Weather

- Follow the instructions of emergency personnel.
- Seek out and secure outdoor objects that might blow away and cause injury or structural damage. Move all balcony or patio items indoors.
- Keep a supply of fresh bottled water on hand in case the storm contaminates or disrupts the community water supply.
- During the storm, remain indoors. Go to a designated shelter area or basement. If there is none, seek shelter in an interior hallway or small room or under sturdy furniture.
- Be prepared for power failures by having flashlights ready. Candles are fire hazards and should not be used. Have a battery-powered radio on hand so you can monitor updates and hear news bulletins.
- Stay away from windows during the storm. If winds are very strong, open windows slightly to alleviate pressure and prevent the glass from shattering.
- Be prepared for possible flash flooding.
- Avoid downed power lines.
- If you smell gas, leave the area immediately; then call the gas company to report the leak.

Your own actions during an emergency will depend on the policies and procedures established by the management company. It is wisest *not* to intervene where you cannot be of help. Often the best you can do is allow the professionals (fire fighters, police, medical personnel) to do their jobs their own way. To make this possible, it may be helpful to keep crowds of spectators well away from the building.

Because of the potential for liability, another important consideration in emergency planning is the public relations policy of the management company. During disasters, media people ask questions. If you are so advised, refer journalists to the appropriate management company representative, the property owner, or a designated public

EXHIBIT 9.3 *(concluded)*

Crime Prevention

- Keep your home locked at all times. Keep doors and windows secured.
- Make your home look lived-in at all times.
- Place a light and a radio on a timer. Avoid coming home to a dark apartment.
- Arrange drapes and blinds so your home looks occupied.
- Do not hide keys under the doormat, windowsill, or elsewhere outside your home.
- Do not encourage intruders by leaving ladders or other objects out in the open. They make climbing through a window easier.
- Be discreet when discussing vacation plans or other times when you will be away. Do not call unnecessary attention to your absence.
- If you are going away for an extended period, arrange to have someone pick up your mail on a daily basis or have delivery stopped. Notify police and the site manager of your absence.
- Do not keep valuables in plain sight, especially in your car.
- Park only in well-lighted areas.
- Lock your car.
- Look under your car as you approach and check the back seat before entering.
- Notify security personnel or the police of any suspicious individuals or vehicles.
- Enroll in a self-defense or crime awareness course.

relations specialist. If there is no one else available to speak, at least avoid saying "no comment"—this response tends to create suspicions. If you have the authority to comment, avoid speculation—state only known facts.

A Specific Emergency—Fire. Of all the major emergency situations faced in real estate management, fire is probably the most common. Because of this, development of a fire disaster plan is imperative. The best approach is to request advice from the local fire department and, insofar as possible, follow their recommendations. In all cases, the first step is to follow all legal requirements for fire prevention. Common causes of fires are careless use and disposal of smoking materials, poor housekeeping, electrical overload, and arson, and almost all of these can be averted. For this reason, fire prevention should be included in the resident handbook and discussed during orientation.

In preparing an emergency plan for fires, the specifics of the prop-

Fires and Fire Extinguishers

- **Class A** fires usually start in materials that burn easily, such as paper, wood, cloth, and rubbish. Put out with water or use a water-type or multipurpose dry chemical-type extinguisher.
- **Class B** fires involve grease or other flammable liquid, such as gasoline, oil, or kerosene. Use a chemical extinguisher, which smothers or blankets the fire. (Water should never be used on Class B fires.)
- **Class C** fires start in electrical equipment. Use a dry chemical or multipurpose extinguisher. (Using water or chemicals that carry an electrical charge may result in injury or death.)
- All classes of fires can be extinguished with an ABC—or multipurpose—dry chemical fire extinguisher.

erty must be considered. These include building size and design, available staff, and the number of residents. You will also play a part in educating staff and residents in appropriate fire response procedures. This entails making sure that residents and staff know how to call the fire department. Both should know the locations and operation of alarm boxes; staff need to know where sprinkler valves (if nonautomatic) and master controls for electrical power and gas are located, as well as how—and when—to turn them off.

All on-site personnel should be trained to use emergency equipment. Having a licensed company give a demonstration is the best way to do this. Many people do not know how to use a fire extinguisher properly (i.e., it should be pointed at the *base* of the fire). By walking through the evacuation procedure with your staff and providing residents with guidelines for what to do in case of a fire, you can make sure all will run smoothly. To be certain, fire drills for residents should be conducted twice a year. (The fire department should be notified beforehand to avoid causing a false alarm.) As an added safeguard, you may want to remind residents to test in-unit smoke alarms from time to time and replace dead or dying batteries. This could be an item in the property newsletter or a notice on the bulletin board in observance of Fire Prevention Week. To be certain, maintenance technicians should make a habit of checking smoke detectors whenever they are in occupied apartments and as a regular part of the turnover process. You also need to maintain fire extinguishing equipment. Fire extinguishers must be inspected periodically to assure that they are properly located (local law may prescribe the height above the floor, the distance between apartments, etc.). They must also be readily accessible, in working order, and fully charged. Because fire extinguishers have to be recharged in accordance with manufacturer's recommendations, they should be taken apart and recharged only by competent experienced personnel. A tag on the extinguisher documents each recharging.

Liability Risk

Real estate management has its share of liability risks. Residents, their guests, visitors to the property, vendors, and the general public may hold the property owner, the managing agent, and the on-site staff liable for damage to personal property, injuries, or death related to the property and its operation. Such liability, as pointed out earlier, is inherent in the other types of risk discussed here. Other types of liability concern discrimination against residents or employees and failure to follow landlord-tenant law. (These issues will be discussed in chapter 10.)

One of the greatest concerns today is liability for injuries suffered at the property. If a visitor slips and falls while on the premises, the property's premises medical insurance would pay his or her medical bills. The insurance would also shield the owner and any other *named insured party* financially if a lawsuit were filed. Liability of the managing agent—including the site manager—arises out of his or her involvement in the day-to-day operation of the property. (Liability insurance will be discussed later in this chapter.)

MANAGING RISKS

Risks such as the ones discussed in this chapter represent potential financial losses for the management company, the property owner, and residents alike. While risk cannot be eliminated altogether, there are ways to deal with it. *Risk management* is the process of controlling or reducing risk to acceptable levels. There are several approaches to risk management, and each one has advantages and disadvantages. Selecting the best approach to a particular risk will require a comparison of the costs and benefits of retaining a risk versus the costs and benefits of changing the condition. As site manager, you will work with the property manager to identify the risks at the property through the inspection process and help determine the reasonable nature of these risks and the value of different approaches to them.

A Preventive Approach to Risk

Whether the risk concerns safety, security, an emergency, or liability, risk management demands a preventive approach in which specific risks are identified and assessed, and the best means of dealing with each of them is determined. A preventive approach to risk—whether the concern is violent crime, vandalism, or accidents—has several components.

1. Educate everyone who needs to know. Before people can reduce their risk, they must be made aware of its existence and its nature.
2. Evaluate the habits or conditions that may contribute to the occurrence of undesirable events. This demands both self-assessment and risk-assessment.
3. Consider alternative methods to reduce risk or eliminate it altogether.
4. Design and implement a risk-reduction program and periodically review prevention efforts.

Maintenance—keeping the property in optimum operating condition—is by far the best method of risk reduction.

Managing Specific Risks

Inspections are the single best means of identifying risks at a property. Your own familiarity with the operation of the property can grow by interviewing members of the site staff to develop the fullest picture of its physical condition. (Inspection procedures were discussed in chapter 8.)

As an illustration, both risks and benefits are associated with having an on-site swimming pool. A pool is a very desirable amenity that will attract prospective renters to a property. Residents can use it to socialize, exercise, or seek refuge on a hot day. Despite these benefits, a pool also poses certain hazards: There is the risk of a person drowning; water on the deck can make it very slippery, creating a slip-and-fall hazard; and the presence of a diving board raises the possibility of severe injuries, which can lead to costly litigation. In deciding how to manage the risks associated with having a swimming pool, you must weigh the benefits for the property and the residents against the potential costs of making changes and the potential for liability if you maintain the status quo. In other words, you will be contributing to a decision whether—and how—to manage the risks involved in having a swimming pool.

There are four approaches to managing specific risks—avoidance, retention, control, and transfer. *Avoidance* is the elimination of a known risk. In the example, the pool could be filled in and the area landscaped. While possible, such a solution may not be desirable because all the benefits of having a pool are lost. The particular risks associated with a pool can be managed much less dramatically.

A second approach is *retention* and acceptance of the associated risks. In this approach, risk is accepted "as-is" because it is unlikely to occur, or the potential for financial loss is minimal. In the example, the decision might be to keep the pool because the benefits of resident enjoyment outweigh the risks of injury or accidental drowning. This is called intentional or active retention. Retention of a risk that is unknown or unobserved—a dangerous condition such as a short in the electrical wiring (invisible because it is inside a wall) or unobserved structural damage within a building (a foundation crack masked by exterior or interior facing materials)—is unintentional or passive retention.

Often, neither pure retention nor pure avoidance is a realistic solution. A more likely approach would be taking action to reduce loss exposure by correcting conditions that pose risk or by using preventive devices or procedures—in other words, *controlling* the particular risk. Control involves reducing the risk while retaining the benefits associated with the condition that creates the risk. Examples of control measures applied to a swimming pool include removing a diving board, installing safety equipment (e.g., a ladder with handrails), hiring a lifeguard, enclosing the pool area with a fence and lockable gates, and posting and enforcing rules. Control measures would reduce pool users' exposure to injury and lessen the owner's and the management company's exposure to liability. In fact, these control measures are commonly mandated by local ordinances.

Other examples of risk control at a residential property include regular fire drills, installation of sprinkler systems, and use of fire-resistent construction and finishing materials. Risk control is also relevant to the workplace: OSHA standards affect the use and storage of hazardous materials and provision of on-the-job first aid.

Another approach is *transfer* of the risk to a professional risk bearer through various types of insurance policies. *Insurance* is a system under which individuals and companies concerned about potential hazards pay premiums to an insurance company. The insurance company then reimburses policyholders (in whole or in part) in the event of a loss. In economic terms, insurance is a means of transferring risk from individuals to a larger group whose pooled funds (premiums) make the group better able to pay for losses experienced by individual members. (Insurance will be discussed in more detail later in this chapter.)

An invaluable component of the risk identification process is a *risk evaluation checklist* (exhibit 9.4). Whether the checklist you use is obtained from an insurance company or an independent risk consultant—or developed by the management company—it should highlight key points for inspection and evaluation. Because real estate management is dynamic and risk varies from one situation to another, a standardized checklist will not cover everything—a list tailored to the property will yield more specific information. Also, a checklist is an important guide, but it is not a substitute for keen attention.

As the site manager, your role will most likely include participating in inspections of the property and collecting information from them as well as retaining records of all company manuals and fire and safety protection standards and procedures. These functions are invaluable to the process of identifying and managing the risks associated with rental property ownership and management.

Because they can save money in several ways (i.e., lessen the likelihood of accidents and lower insurance premiums), risk audits should be conducted regularly. They can be performed by profes-

EXHIBIT 9.4

Sample Risk Evaluation Checklist

Property ______________________________

Inspected by ____________________ Date ______________

The following questions should be answerable YES, NO, or not applicable (NA)

1. Are parking areas free of potholes and tripping hazards?
2. Are handicapped parking spaces clearly marked?
3. Are all parking bumpers and speed bumps secured and painted a bright contrasting color?
4. Are porches, steps, sidewalks, and other exterior walkways in good condition?
5. Are lawn sprinklers positioned so as not to create tripping hazards?
6. If natural gas meters are located outside the building, are they adequately protected from vehicular traffic?
7. Are all fire hydrants capped and free of obstructions?
8. Are fire lanes clearly marked?
9. Are electrical fuse panels cool to the touch?
10. Is the pool fenced and enclosed on all sides, and does the gate lock securely?
11. Is the required life-safety equipment readily accessible near the pool and in working order?
12. Is all poolside furniture clean and free of defects?
13. Is the "Pool Rules" sign clearly visible, and does it provide emergency telephone numbers? (Depending on the resident profile, these signs may have to be printed in more than one language.)
14. Is a "No Diving" sign posted at the pool?
15. Is the playground area free of debris?

sional risk consultants, insurance company representatives, or management personnel. The following are typical of what is evaluated in a risk audit.

- Physical inspections performed regularly.
  - —Professional experts can advise on any hidden potential hazards.
  - —Claims adjusters and local fire and police departments can provide valuable adjunct information.
- Security and safety "systems" reviewed regularly and improvements made promptly.

EXHIBIT 9.4 *(continued)*

16. Is the playground equipment free of worn parts and other defects?
17. Is all interior and exterior lighting adequate, day and night?
18. Does the emergency lighting system function properly?
19. Are all interior hallways, stairs, and walkways free of tripping hazards?
20. Are all fire exits shut and fully operational?
21. Are all fire extinguishers fully charged and tagged, indicating recent service?
22. Are exit signs clearly visible?
23. Are fire hoses properly stored, without obstructions?
24. Are all fire sprinkler heads unobstructed?
25. Are all sprinkler valves in the open position?
26. Have all fire alarms been tested recently?
27. Is the number of electrical outlets sufficient, eliminating the need for extension cords?
28. Is there sufficient clear space around furnaces, water heaters, radiators, and electrical panels?
29. Are all electrical appliances properly grounded?

Other hazards or comments:

Where there have been negative responses, please indicate below what action will be taken to correct the situation and when. Use a separate sheet if necessary.

Repair Item Number	Action Required	Scheduled Date of Repair

- Insurance coverage reviewed periodically to assure adequate and appropriate coverage that reflects new purchases, replacement costs, and inflation.
- Adequate records maintained
  —Building plans and site plans, including dimensions and locations of systems controls.
  —Current occupancy list.
  —Structural, construction, and mechanical systems data and drawings.
  —Equipment operation and repair manuals.
  —Furnishings.

In all cases, an insurance "log" should be established to record the history of insurable losses and personnel risks. Components of the latter should include results of pre-employment screening checks, information on employee substance use or abuse convictions as well as their driving records and references, information on work hazards and security risks related to task assignments, job descriptions, training and supervision, and copies of the company's employment policies.

If independent contractors are hired to work at the property, it is essential to have an indemnification (hold harmless) clause in the contract. The contractor should also be bonded as a guarantee of performance (surety) and provide a certificate of insurance that lists the coverage carried and shows the property owner and the management company as additional named insured parties. (It is best to obtain such certificates directly from the insurer to be certain they are up-to-date and in effect.)

The goal of any risk management program is, of course, to *prevent* losses. Whether the means of achieving this goal involve implementing safety and security measures, planning emergency procedures, or raising resident awareness, an additional "safety cushion" is needed. This is provided by insurance. Regardless of the approach to—and success of—efforts at risk management, insurance is a necessity in real estate management.

Insurance—Transferring Risk

Insurance serves as an additional financial shield against risk. While insurance will not prevent losses, it will offer financial protection against their consequences.

There are two primary types of insurance, casualty and liability. *Casualty insurance* covers property loss from damage to buildings, their contents, and external equipment. Such damage may be caused by fire, storm, theft, vandalism, or malicious mischief. *Liability insurance* covers bodily injury or damage to the property of a third party due to an existing condition or a negligent act. An injury that occurs on the property (a visitor who trips on the carpeting, a resident who is assaulted by an intruder) and damage to someone else's property (a visitor's car dented by a falling tree branch) are examples. Personal injury (e.g., libel) may be covered under general liability or as an added *endorsement* (specified coverage, usually requiring payment of an additional premium).

Most owners purchase policies that provide combined coverage for casualty and liability. Additional coverage may be purchased on an as-needed basis. An *umbrella liability insurance policy,* purchased separately, gives the owner additional liability coverage beyond the basic policy; separate endorsements may be available to meet other specialized needs (e.g., plate glass coverage). In all cases, the management company should be listed as an *additional named insured party* (the site manager would be covered as an employee of the management firm or the property).

Insurance covers such things as property damage, loss of rental income, liability for personal injuries, damage or injuries caused by others on the property, losses from fraud or criminal acts, and liability for actions of vendors or contractors (e.g., a resident's car damaged during installation of a roof). Insurance policies should protect both the owner and the management company; individual real estate managers are commonly protected under the umbrella of the management company, except in cases of gross negligence. Although the management company's insurance policies may cover its employees, it is important that the management company and site personnel are protected first by the property's insurance policy and then by the management company's policy.

Insurance coverage is a product of several factors. In determining how much protection or monetary coverage is appropriate, one must first identify the types and extent of specific risks, including consideration of such things as climatic conditions, property age and condition, nature of the neighborhood, and type of ownership. Another consideration is the owner's attitude toward insurance: How much is he or she willing to pay out directly for a loss, and should the policy be all-inclusive or cover only essentials?

The *type of coverage* is an additional factor. If an apartment building is destroyed, the terms of the insurance policy will dictate how it will be restored. Coverage limits are the maximum amount the insurance company will be responsible to pay—for example, in the event of a fire—but this can take on different meanings according to the terms of the policy. If the policy covers the *actual cash value (ACV)* of the building, the property will not be restored to its former state. Instead, the insurance company will pay the replacement costs minus amounts for depreciation (due to age) and an agreed-upon deductible. (A *deductible* is a minimum dollar amount for which the insured is responsible "out of pocket.") If a portion of the property were destroyed in a fire, and this portion contained five-year-old equipment that was being depreciated on a six-year cycle, the insurance company would pay for only one-sixth of the value of the equipment.

From the perspective of the property owner and the management company, *replacement cost coverage* is preferable. This type of coverage would replace the five-year old equipment with new equipment at its replacement cost—less the established deductible but without consideration of depreciation. The same would be true for all depreciable items.

Insurance coverages should be reviewed periodically. From the perspective of the management company and the owner, insurance should provide the best possible coverage at the most competitive price. Like risk in general, insurance coverage must be weighed in terms of the possible (worst case) and the probable (most likely) losses, with the premium cost as an added factor.

There are also different types of liability insurance. *Owner's, landlord's, and tenants' (OLT) liability* policies will list which liability situations are covered. *Comprehensive general liability* insurance covers all liability claims—bodily injury, property damage, and personal injury—except for specific exclusions.

Today, owners and management companies customarily purchase package policies that include all-risk property coverage and comprehensive general liability. Known as *special multiperil policies (SMP),* they include liability, fire, and extended coverage. This type of policy covers most perils, with the exception of such listed exclusions as floods, landslides, earthquakes, sinkholes, broken plate glass, and sewer backups. Often these exclusions can be covered by special endorsements for an additional premium. A multiperil policy usually covers buildings and some of their contents. Contents coverage is also available separately, and this is a sound investment for the site office and clubhouse and lobby furniture. Signage can also be insured at an additional cost. Often it is possible to arrange for a master policy that covers all properties managed for the same owner. Not only can this result in significant savings on premiums, but it reduces the administrative responsibilities related to insurance.

There are also other types of specific insurance policies that are worthwhile for owners, managers, and property management firms to have. *Errors and omissions insurance* (professional liability) covers errors in business activities, including personal injury, libel, slander, false arrest, invasion of privacy, and malicious prosecution, but not gross negligence. This type of insurance is very expensive, and it usually excludes many management activities.

Another coverage that is very important, yet often overlooked, is the *fidelity bond* (a type of *surety*). In suretyship, one party (the surety) guarantees a second party (the obligee) against financial loss arising out of the dishonest acts of a third party (the principal)—i.e., it applies to specific individuals. Insurance, on the other hand, involves only two parties (insurer and insured). The fidelity bond should be configured as a blanket bond covering all employees, the owner's attorney, and the attorney's employees.

Nonowned and hired automobile coverage (e.g., if an employee uses his or her car for business purposes) is also good to have. This coverage may or may not be part of a general liability insurance policy, and it might be purchased separately under the property's *automobile liability insurance.*

Loss of rental income is especially important coverage in real estate management. This ensures that the owner will have a continuous flow of cash to pay operating expenses, even if rent payments are not collectable, as when units become uninhabitable and rent payment ceases as a result of flood, fire, or a natural disaster. (Premiums are based on gross potential rental income.) Under this coverage, the owner receives the equivalent of rent payments during the restoration of the premises. Rent reimbursement ends, however, once the building is ready for occupancy.

Specific *flood insurance* is also available, but it can only be obtained from the U.S. government through a program called the National Flood Insurance Act. To qualify, a policyholder must be located in a flood plain and meet other specific requirements.

Boiler and machinery insurance covers engines, pumps, motors, compressors, and gears. These policies require equipment to be maintained to a certain standard, and insurance representatives usually inspect the property on an annual basis to verify this. Boiler and machinery insurance covers damage due to accident or breakdown and protects against bodily injury and business interruption if these additional coverages are purchased.

Workers' compensation is a standard policy offering coverage for employees' work-related illnesses or injuries. Many states require employers to participate in a state-administered workers' compensation program; others allow employers to purchase coverage from third-party insurers. The amount of required coverage is determined by state laws. In some states, the terms of the policy may also be mandated. In addition to the work-related medical expenses and rehabilitation costs being paid directly, an injured employee receives a percentage of his or her salary or wages over a stated period of time after becoming partially or completely disabled. In some states, the injured party can elect to take the statutory amount or negotiate or sue for larger settlements from the employer. (One advantage of participating in a state program is that an employee sues the state agency and not the employer.) Sometimes owners and managing agents use different insurance carriers, and state workers' compensation insurance boards will rule differently, depending on whether the injured worker is employed by the agent or the owner. By using the same carrier, there is no need to engage in costly and time-consuming debate on this issue.

Other forms of insurance may be desirable in particular situations. *Premises medical insurance* allows for a no-fault minimum amount to pay for minor injuries to individuals without the need for assigning responsibility. *Host liquor liability* protects the owner and manager from lawsuits brought by people who are injured after consuming alcohol on the owner's premises or at functions hosted by the property.

Mortgage insurance for the benefit of the lender may be required by the financial institution. This type of policy guarantees payment of the mortgage in the event of the property owner's death or disability, or default of the loan. Although the lender's interest is usually covered in the property insurance, the lender may require a "lender's loss payable clause," which specifies that claims collected from the insurer are to be used to repair the property and not used otherwise or kept by the owner. In the case of destruction by fire, for example, the proceeds of an insurance claim would go directly to the lender, who would inspect the property and monitor its reconstruction. The lender would then release funds to the contractor as various phases of reconstruction are completed.

All insurance policies contain a cancellation clause that describes the circumstances under which *the insurer may cancel the policy.* It is important for you to know these circumstances. Insurance can be terminated for the following reasons:

- Nonpayment of premiums.
- Hazards found during inspection (e.g., flammable materials, toxic wastes).
- Deterioration of the insurer's risk, either physical or moral (e.g., change of use or occupancy).
- Misrepresentation prior to the issuance of the policy.

There may be additional reasons for cancellation that are specified by state laws.

Your role in the insurance component of risk management will vary, but the importance of many aspects of real estate management to continued coverage are apparent. These include strict financial administration, careful inspection, prompt response to maintenance requests, deliberate prospect qualification, and honesty.

Controlling Insurance Costs. Site managers rarely select insurance policies, but they can help control insurance costs. Insurance rates and premiums are based on the types of risks present on a property and how they are being managed. The susceptibility of construction materials to fire, the kinds of protective measures in place, and vulnerability to hazards from outside the property are all taken into consideration. The cost of an insurance policy can be reduced if the severity of a covered risk is lessened through such measures as regular employee and resident training in fire prevention and related emergency procedures. Up-to-date documentation that employees are authorized to operate vehicles, have good driving records, and were given safety training may lead to lower automobile insurance premiums. Conducting and documenting regular inspections of the property—i.e., showing that care has been taken to create a safe and secure environment—helps to avoid insurance inspections that uncover additional risk and, thus, have the potential to increase premiums.

Coinsurance is an extremely important topic in risk management. A coinsurance clause requires the policyholder to carry insurance equal to a specified percentage of the value of the building at the time of loss in order to avoid a penalty. If less insurance is carried, the insurer pays for only part of the loss. Under an 80-percent coinsurance

Factors Affecting Insurance Rates and Premiums

- **Construction**—the materials used in building the structure. Interior materials and the layout and design of the building are also evaluated with regard to susceptibility of the materials to fire and their potential for spreading fire. Another consideration is the presence (or absence) of a fire sprinkler system.
- **Condition**—the maintenance status of the property. A sound preventive maintenance program may reduce premiums because risk is reduced. (In addition, insurance companies may discount premiums if a property is professionally managed.)
- **Occupancy**—the number and type of residents and their payment histories. The higher the vacancy rate, the higher the premiums. Also a consideration is the presence of retail tenants who would increase the premium (e.g., because of their use of hazardous or flammable materials).
- **Protection**—actions taken to protect the property and reduce its exposure to loss. Used effectively, systems such as sprinklers, fire walls, and fire doors reduce premiums and lessen underwriting problems. Prevention activities such as fire drills, meetings with residents to discuss fire safety, and periodic inspections of units may ultimately reduce the threat of fire or other losses and help control insurance rates.
- **Exposure**—external hazards that increase the dangers to the property. These include vulnerability to physical hazards such as might result from being located near a chemical manufacturing plant (e.g., property damage and potential liability in the event of an explosion) and weather-related perils such as tornadoes, hurricanes, or hailstorms. Geologic perils such as earthquakes and volcanic eruptions are other considerations.

clause, for example, the insured must have coverage equal to 80 percent of the replacement cost of the building at the time of the loss in order to receive 100 percent reimbursement (up to the policy limit). Otherwise, the policyholder is penalized, and the loss is shared by the insurer and the insured. Coinsurance amounts to a rate reduction.

As an example, under an 80-percent coinsurance clause, a building worth $100,000 must have $80,000 worth of coverage. Provided the building value remains at $100,000, 100 percent of losses will be covered, up to the policy limit. However, if the building value increases to $150,000 and the amount of coverage remains at $80,000, the policyholder would have to pay the difference because the amount of insurance required to cover the building has increased to $120,000 ($150,000 × .80 = $120,000). In this case, the insured would receive only two-thirds of the value for a partial loss ($80,000 ÷ $120,000 =

2/3). For a total loss, the policyholder would receive only $80,000—the maximum value of the policy, which is 80 percent of the original value of the building.

To assure that the building is not underinsured, a policy may contain an *agreed amount endorsement* under which the building is insured for a particular amount for a specified period of time. The policyholder does not have to worry about being underinsured as long as an agreed amount of insurance is carried. An inflation endorsement (sometimes called inflation guard) may also be included so the amount of insurance automatically increases by a predetermined percentage periodically during the policy term.

Deductibles are a means of reducing the costs of claims processing as well as lowering policyholders premiums. Rather than face the costs of processing numerous small claims, an insurance company will set a limit under which the policyholder is responsible for losses out of pocket. The amount can range from as little as $100 to more than $1,000,000. Some owners and management companies set aside funds and self-insure against all but catastrophic losses. Another option is to establish a loss pool among several properties and cover them all under a blanket policy with a sizable deductible. This results in lower premiums because losses below the deductible amount would be reimbursed from the loss pool.

Insurance Claims. Once a loss has occurred, real estate managers have several responsibilities. The site manager's responsibilities will vary from one property to another and from one management company to another. Nevertheless, some basics will apply to all cases.

The soundest practice is to report all losses. Whether a maintenance worker suffers a minor injury, a resident slips on some ice, a guest stumbles on the stairs, or the building is physically damaged, everything you know or can discover about the incident should be reported to the insurance company. Failure to do so may shift liability to the owner or the management company. An injured party may claim injury or seek monetary damages long after the actual event. If it is revealed that you had knowledge of the incident but failed to report it to the insurance company at the time, the duties and obligations of the policyholder may have been breached. To be safe, report all incidents to the property manager, even if you do not have very much information.

Specific documentation of incidents and losses ordinarily involves taking written notes at the time of the incident and identifying witnesses whenever possible. Your notes can be supplemented by photographs or an audiotape or videotape recording. This documentation assists in visualizing the extent of injuries or property damage, which can help defend against lawsuits. Finally, records of prior inspections, maintenance, and repairs help prove reasonable care and reduce both liability risk and insurance premiums.

Most insurance companies provide a checklist of what to do in case of loss, which includes minimally:

- Whom to contact.
- A list of contractors and resources.
- How to secure the property.
- Protecting occupants and employees from injury.
- Preserving the property.
- Protecting the property from additional damage.
- How to make judgments when authorizing necessary expenditures.

Specifics that apply to the coverages on the property should be obtained from the company that issues the particular policies.

In the event of a loss, make sure that any *claims adjuster* arriving at your property has the proper authority to investigate. The adjuster must be an official representative of your insurance company. It often happens that public adjusters will arrive on the scene of a fire or accident and offer their services even though they are not duly authorized by the insurance carriers. You should be wary of any adjuster until the authenticity of his or her credentials and status as a representative of your insurance carrier have been verified.

The following are some general guidelines for handling incidents that do *not* involve injuries to people:

- Notify those people that you have been instructed to contact (e.g., management company, owner, local authorities, insurance company).
- Assist the property manager in any reporting procedures as required by the insurance company.
- If there is damage to the property, secure the area to prevent further damage.

Key Actions Related to Risk Management in Site Management

Primary Functions
- Conduct inspections to assess risks
- Recommend risk prevention measures to property manager and owner
- Implement safety and security programs
- Maintain security in the site office
- Work with local authorities and community groups to develop safety and security programs for the property and the neighborhood
- Collect data for insurance claims

Adjunct Functions
- Report all incidents to property manager
- Implement renters' insurance program for residents

If someone has been injured, several steps are important both to minimize the extent of the injury and limit liability. First, make sure the medical needs of the injured are attended to by calling for paramedics. Once this is done, you can follow the same guidelines described for handling losses that do not involve injuries.

Renters' Insurance. The contents of residents' apartments are not covered under the owner's policies for the building, so residents are responsible for insuring their personal possessions. Because of this, recommending that residents carry *renters' insurance* is prudent and appropriate.

Renters' insurance is so important that it is advisable to include a recommendation to obtain renters' insurance in the lease and to have residents initial that clause during the lease signing. An alternative approach is to include a lease clause stating that they know their personal effects are not covered by the owner's policies. Sometimes the best solution is to facilitate their obtaining renters' insurance by providing residents with information about sources for this type of coverage (insurance company brochures, names and phone numbers of local agents). Some management companies work with insurance agencies to create insurance packages that can be offered to renters at the time they sign their leases. At some properties, renters can purchase insurance by signing a lease addendum. Under this arrangement, the premium can be paid along with their rent. This is subject to state law because a license to sell insurance is required in most states.

SUMMARY

There are risks in site management related to safety, security, emergencies, and liability. Depending on the nature of the risk and the owner's and management company's desires, risk can be managed through a variety of strategies.

Effective safety programs prevent injury, control damage, comply with applicable laws, and limit liability. Like all other risks, prevention is the most important component of managing safety risks.

Security should always be a cooperative effort by management, residents, and police and other local authorities. Once appropriate security policies have been established, they should be followed consistently. The most important elements of security are education of residents, maintenance of the building, and management follow-through.

Emergency procedures should be planned in advance and designed according to the nature of the emergency situation. An emergency may be limited to the property (e.g., fire) or occur on a larger scale (e.g., natural disasters such as an earthquake or hurricane). Preplanned emergency procedures will facilitate responses to emergencies, but their success will depend on the preparedness of the on-site staff and residents.

Liability relates to injuries to third parties—individuals or their property—caused by people, objects, or events at the property. Provision of reasonable security and safety helps reduce potential liability, and the level of risk determines the necessary response.

There are four approaches to managing risk—avoidance, retention, control, and transfer. Avoidance is the elimination of a known risk; retention is the acceptance of a condition "as is"; control is a reduction of risk while keeping the benefits; and transfer is the shifting of risk to a third party. Insurance is an example of the latter.

There are two primary types of insurance—casualty insurance protects against property damage; liability insurance protects against injuries to third parties and/or damage to their property. While the property insurance covers a large number of risks, it is very important that all residents have renters' insurance because the owner's policies for the property do not cover residents' possessions.

The site manager is responsible for many important areas of risk management. Good maintenance and planned responses will enhance security, ensure safety, and help minimize potential liability risk. The observations of the entire on-site staff, accompanied by official inspections, can contribute to effective loss control.

Key Terms

coinsurance
emergency risk
fidelity bond
key control
renters' insurance
risk management
safety risk
security risk
surety

Key Concepts

avoidance
control
deductible
insurance
liability
reasonable care
retention
transfer

Key Points

- How are risks assessed in risk management?
- In what way is property inspection one of the most important components of risk management?
- What are the components of a preventive approach to risk management?
- Why is security a sensitive issue in real estate management?
- Why is key control critical to security?
- What is the difference between casualty and liability insurance?
- Why must the value of the property be carefully monitored when an insurance policy contains a coinsurance clause?
- Why is it important to review insurance policies periodically to see that coverage is still adequate?
- What role does the site manager play in reporting losses or incidents?
- Why is renters' insurance so important?

10

Legal Issues

The relationship between landlord and tenant is formalized by the signing of a lease agreement, but the lease is just one of the many legal documents and issues you must be familiar with as a site manager. In addition to understanding the requirements of lease clauses, lease renewal and nonrenewal, and eviction proceedings, site managers must be familiar with agency law, landlord-tenant law, building codes, occupancy standards, and the Americans with Disabilities Act (ADA). Additionally, your marketing and leasing practices must comply with fair housing laws that may exist at federal, state, and local levels. Qualifying rental applicants is another area of potential discrimination, so every application must be handled in the same way (i.e., if a credit check is made on one applicant, it must be done for all applicants). There are also numerous laws regarding employment that affect the management company as an employer and the site manager as its representative. Laws that pertain to wages and hours, occupational safety, equal employment opportunity, and other specifics of the employer-employee relationship were detailed in chapter 3 and will not be addressed here.

THE AGENCY RELATIONSHIP

The relationship between the management company and the property owner is defined as one of *agent* and *principal.* This legally recognized relationship is based on management's *fiduciary responsibility* to the owner. As an agent, the real estate manager is entrusted to act in the owner's best interests to safeguard the investment. These responsibilities extend to the site manager and the entire on-site staff.

An *agency relationship* is created when a principal (in this case, the property owner) authorizes another person (the real estate manager) to act on his or her behalf. This relationship is nearly always agreed to in writing—in real estate management, the document formalizing the relationship is a *management agreement* (see chapter 1). The management agreement is a contract that authorizes the real estate manager to perform the specific functions, duties, and obligations of the owner. It establishes a fiduciary relationship in which the agent is expected to demonstrate loyalty to the principal and to keep him or her informed about the status and operations of the property. In addition, the agent is expected to follow the principal's instructions—provided they are legal and ethical—and to perform his or her duties diligently.

The management agreement also authorizes the real estate manager to represent the principal in dealings with third parties, and the agent may create new contractual obligations for the owner in the course of business. The agent is to be included as an additional named insured party on the owner's property insurance and may also be *indemnified* (secured against loss or damage) against liability for incidents that occur on the property. The management contract may also contain hold-harmless clauses that protect the agent from acts or omissions of the owner. This does not, however, protect the agent from liability for personal acts of gross negligence or malfeasance—for this type of coverage, the agent should hold its own errors and omissions insurance policy, although such policies are very expensive and have many exclusions. (Management liability was discussed in chapter 9.)

The real estate manager is expected to disclose to prospective tenants that he or she is an agent of the owner. This is important because, while the manager does have certain responsibilities to tenants under landlord-tenant law, the specific fiduciary responsibilities of agency apply only to his or her relationship with the property owner—the real estate manager is an agent of the owner, not the tenants.

LANDLORD-TENANT LAW

Throughout this book, residential tenants have generally been identified as "residents." While this practice is encouraged as a means of fostering a closer relationship between real estate managers and renters, in the eyes of the law, the parties to a lease are known as landlord (*lessor*) and tenant (*lessee*). Because this chapter focuses on the legal context, the terms landlord and tenant will be used throughout.

The respective rights and responsibilities of landlords and tenants are contained in a body of law known as *landlord-tenant law,* and the most widely accepted source for landlord-tenant rights and responsibilities is the Uniform Residential Landlord and Tenant Act drafted by the National Conference of Commissioners on Uniform State Laws. It is intended to provide clarification and foster uniformity among state landlord-tenant laws to protect both landlords and tenants. Many states have adopted this law or some version of it.

The Landlord's Rights and Responsibilities

Under landlord-tenant law, the landlord is obligated to deliver the premises at the beginning of the lease term, maintain the premises in a habitable condition, provide for the tenant's quiet enjoyment of the premises, supply essential services, notify the tenant of any changes to the terms of the lease (including rent increases), notify the tenant before lease expiration, and return the security deposit within the prescribed period after a tenancy ends. In consideration for fulfilling these obligations, the landlord is to receive timely payment in the form of rent. The amount of rent, when it is due, how often it is to be paid, and where payment is to be made should be stated clearly in the lease, along with any fees or other charges (e.g., for late payment of rent).

If the rent is not paid or if the tenant is otherwise in violation of the lease, the landlord has the right to terminate the lease agreement and evict the tenant. Violations of the lease include damage or destruction of property, failure to comply with lease provisions and property rules and regulations, engaging in illegal activities on the premises, or failing to respect the privacy of other tenants. Because the eviction process is very specific, its procedures must be followed carefully. (Eviction will be discussed later in this chapter.)

In return for the tenant's payment, the landlord agrees to provide a habitable apartment. This *implied warranty of habitability* means that an apartment must be safe and clean. Specific standards are usually defined by local building codes and may include the following:

- Maintain the common areas in a clean and safe condition.
- Maintain the apartment in a safe condition.
- Maintain the structure (roof, exterior walls) free from leaks.
- Provide appropriate fixtures and facilities and maintain them in safe working order.
- Supply essential services, including heat, running water, gas, electricity, sewerage, and waste disposal.

In some jurisdictions, the landlord is required to have every vacant apartment inspected prior to allowing occupancy by a new tenant.

The applicable landlord-tenant law may also distinguish between habitability and *essential services,* granting landlords up to two weeks to correct situations where habitability standards are not met, while essential services may have to be restored within 24–48 hours. If the leased premises are not maintained in a habitable condition by the landlord, or essential services are not provided, the tenant may have the right to withhold rent, vacate the apartment without penalty, make repairs and deduct their cost from the rent, and/or collect damages in court based on the landlord's breach of contract. In general, tenants are required to provide the landlord with formal notice of the breach and give the landlord the opportunity to make corrections before exercising any of these remedies; however, the tenant's specific rights and responsibilities under the warranty of habitability are subject to applicable law.

As was discussed in chapter 9, security is a major concern for landlords and tenants alike, and it is relevant to the landlord-tenant relationship as well. The landlord does have some responsibility to tenants and visitors for safety and security of the premises, including the common areas, facilities, and parking lots. However, issues of liability can arise if the landlord expresses—or even implies—a promise of security to a tenant.

Because the landlord controls the common areas and facilities of the property, when an injury is suffered or a criminal act is committed there, the landlord may be held liable if the condition that gave rise to the injury or crime could have been foreseen and prevented. The landlord's best defense is to establish security and safety programs that provide reasonably safe and secure conditions, considering the property, the tenants, and the neighborhood. (The concept of reasonable care was discussed in chapter 9.)

In order to fulfill his or her responsibilities under landlord-tenant law, and to preserve the value of the property and ensure safety, the landlord has the right to enter apartments and make repairs. Known as the *right of re-entry,* this provision allows the landlord to make repairs and improvements and provide agreed-upon services. Within this right, the landlord can also show the apartment to prospective tenants, contractors, purchasers, and lenders, subject to specific limitations.

The landlord also has the right to set *reasonable* policies and rules for the property. These rules generally concern promotion of the convenience and welfare of all the tenants, preservation of the landlord's (owner's) property, and allocation of services and facilities. The rules must be clearly stated so the tenants understand what is and is not permissible, and the landlord must notify the tenants of any changes to existing policies. (Any changes to policies and rules should be reviewed by legal counsel prior to implementation.) The "house rules" should be attached to the lease as an addendum to be reviewed and signed by tenants when they sign their leases. It goes without saying that such rules must be applied to all tenants fairly and uniformly.

The Tenant's Rights and Responsibilities

The tenant's responsibilities include abiding by the terms and conditions of the lease, paying the rent on time, maintaining the leased premises in good condition, disposing of all rubbish properly, and not disturbing other tenants. The tenant is also responsible for the conduct of his or her guests. If a tenant vacates an apartment prior to

Landlord's and Tenant's Rights and Responsibilities

Landlord's Obligations

- Deliver possession of the premises to the tenant at the start of the lease term.
- Maintain the premises in compliance with building and housing codes to keep them in safe and habitable condition.
- Provide for tenants' quiet enjoyment.
- Supply essential services, including heat and hot water.
- Give proper notice of changes to rules and regulations or a change of ownership.
- Notify tenant of lease expiration and/or changes in lease terms such as rent increases.
- Refund security deposits according to applicable state and local laws.

Tenant's Obligations

- Comply with the terms of the lease.
- Maintain the dwelling unit in a clean, safe condition and use the fixtures and appliances appropriately.
- Respect the privacy and right to quiet enjoyment of other tenants.
- Abide by the rules and regulations of the premises, provided their purpose is to promote the welfare of all the tenants and preserve the property from abuse. These rules must be reasonable and apply uniformly to all tenants.
- Grant the landlord reasonable access to the dwelling unit in order to make repairs or show the unit to prospective renters, purchasers, or lenders.
- Use the dwelling unit only as a residence, unless otherwise agreed.
- Give proper notice before vacating the premises.

expiration of the lease, he or she is responsible for the rent and the cost of any damage beyond ordinary wear and tear during the remaining part of the lease term until the unit is re-rented. In exchange for meeting these obligations, the tenant has the right to occupy the premises for the duration of the lease term in the expectation that the landlord will also abide by the lease.

A tenant's right to possess and use the premises is the counterpart of the landlord's responsibility to deliver possession of a leased apartment on a specified date. Delivery of possession by the landlord is an important point. Usually, this is specified in the lease agreement as well as landlord-tenant law. However, there are actually two potential issues involved with possession, and the distinction should be understood. If the landlord has possession of the leased premises at the beginning of the lease term but for some reason is unable to deliver it to an incoming tenant, the landlord may be obligated to abate the rent until he or she is able to deliver the apartment to the tenant. Alternatively, the tenant may elect to terminate the lease and have all prepaid rent, deposits, and fees returned; or the tenant may sue for possession of the premises and recover damages from the landlord (e.g., for the cost of lodging, moving and storage charges, days lost at work). If the landlord does not have possession of the dwelling unit because a previous tenant has not vacated it, the landlord's liability is partially mitigated by that of the current occupant. As in any such complex situation, advice of legal counsel should be sought.

Once occupying the apartment, tenants have the *right to quiet enjoyment* of the premises. This includes the right to privacy, peace and quiet, and lawful use of the apartment, common areas, and facilities. Tenants are expected to respect each others' right to privacy and peaceful enjoyment. It also means that the tenant can occupy the premises free from interference by the landlord, excepting the landlord's obligation to make repairs and right of re-entry.

Just as the landlord is obligated to make repairs as necessary, tenants are responsible for maintaining the leased premises in the same condition as when they initially took possession (allowing for ordinary wear and tear). This includes keeping the apartment clean, using appliances and other features in a safe and proper manner, keeping the apartment free of hazardous materials, and disposing of trash properly. Because *normal wear and tear* can become a serious issue between landlord and tenant, it should be addressed specifically in the lease. Some states define normal wear and tear as deterioration that occurs without negligence, carelessness, or abuse of the premises or equipment by tenants or their guests. This also extends beyond the apartment to include windows and doors, common areas, and facilities.

When something goes wrong in the apartment, the tenant is responsible for notifying the landlord of the problem. He or she must then give the landlord reasonable time to make repairs. If the landlord did know, or should have known, about the problem, he or she may still be held responsible for the repair. If the landlord fails to make repairs or correct unsafe or unhealthy conditions, the tenant may have the right to make the necessary repairs and deduct the cost from the rent. The *repair and deduct* remedy requires the tenant to give proper notice to the landlord (usually in writing) and is predicated on subsequent failure by the landlord to respond within a "reasonable" time (as required under the applicable landlord-tenant law). If the landlord fails to make repairs, the tenant may have the work performed by a third party, who is treated as an agent of the landlord.

In order for the repair and deduct remedy to be legally sound and binding, the tenant must document all requests, including the nature of the problem and the landlord's response (or lack of response). Exercise of this option may require payment of rent into an escrow account until repairs are made, and the tenant must comply with applicable legal conditions and restrictions; otherwise the remedy may be deemed "procedurally" invalid in court. In addition, many states place a dollar limit on the amount that can be deducted from rent. Depending on local law, it usually cannot exceed one month's rent.

From both a legal and a maintenance standpoint, sound maintenance policies should include careful documentation of all repair requests and how they are handled. Failure to make necessary repairs is a serious situation from both a landlord's and a tenant's perspective. If a tenant can document that a landlord was aware of a problem and failed to correct it, this may constitute violation of the implied warranty of habitability, and the tenant may be able to vacate the premises on the basis of *constructive eviction*.

Constructive eviction may also apply if the tenant's right to quiet enjoyment is disturbed by some action of the landlord that renders the leased premises uninhabitable or deprives the tenant of enjoyment of the premises. (The allegation is that the tenant's rights under the lease or under landlord-tenant law were denied by the landlord.) In such a case, a tenant must complain about the habitability of the property or his or her unit or about the lack of essential services or frequent intrusions by the landlord. To uphold a claim of constructive eviction, however, *the tenant must vacate the apartment after notifying the landlord in writing* and allowing the landlord sufficient time (as stipulated by law) to remedy the situation.

The best rule to follow is to never let a maintenance problem get to court. Such a situation does nothing to improve resident relations or resident retention. If a tenant vacates an apartment, the landlord will still have to correct the problem; losing the resident will probably also damage the property's reputation. Such unnecessary turnovers lower staff morale, disrupt the property's income stream, and impose the additional expense of legal fees. Thus, preventive maintenance can yield dividends beyond merely assuring the property's physical functions.

How different types of situations are handled can have serious repercussions as well. If a tenant is asked to vacate his or her apartment after complaining about the condition of the property or for forming a tenants' union, the tenant may allege *retaliatory eviction* by the landlord. In many states, landlord-tenant law forbids retaliation for lawful conduct on the part of a tenant. If a tenant complains in good faith to a governmental agency about building or health code violations and the landlord subsequently refuses to renew a tenancy, increases the rent beyond what is normal for comparable apartments, or reduces the services required by the lease, the tenant may be able to claim retaliatory eviction. However, if the tenant damages the apartment and then asserts retaliatory eviction, the landlord's case is much stronger. The best way to combat the likelihood of any such charges arising is to apply rules uniformly and treat all tenants fairly.

Unless a clause to the contrary is written into the lease, the tenant may have the right to assign or sublet the unit without the landlord's permission. *Assignment* is the process of transferring all unexpired rights of a lease to another person; it essentially replaces one tenant with another. If an assignee fails to pay the rent, the landlord must first attempt to obtain payment from the assignee. If the landlord is unable to obtain payment from the assignee, he or she may sue the original tenant as well as the assignee. *Subletting* is the transfer of part of the rights of the lease to another person. Under a sublease, the original tenant retains some rights and obligations under the original lease—i.e., the original tenant is responsible under his or her lease with the landlord regardless of his or her agreement with the sublessee.

All leases should contain clauses that grant tenants the right to assign or sublet *only with the landlord's written permission.* This enables the landlord to evaluate whether the new tenant is acceptable, according to the property's standard screening criteria. By limiting the tenant's right to assign or sublet, the landlord reduces the potential for legal problems due to nonpayment of rent or because of violations of the lease or house rules.

THE LEASE DOCUMENT

The purpose of the *lease* (sometimes also called a *rental agreement*) is to detail the rights and responsibilities of the parties to the contract. A lease is an agreement that grants a tenant the rights of possession and use of an apartment for a defined period of time. In consideration of these rights, the tenant is required to pay the landlord rent. In order for a lease to be enforceable, it must be legally valid—the apartment must not to used for illegal purposes, both parties must enter into the lease by mutual consent, and it must be signed and dated. Usually the tenant's signature is affixed before the lease is presented to the landlord for acceptance and signature. The landlord and the tenant each receive an original signed copy of the lease.

All leases should be in writing; because so many issues of a lease agreement involve monetary considerations, it is unwise to rely on oral agreements. (If the term is one year or longer, a lease must be written to be valid.) Accuracy is very important because errors in the lease will generally be interpreted in favor of the tenant in a court of law. Oral agreements are potentially very destructive—they are difficult to verify and even harder to enforce. Parties may change in real estate management—owners sell properties, management changes, and tenants move on. Not only is it difficult to keep track of oral agreements, but the perceptions of the events and the agreements themselves will differ from case to case. Often, the *only* way to resolve disputes about oral agreements is costly litigation. Oral agreements also create the potential for charges of discriminatory treatment.

A lease must identify *the parties,* and all occupants of legal age should sign the contract individually, using the *correct legal names of all lessees.* Married couples should sign their own names—as an example, the law would recognize "Lisa Monroe" but not "Mrs. Jack Monroe." Having individual signatures makes all lessees responsible for the lease. In the case of the example, the lease should identify the lessees as "Jack Monroe and/or Lisa Monroe." This creates *joint and several liability*—the obligations of the lease may be enforced against both lessees or either one of them.

In order to sign a lease, a person must be 18 years of age or older. If a minor signs a lease (as often happens in college towns), an adult should co-sign it as *guarantor.* Likewise, the lease should correctly

Advantages of a Standardized Written Lease

- Is more effective in court than an oral agreement, which can be disputed.
- Prevents misunderstanding of the rights and responsibilities of the parties.
- Assigns specific responsibilities to tenants (e.g., payment for utilities).
- Assigns certain liabilities to tenants (e.g., for damage and cleaning costs).
- Reduces the likelihood of charges of discrimination.
- Discourages undesirable actions by tenants (e.g., keeping exotic pets, subletting or assigning the lease).
- Facilitates inspection and repair of apartments.
- Facilitates showing occupied apartments to prospective renters, purchasers, and lenders.
- Facilitates repossession of the apartment when the tenancy terminates.
- Facilitates disposal of unclaimed personal property.
- Extends the period of time within which former tenants can be sued for delinquencies.

identify the lessor as the owner of the property or show the name of the property and the management company, citing the latter as the agent of the owner. The lease must also include a complete *description of the leased premises.* This should include the apartment number and the street address, city, and state.

A lease must state the *duration of the lease term*, including the commencement and expiration dates. Leases are invalid if they do not contain expiration dates. If at all possible, leases should begin on the first day of the month and expire on the last day of a month. (If a lease term is to begin in the middle of a month, the rent for the first month should be prorated.)

The lease must also state the *consideration* (e.g., the rent amount) as well as the terms of payment. This includes when the rent is due, where it is to be paid, when payment is late, and whether there is a "grace period," as well any late fees or charges for returned checks. As was discussed in chapter 4, rent policies should require payment by check or money order. Cash payments should be discouraged because of the potential risk; however, in some jurisdictions refusal to accept cash is illegal, and such refusal could be interpreted as refusal to accept payment.

Because rent collection is important from both a legal and a financial perspective, all payment requirements should be stated explicitly in the lease. The lease should also state that nonpayment is cause for eviction. While it is natural to empathize with a tenant's personal and financial problems, the need for fairness dictates that policies should be applied without preference. Any exception to this would not only be a disservice to tenants who pay their rent on time, but also jeopardize the owner's investment as well as raise the specter of discrimination.

Specific Lease Clauses

The remaining contents of the lease document spell out the various requirements of the parties under the agreement. These are usually identified as a series of specific clauses covering everything from security deposits to requirements for notices.

The *security deposit* serves as a guarantee of the tenant's performance of the lease. It is to be refunded at the end of the lease term unless the tenant fails to make rent payments or does not maintain the premises in good condition. Local ordinances, as well as state landlord-tenant law, may regulate the amount of security deposits and procedures for their refund, sometimes including payment of interest to the tenant.

Generally, security deposit funds can be used only to cover unpaid rent or utilities or the cost of repairs or cleaning after move-out. The deposit should not be useable for the last month's rent, and this should be stated in the lease. If a tenant is in default for nonpayment of rent, the security deposit may not be sufficient to cover both delinquent rent and any cleaning and repair charges. Because of the legal and financial ramifications of security deposits, it is important to document move-in and move-out conditions scrupulously and account for any deductions for cleaning and repairs or unpaid rent. Having tenants sign the inspection forms provides strong evidence in the landlord's favor in the event of disputes about unit conditions and refunds. (Security deposits and their administration were discussed in chapters 4, 6, and 7.)

Leases often contain a *utilities* clause. Typically, the tenant is required to pay for interior utilities (electricity and cooking gas), including air conditioning and, sometimes, heat. Most leases spell out the

Some Common Lease Clauses

Security deposit—explains the purpose of the deposit and the conditions for its return.

Delivery of possession—used to protect the owner in case of inability to deliver possession of the apartment on the agreed-upon date. This would apply to new or rehabilitated properties when leasing predates completion of construction or when a departing tenant has not vacated the apartment and the landlord must use an unlawful detainer action to eject the tenant.

Quiet enjoyment—upon fulfilling the obligations of the lease, the tenant is granted quiet and usually exclusive enjoyment of the apartment.

Maintenance—states the specific maintenance responsibilities of each party under the lease.

Utilities—what utilities will be supplied at the expense of the landlord as well as those for which the tenant is responsible.

Improvements and alterations—the tenant is prohibited from making alterations or improvements to the apartment without the written consent of the landlord. Any permanent installations become the property of the landlord.

Assignment or subletting—prohibits the tenant from letting another person occupy all or part of the leased apartment without the written consent of the landlord.

Default—explains what constitutes default, the procedures to be followed, and what rights will exist in case of default by either of the parties to the lease.

Hold harmless—this clause is to protect the landlord if the tenant or any third party is injured on the leased premises.

Right of re-entry—following its assignment to a tenant by lease agreement, the landlord is permitted to re-enter the apartment for specific purposes.

Holdover tenancy—provides additional terms in case a tenant does not vacate the premises upon expiration of the lease.

Automatic renewal—provides for automatic renewal of the lease, on the same terms or conditions and for the same period of time, unless notice is given by landlord or tenant prior to expiration. This is rarely used because the rent is usually adjusted after each completed term.

This list is not all-inclusive. Residential leases also commonly include provisions that address circumstances arising out of particular situations—among these are destruction of the premises, foreclosure or receivership, and bankruptcy or insolvency of either party.

requirements as set forth in the applicable landlord-tenant law. If the landlord pays the utilities and residents are responsible to pay for their respective shares, the lease should spell out both parties' responsibilities and the procedure for payment as well as the landlord's remedy for nonpayment.

Leases also usually contain a *condition of premises* clause, which states that tenants have inspected the premises and accepted their condition. This is supplemented by the records of move-in and move-out inspections. Related to this, leases often explicitly prohibit *alterations* to the leased premises and stipulate that any plans for decorating or painting must be approved in writing by the landlord. However, under the Fair Housing Amendments Act of 1988, disabled residents must be allowed to make rented apartments accessible at their own expense, and they may have to restore the premises to the original condition, also at their own expense. (Advice of legal counsel should be sought regarding particulars and their applicability in a given situation.)

If the leased premises are *destroyed* by fire or become partially uninhabitable, the tenant's rent may be reduced while repairs are being made. If the building is completely destroyed or condemned, the tenant may have the option of terminating the lease and vacating the premises, in which case all deposits and unused prepaid rent are to be refunded. The landlord often has the right to terminate the lease and return all unused rent monies and security deposits to tenants if the destruction is not total. However, if the damage was caused by the tenant, these remedies are not available to the tenant, and he or she may be required to pay for the repairs. (The potential for this kind of situation to arise is one of the reasons tenants should be encouraged—or even required—to obtain renters' insurance; this issue should be addressed specifically in the lease, as noted in chapter 9.)

The *landlord's right of access* to the leased premises (also called the right of re-entry) should be included in the lease. Landlord-tenant law should be checked regarding this right. Access is usually permitted at any time in case of emergency. Otherwise, proper notice and the tenant's consent are required for the landlord to enter during "reasonable" hours for inspection, repairs or necessary services, or to show the unit to prospective tenants or buyers. If a tenant refuses access, the landlord can seek an injunction in court to compel the tenant to allow re-entry. Out of consideration for your tenants, it is a sound policy to provide 24 hours' notice whenever possible—failure to notify tenants and entering without consent can have serious repercussions, including a lawsuit for breach of contract. Under certain circumstances, a tenant may even obtain an injunction against the landlord for trespassing.

A lease should refer to *house rules and regulations* and make clear that violation of them may be grounds for eviction. To make sure that tenants have read—and understand—their rights and responsibilities under the lease, it is a good idea to have them initial specific provisions or each page of the lease during the lease signing. This also acts as a safeguard in the event of any dispute between landlord and tenant regarding lease terms.

Leases also should contain clauses concerning termination of the lease and the tenancy. A *surrender of premises* clause states that the tenant will vacate the premises when the lease terminates. Often this clause stipulates that if a tenant remains beyond the termination date, he or she has become a *tenant at will* and is obligated to fulfill the terms of the original lease on a month-to-month basis. Tenancy at will can be terminated by a thirty-day notice from the landlord (or the length of time specified by state landlord-tenant law). Failure to vacate following this notice (or at the end of the lease term) creates a *holdover tenancy,* which is grounds for eviction. (These issues will be revisited later in this chapter.)

A lease should never contain any clause that could reasonably be considered *unconscionable.* This refers to any part of a contract that is unenforceable because it is grossly unfair—e.g., a lease clause under which a tenant waived key rights guaranteed under landlord-tenant law. If a tenant contested such a clause in court, a judge could invalidate the entire lease or only the offensive part. An attorney should always review lease forms prior to implementation to identify any such problems.

Pets. One important issue that warrants consideration in leasing apartments is the keeping of pets. Because animals can cause damage to property and injure people, property owners often prohibit them in apartments. However, more than 50 percent of Americans own pets, and such a policy can limit the potential market for an apartment. In addition, while some management companies have strict no-pets policies, civil rights laws that cover discrimination on the basis of disability (e.g., the Fair Housing Amendments Act of 1988) prohibit landlords from excluding guide dogs or other animals that help the disabled. A review of applicable laws and advice of legal counsel can avert problems arising out of this issue. If pets are allowed, the wisest approach is to provide thorough guidelines for maintaining them; these guidelines should be reiterated in a specific clause in the lease—and enforced.

Pet guidelines often set limitations on the type, size, weight, and number of pets allowed and specify requirements for damage deposits, use of leashes, clean up of animal wastes, and pet insurance. Current pet licenses and vaccinations should also be required; these are often prescribed by local ordinances. Sometimes there are also noise ordinances that apply to pets, and these should be noted as well. The following are some points to consider in developing a pet policy.

- *Type of animal*—While dogs can be noisy and cats tend to roam, they are common house pets. However, some types of animals should be excluded as pets: For example, "exotic" animals such as pigs or monkeys are usually prohibited by ordinance.
- *Size of pet*—Specific weight and height requirements should be stated in the rules and regulations of the property so that very large animals may be excluded, especially in the case of small apartments.
- *Number of pets*—A maximum number of pets should be set.
- *Pet deposit*—It is appropriate to require an extra deposit to cover any damage by a pet to the apartment or the property as a whole. This deposit may be nonrefundable; however, a tenant may be less vigilant about a pet's behavior if the deposit is not refundable, reasoning that the deposit will cover any damage. A refundable deposit, on the other hand, serves as an incentive to keep pets in check. Alternatively, residents may be charged additional monthly rent as consideration for allowing them to keep a pet.
- *Pet insurance*—Tenants should be required to carry a policy covering damage or injuries caused by their pets. The property owner and management company should be listed as additional named insured parties.
- *Pet registration*—Tenants should register their pets with the site manager. A description and photograph of the animal, its breed, and its name should be included in the tenant's file.
- *Vaccinations and licenses*—All pets should be required to have appropriate vaccinations and licenses as required by law. An ad-

ditional lease requirement should be proof of vaccination updates (boosters).

- *Leash requirement*—Pets should not be allowed to roam the grounds or the common areas of the property. This policy should state that all pets taken outside must be kept on a leash. Remember that pets can sometimes break loose from their leashes, and the leash requirement is not intended to penalize a resident for this rare occurrence. A limitation on the length of the leash (e.g., not to exceed five feet) may also be appropriate. Animals should wear appropriate identification tags and name tags that include their owner's name and phone number to aid in their return.
- *Cleanup*—Animal wastes are a danger to health and sanitation, and many communities have ordinances requiring pet owners to clean up after their animals. This should be a property policy as well.

In addition, a pet policy may impose limitations on where pets are permitted (e.g., they should be prohibited in the swimming pool and other recreational facilities, laundry rooms, and landscaped grounds). It is also appropriate to limit the use of elevators and front entrances. Because pets require exercise, it may be possible to provide a specific area for tenants to play with their pets. This will also facilitate the enforcement of other rules.

When pets are permitted, pet owners should be required to sign a separate *pet agreement* that becomes an attachment to the lease. The agreement should provide for identification of the pet (including a photograph), state the rules and limitations that apply, and indicate the consideration to be paid by the pet-owning resident (e.g., a pet deposit or additional rent). Exhibit 10.1 is an example.

LEGALITIES OF LEASE RENEWAL OR NONRENEWAL

A lease transfers the right of possession and use from the property owner (landlord) to the tenant. In doing so, it may create one of four types of tenancy: tenancy for years, tenancy from period to period, tenancy at will, or tenancy by sufferance.

The most common type of tenancy is *tenancy for years*. It specifies

EXHIBIT 10.1

Sample Pet Agreement

Tenant name ______________________ Date ____________
Lease Term Commencement Date ________ Termination Date ____________
Address ______________________ Unit number ____________

The landlord and tenant agree that the landlord will allow the tenant to have the pet described below in the designated premises under the following agreed terms and conditions:

1. Description of pet (type, breed, size, color, name): ______________________
   ____
2. The pet will not be allowed out of the apartment unless it is in the custody of the tenant and on a leash.
3. The tenant will not use the elevators, but will use the side stairwells in leaving and entering the apartment building.
4. The pet will be curbed on the property.
5. The tenant will furnish the landlord with a copy of a comprehensive personal liability insurance policy to cover any loss or personal injury to any tenant, guest, or employee of the property.
6. The tenant will permanently remove the pet from the premises if its noises or barking cause any complaints from other tenants, it damages the building or apartment unit, or it bites or injures any person on the premises.
7. The tenant agrees to pay for any damage to the building or its grounds caused by the pet. The tenant acknowledges full responsibility for his or her pet and agrees to pay all costs involved in restoring any damaged areas to their original condition. If the damage cannot be removed (stains or other destruction of property), the tenant agrees to pay the full cost of replacing the materials.
8. The tenant will pay the landlord a refundable pet deposit in the amount of $ ____________.

______________________________ ______________________________
Tenant Date Landlord Date

NOTE: It is important that management have a description of the particular pet covered by this agreement (a photograph is also desirable). If anything happens to the animal, the pet owner has to sign a new agreement for another pet.

the period of time for which the tenant may use the property (e.g., one year). At the end of the term, the tenancy terminates and the tenant must surrender possession to the landlord unless a new lease is signed. By contrast, *tenancy from period to period* specifies the period (e.g., month-to-month) and states that the tenancy will automatically renew at the end of each period until notice is given by the landlord or the tenant. Depending on the provisions of the lease and applicable landlord-tenant law, a tenancy for years may automatically become a tenancy from period to period at the expiration of the original lease term.

A lease may provide specifically for *holdover tenancy*—a tenant remaining beyond the original lease term. If the tenant remains with the landlord's permission, he or she is said to be a *tenant at will.* This gives the tenant possession for an indefinite period of time subject to renegotiation of the lease terms. On the other hand, *tenancy by sufferance* occurs when a tenant remains *without* the landlord's permission. A tenant by sufferance is subject to immediate eviction.

Lease Renewal

Lease administration and renewal efforts have many legal implications. One of your main responsibilities as site manager is to monitor lease expirations and offer new leases to tenants in a timely fashion. As the date of a tenant's lease expiration approaches, it is important to review his or her rental record—i.e., payment history, records of housekeeping and unit condition, and other information. If the tenant meets the criteria for lease renewal, tenancy may be renewed with either a new lease or a lease *rider*—an addendum to the original lease. The advantage of an entirely new lease is that it enables the landlord to update lease terms and assures consistent documentation and lease terms for all tenants.

Ordinarily, landlord-tenant law requires 30–90 days' notice for lease renewals and changes to the terms of a lease. All renewal correspondence should provide notice of any rent increase or changes in the amount of the security deposit, consistent with established management policy. Reasons for rent increases should also be explained. In many areas, it is common practice to require a security deposit equal to a month's rent, and additional deposit funds may be required when the rent is increased.

Following receipt of the renewal notice, the tenant must notify the landlord of his or her decision to stay or move out. Depending on local law, if a tenant does not notify the landlord and does not move out, the tenancy may continue on a month-to-month basis at the increased rent described in the renewal letter. However, such holding over may create a tenancy by sufferance. To avoid the confusion—and possible confrontation—that can arise in such a situation, it is important to pursue renewal efforts vigorously and to follow up on correspondence with telephone calls or personal visits.

Renewal of leases is one of the site manager's most important responsibilities because the attendant rent increases are a critical element in increasing the property's NOI. While personal efforts are often much more effective than form letters in achieving lease renewals—as noted in chapter 7—such personal contacts also assure that the legalities are being followed. The site manager will also be better able to anticipate problems arising out of a possible holdover if the tenant does not renew the lease.

Nonrenewal of Leases

If a tenant decides not to renew a lease, it is important to know that fact in advance. Because turnover times can be difficult to predict, you will want to arrange to start showing apartments as soon as possible. Although landlord-tenant law grants the landlord the right to show apartments (this point should be stated in the lease) and tenants cannot refuse permission, you should try to respect the departing tenant's privacy, and times for showing the apartment should be arranged in advance.

Sometimes a landlord will decide not to renew a tenant's lease. This may be done for any number of reasons. If a property needs major rehabilitation, it may be easier to do the work in the absence of tenants. Often, however, nonrenewal is the result of a tenant's behavior—e.g., an erratic payment history, excessive damage to the premises, or failure to respect other tenants. Because the landlord has the legal right to repossess the premises at the end of a tenancy, there is no need to provide justification for nonrenewal *(no-cause termination).* Nevertheless, you should send the tenant a brief statement notifying him or her that the lease is expiring and stating when the tenant is expected to vacate the premises because the lease will not be renewed. It is wisest to avoid explaining reasons for nonrenewal. Otherwise a tenant can contest the action by claiming in court that the landlord was retaliating against him or her or breaching the lease *(termination for cause).*

Terminating a Lease. Usually a lease may be terminated by either party because of a breach by the other. However, part of the rationale

Reasons for Terminating a Lease

Breach of Contract by the Tenant
- Failure to pay rent.
- Failure to comply with the lease requirements.
- Failure to abide by property rules and regulations, lease covenants, and landlord-tenant law.

Breach of Contract by the Landlord
- Failure to maintain the leased premises in a habitable condition.
- Failure to deliver possession to the tenant.
- Unlawful removal of the tenant by the landlord.
- Destruction or condemnation of the premises.

Specific Early Cancellation Provisions
- Transfer clause—may require several months' notice and proof of transfer, and landlord may impose a penalty or "buy out."
- Home purchase clause—may require several months' notice and landlord may require a "buy out."
- Death clause—states number of months an estate would be obligated for rent.
- Military clause—may require advance notice, proof of transfer orders, and up-to-date rent payment.
- Condemnation—acquisition of the property by a government agency for public use (eminent domain).

for having a lease is to establish occupancy for a specific period of time. Because people's circumstances can change, it may be necessary (or desirable) to be able to accommodate some types of changes.

If tenants are not permitted to terminate a lease legally, some will do so illegally. Management companies can reduce the number of tenants who "skip out" on leases—and the attendant litigation—by providing reasonable alternatives within the lease itself. Whether your standard lease requires a departing tenant to find a replacement, or the landlord assumes this responsibility, the lease should contain a subletting clause. For example, if a new tenant is found, and the individual meets all of management's tenant selection criteria, either the old lease can be canceled outright, or the new tenant may be permitted to sublease the apartment under the original agreement. If the second option is chosen, the original tenant must understand that he or she is still liable for all covenants of the original lease.

If management policy allows tenants a right to terminate their

EXHIBIT 10.2

Sample Transfer Agreement/Cancellation of Lease

This rider is attached to and made a part of a lease dated ______________
between ______________, lessor, and ______________,
lessee, for an apartment at ______________.

This lease may be canceled by mutual agreement between Lessee and Lessor in the event that Lessee's employer transfers Lessee to another business location and such transfer requires Lessee to relocate his/her residence, subject to the following conditions:

Lessee must give Lessor ______________ (________) days prior written notice of transfer.

Such notice to Lessor must be accompanied by a copy of the transfer orders from his/her employer.

It is also agreed and understood that this transfer clause may be executed only after ______________ (________) months have elapsed and provided Lessee pays an additional fee of $ ______________ at the time the Notice of Transfer is submitted to Lessor.

It is also agreed and understood that Lessee will pay Lessor for any and all damage in the apartment which may be discovered by Lessor when Lessee vacates the apartment.

For lessor	Lessee
______________	______________
Date ______________	Date ______________

leases prematurely, this should be handled on the basis of a standing policy, which will reduce the likelihood of inconsistent treatment. It may also be appropriate to address particular situations that are likely to arise and to indicate a requirement for extra consideration. Tenants may seek to terminate a lease for many reasons, including marriage, divorce, or a job transfer. Because job transfers are not always in the individual's control, it is a good idea to provide for this occurrence with a transfer or cancellation rider that can be added to the lease (exhibit 10.2). Also if a tenant has personal (financial) problems that may preclude him or her from honoring the lease obligations, it may be to the advantage of the management company to find a replacement tenant before the lease expires. Whether the new tenant subleases the apartment or signs a completely new lease, the management company will be protected by replacing the first tenant with one who has a better financial footing.

EVICTION

Sometimes it may be necessary to take legal action to remove a tenant from the leased premises. *Eviction* of tenants is a very serious undertaking. Although it can be unpleasant, it is sometimes necessary in site management. Because the specific legal requirements of eviction vary from state to state and even between municipalities within states, you must be familiar with the particular requirements in your jurisdiction and confer with legal counsel prior to initiating eviction proceedings against a tenant.

Reasons for Eviction

The most common reason for eviction is nonpayment of rent. In many states, the only defense a tenant can offer for nonpayment of rent is *constructive eviction* (i.e., that the landlord's actions violated the tenant's rights under the lease or failed to provide for the habitability of the unit or essential services, and the tenant has been forced to vacate the leased premises).

Other grounds for eviction are violation of the lease terms, including nonpayment of monies other than rent (e.g., utilities, deposits, fees), misuse of the facilities, destruction of property, failure to maintain the premises, and creating a nuisance (for example, unlawful activities, persistent noisy behavior, keeping a pet in violation of the lease, or improperly disposing of wastes). These are all examples of *eviction for cause* (other than nonpayment of rent). A *no-cause action,* on the other hand, is the landlord simply calling an end to the lease, usually a month-to-month lease which either party can terminate with sufficient notice. If a tenant fails to move out at the end of a tenancy, an *unlawful detainer* action may be required to terminate what has become a holdover tenancy. (More details are provided in the discussion of eviction for nonpayment.)

Because eviction procedures and definitions of cause and no cause are prescribed by statute, real estate managers must be familiar with both law and practice. In particular, local law may be more favorable to tenants than to landlords.

Handling Delinquencies. Because the most common reason for eviction is delinquency or outright nonpayment, the best practice is to encourage timely payment of rent, beginning with the qualification process (checking on past performance) and then reiterating management's collection policies during orientation. This should include actions that will be taken in case of delinquency. (Tenant selection criteria were described in chapter 7.) However, even the most exacting qualification processes will occasionally miss an irresponsible person.

Some real estate managers are hesitant to pursue delinquencies, especially in a soft market. They fail to realize that an occupied apartment for which no rent is being collected is more costly than a vacant one—a vacant unit is not subject to damage and its utility costs are negligible. More importantly, vacancy allows the real estate manager to find a new tenant who will pay the rent.

You should not be afraid to pursue collections aggressively. The effectiveness of a collection process depends on the diligence of the people implementing it. You should make sure the site personnel who deal with collections are familiar with company policy and apply it uniformly, without exception. In most situations there is a nominal grace period (e.g., 3–5 days) to allow for mail delivery of payments. Then, in keeping with established policy, a notice should be sent to tenants on the first day the rent is delinquent. This should be a strongly worded but friendly *reminder notice.* Because the check may be delayed in the mail, the notice should simply state that the office has not received the rent payment and ask the tenant to contact the office about the matter (exhibit 10.3). In addition, the site manager should contact the tenant by telephone or in person.

If there is no response to the reminder notice, the next step is to send another notice and visit the tenant personally. The notice may be either an eviction notice or a second reminder notice as required by local law. It may demand that the tenant pay the delinquent rent or vacate the premises. By law, such a *notice to pay or quit* is usually the first step in a formal eviction proceeding, and notarization and proper service may be required. Because this may automatically terminate the lease, its implications must be understood completely before you send it.

State and local laws prescribe the period of time allowed and the form and content of the notice to pay or quit, as well as how it is to be served and witnessed. This notice should also state any late or legal fees, if they are permitted. Generally, the landlord may not be able to accept partial payment without jeopardizing the effectiveness of the

EXHIBIT 10.3

Sample Late Rent Reminder Letter

Date

Name of Tenant(s)
Address
City, State, Zip Code

Dear Resident:

Our records indicate that your rent for the month of ________________ is past due. Perhaps you have overlooked this obligation.

In accordance with your lease, a late fee of $ ______________ is due in addition to your rent payment of $ ______________. Your total unpaid balance is $ ______________.

Please be advised that if all monies due are not received in our office within five days of the date of this letter, legal actions will commence.

Thank you for your prompt attention to this matter.

[NAME OF MANAGEMENT COMPANY]

____

Site Manager

notice or the right to bring suit; however, local requirements differ so widely that an attorney should be consulted to determine what applies in your jurisdiction. If the tenant refuses to pay all the delinquent rent, you can begin eviction proceedings (with the management company's approval).

Eviction for Nonpayment. In the case of eviction for nonpayment, if the tenant has not complied with the demand for payment within the time allowed, a complaint must be filed in court. This should be done by an attorney; however, in some jurisdictions, the owner's agent (e.g., the property manager or site manager) may be able to file the complaint without an attorney accompanying him or her. When the complaint is filed, the judge will issue a summons to appear in court, and this document and the complaint are served on the tenant by a third party (e.g., a sheriff or process server or the owner's agent or the site manager, depending on local law). If the summons and complaint cannot be delivered to the tenant personally, state or local law will specify alternate procedures. Sometimes a notice may be affixed on the front door of the premises or in another conspicuous place.

The prescribed procedures must be followed to the letter, or the entire eviction proceeding may be invalidated. Even a minor procedural inconsistency may permit the tenant to avoid the eviction, and the process will have to be restarted. Harassment or intimidation of the tenant should be avoided at all costs—denying the tenant access to or use of the apartment (lockout) or denying or limiting specific services (e.g., maintenance) would be considered harassment and could be cause for a countersuit.

In court, the judge may give the tenant an opportunity to pay the rent. State and local laws determine whether the landlord has any *legal obligation* to accept payment at this point. If the tenant offers to pay, the judge may direct the landlord to accept payment. If the tenant cannot pay, the judge will usually award judgment in favor of the landlord. This award often includes possession of the apartment, rent due, and court costs, depending on the judge. As part of the judgment, the tenant will be given a date by which to vacate the premises.

If the tenant does not vacate the apartment by the specified date, he or she may be guilty of *unlawful detainer* (remaining in possession of the premises after proper notice to vacate has been served), and further action will have to be taken. Here again, specific procedures are dictated by applicable local law. In some jurisdictions, removal by the sheriff follows automatically; in others, the landlord's attorneys must obtain a writ of possession, and if that is ignored, they have to return to court for a writ of eviction, which orders an officer of the court to physically eject and dispossess the tenant.

Eviction is a costly and time-consuming remedy. Even in the best of circumstances, it may take several months to complete the process although, in some states, eviction can take place in as few as ten days. The best way to minimize the need for eviction is to be diligent in screening prospective tenants—checking credit references and verifying all information provided on the lease application. In the course of a tenancy, documenting tenants' payment records, being respectful of their privacy, and performing (and documenting) maintenance promptly, are the best ways to maintain harmony on the property (as well as counter a tenant's defense of nonpayment in court). If this is done, the majority of tenants will observe the requirements of the lease.

Eviction from Government-Assisted Housing

The rules governing eviction are somewhat different for landlords of properties administered through the U.S. Department of Housing and Urban Development (HUD) or under Section 8 of the Housing Authority Act of 1937. Each federally subsidized housing program is regulated by provisions of federal law that contain specific procedures the landlord must follow to recover possession of a dwelling from a tenant. Because evictions put tenants at risk of losing not only their leases, but also their right to participate in federal subsidy programs, the regulations covering such lease terminations contain numerous safeguards for the tenant that exceed most state laws.

Typically, there must be good cause to evict a tenant from federally subsidized housing. The notice requirements differ according to the type of lease violation. *Material violations* include nonpayment of rent and any threat to the health or safety of other tenants or employees. State law usually prevails regarding notice requirements in these cases. For *nonmaterial lease violations* (violations not related to money), a thirty-day notice is usually required for lease termination. Notices must be hand delivered or mailed, and they must be sent to both the tenant and HUD.

Regulations also require the termination notice to state the specific grounds for terminating the lease so the tenant is able to prepare a defense. The termination notice usually allows for a meeting with the landlord prior to review of the eviction and for a pretermination administrative review. The notice must also state that the tenant may retain the services of an attorney.

If the tenant is still in breach of the lease after the termination notice period has expired, the landlord can proceed with an unlawful detainer action. Unlawful detainer occurs when a tenant intentionally holds over the leased premises without rights beyond the lease term. The procedures here are quite similar to those used to regain possession of privately owned property.

OTHER LEGAL CONSIDERATIONS

In addition to the legal issues already discussed, site managers must occasionally deal with situations in which tenants have abandoned their apartments, sometimes leaving behind personal possessions. In these and other circumstances, efforts must be made to collect delinquencies as well as dispose of abandoned personal property. More rarely, the site manager may have to deal with the death of a tenant. The civil rights of tenants—especially as they concern the requirements of the Americans with Disabilities Act and fair housing laws—are also a consideration.

Dealing with Abandonment

On occasion, the site manager may have to deal with abandonment of an apartment and the tenant's personal property. This poses several legal challenges. *Abandonment* is defined as the voluntary intentional surrender of property, or a right to property, without naming a successor as owner or tenant. Nevertheless, the tenant is not relieved of lease obligations unless the landlord accepts the abandonment and does not pursue the case further.

While abandonment may eliminate a troublesome tenant, the issues of unpaid rent and disposal of the tenant's personal property remain, and the landlord may be liable for damages if the tenant's personal property is not disposed of properly. *Abandonment of the leased premises* may be indicated by one or more of the following signs:

- An extended period of inactivity or apparent absence and failure to pay the rent during this time.
- Return of keys by the tenant.
- Failure to elicit a response during repeated attempts to communicate by letter, telephone, or knocking at the door.
- Finding the unit unoccupied upon entering it.
- Utilities (electricity, gas) turned off.
- Absence of mail (mail being forwarded).

Because abandonment of the leased premises constitutes *default* of the lease, there should be a clause in the lease defining abandonment and its consequences. Under such a clause, a tenant may be required to give notice of his or her intent to be absent for an extended period. If rent is unpaid *and* a unit appears to be abandoned, you should initiate the usual eviction process. This is a good precaution against an unlawful entry suit by the tenant.

Disposition of *abandoned personal property* requires a different approach. The landlord should store abandoned property appropriately. This includes inventorying, tagging, and storing all items left behind in the rented space. State or local law may require witnesses to this procedure. If that is the case, their names, signatures, addresses, phone numbers, and social security numbers should be recorded. If possible, photographs should be taken for documentation. This can serve as evidence if the tenant charges theft or destruction of his or her property.

The holding period and disposition procedures are usually prescribed by law. Storing abandoned property creates a lien against that property for moving and storage costs. However, this amount must be reasonable; otherwise the tenant can challenge it in court. The tenant must be notified of the storage and intended disposition of the abandoned property. Because the specific procedures and time frame for this notice may also be prescribed by law, an attorney should be consulted before you take any action. Delivery of the notice via certified mail, return receipt requested, to the last known address of the tenant may be required. If the tenant reclaims the property and pays whatever is owed, the problem is solved; however, if the tenant does not do this within the prescribed period, the property may be sold, donated, or discarded. (It is important to keep accurate records of their disposition in case any questions arise.) Note, however, that a tenant's abandoned property should never be "held hostage" in an effort to force payment of back rent. Landlords can only collect for packing and storage; back rent is a separate issue.

In the same vein, *abandoned vehicles* are another issue you may have to face. A vehicle is presumed abandoned by its owner if (1) it is not moved for a specified period of time (unless the landlord has notified its owner regarding the lack of use), (2) it appears to be disabled, (3) it does not show a required parking sticker (on-site parking or other permit), or (4) it has no local (municipal) sticker or state license plate. If a vehicle is abandoned, it must be removed from the property. Local ordinances usually outline specific requirements, such as posting signs that say "unauthorized vehicles will be towed." Even if not required by law, you should notify the police of abandoned vehicles and their disposition.

Collections

Collecting rent after a tenant has abandoned an apartment or been evicted can be difficult. The landlord has several options, including use of a *collection agency.* The management company may have a standard procedure for determining whether this option is financially viable. Of course, the agent does have a fiduciary responsibility to attempt to collect delinquent rent. Collection agencies typically charge a fee that is a percentage of the amount recovered. Although the fee reduces the amount of money collected, collecting some money is better than collecting none or spending valuable time pursuing delinquent tenants. Collection agencies assume responsibility for all legal costs, which is an advantage of using them. The landlord is not relieved of liability, however, and can be sued if the agency harasses a former tenant.

In some states, the real estate manager may be able to pursue collections in small claims or "housing" court. In *small claims courts,* the dollar amounts and procedures vary by jurisdiction: Dollar limits may be as low as $500 or as high as $5,000. Depending on the amount owed, the costs of a court appearance (manager's time, attorney fees) may limit the effectiveness of this option. If you appear in court, you should be prepared to document the manager's authority by being able to show a copy of the contract that authorizes you to act for the property owner. Because technicalities can be the basis for dismissal of a case, requiring it to be refiled, you should always make sure that proper notice has been given to a tenant in a letter or legal document that outlines the complaint—i.e., the amount that is owed and the period of delinquency. You should also know how the tenant responded and be prepared to refute any false claims. It is a good idea to document the exact sequence of events. Being able to furnish supporting documents is essential; extra copies should be prepared in advance of a court appearance. Not only will this save time and legal fees in the preparation of a formal complaint by an attorney, it will help focus the judge's attention on the primary issue. Photographs and the testimony of witnesses may also be important to a case.

Dealing with the Death of a Tenant

Occasionally site managers must deal with the death of a tenant. This unpleasant experience is made more difficult by the legal responsibilities associated with it. The first step is to notify the appropriate authorities (e.g., the police). After that, you should secure the apartment because the manager or landlord may be liable for the safety of personal belongings until the proper authority takes over. Authorities will most likely secure and seal the apartment while they investigate the cause of death. Because the estate may be under the supervision of a local public administrator until processing is completed, it could take as long as a month before you can regain possession of the premises. Administrative details—e.g., notifying the tenant's next of kin (identified in rental records)—must also be handled properly. Following a careful accounting of any charges to the tenancy and removal of the deceased tenant's property, the security deposit—less charges for excess damage—can be returned to the tenant's estate.

Civil Rights Issues in Real Estate Management

Site managers have to be concerned about complying with fair housing laws and the Americans with Disabilities Act (ADA). These laws have been discussed earlier (see chapters 3, 6, and 7), but their legal implications require additional review. Failure to comply with them can have serious implications for the management company and the property owner.

The *Fair Housing Amendments Act of 1988* expanded the number of "protected classes" subject to Title VIII of the Civil Rights Act of 1968. Title VIII formerly prohibited discrimination in the sale, rental, and financing of dwellings based on race, color, sex, religion, or national origin. The new law also prohibits discrimination on the basis of physical or mental disability and familial status. (Other protected classes based on lifestyle or sexual orientation may be established under state or local fair housing laws.) Because advertising and other marketing activities can be perceived as discriminatory, the Fair Housing Amendments Act also addresses words, phrases, and symbols to be avoided.

Under provisions of the 1988 Act, a landlord cannot refuse to permit a disabled tenant to modify the leased premises at his or her own expense, as long as the modifications are necessary to allow full enjoyment of the premises. Nor can a landlord refuse to implement reasonable rules and policies that will allow a disabled person the same right to use and enjoy the dwelling as tenants who are not disabled. Finally, certain multifamily dwellings designed and constructed after March 13, 1991, must be accessible to people with disabilities.

Discrimination on the basis of familial status refers to people under the age of 18 who live with a parent, legal guardian, or any person

Key Actions Related to Legal Issues in Site Management

Primary Functions
- Fulfill the obligations of agency described in the management agreement
- Fulfill the obligations created under landlord-tenant law and the lease
- Administer leases fairly
- Monitor lease compliance and enforce lease provisions
- Monitor lease expirations and initiate renewal efforts
- Implement nondiscriminatory policies and practices related to fair housing and ADA requirements
- Pursue collections diligently

Adjunct Functions
- Administer security deposits
- Participate in eviction proceedings
- Investigate abandonment of leased premises and deal with abandoned personal property

designated by law to have custody of a child. This includes pregnant women and anyone who is in the process of securing legal custody of a child under the age of 18. The law applies not only to the sale and rental of housing, but also to financing for housing.

Prior to the Fair Housing Amendments Act, the U.S. Department of Housing and Urban Development (HUD) had the power to enforce Title VIII requirements only by informal conciliation efforts. Under the 1988 Act, however, this agency has much greater discretionary power. If HUD learns of a discriminatory practice by a landlord, it may investigate and bring action against him or her. In addition, anyone who is alleged to have suffered discrimination may file a complaint with HUD, which may ultimately be referred to the federal court.

The penalties for violating fair housing laws are severe. If found guilty under the federal act, a landlord may face a fine of $10,000 for the first offense, $25,000 for the second offense within five years, and $50,000 if the statute has been violated more than twice in seven years. A landlord found guilty in federal court may be assessed punitive damages in addition to any civil penalties imposed.

In addition to the federal laws, fair housing laws may be enacted at the state and local levels, and you will need to know their compliance requirements as well. As with all multilevel regulations, in practice the most stringent requirements will prevail.

The *Americans with Disabilities Act (ADA)* prohibits discrimination against qualified disabled persons in job application procedures, hiring, promotion, compensation, job training, or discharge because of a physical or mental impairment (disability) that substantially limits one or more of a person's major life functions. The employee policies in place on site should foster compliance with ADA requirements. The ADA also addresses accessibility of public accommodations, which may apply to building entrances and the leasing office as part of the common areas of the property. Required changes to the common areas (e.g., access ramps, special parking provisions) are the landlord's expense.

SUMMARY

Site managers have few responsibilities more important than those concerning the many legal issues related to real estate management. The management agreement creates an agency relationship. As an agent of the owner, the management company—and therefore the site manager—has a fiduciary responsibility to act in the owner's best interest. Part of this responsibility includes familiarity with and understanding of the landlords' and tenants' rights and responsibilities that are contained in the applicable landlord-tenant law and reiterated in the lease agreement.

Landlord-tenant law governs lease requirements. To be legally binding, a lease must identify the parties, describe the leased premises, define the lease term (including the commencement and termination dates of the tenancy), state the rent and how it should be paid, and spell out the respective rights and responsibilities of the parties.

Lease clauses address specific issues relating to those rights and responsibilities, including requirements for security deposits, maintenance of the premises, subletting and assignment, notice requirements for renewal and nonrenewal, and conditions under which a tenant (or landlord) would be in default of the lease. The advantages of a written lease over an oral agreement include the clear establishment of specific performance requirements that minimize liability for the parties to the agreement.

Eviction is a serious action, but it may be the only solution to a problematic tenancy. Because the site manager's participation in eviction proceedings is essential, you must be familiar with the legal requirements and procedures necessary to regain possession of an apartment in your area. The requirements for eviction from government-assisted housing differ from those for privately owned apartments.

As site manager, you must also be able to deal with abandonment of apartments by tenants. There are certain requirements that you must meet to regain possession of the premises legally, and these must be followed carefully to protect the owner and the management company from liability. Because abandonment often goes hand-in-hand with delinquency, you also have to be familiar with procedures for collection of back rent when a tenant "skips." The legalities of collection demand careful assembly of evidence that will be presented in court. Abandoned personal property and the death of a tenant are other situations for which there are legally mandated procedures to be followed. Site managers must also be familiar with the compliance requirements of fair housing laws and the Americans with Disabilities Act.

Key Terms

agent
breach of contract
consideration
default
delinquency
lessee
lessor
notice to vacate
principal
security deposit
small claims court
Uniform Residential Landlord and Tenant Act
wear and tear

Key Concepts

abandonment
assignment
constructive eviction
essential services
eviction
fiduciary responsibility
habitability
retaliatory eviction
nonrenewal
right of re-entry
sublet
tenancy at will
tenancy by sufferance
unlawful detainer

Key Points

- What is the real estate manager's fiduciary responsibility to the property owner?

- What are the landlord's rights and responsibilities under landlord-tenant law?
- What are the tenants' rights and responsibilities under landlord-tenant law?
- Why is it important to use a written lease?
- What are the grounds for evicting a tenant?
- What are the grounds for not renewing a tenant's lease?
- What constitutes abandonment of leased premises? Of personal property?
- What classes are protected under the federal fair housing law?

11

Implementing Professionalism in Residential Management

In the preceding chapters, you have read about the many aspects of residential site management and seen that contemporary site management is much more than showing and leasing apartments and collecting rent. In order to meet the challenges of today's complex and ever-changing real estate management markets, you have to take into account all the components of management.

Property owners also recognize the complexity and challenges of managing real estate, and they look to professional real estate managers to meet them. Whereas property owners once commonly looked upon real estate ownership merely as a tax shelter, they now seek competitive returns on their real estate investments. Value enhancement—maximization of cash flow and continual improvement of the physical asset—are now routinely expected by property owners.

In a survey conducted for the Institute of Real Estate Management Foundation, property owners were asked to rate the importance of several different characteristics when selecting professional management. Integrity and reliability were considered the most important, followed by the quality of individual real estate managers, timeliness of reports, and knowledge of local market conditions. In this case, the quality of the individual was related to property management tasks rather than personal traits. Next in importance were specific real estate management skills and knowledge: maintenance, budgeting, quality and scope of reports, marketing strategies and programs, and record keeping. Finally, owners look for *professionalism*—education and training—in their real estate managers.

In order to achieve the high standards that owners set, real estate managers have to understand the management process at two levels: real estate management in the broad sense and the demands of managing a particular property and meeting the specific goals of that property's owner. This requires consideration of customers and how to respond to their needs as well as the needs of the property.

DEFINING THE CUSTOMER—THE KEY TO SERVICE

Many businesses have difficulty defining their customer: To whom does their product or service appeal? How can a product or service be improved? In the simplest terms, a customer is anyone who benefits from the product or service a company offers. In residential real estate management, there are two very different customers. The primary customer is the property owner: The manager's responsibilities to this customer are detailed in the management agreement, which makes fiduciary duties concrete. The secondary customer is the resident. The challenge of management is to meet both of these customers' expectations.

Although the two customers' demands differ—sometimes widely—they cannot be viewed separately. The property owner wants to profit from a real estate investment, while residents want value and service in exchange for their rent dollars. In turn, fulfillment of the owner's desires depends on satisfied residents who pay their rent on time, take care of their homes, and renew their leases. To satisfy both sets of demands, the site manager has to weigh and assess how they best can be met. The role of "balancer" is central to the site management position. One of the most important tasks of real estate management, then, is identifying customers' requirements and finding a way to balance them.

The first step in this process is recognizing that the demands of both kinds of customer are not mutually exclusive. It is more realistic—and more productive—to adopt an approach that allows for "win-win" solutions to management challenges. The property owner *could* extract enormous income from a property in a short period of time by reducing maintenance expenses while keeping rents high. Indeed, this strategy would result in high short-term profits. In the longer term, however, such a strategy would have severe repercussions. Neglect and deferred maintenance would drive out better residents, leaving behind only those residents who do not care about the condition of the property, who are less likely to pay their rent reliably and more likely to damage their apartments. In the end, the property's NOI would decline, cash flow would dwindle, and the value of the property itself (as demonstrated in the capitalization rate equation discussed in chapter 4) would suffer.

In real estate management, there are many factors that must be weighed in the balance. A site manager must consider the needs and expectations of the owner, the physical needs of the property, the residents' expectations and desires, and the financial realities of the marketplace and the property. Finding an equilibrium among all these factors is the key. Also, because the demands are constantly evolving and changing, the equilibrium will have to be readjusted along the way.

In the process of balancing these demands, expectations, and desires, the manager also has a series of formal responsibilities to different parties. The fiduciary responsibility of the management agreement spells out legal and ethical standards that must be upheld as part of the agency relationship. Real estate managers also have a responsibility to achieve property owners' financial objectives. In addition, the site manager has legal and ethical responsibilities to residents. These are prescribed by landlord-tenant law and fulfilled by complying with that body of law, subscribing to a professional code of ethics—such as that of the ACCREDITED RESIDENTIAL MANAGER® (ARM®) service award granted by the Institute of Real Estate Management—and demonstrating personal character and integrity. As a site manager, your responsibilities will vary from one property to another and from one management firm to another, but the need to be professional and do your job well is a constant.

SITE MANAGEMENT AS A PROCESS

In a competitive rental market, all the components of real estate management must come together seamlessly. Because of this, the site manager is the critical link in the management chain. His or her conceptual skills (seeing the "big picture"), technical skills (implementing the details of real estate management—the specifics of marketing and leasing, maintenance, and resident retention as well as attention to risk management and legal issues), and interpersonal skills (coordinating the efforts of the entire on-site staff and communicating with residents) are all necessary for success.

One of the most important roles site managers play is that of *team manager,* bringing together the strengths of all the members of the on-site staff and creating a supportive environment in which information is shared and everyone has a chance to contribute. To achieve this, information must be shared and presented appropriately. The cascade effect can be demonstrated by an example related to leasing. If traffic reports are not completed properly, sources of prospects could be misidentified with the result that marketing dollars would be misspent and future prospects lost. The ramifications of this are serious—occupancy rates could begin to decline as a result, reducing the amount of income the property generates. Thus, the potential damage to the financial integrity of the property from something as simple as erroneous or incomplete traffic reports is quite serious.

Team management begins with some rather simple—but very important—concepts. First an understanding on the part of each member of the team that everyone has to work together, along with a willingness and desire to make it happen. This is something like the saying about the left hand knowing what the right hand is doing. In residential management, all personnel need to know what has to be done when: What are the goals for the week, the month, the quarter, and the year? Part of this understanding involves replacing "me" and "I" with "us" and "we." This is not easy for some people, and resistance can be expected. However, given time and support, employees will begin to thrive under team management.

The success of a residential rental property depends on the site manager's understanding of management at the conceptual level and his or her ability to achieve the owner's goals. These goals must be realistic; and once they have been set, their achievement will depend on the daily operations of the property. In day-to-day operations, the conceptual plan for the property is outlined in a management plan, reflected in the operating and capital improvements budgets, and implemented through the real estate manager's technical and interpersonal skills.

Another part of effective management is the manager's ability to motivate all types of employees. A successful manager knows the players, their strengths and weaknesses, and how to bring together the different personalities to work better by complementing and supplementing each other. In addition, the site manager has to know how to talk to each employee, what motivates him or her, and what will invite and sustain everyone's cooperation. Words are powerful tools, and, used correctly, they can stimulate people to great achievements.

The Conceptual Level—Management Planning as a Design for Success

A management plan may comprise an exhaustive analysis of the physical, financial, and operational conditions of a property, or it may consist of only an operating budget, a list of goals, and a property manager's observations about a property. The specific emphasis of any management plan will depend on the owner's goals, the property type, its physical and financial condition, and any problems that management must resolve.

The property owner sets broad goals (e.g., capital appreciation or income), and the property manager establishes narrower, more specific goals aimed at realizing those set by the owner. The site manager works with the property manager in deciding how to carry out these various goals for the property, setting his or her own personal goals within that broader perspective. Because of the unique aspects of each property, each real estate manager's management style, and each owner's expectations, particular aspects of management plans will differ; however, the basic demands and format are quite similar. If the owner seeks rapid capital appreciation from the property, the management plan may recommend improvements that can be made in a short time.

For owners who want consistent income from their investment, the plan might comprise a schedule of gradual improvements that will develop and maintain a higher occupancy rate, creating the potential for steadily increasing cash flow.

The preliminary analytical components of a management plan, as described in chapter 2, are:

- Regional analysis
- Neighborhood analysis
- Property analysis
- Market analysis—the competition

Often an analysis of alternatives and a cost-benefit analysis, drawing from these a series of general conclusions and recommendations, are included.

Analysis of Alternatives. Some properties require fundamental changes in their operations or administration, or their physical components, to enable them to generate maximum NOI. In the effort to improve the performance of a property, a real estate manager investigates the range of possible changes and evaluates their anticipated effects—an *analysis of alternatives.* Because each proposed change carries a cost, it is also important to compare the costs and benefits of each proposal or combination of proposals.

Changing the operations of a property is a common component of any management plan. The intent is usually to alter or modify procedural methods or increase efficiency without changing the physical makeup of the property. The aim may be to reduce operating expenses and thereby increase NOI. Operational changes can range from raising rents so they will be more in line with market conditions to adopting low-cost or no-cost energy-saving measures of the type discussed in chapter 8.

Even though the intent of operational changes is to reduce operating expenses as a percentage of gross income, quality should never be compromised. Not only will residents notice the difference, but competitors will readily seize the advantage created for them by such a move. Any recommendation that sacrifices particular services may be more costly than the savings that are achieved. On the other hand, studying the competition may lead to discovery of new methods that will reduce costs while preserving or enhancing service standards.

Administrative changes can have a profound impact on a property as well. A few examples will illustrate this point. Changing the grace period during which rent can be paid before late fees are assessed from 5 to 3 days may increase delinquencies at the start, especially if a high percentage of residents have limited incomes; over the long run, however, it will allow you to collect money sooner, allowing for greater control and better financial management. Raising security deposits with the intention of attracting better-qualified renters may achieve its objective. On the other hand, such a move may result in longer turnaround times for vacant apartments. Finally, charging residents additional rent for the privilege of month-to-month tenancy may motivate residents to renew leases—but it may also increase turnover.

Physical changes to the property may be considered as well. Rehabilitation and modernization, for example, can lengthen the economic life of a property. Installation of new carpeting, new appliances, or equipment that is more energy-efficient—any physical improvement that does not alter the use of the property—is considered rehabilitative. Rehabilitation and modernization are attractive because, depending on local market conditions, the costs of financing and building new structures may be prohibitive. When physical changes are proposed, a capital budget must show how funds for the change will be allocated, and the manager must estimate the impact of the change on NOI and property value and project how long before a financial benefit will be realized.

The most drastic alternative is a change in use. A recommendation to change the use of a property must be well-founded because such a procedure is complex and expensive, and once it is implemented, it is usually impossible to return to the original state. As with any such measure, the improvement in performance expected from a change in use must always be weighed carefully against the risks involved. The most common change for residential properties is condominium conversion. Other kinds of change in use include adaptive use (e.g., turning an old factory or warehouse into loft apartments) and demolition of existing structures to allow for new development.

Cost-Benefit Analysis. Changing a property or its operations always involves costs. The amount and extent of the costs will depend on the scope of the changes being made. Establishing a new accounting procedure may only require training of staff and replacement of a current form, but these can have measurable costs—in terms of personnel time, in particular—and the costs of such a change should be considered in light of the expected benefit of increased employee efficiency. On the other hand, physical changes—whether rehabilitation or other structural alterations—can be very costly and can cause interruption of all or part of the rental income stream while the work is being done. Even a recommendation to maintain the status quo has to be justified financially.

In order to determine whether a specific recommendation will improve the property's income, the real estate manager performs a *cost-benefit analysis.* Each proposed alternative is evaluated to determine whether it would indeed yield higher levels of NOI and cash flow than if the property were left unchanged. There is also the matter of recovering the costs of making the changes plus repayment of borrowed funds, with interest. Clearly, the benefits of increased income and increased property value must outweigh the costs of a change if a recommendation is to be feasible. This means the *payback period*—the amount of time for the change to pay for itself—has to be evaluated as well.

The Technical Level—Skills in Action

Site management develops mastery of many seemingly unrelated skills. In practice, administrative functions are intermingled with maintenance of the property as well as effective marketing and leasing.

Financial Aspects. In order to meet the owner's investment goals, realistic operating budgets must be developed, and budget projections for income and expenses must be met. Income can be increased by raising rents, lowering vacancy rates and reducing rent losses, shortening turnover times, and increasing closing ratios and renewal rates. Expenses can be controlled by reducing or stabilizing operating expenses—without sacrificing the physical integrity of the property. Efforts to do this include bulk purchasing, competitive bidding for quality products and services, maintenance management (including closer scheduling and better coordination and monitoring of maintenance personnel), and general preservation of the physical condition of the property.

Several specific steps can be taken to strengthen the financial integrity of the property:

1. Collect rents and late fees on a timely basis, shorten grace periods, reduce delinquencies and bad debts, and vigorously enforce rent collection and eviction policies.
2. Establish and maintain credit check policies and procedures in the resident qualification process. The result will be better-qualified residents who will pay their rent on time and will not break their lease agreements or precipitate evictions.
3. Maintain accurate and timely financial records for inclusion in monthly reports to owners. Review these records with the staff to identify problem areas that can be corrected.
4. Observe and report trends in marketing, leasing, turnover, delinquency rates, and activities of competing properties to ensure that the property is well positioned in the market place and that it maintains a competitive edge. Seek staff observations and input.
5. Contribute to the efficient operation of the property through comprehensive maintenance planning, scheduling, and implementation within budget guidelines (preventive maintenance). This entails pacing of expenses based on income flow and monitoring maintenance and repair work.
6. Maintain accurate maintenance and repair records that will facilitate accuracy in the preparation of operating budgets. Part of this will involve reporting to the property manager anticipated need for major repairs or replacements (capital expenditures) or other extraordinary requirements for maintenance or repairs to preserve the property or make it more competitive.
7. Create new programs to retain residents. This could involve training staff in how to renew leases and demonstrating the importance of quality in value enhancement to create an atmosphere that fosters resident retention.

These types of actions underscore the fact that viewing any one component of site management in isolation will yield a distorted picture. Successful site management requires understanding of the connections between all of your responsibilities. Marketing and leasing affect the financial integrity of the property. Maintenance and repairs influence resident satisfaction, which, in turn, strengthens or weakens the financial position of the property.

With the exception of debt service and capital expenditures, which are paid out of NOI, the site manager's actions directly affect the other seven components of cash flow. (Debt service is affected by NOI whenever an owner seeks to refinance his or her mortgage—NOI determines the property value as the basis for a loan—and capital expenditures are a direct result of the aging of the property or lack of diligence in performing maintenance.) In order to help maximize the property's NOI, the site manager must strive for the highest possible level of collected income and the lowest possible level of operating expenses without sacrificing the physical needs of the property. Deferring maintenance may increase NOI, but only at the expense of the property's physical condition, and that would be an undesirable outcome.

Site managers' contributions to the budgeting process can be invaluable. First, site managers can monitor what the competition is doing in terms of rent increases, deposits and fees they collect (additions, reductions, new fees), rehabilitation, and the addition of amenities. This information provides a better basis for comparison and enables the management company to determine what changes must be made to remain competitive, which advertising media are successful, and how much rent can be charged. *Shopping the competition* provides information about the strengths or weaknesses of particular apartment types in the local market as well as the point at which residents will probably reject rent increases and start to move out.

Maintenance and Other Costs. You are in an excellent position to identify necessary maintenance and repairs and what they should cost. Site managers can foresee trends in terms of the physical condition of the property (deterioration, obsolescence), and inspection reports help predict the need for maintenance and repairs—the key to preventive maintenance. A site manager is also in a position to estimate the costs of turning over vacant apartment units—in terms of both labor and materials.

Cost savings, as such, are a major component of your responsibilities. Examples of this include identifying jobs that can be consolidated

The Components of Cash Flow

	Gross Potential Rental Income
minus	Vacancy and Rent Loss
plus	Miscellaneous or Unscheduled Income
equals	Effective Gross Income
minus	Operating Expenses
equals	Net Operating Income (NOI)
minus	Debt Service (mortgage principal + interest)
minus	Capital Expenditures (budgeted separately)
equals	Cash Flow (the owner's proceeds)

to reduce labor costs, supply houses offering better prices and greater depth of inventory, techniques for maintenance and repairs that are more cost-effective—i.e., achieve the same results, for less money—and equipment and materials that can be purchased or used to reduce the costs of both labor and material without compromising quality.

Marketing and Leasing. Effective marketing requires the skills of many people. Beyond the conceptual level, the performance of market surveys, understanding of the competition and changing demographic factors, and the ability to relate these types of information to specific marketing strategies are essential. *Positioning* the property is the process of bringing together the pieces of the marketing puzzle, including the regional, neighborhood, and property analyses and the resident profile. The interpersonal skills of salesmanship and communication that are required elsewhere in site management also come into play.

A successful marketing program does not value marketing to new residents over retention of those already in place. Resident retention is an essential component of successful marketing. In fact, marketing and resident relations are inseparable. Marketing is a way to understand how to create, develop, and implement a better resident retention program. The greater the number of residents whose leases are renewed, the lower the turnover rate and the stronger a property will be—both financially and in terms of its sense of community. This, in turn, changes your marketing strategy for attracting new residents. Marketing forces you to understand the property in its environment and in comparison with its competition.

As an extension of marketing efforts, leasing requires you to share information with the staff, discuss goals, and develop approaches to achieving the planned results—together. Being more involved will increase staff members' feelings of satisfaction and result in higher productivity and greater achievement.

A Soft Market. Different market conditions place different demands on management. For example, when the market is soft—i.e., there are too many vacant apartments and too few renters—marketing efforts must be more focused to reach the desired target market effectively. A soft market can be the ultimate test for the entire on-site staff as well as the management company. In a soft market, there is a tendency to reduce economic standards—lower rents, offer more concessions, relax qualification requirements. In the short run, this may fill empty apartments, but in the long run, the results can be very undesirable. When economic conditions improve and the market is no longer "soft," rents can be increased. However, those residents who were accepted based on reduced standards may be unable to pay the higher rents, and delinquencies and vacancies will increase. In effect, all you have done is deferred future vacancies and reduced the property's NOI through concessions.

When the market is soft, it may be more effective to rely on fundamentals. Before apartments can be rented, prospects must be attracted to the property. Thus, efforts to increase traffic should be a priority. Reviewing the basics of marketing is an important first step: Signage, curb appeal, knowledge of the target market and renter profile, effective advertising, and a resident referral program are all fundamental to positioning the property.

In a soft market, you must use everything you have learned. Evaluating competitors' advertisements and signage—as well as your own—for fresh ideas and ways to increase the appeal of the property is a good starting point. Increasing public relations stories and implementing resident retention programs are also important. Teaching the on-site staff how to lease and close—to actively "sell" apartments rather than be mere "order takers"—may require formal training in the form of seminars on leasing, retention, or communication. Providing feedback is especially important, so staff members' performance should be evaluated regularly. Because retaining current residents is even more important in these times, good relations with residents should be stressed to all employees. The higher the retention rate, the stronger the financial condition of the property.

The Interpersonal Level—"People Skills" and Team Management

Management combines policies and procedures with administrative strategies, working closely with the people who make the decisions, and providing the necessary supervision to implement an owner's business objectives and achieve financial stability and growth. The key to success is recognizing that, in practical terms, *management is a process of achieving planned results through people.* Residential real estate management is no exception. In order to be a successful real estate manager, you have to be able to bring together the strengths of all the staff members—i.e., the team.

Teamwork and Goals. A teamlike atmosphere is essential to on-site success. In large part, this atmosphere will evolve out of your role as teacher and coach. As a manager and supervisor, one of your most important tasks is expanding your own knowledge so you can teach the on-site staff to do their jobs as well as possible. Teachers often can learn a great deal from their students, so you should expect to learn from the personnel you manage. They will also learn from each other.

Team management means sharing information, which places a premium on communication. In a team, the players complement one another to achieve greater goals than they could individually. You will have to communicate the goals of management to the entire on-site staff, as a group and individually. Not only will this enable personnel to visualize larger goals—and their roles in realizing them—but it will give them a greater sense of involvement and accomplishment. Just as you depend on communication from the management office, the on-site staff depends on communication from you.

Communication of goals can be accomplished in a variety of ways. One of the most effective is regularly scheduled meetings. Meetings can be very effective management tools, but without clear agendas they can become vague "bull sessions." Meetings are opportunities to report on progress toward meeting specific goals, recognize accomplishments by the team or individuals, and update overall goals. The way a meeting is conducted can convey expectations for time management and achievement, so you should use these opportunities to solicit suggestions from staff members on how they can do their jobs better and encourage feedback from other members of the team.

The result of such a supportive and challenging environment will be satisfied employees who achieve success together. The combination of involvement and peer pressure that develops spontaneously in an atmosphere where every member of the team has to pull his or her share of the load can be very rewarding and will generate further innovation. All along the way, you should keep track of the various goals and make sure members of the on-site team are informed of the progress toward meeting them.

Communication and Leadership. Clear, effective communication is essential. As site manager, you will use both verbal and nonverbal, formal and informal, communications in your dealings with the management company, the site personnel, outside contractors, and residents. The method and manner of communication will depend on the particular situation and the goal to be achieved. They will also depend on the structure of the management organization, in particular the number of layers through which communications must pass.

Effective communication has to start with the site manager who, in turn, trains the staff. A site manager will not be very successful if the other staff members do not practice good communication skills. An otherwise excellent employee who is unable to communicate information to other team members and residents will be a liability rather than an asset. Effective communication will not only increase the efficiency of staff responses to different situations, it will also facilitate resolution of both real and potential problems before they become difficult to manage.

Successful site management also requires you to be a good motivator. Motivation is more than directing a group of individuals. Employees must be coached and nurtured so they will greet challenges with energy and enthusiasm and seek creative solutions to problems that arise. Thus, a manager must possess *leadership qualities:* judgment, flexibility, knowledge, the strength to stand behind decisions, and personal and professional integrity—in effect, he or she must set a good example.

Successful leadership requires a clear vision of the importance of individual tasks, understanding of the skills necessary to perform them (and the education and training needed to develop these skills), and professionalism that sets high standards and expectations. All of these qualities are needed to build a collaborative team, involve employees and gain their personal commitment, generate new ideas, help initiate needed change, and develop innovations, all of which are prerequisites to achieving management goals through service.

The energy you bring to the job will be contagious: If you bring enthusiasm and high expectations, your staff will respond positively; if you have a negative attitude and expect the worst of your staff, they will "work down" to that level. By communicating positive expectations to staff members, site managers can avoid self-fulfilling prophecies that rob employees of satisfaction, residents of value, and property owners of income. A *self-fulfilling prophecy* is a situation that is caused by the belief that it will occur. Providing employees with positive expectations and direction will help them to succeed while even subtle hints that failure is expected will increase the likelihood of failure. Too often people are set up to fail, and when they do, the response is, "See, I told you so." As site manager, one of your most important roles is to hire people with the level of skill required, communicate expectations clearly, and then support employees who sincerely and diligently try to meet them. In other words, attitude is often as important as aptitude.

Leasing and Management. Communication skills are absolutely critical in the leasing process as well. They become especially important during closing, when you or a leasing agent are trying to persuade a prospect to complete a lease application. A closing has to be natural, above all, and it must suit the individual's personality. You have to be comfortable with what you say and how you say it. Closing is really nothing more than a summary of what the prospect has seen. It serves to highlight all of the tangible and intangible features of the property and a particular apartment that have impressed the prospect directly or been signalled to you as things the prospect values (through your interview or general conversation). An effective closing means you have observed and listened to the prospect and tied together every relevant point, thus demonstrating your empathy with the prospect. To be good at leasing, you have to enjoy being with people; your energy and enthusiasm must be apparent—and infectious.

In the same vein, lease *renewal* efforts begin the first time a prospect walks through the door of the site office. Everything you and the on-site staff do or do not do becomes part of a resident's history that will encourage or discourage lease renewal. There is a tremendous difference between trying to renew a lease in the last 60 days of a resident's tenancy and turning all of marketing, leasing, and resident relations into a continuing renewal effort. In scrambling to renew a lease in its final weeks, you may find out for the first time that a resident is unhappy with the way management responds to maintenance requests. After the impression that management simply does not care has been allowed to take root, it will not be easy to convince a resident to renew his or her lease. Undoing damage is much more difficult than preventing it. As pointed out in earlier chapters, prevention is critical in most areas of real estate management, from maintenance to new resident orientations to surveys of residents designed to identify potential trouble spots around the property. Effective communication leads to more efficient performance of everyone's duties and functions: Jobs are more likely to be done right the first time, saving both time and money. Residents will see and appreciate consistently higher levels of performance and be more inclined to renew their leases.

Effective communication is important to all aspects of management—personnel relations, financial administration, marketing and leasing, resident relations, maintenance, risk management, and the handling of legal issues. High professional standards are achieved through effective communication.

Confidence—The Key to Success

As in any profession, those who excel in residential real estate management have confidence in their own abilities. They have developed professional competence as a result of hard work. You can develop competence—and confidence—by following these steps:

- Master your subject—Self-confidence comes from hard work and experience, so become good at whatever you do.
- Surround yourself with good teachers—Good teachers will train you well and remind you to examine your own work and insist on doing your best.
- Organize what you learn—By organizing what you know, you will be able to take it apart and put it together to suit your needs.
- Practice—Competence comes with repetition. The more you do something, the better you will become at it.
- Seek feedback—Honest feedback is essential for building con-

fidence. The candor of those you respect and trust will help you do a better job each time.

- Be self-critical—Scrutinize your own work. Is there room for improvement? This will ward off complacency—a tendency to self-satisfaction, *in spite of* flaws and shortcomings.
- Keep learning—If you add to what you know, you will add to your confidence.

None of this is easy, but the results will be worth the effort.

While there are no shortcuts to success, there are things you can do that will be of immeasurable value. Get support from someone you trust who can make a difference. Try to find a mentor in your chosen field who can help guide you and encourage you along the way. At the same time, honestly evaluate your own abilities. Be realistic. Apply yourself where you are most likely to succeed, and seek help from others in developing other talents. This must be accompanied by a willingness to learn. Finally, learn to thrive on challenges. Whether you succeed or fail, experience is the best teacher.

SUMMARY

Residential site management is a very challenging and rewarding field. From one day to the next, the job is never the same. Whether filling an open staff position, leasing apartments, responding to an emergency maintenance request, or seeking a lease renewal, a site manager's responsibilities are always changing. This is what makes the job challenging. It is also what makes it satisfying and exciting.

All of a site manager's duties—administration and operations, staffing, marketing, leasing, maintenance, risk management, and the attendant legalities—contribute to the success or failure of a property. Whether you manage a high-rise, low-rise, or condominium building, or a portfolio of single-family homes, your contributions are vital to the success of the property owner's investment. In the end, site managers are on the front line, and their efforts are instrumental in achieving value enhancement as well as creating a sense of home for the residents.

Key Terms

analysis of alternatives
change in use
cost-benefit analysis
physical change

Key Concepts

leadership qualities
management planning
professionalism
team management
self-fulfilling prophecy

Key Points

- What do property owners look for in real estate managers?
- Who are site managers' customers?
- What is a cost-benefit analysis?
- What does it mean for a site manager to be a "balancer?"
- What is the relationship between the conceptual, technical, and interpersonal levels of real estate management?
- Why is communication the critical ingredient in building an effective team?

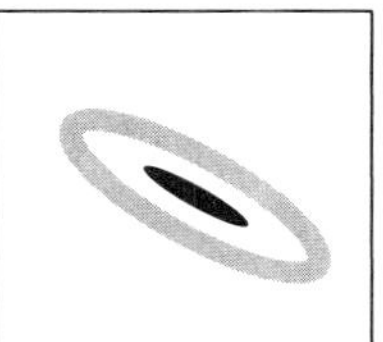

Glossary

Abandonment A relinquishment or surrender of property or rights to it. In real estate management, abandonment of leased premises refers to the relinquishing of the premises by the tenant before the lease expires without consent of the owner. The term is also applied to personal property left behind by a tenant, a situation that has legal implications regarding the removal and storage or disposition of such property.

Abatement In real estate, a reduction of rent, interest, or amount due. Also an environmental term meaning partial or complete reduction of the intensity of concentration of a contaminant (e.g., removal of asbestos).

Absorption rate The amount of space of a particular property type that is leased compared to the amount of that same type of space available for lease within a certain geographic area over a given period.

Accounts payable Monies due others for services rendered or goods ordered and received.

Accounts receivable Monies due for services rendered or goods ordered and delivered.

ACCREDITED MANAGEMENT ORGANIZATION® (AMO®) A designation conferred by the Institute of Real Estate Management on real estate management firms that are under the direction of a CERTIFIED PROPERTY MANAGER® and comply with stipulated requirements as to accounting procedures, operating standards, ethical practices, and protection of funds entrusted to them.

ACCREDITED RESIDENTIAL MANAGER® (ARM®) A professional service award conferred by the Institute of Real Estate Management on individuals who meet specific standards of experience, ethics, and education in the management of residential real estate.

Accrual-basis accounting The method of accounting that involves entering amounts of income when they are earned and amounts of expense when they are incurred even though the cash may not be received or paid. (Compare *cash-basis accounting.*)

Actual cash value (ACV) Insurance that pays a claim based on the purchase price of the item, minus a stipulated deductible, and allowing for depreciation because of age and use. (Compare *replacement cost coverage.*)

Agent A person who enters a legal, fiduciary, and confidential arrangement with a second party and is authorized to act on behalf of that party.

All-risk insurance Insurance that pays for any losses unless risks are specifically excluded in the policy.

Americans with Disabilities Act (ADA) of 1990 Civil rights legislation prohibiting discrimination against the disabled. Of the five sections or titles, two are directly applicable to real estate managers: Title I addresses employment procedures and policies and prohibits discrimination against *qualified* disabled applicants if they can perform the *essential functions* of a job with or without *reasonable accommodations;* the goals of Title III are removal of architectural and communication barriers (architectural barriers must be removed in areas of *public accommodation*), provision of auxiliary aids and services to assist in communication, and modification of discriminatory policies, procedures, and practices.

Amortization Gradual reduction of a debt (or principal), usually through installment payments.

Ancillary income See *unscheduled income.*

Assessment An amount charged against each owner or tenant of a property to fund its operation; also, the amount of tax levied by a municipality, as against real property (i.e., real estate taxes).

Assignment The transfer, in writing, of an interest in a bond, mortgage, lease, or other instrument. The *assignee* is the person to whom some right or interest is given, either for the individual's own enjoyment, or in trust, while the *assignor* is the one giving the right or interest. The assignor of a lease remains liable unless released by the landlord. (Compare *sublet.*)

Bankruptcy A state of financial insolvency of an individual or organization (i.e., liabilities exceed assets); the inability to pay debts. The objective of bankruptcy is a court action providing for the orderly and equitable settlement of obligations.

Blanket policy A single insurance policy covering a variety of risks or more than one kind of property at the same location, the same kind of property at multiple locations, or both.

Board of directors The governing body of any corporation, including a condominium, or other common interest realty association. (See also *corporation.*)

Bond An agreement stating that one party (surety or guarantor) will answer for the acts or omissions of a second party (principal) who has agreed to perform in some manner for a third party (obligee); the third party is indemnified in case the second party does not perform—a *surety bond* also called *performance bond* or *contract bond*. A *fidelity bond* may be obtained by an employer to protect against the economic loss (money or property) due to dishonest acts of employees.

Budget An estimation of income and expenses over a specific time period for a particular property, project, or institution. (See also *capital budget* and *operating budget*.)

Budget variance The differences between projected and actual amounts of income and expenses. Higher income and lower expenditures than expected constitute favorable variances, while lower income and higher expenditures are reported as unfavorable variances.

Bylaws Regulations that govern specific procedures for handling routine matters in an organization such as a condominium association.

Capital budget An estimate of costs of major improvements or replacements; generally a long-range plan for improvements to a property.

Capital improvement A structural addition or betterment to real property that has a life in excess of one year, the cost of which can be depreciated for income tax purposes. (See also *depreciation*.)

Capitalization The process employed to estimate the value of a property by the use of a proper investment rate of return and the annual net operating income produced by the property, using the formula:

$$\frac{\text{Net Operating Income (I)}}{\text{Rate (R)}} = \text{Value (V)}$$

Capitalization rate A rate of return used to estimate a property's value based on that property's net operating income. This rate is based on the rates of return prevalent in the marketplace and represents the degree of risk associated with an investment. Also the rate of return produced by a property when comparing income to value.

Cash-basis accounting The method of accounting that recognizes income and expenses when money is actually received or paid. (Compare *accrual-basis accounting*.)

Cash flow The amount of cash available after all payments have been made for operating expenses, debt service (mortgage principal and interest), and capital improvements.

Casualty loss In insurance, any property loss from damage to buildings, their contents, and external equipment by fire, storm, theft, vandalism, or malicious mischief.

CERTIFIED PROPERTY MANAGER® (CPM®) The professional designation conferred by the Institute of Real Estate Management on individuals who distinguish themselves in the areas of education, experience, and ethics in property management.

Chart of accounts A classification or arrangement of account items by type (e.g., advertising, insurance, maintenance).

Coinsurance clause Insurance coverage that requires the insured (e.g., the property owner) to maintain the insurance amount at a specific level (e.g., 80% of the property's value) in order to receive the full value up to the limits of the policy in case of a loss, in exchange for a lowered premium rate. However, failure to keep that level of insurance coverage will reduce the amount reimbursed (in proportion to the property value).

Commingle To mix or combine; to combine the money of more than one person or entity into a common fund. In real estate management, this practice is prohibited.

Common area Areas of a property that are used by all tenants or owners; in a condominium, the areas of the property in which the unit owners have a shared ownership interest (lobbies, laundry rooms, etc.).

Comparison grid A form of price analysis in which the features of a subject property are compared to similar features in comparable properties in the same market. The price (or rent) for each comparable property helps to determine an appropriate market price (or rent) for the subject property.

Concession An economic incentive granted by a landlord to encourage the leasing of space or the renewal of a lease.

Condemnation A legal action by which government takes private property for public use, and the owner is compensated under *eminent domain*. A declaration that a structure is unfit for use.

Condominium A multiple-unit structure in which the housing units are individually owned and the common areas are proportionately owned; a unit in a condominium property.

Condominium association Usually a not-for-profit corporation comprised of the unit owners of a condominium that governs its operation. The operation of a condominium association is governed by legal documents known as the declaration (also called *covenants, conditions, and restrictions*), by-laws, and articles of incorporation.

Consideration Something of value exchanged for a promise or for performance of a service that makes an exchange legally binding, such as paying rent in exchange for use of a property.

Constructive eviction Inability of a tenant to obtain or maintain possession because of conditions of a property that make occupancy hazardous or the premises unfit for its intended use. To apply in a landlord-tenant dispute, the tenant must vacate the premises prematurely because of the conditions.

Conversion ratio The average number of prospects who visit a rental property compared to the number who sign a lease. The number of prospects who must be seen in order to obtain a signed lease.

Cooperative Ownership of a share or shares of stock in a corporation that holds the title to a multiple-unit residential structure. Shareholders do not own their units outright but have the right to occupy them as co-owners of the cooperative association and through proprietary leases.

Corporation A legal entity that is chartered by a state and is treated by courts as an individual entity separate and distinct from the shareholders who own its stock.

Corrective maintenance See *maintenance.*

Cosmetic maintenance See *maintenance.*

Cost-benefit analysis A method of measuring the benefits expected from a decision (e.g., a change in operating procedures) by calculating the cost of the change and determining whether the benefits outweigh the costs.

Curb appeal General cleanliness, neatness, and attractiveness of a building as exemplified by the appearance of the exterior and grounds and the general level of housekeeping.

Death clause A special clause in a lease that provides for termination of the lease before its expiration date in the event of the tenant's death.

Debt service Periodic payments of principal and/or interest on a loan.

Declaration A legal document that creates a condominium. The document describes the condominium, defines the method of determining each unit owner's share of the common elements, and outlines the responsibilities of the owners and the association.

Deductible In insurance, a specified amount the insured party must pay before the insurer pays on a claim.

Default Failure to fulfill an obligation; the nonperformance of a duty, such as those required in a lease or other contract. Sometimes called *breach of contract.*

Deferred maintenance See *maintenance.*

Delinquency Failure to make payment on a debt or obligation when due.

Demographic profile A compilation of social and economic statistics for a specific population (including population density, age, education, occupation, and income), usually within a geographic area (as a metropolitan area or a region).

Department of Housing and Urban Development (HUD) A department of the federal government that supervises the Federal Housing Administration (FHA) and a number of other agencies that administer various housing programs.

Depreciation Loss of value due to all causes, including physical deterioration (ordinary wear and tear), structural defects, and changing economic and market conditions (see also *obsolescence*). The tax deduction that allows for exhaustion of property.

Economic obsolescence Impairment of desirability or useful life, or loss in the use and value of property, arising from economic forces outside of the building or property such as changes in optimum land use, legislative enactments that restrict or impair property rights, and changes in supply-demand relationships. (See also *obsolescence.*)

Economic vacancy The number of units in a building or a development that are not producing income. This includes vacancies, models, offices, delinquencies, staff apartments, cannibalized units, and units being used for storage; usually expressed as a percentage of the total number of units. The rent dollars lost from those units, expressed as a percentage of the gross potential rental income of the property. (Compare *physical vacancy.*)

Effective gross income The total amount of income *actually collected* during a reporting period; the gross receipts of a property.

Emergency maintenance See *maintenance.*

Eminent domain See *condemnation.*

Employee handbook A detailed accounting of the personnel policies and procedures of the management company and the site office.

Endorsement An attachment to an insurance policy that provides or excludes a specific coverage for a specific portion or element of a property; also called a *rider.*

Environmental Protection Agency (EPA) The agency of the United States government established to enforce laws that preserve and protect the environment.

Equal Employment Opportunity Commission (EEOC) A U.S. governmental body that enforces Title VII of the Civil Rights Act, which prohibits discrimination in the work place.

Equity The value of real property in excess of debt.

Errors and omissions insurance See *professional liability insurance.*

Eviction A legal process to reclaim real estate, usually from a tenant who has not performed under the agreed-upon terms of the lease.

Eviction notice A written notice to a tenant to cure a breach of the lease immediately or vacate the premises within a specified period.

Extended coverage (EC) An endorsement to a standard fire insurance policy which adds coverage against financial loss from certain other specified hazards beyond those of fire and lightning. Examples typically include damage from windstorms, civil commotions, smoke, hail, aircraft, vehicles, explosions, and riots. However, coverage for water damage from most causes, including broken pipes and fire hoses, may have to be obtained as a separate endorsement.

Fair Credit Reporting Act A federal law that gives people the right to see and correct their credit records at credit reporting bureaus. It also requires real estate managers to inform applicants if a credit bureau is contracted to investigate their credit.

Fair housing laws Any law that prohibits discrimination against people seeking housing. There are federal, state, and local fair housing laws. Specifically, Title VIII of the Civil Rights Act of 1968 prohibits discrimination in the sale or rental of housing based on race, color, religion, national origin, or sex; the Fair Housing Amendments Act of 1988 further prohibits discrimination on the basis of familial status (children) or mental or physical disability.

Fair Labor Standards Act (FLSA) The federal law that establishes a minimum wage per hour and maximum hours of work. In addition, certain employees who work more than forty hours per week are to be paid one and one-half times their regular hourly wage. Frequently referred to as the Wage and Hour Law.

Federal Housing Administration (FHA) An agency, part of the U.S. Department of Housing and Urban Development (HUD), that administers a variety of housing loan programs.

Fidelity bond See *bond*.

Fiduciary One charged with a relationship of trust and confidence, as between a principal and agent, trustee and beneficiary, or attorney and client, when one party is legally empowered to act on behalf of another.

Fire insurance Insurance on property against direct loss or damage by fire. (See also *extended coverage*.)

Garden apartment building A low-rise building, one to three stories tall, designed for multifamily living, often referring to developments in a suburban area.

General liability insurance An insurance policy that protects the property owner and those involved in the property's operation (e.g., managing agent) from claims arising out of injury or damage to property of third parties as a result of accidents or existing conditions on the property. *Comprehensive general liability insurance* covers all claims *except* those listed as exclusions or in cases of negligence by the insured.

General partnership See *partnership*.

Government-assisted housing Residential rental property in which the lessor receives part of the rent payment from a governmental body, either directly from the government on behalf of a resident or indirectly from a grant to a public housing authority, or from the residents in the form of a voucher. (Compare *public housing; subsidized housing*.)

Gross potential rental income The maximum amount of rent a property can produce; the sum of the rental rates of all spaces available to be rented in a property at 100% occupancy.

Habitability The state or condition of being safe and sanitary and fit for living. Under landlord-tenant law, the landlord is bound by an *implied warranty of habitability,* by which he or she warrants the condition of the leased premises at the time the tenant takes possession and during the period of tenancy.

Heating, ventilating, and air conditioning (HVAC) system The unit regulating the internal environment of a building for even distribution of heat, air conditioning, and fresh air.

Highest and best use That use of real property which will produce the highest property value and develop a site to its fullest economic potential.

High-rise apartment building A multiple-unit dwelling ten or more stories tall.

Hold harmless A declaration that one is not liable for things beyond his or her control; a specific clause in a management agreement or other contract.

Holdover tenancy A tenancy whereby the tenant retains possession of leased premises after his or her lease has expired, and the landlord, by continuing to accept rent from the tenant, thereby agrees to the tenant's continued occupancy as defined by state law. Some leases stipulate that such holding over may revert to a month-to-month tenancy.

Household All persons, related or not, who occupy a housing unit.

Indemnification The legal action of securing (or holding harmless) against injury, damage, or loss. The same as a *hold-harmless* agreement.

Independent contractor A person who contracts to do work for another by using his or her own methods and without being under the control of the other person regarding how the work should be done. Unlike an employee, an independent contractor pays his or her own social security and income taxes and receives no employee benefits.

Inflation An economic condition occurring when the money supply increases in relation to goods, resulting in substantial and continuing increases in prices.

Institute of Real Estate Management (IREM) A professional association of men and women who meet established standards of experience, education, and ethics with the objective of continually improving their respective managerial skills by mutual education and exchange of ideas and experience. The Institute was founded in 1933 and is an affiliate of the NATIONAL ASSOCIATION OF REALTORS®. (See also *CERTIFIED PROPERTY MANAGER®*, *ACCREDITED MANAGEMENT ORGANIZATION®*, and *ACCREDITED RESIDENTIAL MANAGER®*.)

Insurance An agreement by one party (the insurer, carrier, insurance company, etc.) to assume part or all of a financial loss in the event of a specified contingency or peril (e.g., liability, property damage) in consideration of a premium payment by a second party (the insured).

Interest A share in the ownership of property; a payment for the use of money borrowed.

Joint venture An association of two or more persons or businesses to carry out a single business enterprise for profit.

Jurisdiction The geographic area of authority for a specific government entity.

Landlord One who owns real property and/or personal property that is leased to a tenant. (See also *lessor.*)

Landlord-tenant law Laws enacted by various jurisdictions that regulate the relationship between landlord and tenant.

Lease A contract, written or oral, for the possession of part or all of a landlord's property for a specified period of time in consideration of the payment of rent or other compensation by the tenant. (A residential lease is sometimes called an *occupancy agreement.*) Leases for more than one year generally must be in writing to be enforceable.

Lease renewal A goal of marketing in which qualified residents are encouraged to renew their leases. The benefits of lease renewal include reduction or elimination of marketing costs, lower turnover costs, and assured income from an apartment unit.

Leasing agent A person who is directly responsible for renting space in assigned properties.

Lessee The tenant in a lease.

Lessor The landlord in a lease.

Liability insurance Insurance protection against claims arising out of bodily injury (or death) of third parties or damage to their property.

Limited partnership See *partnership.*

Low-rise apartment building See *garden apartment.*

Maintenance The upkeep and repair of buildings and equipment. In real estate management, several types of maintenance are differentiated. *Corrective maintenance* is the ordinary repairs made on a day-to-day basis; when this work is not done, such *deferred maintenance* negatively affects the use, occupancy, and value of the property. *Routine maintenance* (also called *janitorial maintenance*) is the day-to-day upkeep—mopping and waxing floors, washing windows, polishing fixtures, and generally keeping the interior and exterior of the building clean—that is essential to preserving the value of a property. While *emergency maintenance* refers to unscheduled repairs that must be done immediately to prevent further damage or minimize danger to life or property, *preventive maintenance* is a program of regular inspection and care designed to detect and resolve potential problems *before* major repairs are needed. *Cosmetic maintenance* does not affect function; rather, it makes the property more appealing in appearance.

Management agreement A contract or agreement between the owner(s) of a property and the designated managing agent, defining the term (duration) of the arrangement; describing the duties and establishing the authority of the agent; and detailing the responsibilities, rights, and obligations of both agent and owner(s).

Management fee The monetary consideration paid to the property manager or the management company, monthly or otherwise, for the performance of management duties.

Management plan An outline of a property's physical and fiscal management that is directed toward achieving the owner's goals within a certain time frame.

Market analysis A determination of the demographic characteristics (age, income, etc.) of prospective residents for a particular property and an evaluation of the features of the property according to that market's standards for leased space.

Marketing All business activity (advertising, packaging, selling, etc.) used by a producer to expose potential consumers to available goods and services. In real estate leasing, methods used to rent apartments and other space and retain current residents.

Market value The highest price a ready, willing, and able buyer, who is not compelled to buy, would pay and the lowest price a ready, willing, and able seller, who is not compelled to sell, would accept for a good or service.

Mechanic's lien The right of one who provides services or supplies in connection with improvements to real property to seek a judicial sale of the property to satisfy unpaid claims.

Mid-rise apartment building A multiple-unit dwelling between four and nine stories tall. Although some older four-story buildings only have stairs, most mid-rise apartment buildings have elevators.

Miscellaneous income See *unscheduled income*.

Mobile (manufactured) home A dwelling built in a factory, transported to and anchored on a site, and generally used as a year-round residence. All manufactured homes must be in compliance with the federal Manufactured Home Construction and Safety Standards Act of 1974 (the HUD code), which became effective in 1976. The term "mobile home" is commonly used to identify such housing even though the legal nomenclature is "manufactured homes" for units built after the enactment of the HUD code.

Modernization The process of replacing original or outdated equipment with similar items that are up-to-date in design and more technically advanced.

Month-to-month tenancy An agreement to rent or lease for consecutive and continuing monthly periods until terminated by proper prior notice by either the landlord or the tenant. The time period of prior notice is usually established by state law or by the lease agreement. (See also *holdover tenancy.*)

Mortgage A conditional transfer or pledge of real property as security for the payment of a debt. The document used to create a mortgage loan.

Neighborhood analysis A study of a neighborhood, comparing it with the broader economic and geographic area of which it is a part, to determine why individuals and businesses are attracted to the area.

Net operating income (NOI) Total collections less operating expenses.

Obsolescence Lessening of value due to being out-of-date (obsolete) as a result of changes in design and use; an element of depreciation. *Physical obsolescence* is a condition of deferred maintenance; *functional obsolescence* is a condition of obsolete design or use of a property, and *economic obsolescence* is the state of a property that cannot generate enough income to offset operating expenses.

Occupancy agreement See *lease.*

Occupational Safety and Health Act (OSHA) of 1970 A law requiring employers to comply with work place safety and health standards issued by the U.S. Department of Labor.

Operating budget A listing of all anticipated income from and expenses of operating a property, usually projected on an annual basis. While funds for accumulation of capital reserves would be considered an expense item, actual expenditures of such reserve funds would be anticipated in a *capital budget.*

Operating expenses All expenditures made in connection with operating a property excepting debt service, personal income taxes, contributions to reserves, and capital expenditures.

Owner by choice An entity who actively invests in real estate. Examples include individual investors, corporations, and partnerships.

Owner by circumstance Ownership acquired other than by choice. Examples include individuals who inherit property from relatives or others and REO (real estate owned) departments of financial institutions that hold property acquired through foreclosure.

Owner, landlord, and tenant liability (OLT) An insurance policy that protects a property owner, a landlord, or a tenant against claims arising out of bodily injury to a person or damage to the property of a third party occurring at a subject property, including the improvements on the land and other contiguous areas for which the insured is legally responsible, such as sidewalks.

Partnership An agreement between two or more individuals or entities to go into business together. In a *general partnership,* the partners agree to pool their capital and talents, to divide the profits and losses (according to a set formula), to commit the partnership to certain obligations, and to assume unlimited liability for the partnership. In a *limited partnership,* some partners have a passive role. The partnership is managed and operated by one or more *general partners* whose liability is unlimited, while the liability of the *limited partners* may not exceed the amount of their investment, and they have no voice in management.

Personal property Movable property belonging to an individual, family, etc., that is not permanently affixed to real property, such as clothing, fixtures, and furnishings. In real estate, the furniture, blinds and drapes, office equipment, appliances, etc., that belong to the property owner apart from the land and the improvements to it. Also, the items owned outright by the tenant in leased premises.

Pet agreement A lease addendum that authorizes a tenant to keep a specific pet on the premises as long as certain conditions are met.

Physical vacancy The number of vacant units in a building or development that are available for rent, usually expressed as a percentage of the total number of units. (Compare *economic vacancy.*)

Planned unit development (PUD) A single development in which most residents own their dwellings and the land they occupy as well as an individual share of the common areas within the PUD. A zoning classification that allows flexibility in the design of a subdivision, usually setting an overall density limit which allows clustering of units to provide for common open space.

Preventive maintenance See *Maintenance.*

Principal In real estate, one who owns property; in real estate management, the property owner who contracts for the services of an agent; in finance, the amount of money borrowed as distinct from the interest paid on it.

Professional liability insurance In real estate management, insurance to protect against liabilities resulting from honest mistakes and oversights (no protection is provided in cases of gross negligence); also called *errors and omissions insurance.* Policies protecting directors and officers of corporations are also available.

Property analysis A study of a property referring to such items as land location and zoning, exterior construction and condition, facilities, plant and equipment, unit mix, deferred maintenance, functional and economic obsolescence, and expected income and expenses.

Prospect A potential resident or management client.

Public housing The principal form of low-income housing available in the United

States and owned by and/or managed for a local or state governmental agency. (See also *subsidized housing* and *government-assisted housing.*)

Purchase order Written authorization to a supplier to deliver specified goods or services at a stipulated price. Once accepted by the supplier, the purchase order becomes a legally binding contract.

Qualification The process of evaluating a prospective tenant's financial or credit information to determine whether a prospect can afford the unit applied for and has a good history of bill payments (including rent); landlord's also want to know that a tenant will take good care of the leased premises and not disturb the other occupants of the building.

Quiet enjoyment The use of real property by a tenant without illegal or unreasonable interference or annoyance by the landlord or others—a right granted under landlord-tenant law (the right to privacy, peace and quiet, and use of the apartment, common areas, and facilities).

Real estate Land and all improvements in, on, or attached to it.

Real estate investment trust (REIT) An entity that, like a corporation, sells shares to investors and uses the funds to invest in real estate or mortgages; however, it is not subject to the double taxation imposed on corporations, provided it meets certain tests and distributes 95% of its income to shareholders.

Real estate management A profession in which someone other than the owner (a property manager) supervises the operation of a property according to the owner's objectives or consults with the owner on the definition of those objectives and strategies to maximize the property's profitability. A *site manager* is a type of real estate manager.

Recycling Reprocessing of used items or materials to create new products.

Referral program A marketing vehicle that offers residents incentives to refer others to a property. If a prospect is accepted for tenancy, the referring resident receives some material benefit such as an improvement to his or her apartment.

Regional analysis A detailed study of the population growth and movement, employment, industrial and business activity, transportation facilities, tax structures, topography, improvements, and trends within a defined geographic area, usually surrounding and including one or more neighboring cities but, today, typically a metropolitan statistical area (MSA) as defined by the census bureau.

Rehabilitation Restoration of a property to a state of functional efficiency and sound management.

Renewal See *lease renewal.*

Rent In real estate, payment for the use of space or personal property; the periodic payments to the landlord under a lease.

Rental agreement See *lease*.

Renters' insurance Insurance coverage for tenants' personal possessions. This is important because residents' personal property is not covered by a landlord's insurance policies.

Rent loss The loss of income due to vacancies, bad debts, etc.; the difference between the gross projected rental income (for a given period) and the actual amount collected.

Rent loss insurance A coverage that provides for lost income when damage from a fire or other peril interrupts or terminates the flow of rental income to the property.

Rent roll A listing of all rental units showing the rental rate, tenant's name, and lease expiration date for rented units as well as notations for unoccupied units, which are listed as vacant; also called *rent schedule*.

Replacement cost coverage Insurance to replace or restore a building or its contents to its pre-existing condition and appearance using new materials. In this type of coverage, no allowance is made for depreciation and the policy holder must pay a deductible. (Compare *actual cash value*.)

Reserve fund Money set aside to provide funds for anticipated future expenditures, usually applied primarily to capital expenditures.

Resident One who lives (or resides) in a place. Referring to residential tenants as "residents" is preferred by many real estate professionals. (Compare *tenant*.)

Resident handbook Minimally, a compilation of house rules and other information apartment occupants need for ready reference. Ideally, such a handbook will inform residents of their basic rights and responsibilities, covering basic lease provisions (e.g., when rent is due) as well as management's policies regarding use of the facilities at the site (swimming pool, exercise room, laundry room), the keeping of pets, and requests for maintenance or other services.

Residential manager One who manages a residential property or properties; see also *site manager*.

Resident profile A study and listing of the similar and dissimilar characteristics of the present residents in a property; used to assist the real estate manager in positioning the property in the market.

Retaliatory eviction Requirement by a landlord that a tenant vacate leased premises in response to a complaint from the tenant concerning the condition of the building or efforts to form a tenants' union. Landlord-tenant laws in many states forbid such evictions.

Rider An amendment or attachment to a contract such as a lease or management agreement. (See also *endorsement*.)

Right of re-entry A right granted to the owner of leased property under landlord-tenant law so that leased premises can be inspected, maintained, or shown to others at reasonable hours; sometimes called *right of access.* Also the right of the owner to terminate a lease and resume possession of the leased premises for nonpayment of rent or breach of any of the lease covenants by the tenant within the limits of state laws.

Routine maintenance See *maintenance.*

Section 8 housing Privately owned residential rental units that participate in the low-income rental assistance program created by the 1974 amendments to Section 8 of the 1937 Housing Authority Act. Under this program, the U.S. Department of Housing and Urban Development pays a rent subsidy to the landlord on behalf of qualified low-income residents so they pay a limited portion of their incomes for rent (voucher program). Alternatively, residents may receive rent subsidies for the entire rent and not pay any portion of the rent themselves (certificate program).

Security deposit An amount of money advanced by the tenant and held by an owner or manager to ensure the faithful performance of the lease terms by the tenant. Part or all of the deposit may be retained to pay for rent owed, miscellaneous charges owed, unpaid utility bills, and damage to the leased space that exceeds normal wear and tear. Limitations on withholding may be imposed by local and state laws, and the landlord may be required to pay interest to the tenant during the holding period.

Site manager An employee who oversees and administers the day-to-day affairs of a property in accordance with directions from the property manager or the owner. A site manager may live in the building being managed or off site.

Sole proprietorship A business enterprise carried on by one person.

Special multiperil (SMP) insurance policy A commercial insurance contract that provides property and liability insurance under a single policy. Crime insurance and boiler and machinery insurance are optional additions to this policy.

Steering An illegal discriminatory practice that conceals vacancies from a prospect, shows prospects only a portion of a site or area, or encourages a prospective tenant to look at another site for housing.

Sublet The leasing of part or all of the premises by a tenant to a third party for part or all of the tenant's remaining term. Under a subletting agreement, the original tenant is responsible for rent not paid or damages committed by the subtenant regardless of his or her agreement with the subtenant. (Compare *assignment.*)

Subsidized housing Usually privately owned rental property for which a portion of the return on the owner's investment may result from additional tax advantages granted for development, for leasing part of the property to residents who are eligible for housing subsidies, or for leasing to a local housing authority. The National Housing Act, which has been amended substantially over time, includes provisions for subsidies to landlords via low mortgage rate loans and for payment of rent on behalf of qualified individuals. (Compare *government-assisted housing* and *public housing.*)

Surety See *bond.*

Syndicate Individuals or companies who join together to pool their capital and talents and invest in a project on a scale they are unable or unwilling to pursue alone. *Syndication* is a form of partnership that permits investment in very large projects by spreading risk among a larger number of investors.

Tax An amount assessed by a government body for public purposes, usually based on income or the relative value of real or personal property. Taxes take many forms, including *real estate tax* (an operating expense before NOI), *sales tax* (paid on goods and equipment needed to run the property), and *personal income tax* (paid by the owner from the proceeds or cash flow generated by a property).

Tax shelter Any device used to reduce tax liability by providing a taxpayer with deductions or credits that may be applied against taxable income.

Tenant A legal term for one who pays rent to occupy real estate; the lessee in a lease. Property managers often refer to residential tenants as "residents," which is also a marketing term. (See also *lessee, resident.*)

Tenant organization A group of tenants who join together to use their collective powers against an owner to achieve certain goals such as improved conditions, expanded facilities, and lower rent.

Term The duration of a lease, mortgage, or other contractual arrangement, defined by the starting and ending dates of the agreement.

Townhouse A one-, two-, or three-story dwelling with a separate outside entryway sharing common or partitioning walls with other similar dwellings.

Traffic report A record of the number of prospects who visit or make inquiries at a property and the factors that attracted them to it, often used to measure the effectiveness of advertisements and other marketing vehicles as well as closing techniques.

Trust account A separate bank account, segregated from an agent's own funds, in which the agent is required to deposit monies collected for the client; in some states called an *escrow* account.

Turnover rate The number of units vacated during a specific period of time, usually a year, typically expressed as the ratio between the number of new tenancies and the total number of units in a property.

Umbrella liability insurance A policy that provides liability coverage above and beyond the limits of a basic liability policy.

Unconscionability Gross unfairness. Under landlord-tenant law, a lease may be struck down if it is found in court to contain an unconscionable clause. Alternatively, only the offending clause may be found unenforceable.

Unlawful detainer Failure of a tenant to move out at the end of a tenancy or following lawful eviction.

Unscheduled income Income from sources other than rent, such as coin-operated laundry equipment, vending machines, late fees, forfeited security deposits, etc.; also called *miscellaneous* or *ancillary income.*

Vacancy An area in a building that is unoccupied and available for rent or could be made ready for occupancy.

Valuation An estimation or calculation of the worth of an object. In real estate investment, value is typically based on the income stream generated. (See also *capitalization.*)

Variance See *Budget variance.*

Wage and Hour Law See *Fair Labor Standards Act.*

Walk-up An apartment building of two or more floors in which access to the upper stories is solely by means of stairways.

Workers' compensation insurance Coverage obtained by an employer to pay an employee medical and disability benefits and lost wages in the event of employment-related sickness or injury.

Work order A written form, letter, or other instrument for authorizing work to be performed; a means for controlling and recording work ordered. The paperwork attendant on service requests initiated by residents, real estate managers, or property owners.

Zoning Restriction of the character and use of property by areas or "zones," usually by local (municipal) government.

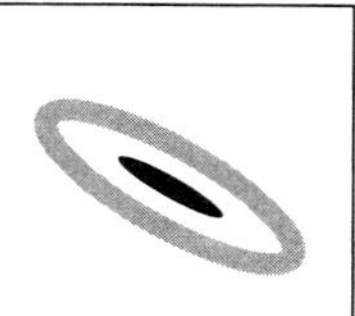

Index

S